A352·38   737100

Digital Governance

The application
(ICTs) to reforn
tion is widely
reinvigorate de
this timely and
assumptions u
the financial ex
and other organ

This book ex
to digital or d-g
pation and infc
self-governance
extension of IC'
service delivery
information tec
The shift from
tion is viewed
quality: digital
reduce costs, n
goals.

Michael E. Mil
Studies at the U

Digital Governance
New Technologies for Improving Public Service and Participation

Michael E. Milakovich

Routledge
Taylor & Francis Group

NEW YORK AND LONDON

First published 2012
by Routledge
711 Third Avenue, New York, NY 10017

Simultaneously published in the UK
by Routledge
2 Park Square, Milton Park, Abingdon, Oxon OX14 4RN

Routledge is an imprint of the Taylor & Francis Group, an informa business

© 2012 Taylor & Francis

Library of Congress Cataloging-in-Publication Data

Milakovich, Michael E.
Digital governance : new technologies for improving public service and
participation / Michael E. Milakovich.
    p. cm.
Includes bibliographical references and index.
1. Internet in public administration. 2. Electronic government
information. 3. Public administration–Technological innovations.
4. Political participation–Technological innovations.
5. Public administration–Citizen participation. I. Title.
JF1525.A8M56 2011
352.3'802854678–dc23   2011024012

ISBN13: 978-0-415-89143-1 (hbk)
ISBN13: 978-0-415-89144-8 (pbk)
ISBN13: 978-0-203-81599-1 (ebk)

Typeset in Garamond
by Cenveo Publisher Services

Printed and bound in the United States of America on acid-free paper by
Edwards Brothers, Inc.

SUSTAINABLE FORESTRY INITIATIVE
Certified Fiber Sourcing
www.sfiprogram.org

To my colleague, friend, mentor, spiritual adviser and writing partner, George J. Gordon, for his confidence and infinite patience.

In memory of Eli M. Milakovich.

As always, to Cindy, Nicole and Tiffany for their loving support.

Contents

Figures

Tables

Boxes

Preface

Computer-assisted *information and communications technologies* (ICTs) are impacting all aspects of public and private services worldwide. Although public sector applications in the United States have trailed private firms as well as other economically developed nations in Asia and in Europe, many U.S. governments are moving away from agency-centric bureaucracy and towards a *citizen-centric* approach to delivering services. The motivation for adopting ICTs is the harsh reality of fiscal austerity: steep cuts in revenue brought on by global financial crises, lower property values and job losses. Although financial desperation (sometimes) fosters innovation, existing governmental structures and those who lead and manage them sometimes fail to recognize the need for change. Integrating complex governmental structures with high-tech information systems is a merger that many governments have attempted, but few have yet completed. An important question raised in this book is: why do some government officials accept change while others resist?

Elected officials, public administrators and managers, civic reformers, government contractors and regulators—in concert with informed citizens and other interested stakeholders—need current knowledge of ICTs to adapt traditional governmental systems to reach higher levels of administrative efficiency and citizen satisfaction. Accomplishing this transformation is the subject of this book.

Historically, social and technological innovations have rendered existing structures and organizational behaviors obsolete. As societies advance technologically, citizens expect access, convenience, reliability and speed of service transactions to rise correspondingly. Change in the public sector is limited by internal and external factors, including, among others: bureaucratic protectiveness, existing laws and regulations, political interference, privacy concerns, obsolete technologies and infrastructures unsuited for the adoption of high-level technologies. In addition, accountability, transparency and lack of trust are major problems facing nearly all governments, especially in the United States. Recent initiatives advocating citizen-oriented strategies supported by digital governance are designed to respond to the multiple challenges facing public agencies.

Digital governance is broadly defined as the advanced use of ICTs as enabling strategies for improving organizational performance. Customer-centric and mission-driven governments use the power of the internet to more closely link citizens with public service providers. Transaction costs are lowered and processes streamlined by offering more accountable, capable, competent and responsive services. Digital governance is a strategy for governments at all levels to achieve economic recovery goals, reduce costs and meet citizen expectations. Many public agencies are (albeit slowly) adopting standardized procedures to meet customer service quality expectations created by the Digital Revolution. Successful cases are presented in this book as examples for others to follow.

The rapid evolution of ICTs and their success in the private commercial sector brought the concept of electronic—and now digital—commerce to the forefront. During the past three decades, most governments connected basic informational resources to the World Wide Web; others have built comprehensive 'portals' allowing citizens to access information and conduct transactions online. Several alternatives have been proposed to guide the transition, although more needs to happen before full-scale government-to-government (G2G) and government-to-citizen (G2C) linkages are established and fully utilized. Several conditions must be present before such integration occurs.

First, transformation of citizens into "netizens" must enhance, not damage, democratic governance; applications must increase trust in government and promote public administration accountability and responsible citizenship. Second, "digital divides" resulting from unequal access to the internet should be reduced. Implementation should occur with an awareness of the overall values and *raison d'être* of the public sector and a recognition of government's role in securing both the *equality* and *quality* of public services. Third, the role of third-party consultants or intermediaries must be carefully monitored and regulated. And last, various innovative incentives such as applied quality theories, prizes and the expanded use of social networking can be used to guide ICT strategies, redefine roles and responsibilities and, where appropriate, transfer the best practices of both private and public organizations.

Through the adoption of standards guided by these principles, public agencies can initiate, evaluate and expand the use of ICT applications and digital technologies. Applying service quality standards to achieve citizen-oriented online government, particularly in the U.S. federal system of fragmented accountability and dispersed responsibility to govern, presents unique challenges for reform-minded citizens and public officials.

The continuing global effort to improve government performance heightens expectations that public services will be comparable to those provided by the private sector. In theory, awareness of successful customer service efforts should convince public officials to respond to citizens in the most efficient and straightforward manner. Government is different, however, and public administrators must adhere to strict legislative and regulatory standards, respect the rights and responsibilities of citizenship and respond to demands from recipients for better service quality at lower costs. Regardless of the level of technology used, the ability of any government to function more effectively is compromised when there is insufficient articulation of program goals, inadequate information on program performance, weak evaluation and limited oversight. Expanded use of digital governance increases citizen access to information at reduced costs and enables citizen-oriented virtual government services. Demand for more accessible and efficient (that is, cost-effective) government, combined with higher budget deficits and shrinking governmental resources, creates opportunities for the expansion and broader public access through the use of ICTs. When fully operational, digital governance increases civic knowledge, improves confidence in government and enhances the quality of information conveyed and received.

Requests for public services will always outweigh resources and revenue available to meet those demands. Everyone wants more, feels justified in seeking more and organizes special interest groups to lobby for more. That is the nature of human political behavior. Better program management online or in person won't alter that reality. Nor will audits, evaluations or efficiency measures alone close the gap between available revenues and requests for spending. Budgeting in times of economic scarcity requires prioritizing spending decisions to overcome the impacts of declining revenues. Changes in budgetary processes can also make elusive problems more obvious and solutions easier to implement. This creates a focus on achieving results, the ultimate yield of technology.

The basic purpose of digital governance is to improve public services using a common set of performance standards. Most governments have expanded both electronic and digital access to citizens, businesses and other governments; over two-thirds of all Americans say they have visited a government portal or website. Although most transactions are basic data inquiries or information searches, many public agencies are conducting higher-level complex G2C or G2B (government-to-business) transactions. Digital governance's full potential will only be realized when governments have eliminated entry barriers and deployed software for full service interactions, thereby reducing duplication and eliminating inefficiencies and redundancies.

New Media technologies such as the internet link together governments, businesses and citizens by facilitating two-way "open-source" communication. Web-based education, or virtual learning, is an advanced educational model which promotes civic participation by allowing students' access to online classrooms from anywhere on the globe, at any time. Virtual learning encourages the overall use of information technology in education, state and local government's largest expenditure. When authenticated and validated, New Media applications provide a rich forum for information exchange and discussion of political issues. Not all citizens, however, have equal access to computers nor is everyone (including teachers and public managers) equally capable of understanding how to use them. Although ICTs facilitate wider citizen participation, they pose challenges as well as opportunities for governments in adopting a citizen-focused participatory approach to co-producing public services. Whether ICT strategies can be used by political candidates or converted to the administration of public programs remains to be seen.

Citizens' opinions about government are also affected by fundamental changes occurring in their societies. Broader global trends increase the speed at which goods, knowledge and services cross international borders. Globalization of the world economy has fundamentally changed relationships among individuals, businesses and governments. What was once a controlled and gradual shift in the world's balance of economic and political power drastically accelerated (then abruptly stalled) in the first decade of the 21st century. As corporations globalize, they not only affect regional cultures but also breed hostility in countries (at various levels of economic development) where disaffected citizens are taking anti-globalization and (sometimes) anti-democratic actions to preserve their local cultures, traditions and values. Fast food lifestyles are being challenged by the slow food movement. As more citizens are discontented in some way by the effects of globalization (especially job losses), governments and public administration assume greater responsibilities for guaranteeing educational and economic policies to redress inequities produced by this inexorable trend. Whether we ignore, oppose or support it, globalization is having a significant impact on the roles and responsibilities of business, government and society.

In the downsized, flattened, hyper-competitive and mission-driven global economy, all organizations search for models to promote innovation, measure performance and raise customer service quality standards. The full implementation of digital governance requires fundamental changes in the relationship between citizens and state, using ICTs as catalysts for political as well as administrative communication. This entails attitudinal and behavioral changes and less dependence on formal bureaucratic structures (covered in Part I of this book); transformation of administrative, educational, political systems to manage public services in a more citizen-centric way (Part II); the integration of advanced digital communication systems with broadband wireless internet services (Part III); and the creation of new forms of global interactive citizenship and self-governance (covered in Part IV). This book concludes with recommendations for further improvement and civic actions to stimulate this important instrument of governance and public administration. Success of such efforts increasingly depends on leadership, technical competence and tenacity of federal, state and local government officials: it is to all of them, teaching faculty as well as current and future students, that this book is dedicated.

Educational professionals everywhere find themselves coping with new challenges resulting from the knowledge explosion and application of information systems created by the growth of the internet. Faculty and students generally familiar with ICT applications will recognize the subjects in this book as a continuous work in progress. For most of us, traditional content delivery methods are changing. We are now incorporating clickers, blogs, e-books, ICTs, multi-media systems, social networking and e-quizzes into our courses. We have joined learning communities and are trying keep up with the latest instructional technologies necessary to more effectively communicate with our students. Hopefully, this contribution will further that quest.

Acknowledgments

This book began to take form in 2002, shortly after the millennial dot-com bust and the Y2K panic. As some readers will remember, the expected damage to computers did not occur and, at the time, the only survivors of the failed internet revolution appeared to be an online bookstore and an electronic swap meet. Everything has changed in less than 10 years. Privacy and security concerns have dissipated and we now bank, communicate, file legal forms, learn, pay taxes, stay informed, shop, receive benefits and perform a multitude of other tasks on our personal data devices (PDAs), computers and smart phones. New applications integrate organizational practices with technology and add more value to the burgeoning global communication system known as the internet. Innovation is accelerating and multi-billion dollar industries have emerged from the advent of social networking. Thousands of commercial online retailers, including Amazon.com and eBay, are thriving with the dissemination of new technologies. The public sector is now facing the same challenges that private businesses confronted a decade ago: public distrust, financial depletion and recession. There is a new urgency for governmental reform resulting from a prolonged economic downturn, the mortgage meltdown and taxpayer's anger—many agencies are being forced to change in order to survive. Public administration has a unique opportunity to renew confidence and redesign basic governance systems using new digital information and communications technologies to more effectively deliver public services.

Many people have generously contributed to this project. I am grateful to have been invited to present peer-reviewed papers at several international conferences, including the Knowledge Management in E-Government Conferences in Copenhagen in May 2002 and in Krems, Austria, in May 2004, the e-Government meetings at Corvinis University in Budapest in March 2005, the Electronic Government Conference in Copenhagen in August 2005 and the International Association of Schools of Public Affairs and Administration (IASIA) meetings in Lake Como, Italy, in 2006. Portions of Chapter 2 received excellent criticism at an Electronic Democracy Conference in Vienna in September 2009 in a paper entitled

"From Representative to Digital Democracy: The Internet and Increased Citizen Participation in Government," in Alexander Prosser and Peter Parycek (eds.) *EDEM 2009—Conference on Electronic Government*, Vienna, Austria: pp. 91–100. A revised version of the paper was published in 2010 as "The Internet and Increased Citizen Participation in Government," *eJournal of eDemocracy and Open Government*, 2 (1): 1–9. Portions of Chapter 5 were drawn from an earlier version of an article "Balancing Customer Service, Empowerment, and Performance with Citizenship, Responsiveness, and Political Accountability," *International Public Management Review*, 4 (1) 2003: 61–83. Concepts in Chapter 6 were presented at the E-Government and Information Technology in the Public Sector at East European E-Government Days, Prague, Czech Republic, April 2007 and draft versions of portions of Chapter 9 were discussed at the 27th International Congress of Administrative Sciences in Abu Dhabi, UAE, July 11–14, 2007. I wish to thank all those at these and other professional meetings who offered constructive criticisms.

Many colleagues provided examples and offered suggestions for improving the content of the book. Special thanks to Thomas Holstrom, Nele Leosk, Matt Poelmans, Peter Parycek, Alex Prosser, David Newman, Bettina Larsen, D. Marshall Nelson, Esq., Mary Griffiths, Axel Bruns, Roland Traunmüller, Maria Wimmer, Bill Vilberg and the FLC gang at UM, Allen Rosenbaum at FIU and Diane George at Va Tech. Students in my POL 558 seminars in spring and fall 2010, especially Andrew Chatzsky, Amber Stephens and Andrew Verblow, also assisted in reviewing final drafts.

Part I

Introduction and Overview

From Formal Bureaucracy to Digital Democracy

Digital information and communication systems are widely viewed as the 21st century "savior," *the* enlightened way to reinvigorate democracy and improve the quality of citizen services. Electronic government (e-gov) has been touted (perhaps naively) as a means to reform politics, government and public administration. Advocates for more online interactions among businesses, citizens and governments assert that civic interactions are enhanced and that the costs and time associated with delivering public services can be reduced. Chapter 1 examines the assumptions underlying the "e-government revolution" in light of the financial exigencies facing many commercial enterprises, public agencies and other organizations resulting from the harsh effects of economic globalization, loss of tax revenue, lower property values and greater debt incurred to deal with persistent fiscal crises.

1 The Transition from Electronic Government to Digital Governance

The expanded use of internet-driven technology to meet budgetary and deficit challenges is rapidly changing traditional boundaries of commerce, politics and public administration. As a result, global markets are increasingly interconnected and the costs of installing and accessing new **information and communication technologies (ICTs)** are decreasing, allowing greater numbers of online participants to become more closely linked together. (**Bold print** denotes key term listed at back of chapter and defined alphabetically in the Glossary.) As the **knowledge revolution** expands, geographically isolated parts of the world are interconnected via cellular/mobile phones, fiber optic cables, social networking, teleconferencing and satellites. Businesses, both large and small—as well as many governments and non-profit organizations of all purposes and sizes—are revising performance management strategies, personnel systems and technology standards to respond to customers in a more "wired" but less stable world economy. Spurred by growth of the global economy, ICTs are expanding faster than many organizations are able to cope with or pay for the changes necessary to fully benefit from the knowledge revolution.

Globalization of the world's economy is altering how businesses, individuals and institutions communicate, collaborate and compete. The effects of globalization began impacting the world economy almost a generation ago—around the time the Berlin Wall fell and the Soviet Union collapsed. Since Europe began to unify in the early 1990s, the economic impact of globalization has empowered billions of individuals who would otherwise have been excluded from the material benefits of free enterprise capitalism (Bhagwati, 2004; DeSoto, 2000; Friedman, 1999, 2005; Prestowitz, 2006). Durable goods and services, such as automobiles, computers, consumer electronics, tourism, service call-centers, smart phones and many other commercial products are now being mass produced and distributed less expensively on a larger scale than ever before. Improvements in technology, telecommunications and transportation permit billions more people to participate in what Thomas L. Friedman calls a "hot, flat and crowded" world, one that is more level and less hierarchical—but also more dangerous and unstable—due to the driving forces behind globalization and its dissidents (Friedman, 2005, 2008; Milakovich, 2006a; Stiglitz, 2003). Opinions about the long-term impacts of these trends differ. Unquestionably, globalization has accelerated with the growth of ICTs—forming complex linkages among business, government and society which did not exist a generation ago—impacting economies and politics worldwide in both positive and negative ways (detailed in Chapter 8).

The negative effects of globalization have included bank failures, corporate bailouts, declining tax revenues, financial crises and shrinking profit margins. In many instances, revenue losses have forced governments—often with opposition from counterparts in private industry—to lower access costs, remove "unnecessary" regulations (and strengthen "necessary" ones) to stimulate economic growth and streamline service delivery. Generally more advanced and technologically sophisticated than what is commonly known a **Web 2.0**, ICT-driven changes in economic, political *and* societal relationships are being accomplished with less labor-intensive and more cost-effective electronic and digital communication systems. To succeed, the transformation requires widespread adoption of digital ICTs capable of connecting governments with citizens who can apply additional knowledge and understand how to interact with newer forms of technology. For those unable or unwilling to learn how to access new technology-driven ICTs, massive re-education and training efforts must accompany the transition (Chapter 4).

All types of service organizations are adapting to rapid **technological change** brought about by new applications and the exponential growth of **social networks**, including among many others *Facebook*, *YouTube*, *Twitter* and *MySpace*. Governments in particular are coping with contemporary economic, fiscal and social problems—often *without* the benefit of post-modern information technologies, structural reforms or adequate managerial and technical skills. Despite the best intentions, many public agencies are still encumbered by antiquated command-and-control mindsets, outdated equipment and procedures, rigid hierarchies and traditional boundaries which define "necessary regulations"—often better suited for 20th century internal procedural reporting requirements than for 21st century accessibility, economy, flexibility, networking and mobility. Unlike many of their counterparts in private industry, government agencies have been slow to adopt ICTs as a means to achieve results, improve administrative efficiency or enhance work processes.

The knowledge revolution has raised numerous new concerns within the fields of public and private administration, affecting how organizations interact with each other, businesses, citizens and customers in new and often unfamiliar ways. For example, equipment replacement schedules and employee skills within all types of organizations—not just governments—have not kept pace with developments in **information technology (IT)**.

In many instances, public agencies have had to divert resources in order to "pick up the pieces" of fractured economies and damaged eco-systems caused by unregulated corporate globalization (Chapter 9). These expenditures further deplete already bare-bone government budgets, increase taxes and add to burgeoning public debt. Adopting new technologies and adapting local environments to adjust to these seismic changes are vital capacity-building exercises for all types of organizations, especially sub-national units such as states and local governments. Demands for better integration of ICTs with public administration have increased since the worldwide global recession began in late 2007, adding even more debt to already financially strapped public agencies. The challenges for public administration are to meet these demands with existing or more often declining fiscal resources.

Globalization and the knowledge revolution have converged to create opportunities for ICT-driven innovations in a wide variety of public policy disciplines, including health care, education and social services: this has contributed to the expansion of government-sponsored and private scientific research on digital applications in government and public administration. This merger has not yet, however, resulted in the widespread use of ICTs to transform online government service delivery systems. The conversion from traditional public administration service delivery systems and the expanded use of digital governance is more likely to occur as a result of the dire financial conditions facing nearly all governments.

New Media Technology and Public Administration

As an academic discipline and also a sub-field of both political science and management, **public administration** combines theory with practical applications to improve efficiency of government operations. Public administration can be distinguished from purely private management by its emphasis on civic governance and political institutions, concern with equity, ethics, decision making and fairness in the distribution of resources as related sub-fields of study. Unlike the private sector, public agencies in the United States are bounded by designated **geographic districts** and heavily dependent on nearly 90,000 elected representative institutions (the U.S. Congress, state legislatures, county commissions, city councils, as well as other governments, special district boards and commissions) for much of their operating revenues. Governmental institutions are highly structured and tightly bound, limiting their capacity for flexible responses to 21st century Information Age challenges. Among the primary advantages of applying **New Media** to organizational operations is its lack of geographic borders: technical expertise and specialized knowledge are required to accomplish these reforms.

On the one hand, specialization is regarded as a core value in traditional conceptions of public bureaucracy—greater occupational specialization in

ICTs represents an extension of this trend. On the other hand, specialized communication is one of the major reasons for the compartmentalization and fragmentation of decision making, an often criticized feature of formal Weberian bureaucracy.[1]

Specialists in politics and administration—both within and outside of government—are forging closer working relationships as part of policy-making processes through New Media networks variously known as web **blogs**, **portals** and **wikis**. These and other internet links allow contact between computer or smart phone users, exchange of information and the formation of mutually supportive issue networks as alternatives to information provided by traditional business, government and media sources (Barlow, 2007a; 2007b; Feld and Wilcox, 2008; Gill, 2004; Kahler, 2009). Portals such as the **USA.gov** website are organized from a citizen-centric perspective. The website is a virtual one-stop-shop to government services and information.[2] In the pre-internet era, citizens would have to contact individual government offices to apply for and receive information—a time-consuming task which would discourage all but the most tenacious. The one-stop-shops, whether they are virtual or physical, represent an organizational change from department-task orientation to citizen-oriented service. Blogging and social networking have accelerated this trend and become pervasive sources of citizen participation covering a wide range of political and social issues.

Although its full influence is still unknown, millions of participants in the developing public space or "blogosphere" are influencing political processes by acting as grassroots observers, reporters, reviewers and fact-checkers (Gill, 2004: 5; Habermas, 1991; Keren, 2006; Richardson, 2006). Citizens are using blogs, e-mail, smart phones and social networking to participate in web-based political and social activities and express their views and positions on a wide range of policy issues. This new type of amateur journalism and political and social commentary challenges established news outlets and opinion sources by promoting a more open, participatory culture in nearly every aspect of society. As a result, demand for expertise in decision making and policy analysis has increased, reflecting human resource systems based on job-related competence, expanded ICT networks and the need for advanced knowledge of New Media technologies. At the same time, interest groups, politicians and public officials are also applying these same technologies to conduct political campaigns, communicate with constituents and recruit new members and voters (Hill, 2009; Miller, 2008). Mastery of the new technology—in all its forms—has become a virtual prerequisite for successful lobbying, winning political campaigns and providing better service to constituents (Chapter 2).

The 2008 U.S. presidential election represented a major breakthrough in the application of New Media technologies to politics and political campaigns. The extensive use of ICTs for political communication began even earlier with former presidential candidate Howard Dean's failed run for the presidency in 2004 (Hindman, 2006). After being appointed Democratic National Committee (DNC) Chair in 2005, Dean (together with President Obama's tech-savvy campaign advisers) used ICTs so effectively during the Democrats' grassroots 2008 campaign that they may have significantly impacted the results of the presidential election. Chapter 2 shows how this type of e-campaigning uses ICTs as a means to disseminate information, mobilize volunteers, raise funds and otherwise pursue electioneering functions (Garson, 2006: 69–72). Plainly, ICTs played a significant role in promoting additional citizen participation during the recent U.S. elections. The causal linkages between decision making, fund raising, party identification, political activism, social networking and voter turnouts are more difficult to establish with precision: they are currently being explored in more depth by communications experts and political scientists. Recent studies suggest that more Americans are using ICTs to access information, ask questions and receive government services online (Pew Internet and American Life Project, 2010).

All forms of political and administrative data collection and decision making involve analysis of risks and investments of time and resources. The realities of these **sunk costs** represent an additional factor to be taken into account in making and implementing decisions. The term has two meanings: first, a given resource or commodity, once spent, cannot be used again. For example, land committed for as an airport runway cannot be used as a hospital site. Second, once a decision has been made to proceed in a particular policy direction, additional costs would be incurred if that direction were later reversed (Milakovich and Gordon, 2009: 221). Investment of extra resources and greater political risk-taking are required to reverse a bad policy direction. Therefore, it is often easier to maintain a given policy course than to change. This explains why administrative agencies resist innovation or modification of previously decided policies, regardless of so-called "cost overruns." However, if the costs of *not* changing direction exceed the costs of changing, then public officials or politicians would be far more likely to adopt a new policy. Technical specifications often dictate initial and continuing sunk costs, putting governments—especially hard-pressed state and local agencies—at a distinct fiscal and recruiting disadvantage vis-à-vis private employers. In addition, the dollar costs of equipment and supplies are relatively easier to measure than the loss of faith and trust that often accompany failed government programs.

The networked high-tech approach to politics and public administration reinforces diverse patterns of accountability, communication, decision making and social organization: that is, *less centralized* decision making due to greater specialization, wider use of technology and the limited capacity of leaders to fully comprehend the specialties of everyone in their organizations. Among the empowering capabilities of ICTs is their ability to assist marginalized individuals and groups—those who would otherwise be silent and invisible—to be heard and seen: precisely what happened during Obama's 2008 presidential campaign. Expanded use of ICTs reveals social diversity, a range of opinion that has always existed but was previously without voice in public decision making. This is due in part to the fact that ICTs facilitate the dispersal of power away from centralized governments with the added result that institutions are challenged as a sole means of service delivery and social control. In what appears to be a worldwide phenomenon, political institutions are losing their monopoly over key sources of power, information and the capacity for surveillance, permitting alternative voices in civil society to emerge. This is consistent with changing patterns of bureaucratic hierarchies and the creation of new social networks rapidly altering traditional communication patterns and organizational roles (Friedman, 2005; Kettl, 2002, 2009; Smith, 2004: 136).

New Media technologies have become highly advantageous outlets for formerly disenfranchised citizen activists, non-governmental organizations (NGOs) and new social movements that seek to challenge and occupy new public spaces. These new public spaces also pose challenges to the contribution of the leading theories of the public sphere, or the **polisphere**.[3] Expanded internet coverage also facilitates the proliferation of an unlimited number of alternative public spaces, as well as the growth of a common forum for discussion and deliberation. The expansion of polispheres permits the expression of a much wider range of opinions and options than those possessed by earlier 19th and 20th century public organizational media. For those who feel their opinions are not reflected in the dominant public media, the internet—with its estimated 30 *billion* websites and 112 *million* blogs—offers rapid access to an alternative world of expression, networking and organizing. Some of the best examples of using ICTs to create new public spaces are found in developing countries, especially those under authoritarian or dictatorial regimes. New forms of communication intensify the postmodern challenge to traditional authority structures in developing countries such as China, Cuba, Egypt, Iran, Jordan, Mexico, Tunisia and Venezuela.[4] The availability and lower costs of communication PDAs (personal data assistants), computers and internet connectivity encourage broader decentralized participation from a wider range of individuals and groups.

Knowledge Management and Digital Governance

New patterns of decentralized and networked ICT exchange have accelerated with the emergence of advanced internet technologies. The use of **knowledge management** tools characterizes networked, non-hierarchical systems of modern technology-driven organizations and encourages the transition from electronic government to **digital govern-ance** (Barquin, Bennet and Remez, 2001; Phusavat, Anussarnnitisarn and Rassameethes, 2008; United Nations, 2007, 2010; Wimmer, 2004). Knowledge management also heightens the search for more effective ways to motivate public employees. The ability of individuals to organize without organizations was dramatically illustrated by volcanic eruptions in Iceland, which disrupted travel in Europe for several weeks during spring 2010. Government and private institutions were powerless to help stranded passengers. Frustrated by the failure of commercial air, rail and highway transportation, many New Media users self-organized and arranged carpools and lodging to get to their destinations.

Successful service innovation and multi-channel delivery systems depend on strategies, policies and digital architectures that connect data, IT systems and business processes (United Nations, 2008). Within this context, the concept of digital governance is a broader umbrella term refer-ring to the networked extension of ICT relationships to include faster access to the Web, mobile service delivery, networking, teleconferencing and multi-channel information technologies to accomplish higher-level two-way transactions. The concept is similar to "connected government" which emphasizes systematic approaches to collection, reuse and sharing of data and information (United Nations, 2010). The key platform upon which digital governance is built is **interoperability**, the capacity of governmental organizations to share and integrate information using common standards (Chapter 7). Few governments have yet harnessed the full power of existing technologies to achieve higher levels of two-way interactions with businesses, with citizens or with other governments. Even fewer citizens recognize the future necessity of interaction through the use of ICTs to deliver more cost effective public services and government benefits.

The Emergence of Electronic Government

An important outgrowth of the information explosion accompanying globalization was the emergence of **electronic government**, an umbrella term which variously describes the integration of disparate data sources into one-stop websites or portals to improve access and communication between governments, businesses, citizens and other related interests. During its early era of development, four general types of e-government relationships were identified and are still useful in classifying interactions between governments and their various stakeholders:

1) **Government-to-Government (G2G)**: Represents a main pillar of electronic government, the linkages among government bodies and agencies working together and providing information and services to each other. Increased interest in better customer service, fiscal

accountability, environmental protection, more efficient government operations, improved performance and the adoption of "best practices" are also among the driving forces behind the implementation of G2G services.

2) **Government-to-Employee (G2E)**: Refers to the online relationships between government agencies, employees and contract workers. This is an important and generally understudied linkage, with risks to public accountability and transparency accompanying the use of consultants, intermediaries, outsourcing or private sector partnerships.[5] G2E relationships also facilitate the management of civil service rules and internal communication with governmental employees as well as citizens and non-governmental contractors.

3) **Government-to-Business (G2B)**: Interaction between government and business takes place by exchanging information, oversight, purchasing and regulatory enforcement. During the 2009 fiscal year, the U.S. federal government alone spent over $70 billion on known IT expenditures, with much of the largesse used for government contracts that by most accounts have not performed well (U.S. Government Accountability Office, 2009). As part of a broader trend in public administration, G2B can be understood from a market-based perspective as a reform "aimed at both improved [citizen-centered] customer service and cost-savings through innovations borrowed from the private sector ... e-government can be a recognized reform that emphasizes the ability of the public sector to overcome many, if not most, of its perceived deficiencies through the adoption of private sector practices" (Morgeson and Mithas, 2009).

4) **Government-to-Citizen (G2C)**: This type of e-government facilitates citizen interaction with government, considered by many as the main goal of public service. How legislation, policy implementation and regulation create avenues for applying electronic and digital governance to improve the quality of citizen services is covered in Part III (Chapters 5, 6 and 7) of this book.

In all its forms, electronic government and now digital governance focus on the use of multiple information and communication technologies (ICTs) such as broadband, e-mail, fiber optics, text messaging, 4G, search engines, teleconferencing and WiFi to more rapidly deliver information and services to citizens, businesses and other governments (Bhatnagar, 2004; Carter and Belanger, 2005; Chadwick, 2006; Heeks, 1999; Hernon, Cullen and Relyea, 2006; Ho, 2002; Holden, Norris and Fletcher, 2003; Homberg, 2008; Roucheleau, 2006, 2007; West, 2005). Although many governments recognize the need for technological change, political leaders must negotiate within a maze of conflicting interest groups to achieve lasting results. This is becoming more difficult as public budgets decrease and public debt increases.

Budgets, Politics and Public Administration

Drastic changes in the technical capacities and social responsibilities of government have permanently affected fiscal and monetary policy and (perhaps) even altered the fundamental purposes of public administration. Government participation in, support for and regulation of increasingly complex policies and processes (especially those affecting banking and financial industries, credit markets, energy resources, health care delivery systems, environmental pollution and toxic wastes, and stem cell research—to name just a few) require more specialized and sophisticated bureaucracies linked together with networked ICTs. New patterns of decentralization and specialization have become significant components of the global knowledge revolution and are embedded in multi-faceted systems of information access and communication among public agencies (Milakovich and Gordon, 2009: 36).

Political decisions to address new problems (or to identify *as problems* conditions already present in society), expand the responsibilities of specialized public administrative bodies. Many of the challenges under-taken by the Obama administration as initiatives requiring "immediate" attention and additional federal resources (including economic stagnation, financial reform, unemployment, immigration reform, mortgage fraud, the banking crisis, health insurance reform, environmental pollution, energy use and conservation, population growth and stability, and mass transit—to name only a few of the major ones), have actually been with us for some time. In all of these cases, changes in economic conditions and societal values preceded identification of these issues as problems meriting further governmental attention. Even though certain other situations—such as the need for regulatory reform, mortgage refinancing assistance and curbs on excessive executive compensation—have not been as widely regarded as areas requiring public action, intense partisan debate continues over the scope and nature of particular governmental actions to address them (or, from the conservative perspective, whether government should deal with them at all!).

Administrative entities legally empowered by statute or regulation to confront these and other public issues are often drawn into political controversies surrounding the nature of the problems themselves as well as the methods proposed to resolve them. (Objections from fundamentalist Christian groups successfully thwarted embryonic stem cell research during the Bush administration.) Several factors encourage or discourage government from adopting new policies and management reforms to address them. These include, among others:

1) high unemployment rates and a "soft" private sector job market attracting more tech-trained personnel to the public sector;

2) criticisms from both the political left and right of unresponsive "bureaucratic" mentality;
3) low public esteem of government and public service in general; and
4) pervasive financial crises brought on by the failures of unregulated private financial markets.

Earlier versions of ICTs were used by previous administrations to promote their policies. Using different approaches, both presidents Bill Clinton (1993–2001) and George W. Bush (2001–2009) initiated "top-down" management reforms, including electronic government (e-gov) strategies to address many of these same issues, "reinvent government" and better manage "results-driven" federal programs and policies. For different reasons, both initiatives failed to fully integrate budgetary, information and performance management systems to achieve policy goals. As detailed in Chapter 5, many of these well-intended **incremental** policies were often co-opted by bureaucratic interests or guided by external ideological considerations.[6] The choice of incremental versus other approaches to policy implementation reflects compromises to achieve program priorities. Such compromises reinforce the limited scope of governmental activity in a staunchly capitalist free-market-based economy. At least that was the strategy prior to the financial meltdown beginning in 2007.

Politics and public administration are inextricably intertwined. Large bureaucracies always become targets for opposition political groups (particularly fiscal conservatives) who disagree with activist policies of reform administrations (typically Democratic). Thus, important national policy issues tend to be "recycled"—for example, health care reform during the Clinton administration in the mid-1990s and the health care affordability laws enacted by Congress and the Obama administration in 2010. Unlike past presidential administrations, however, younger tech-savvy public administrators, like the new voters recruited during the 2008 presidential campaign, are more familiar with and more likely to use new technology; more than older generations of citizens and public administrators, they see the potential value to be added by adopting web-based ICTs to achieve cost effective reform goals such as data collection and analysis, internet voting, performance management, revenue enhancements and measurement of results.

Barack Obama has attempted to initiate massive policy reforms which depend heavily on **innovative** change and expanded use of ICTs for successful implementation.[7] Such changes are rarely welcomed by current job occupants (especially state and local politicians and "old-time" public administrators), but they are evident in a wide variety of fields, especially applied information and communication technology. Among the systems transforming government processes are computer-aided ICTs, cloud computing, customer relationship management, open-source technology, webcasting and other network technologies: e-commerce, mobile computing and electronic fund transfer (EFT) (Chen and Thurmaier, 2008; Pirog and Johnson, 2008)—all are designed to reduce costs, enhance program participation and facilitate communication between governments and citizens. Applications which encourage citizens to self-organize on the Web also help governments improve cyber-security, reduce procurement time and keep from getting locked into sole-source contracts with single vendors, all of which have been identified as persistent problems for public agencies. They may have caused profound and lasting impacts on intergenerational politics as well.

The expanded use of ICTs, the internet and personal data assistants (PDAs), especially by younger tech-savvy voters, has created expectations for better, faster, safer and more efficient "virtual" government. Reasons for this include the influx of over 8 million new voters in the 2008 U.S. presidential elections, and renewed interest in politics among the **Net Generation**, younger voters born after 1982 with insatiable appetites for more information and social interaction over the internet. Some local governments and a few state governments have managed to move with this trend, but the vast majority of public agencies in America still lack the capacity, motivation and standardization required to fully utilize digital technology. (For state rankings, see Tolbert, Mossberger and McNeal, 2008.) Nonetheless, future trends are clear: more people of all ages are using New Media to connect with government. According to the Pew Research Center's Internet and American Life Project, over half of all adults in the United States used the internet to ask questions and obtain information about candidates and issues during the 2008 presidential election.[8] Still, many state and local government websites are limited to providing a narrow range of basic one-way informational and limited transactional services (Coursey and Norris, 2008; Ho, 2002; Holden, Norris and Fletcher 2003; Norris and Moon 2005). Furthermore, many websites are cluttered, difficult to use and incapable of connecting with other portals (Pew Charitable Trusts, 2008). Informed government officials are looking for applications in their home regions as well as other countries for successful cases of ICT policy implementation (Chapters 4 and 8).

The conversion from an **Industrial Age** bureaucracy-centered government to **Information Age** citizen-centered networked digital governance affects various generations differently; the transition will not proceed smoothly and requires advanced specialized technical skills as well as inspired forward-looking political and administrative leadership (Chapter 10). Appointed and elected officials must be committed to change and willing to guide the transition. Broadband internet connectivity, mobility and real-time contact, with their low cost of access to information and instant exchange of data, files and information, are among the powerful advantages that technological improvement brings to individuals, organizations and (eventually) governments. Although personnel, hardware and software investments must be carefully made, this book argues that the key impediments to applying such innovations across existing geographic and generation boundaries are political and organizational—rather than technological. The technology is available: what is lacking is the leadership and political will to apply ICTs to restructure existing political and administrative processes.

The Transition from Electronic Government to Digital Governance

Electronic government is a relatively new concept derived from the expanded use of ICTs in everyday exchanges and transactions. Although its study and practice are rapidly expanding, experts still disagree about a precise definition and the scope of the field. Much of the research has been eclectic and multi-disciplinary, lacking a consistent theoretical focus and integration with theories of public performance. Although those working in the field debate its precise meaning, one aspect is agreed upon: electronic government and its derivatives should be far more than simply making reams of public information available to citizens via an internet portal.

The vast majority (over 90%) of governments in the United States and other economically developed nations report that they are "present" on the internet and provide information to citizens via portals or websites (see Figure 1.1 below). This is an important and necessary threshold—but much more needs to be done before public agencies can fully utilize the

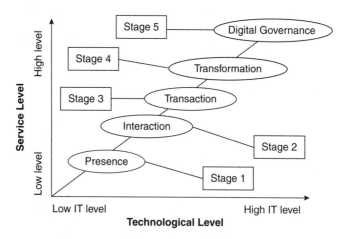

Figure 1.1 Stages of E-Government: Connections between Level of Technology and Quality of Service
Source: Adopted from generic models

capabilities available through existing New Media information technologies. Assessments of e-government sophistication have relied on a sequential approach that implies different degrees of e-government readiness and sophistication (Al-Hakim, 2007; Giuliani, 2005; Moon, 2002; Petroni and Tagliente, 2005; West, 2004, 2005). Depending upon its level of development within individual agencies, e-government has been generally categorized in 4–5 stages (Figure 1.1):

1) **Presence**: This first stage of e-government establishes a "placeholder" to deliver information in the future. It is a simple and less expensive entrance into e-government, but lacks interactive capabilities. An example would be a website where agencies post hours of operation, addresses and phone numbers of elected and appointed public officials.

2) **Interaction**: This stage provides information to help citizens avoid a trip to an office or the need to call for commonly requested information, forms and instructions for obtaining services available around the clock. Successful examples are free online e-filing of simple federal and state tax returns by the Internal Revenue Service (IRS) in cooperation with private tax firms and with several state taxing authorities.

3) **Transaction**: Enables citizens or customers to complete entire tasks electronically 24/7. It creates self-service operations for tasks such as license renewals, paying taxes and fees and submitting bids for procurement contracts. The flow of information can be two-way but is usually one-way (Signore, Chesi and Palloti, 2005: 4).

4) **Transformation**: In earlier studies, this was the highest order of evolution for e-government initiatives using the full capacities of technology to transform government service delivery (Seifert, 2003: 14). This stage facilitates government-to-government (G2G) flow of information and decision-making processes between federal, state, local, public and private institutions. Organizational barriers are removed and service becomes citizen-centric (Chapter 3).

5) **Digital Governance**: As represented by Stage 5 in Figure 1.1, this more advanced interactive and transactional exchange combines technological development with the highest levels of service quality to provide multi-channel two-way service delivery to all citizens. Recipients of government services are expected to make informed choices of alternatives. There are currently few examples of Stage 4 or Stage 5 initiatives.

In addition, greater e-participation and citizen engagement are supported and encouraged by Stage 5 digital governance decision-making processes. In 2002, A. Jae Moon used a similar sequential five-stage methodology to categorize e-government practice in local government (Table 1.1). Each of these stages was viewed as a barrier to implementation and included

Table 1.1 Practices, Effectiveness and Barriers to ICT Implementation in Government

E-Government in Practice	*Real World Applications*
Stage 1: One-Way Communication/Information Dissemination	• Website information posting on "portals"
Stage 2: Two-way Communication	• Registration for programs/services, parks and recreation facilities • Requests for government records; services: sidewalk, streetlight, pothole repair, etc.
Stage 3: Services and Financial Transactions	• Property registration; Business license and permit application/renewal • Online payment of fines, taxes, utility bills, license/permit fees • E-procurement: purchase/online request for proposal (RFPs)
Stage 4: Integration	• The Howard Dean (2004) and the Barack Obama (2008) campaigns
Stage 5: Political and Administrative Participation	• Successful use of ICTs to promote active electoral participation with constituents • Use of technology to co-produce public services

Source: Adapted from Moon, 2002: Barriers to e-government: Personnel capacity, technical capacity, financial capacity and legal issues

personnel, technical and financial capacities and legal issues (Moon, 2002). At the time the article was written, there were too few examples of the integration and political participation stages to be included. This has irreversibly changed since the 2004 presidential election.

Governments worldwide utilize e-government as an enabling strategy to increase efficiency, encourage participation, enhance transparency, collect more revenue and facilitate public sector reforms. Increasing decision-making transparency is especially important in countries such as the United States, where a constitutional system of federalism grants substantial independent powers to states and local governments. Despite available technology, only 32 U.S. states permit citizens to view budgetary decisions, and the websites containing such information for many others are difficult to access (Public Interest Research Group, 2010). While e-government will never be a panacea guaranteeing citizen satisfaction and flawless public sector performance, it is a powerful tool which has aided many governments in achieving administrative reforms (Traunmüller, 2004; Traunmüller and Lenk, 2002; Wimmer, Scholl and Ferro, 2008). Although e-government can be a catalyst for change, it will never be a complete solution without a broader commitment to reform in the public sector. At the very least, three factors are critical for successful implementation: 1) willingness to initiate reform; 2) availability of an information and communications technology (ICT) **infrastructure**; and 3) the institutional capacity to absorb and manage change (Bhatnagar, 2004: 13). In addition, leadership committed to change and backed by knowledgeable constituent support is required to fully overcome resistance and extend the promise of technological innovation to enhance government services.

While it is impossible to fully define the continuously evolving scope of online government, several researchers have offered suggestions to distinguish basic data and information exchange functions from higher-level governmental activities, referred to as digital governance. Professor Donald F. Kettl (2002b: xi) provides an etiology of American Public Administration distinguishing connected government institutions from *governance* as "the way government gets the job done" referring not only to electoral politics but to "the outcomes of the interaction of government, the public service and citizens throughout the political process, policy development, program design and service delivery." Thomas B. Riley, the Executive Director of Canada's Commonwealth Centre for e-Governance, defines e-governance as a choice among citizens and institutions about how they wish to communicate with each other:

> e-governance [is] about the use of emerging information and communication technologies to facilitate the processes of government and public administration. In reality, though, e-governance is really about choice. It is about *providing citizens with the ability to choose the manner in which they wish to interact with their governments* [emphasis added]. And it is about the choices governments make about how information and communication technologies [ICTs] will be deployed to support citizen choices.
>
> (quoted in Oliver and Sanders, 2004: vii)

The limited use of ICTs by citizens is especially prevalent in decentralized, fragmented and locally controlled systems of **federalism** (practiced in the United States and a few other countries) which independently elect public officials, have aggressive business lobbies, separate taxation and revenue-streams and weak local and state institutions. These political systems were never designed to achieve national political objectives and have, in the past, thwarted many centrally directed solutions to issues defined as public problems (Chapter 7). Fragmented systems are inefficient and permit decisions to be made by widely dispersed state and local officials, protected by constitutional institutions from potentially necessary (or repressive) actions by national governments. In such systems, just because a central authority sets a deadline for making some change, there is no guarantee that state and local institutions will follow. Likewise, the conversion from electronic government to digital governance cannot be achieved by setting a deadline for installing new equipment and facilities. Putting public services online and facilitating citizen-to-government (C2G) transactions (Stages 1 and 2) are insufficient to achieve productivity gains. Governments must find other ways, primarily through education, legislation and regulation, to encourage citizens to seek out and use self-directed added-value services.

As in the private sector, changes in the "front office" are preceded by substantial "back office" reorganization and investments in technology and human capital. Operations must be seamlessly integrated into one system for effective implementation. This cannot be dictated centrally: it can be achieved only through the creation of mutual trust-based environments within the public service "which is not suspicious, but supportive of innovation" (Liikanen, 2003: 68).[9]

The transition from e-government to digital governance requires the collection and dissemination of vast amounts of information, assurances of privacy, secure websites and decisions to deliver services more economically, thereby reducing operating costs. Most government agencies now provide basic services over the internet, including the capability to apply for government jobs and contracts, obtain or renew licenses and passports, request government loans and submit employment information (Appendix A).[10] Moving from basic to higher levels of digital governance requires the implementation of advanced digital interchange, lessons in self-service and greater trust among businesses, citizens and public agencies—conditions unfortunately lacking in most governments and many societies.

The Benefits of Digital Governance

Ever since governments began offering online services several decades ago, many have, in varying degrees, succeeded in turning early visions of the information super-highway into reality, albeit severely restricted by existing bureaucratic infrastructures, citizen distrust, local politics, opposing group interests, privacy concerns and resource constraints. Savings resulting from making public services available online are among the main benefits associated with the implementation of e-government. Other proposed benefits include ease of access, reduction of corruption by making processes more open and transparent, greater convenience for agencies and citizens, revenue growth and full-scale citizen participation. Several studies referenced in individual chapters and in the Bibliography at the end of the book argue for ICTs as a means to, among other goals, improve service quality by better utilization of scarce financial resources. Others dispute this facile notion.

Unless the issue of *how* money is spent is addressed, simply allocating more resources for information and communication technology will not necessarily result in more efficiencies or reduced inequities in the delivery of public services. Plainly, many new ICTs require significant expenditures. In addition, interested stakeholders also demand hard statistical evidence of positive outcomes before any further outlay of public funds. Efficiency, economy and quality in resource allocation must be seriously evaluated as new competitive providers offer alternatives to traditional bricks-and-mortar, hierarchical and geographically bound public services.

Efficient management of financial and human resources contributes to success in any segment of the economy, especially the public sector where funds are always limited and citizen demands are notoriously difficult to meet. One of the best ways to ensure quality resource utilization is **cost-benefit analysis** to maximize net benefits to society, thereby providing the greatest good for the greatest number of citizens. Thinking in broader cost-benefit terms when allocating public sector resources is especially important because most public services are paid for directly as taxes or indirectly as user fees by citizens. Nonetheless, very few states or local governments utilize cost-benefit analysis for resource utilization. Until there are acceptable analyses of how public resources are being used, it is difficult to know which among many alternatives (additional resources, competition, partnerships or regulation) result in service quality improvement. Such analyses should include stakeholders closest to the situation to provide an accurate measure of the benefits obtained. Quality resource and results management is too difficult for any one particular public or private entity: everyone must be involved and work together to make necessary improvements (Chapter 3).

The extent to which traditional public administration is eventually transformed into digital governance depends on the *ability* and *willingness* of elected and appointed public officials to demonstrate the **value added** to individual processes from each of the factors discussed in the chapters below.[11] The value-added benefits of a digital ICT strategy are apparent, at least in theory: clearer, cheaper, faster, more personalized services that can be accessed 24 hours a day, seven days a week—literally whenever needed. As a result, governments should (ideally) decrease costs, become more productive, improve services, engage citizens, share information, regain trust and make decisions in a more open and transparent manner. Further development of online digital governance could also enhance public productivity through co-production of services and cost reductions in standard operating procedures. This is widely understood in the commercial sector, but less publicized (although no less important) in the public sector. Simply put, if businesses have benefitted from the internet, why aren't more government organizations taking full advantage of ICTs as well?

One of the primary reasons for this paradox is that there is considerable partisan disagreement among politicians about which sector—public or private—should lead productivity growth efforts in the digital revolution. This stems in large part from varying political definitions of the appropriate and necessary role of government in the private economy.

Open Government Accountability, Privacy and Transparency

All democratic institutions and initiatives require the oxygen of information to be viable. Excessive secrecy or unnecessary emphasis on protecting the privacy of public officials stifles the flow of oxygen, diminishing accountability, transparency and trust. More dangerous and toxic, however, is the potential threat posed by poor information management practices. When records are not created, deliberately destroyed or misplaced, any notion of governmental accountability and transparency loses all meaning. There is a real danger that government websites and public archives are threatened by hackers and lack of storage for increasing volumes of electronic communications (Gorman and Ramstad, 2009). Expanded use of digital governance can open up internal government processes to public scrutiny; information processes and services should be of high quality and engage citizens in policy processes. Information quality standards and feedback mechanisms such as focus groups help maximize the usefulness of information provided and strengthen citizen participation.[12] One successful example is *Citilink* (Burgerlink) a Dutch government initiative to improve the performance of the public sector by involving citizens. *Citilink* provides quality standards, measures citizen satisfaction and stimulates participation; it will run from 2008 to 2010 as part of the expanded Dutch government ICT effort.[13]

The Information Age has brought with it more demands for accountability from larger numbers of sources. Demand is being driven by the infinite expansion of the internet, where there is now so much discourse, exchange of information and alternative sources that it is easy to get lost. The internet is still an expanding network which is being fueled by the development of **open-source** information environments. This idea is spreading to society as a whole, resulting in expectations of more assurances of accountability from all public and private sector organizations. Accountability arrangements should ensure that it is clear who is responsible for shared projects and initiatives.

The vast amount of information available online heightens concerns about information rights applied by and to governments, courts, interest groups and citizens. As average citizens become armed with more knowledge (or at least the capacity to obtain such knowledge), then it will be private sector organizations, along with governments, that are pressured to become more forthcoming about the information held in organizational databases. (The private sector here means not just large corporations or businesses, but all non-governmental organizations, including non-profits.) Just as privacy moved from the exclusive domain of the private sector 30 years ago, when Sweden passed the first data protection law, so will the right of access to information become a part of the public sector domain.

Unlike much of the private for-profit commercial sector, when governments put content online, numerous policy issues immediately emerge. Who has access to the information and for what purposes? What happens to digital records once they have been used? Who is accountable for maintaining "paper trails" to establish accountability when decisions do not result in anticipated results? With so many incidents of identity theft and privacy violations rampant on the internet, many potential users are rightfully apprehensive about the security and validity of certain information contained in public records. The private sector learned the importance of guaranteeing privacy in the early days of the evolution of the World Wide Web. The growth of online marketing and e-commerce brought with it major copyright, ethical, intellectual property and privacy issues as well. For citizens whose online requests for government information are rejected, the issue becomes: what are the reasons why? Public agencies and departments decide in advance what information can be made public, based on their respective laws and policies. Federal open government laws are aimed at balancing privacy rights with an individual's right to access public records (Chapter 6).

Any doubts about the reliability or validity of information contained in "official" websites undermine public confidence and limit the higher-level (Stages 4 and 5) uses of communication and information technology. For such online consultation to succeed, it is important that citizens can access necessary background briefings, documents and policies on issues being discussed. Not only must information be accurate and quality assured, but individual citizens or groups must know and understand how an issue affects them in order to respond appropriately. If governments can show how privacy, security and transparency policies are accurate and evidence-based, then more people will communicate, conduct transactions and perhaps even vote online. Distrust of government remains a primary impediment to applying ICTs to conduct elections, share information, improve service and increase productivity.

Despite attempts to heighten security and transparency, instant access to data may have actually weakened accountability and oversight. The results of the private sector's abdication of accountability standards were visible after the dot-com bust in the late 1990s, followed by revelations of financial malfeasance by large corporations and the spectacle of senior corporate officials being arrested, prosecuted and jailed for financial crimes. The proliferation of so-called "white collar" crimes such as credit card fraud, identity theft, mortgage and securities fraud and brazen multi-billion dollar Ponzi schemes has contributed to the global economic crisis and made it more difficult to establish trust between businesses, citizens and government necessary to nurture digital discourse.

For some types of public services such as patent applications, tax collection and Social Security distributions, e-filing and electronic transfer of benefits are already accepted as the more efficient means of filing all types of forms and receiving benefits by direct deposit.[14] Concerning overall satisfaction with electronic government, a report from the University of Michigan's American Customer Satisfaction Index (ACSI) E-Government Satisfaction Index evaluated 83 federal government websites and revealed that levels of satisfaction were steadily increasing before a slight downturn beginning in early 2009 (Figure 1.2). Furthermore, research shows that improving citizen satisfaction can increase government efficiency and offset negative attitudes about corporate bailouts and economic stimulus expenditures.

Improvement in the quality of government services significantly impacts acceptance, legitimacy and utilization of digital governance. At the same time, the transition to a parallel customer service approach requires new ways of thinking within organizations providing online services to citizens. Top management support and incentives involving both service providers and citizens are fundamental elements in the transformation. To achieve a citizen-centric perspective, information and services should be provided based on the interests and needs of

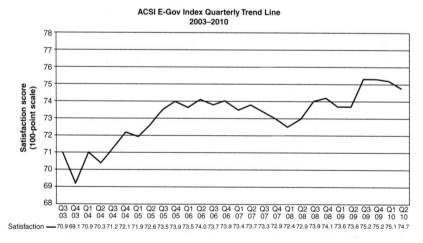

Figure 1.2 Quarterly E-Government Satisfaction Scores Over Time (2003–2010)

Source: foreseeresults.com. Available at:www.foreseeresults.com/research-white-papers/_downloads/foresee-results-acsi-egov-index-q2-2010.pdf

constituents. Although required to stay up-to-date in the technological aspect, public service managers and employees also need adequate training to provide professional point-of-contact service to citizens (see Box 5.1, Chapter 5). Despite some apparent risks, digital governance offers a wide range of benefits and opportunities for all levels of government, including:

1) enhanced direct access to a wider range of government services with more convenient online access via computers, PDAs or mobile phones;
2) better informed citizens who, as they become more proficient with the use of new technology and satisfied with improved service provision, are more likely to participate in the other activities of government;
3) integrated operations across public agencies, departments and jurisdictions, helping to increase intra-agency efficiency and productivity;
4) lower costs when compared to traditional face-to-face services which consume more resources and personnel than online services;
5) reduced layers of organizational processes; and
6) improved effectiveness, trust and quality of service by performing faster transactions, improving accountability and maintaining faster processes.

About the Book

This book explores the transition from traditional forms of public service enhanced by electronic government to new forms of digital governance, emphasizing the importance of citizen participation and information technology to accomplish the change. Chapters concentrate on strategies for public administration and organizational transformation and implications for improved and measurable government performance. Chapter 2 raises critical questions about the integration of ICTs within existing electoral and political structures. The shift from the bureaucracy-centered to customer-centric networked model is viewed as a means to both restore public trust and improve service quality. Cases presented in Chapter 3 show how some governments are transforming service delivery systems with four different, yet interrelated, customer relationship management (CRM) strategies and how the concept is being applied to the public sector as citizen relationship management (CzRM). Chapter 4 stresses the importance of reforming educational and training systems and applying for quality awards to improve service quality. Chapter 5 shows how fulfilling budgetary, legal, political and regulatory obligations and "putting customers first" requires a comprehensive bottom-up re-examination of long-standing public management practices, genuine employee empowerment, responsiveness to citizens as valued customers and changes in the management and oversight responsibilities of public officials. Chapter 6 traces the evolution of laws and regulations for delivering virtual public services and shows how ICTs have influenced public attitudes about traditional governmental functions. Chapter 7 discusses legal, political, structural and regulatory constraints on applying e-commerce and cites working examples of digital governance as a means to enhance interoperability of services. Chapter 8 describes the comparative ranking of various countries in terms of their use of the internet, access to high-speed broadband service and integration of information technology with public services. Chapter 9 returns to the theme of globalization and public administration and Chapter 10 summarizes lessons learned and future challenges.

Digital governance is a rapidly expanding administrative and management practice which offers opportunities to transform public sector service delivery in numerous ways. New Media technologies increase accessibility and convenience of public services and the citizen-centric approach provides incentives for greater numbers of citizens to participate in administrative and political processes. Obstacles such as lack of computer literacy and the **digital divide** must be addressed and overcome to achieve the goal of accessibility for all sectors of society (Mossberger, *et al.*, 2003). Successful transformation of public service delivery systems has to take place within organizations with clear policies supported by effective leaders and active citizens. By providing clear, relevant and transparent ICT services, public agencies can regain trust from constituents by offering new and more effective ways of thinking and interacting with local, state and federal governments. The following chapters outline a road map for governments and public agencies to become more proactive and use the many advantages of ICTs to implement positive organizational changes and improve the quality of citizen services.

Key Terms

information and communication
  technology (ICT), 3
knowledge revolution, 3
globalization, 3
Web 2.0, 4
technological change, 4
social networks, 4
information technology, 4
public administration, 5
geographic districts, 5
New Media, 5

portals, 6
wikis, 6
blogs or weblogs, 6
USA.gov, 6
sunk costs, 7
polisphere, 8
knowledge management, 8
digital governance, 9
interoperability, 9
electronic government, 9
incremental, 12

Part II

Politics

Transforming Democracy and Bureaucracy

Rapid breakthroughs in applications of digital technologies have empowered greater numbers of citizens to contribute directly to electoral processes, affecting political outcomes in a variety of different ways. Increased access to computers and smart phones allows more people to become active participants in economic, political and social development via the burgeoning global information infrastructure known as the internet. Chapter 2 shows how electronic and digital applications emerged with the spread of new communication technologies and accelerated during recent political campaigns. The chapter also describes how traditional political linkages between citizens and governments are changing, outlines a model of how information and communication technologies (ICTs) facilitate wider citizen participation and highlights cases showing how ICTs enhance deliberative and participatory democracy.

Implementation of any ICT-enabled transformation is burdened with a multiplicity of challenges—financial, structural, technical and, above all, political. Different incentives are being used to encourage public managers, especially those at the state and local government level, to reorient bureaucracies to become customer-focused and results-driven. E-government efforts are bolstered by initiatives intended to apply new and emerging technologies to transform the operations and scope of government. In some instances, promises made by advocates of electronic government have exceeded actual levels of performance and results. Chapter 3 explains how moving from a traditional hierarchical, paper-intensive and rule-driven environment (public administration as we know it) to a more horizontally integrated, networked and citizen-centered system, entails internal transformations as well as an informed and educated electorate (voting public) able to access government services online.

Chapter 4 discusses the evolution of web-based virtual learning and cites recent evidence supporting the value of virtual education and training as alternatives to traditional teaching methods. Virtual delivery is emerging as a viable alternative not only because of its lower costs, but its greater flexibility in achieving learning goals and potential to close the digital divide. Quality awards and national accreditation standards also provide a rich and varied resource for governments to define their main missions and purposes and reach out to all citizens. Rewards help improve the quality of public services, focus attention on new performance measures and emphasize process improvements. The competitive challenge and distinction accompanying the pursuit of an award or a prize can also be a source of employee motivation and pride. The application process enhances in-house customer service quality initiatives, helps identify areas needing improvement and generates data that can help develop models and theories to assist public managers in determining strategies best suited for application in specific areas of the public sector.

2 From Representative to Digital Democracy

Using the Internet to Increase Citizen Participation in Governance

I know of no safe depositor of the ultimate powers of the society but the people them-selves; and if we think them not enlightened enough to exercise their control with a wholesome discretion, the remedy is not to take it from them but to inform their discretion. Every government degenerates when trusted to the rulers of the people alone. The people themselves are its only safe depositories.

Thomas Jefferson

What roles do information and communication systems play in fostering greater citizen participation, influencing election outcomes and informing the day-to-day operations of government? Unlike previous forms of New Media, ICTs facilitate two-way communication, encourage interaction among stakeholders and provide a rich forum for information dissemination, decision making and discussion of political issues in technologically advanced societies. The internet facilitates debate by simultaneously acting as a worldwide broadcasting network, a platform for information dissemination and a low-cost medium for collaboration and interaction among individuals and groups via their computers, laptops, iPhones and mobile phones—without regard for geographic boundaries or time zones. Whether or not this technological revolution is being used effectively by citizens to change political processes is still an open question, one without a simple yes or no answer.

This chapter opens with a description of the origins of participatory democracy and discusses how modern concepts of democracy encourage online **citizen participation** and how newly created spaces on the internet are being used by political activists and candidates to facilitate wider collaboration with potential supporters. The chapter also describes traditional political linkages between citizens and governments, offers a model of how ICTs and the internet facilitate citizen access and participation and highlights cases where information technology has enhanced collaboration. The following questions are addressed: What role does the internet play in fostering and aiding citizen participation in government? Does increased citizen involvement lead to greater trust and confidence in government? What role did information technology play in apparently reversing a 40-year trend of low voter turn outs by drawing over 8 million new voters to the 2008 U.S. presidential election? This chapter demonstrates how information technology facilitates broader democratic citizen participation as well as highlighting the challenges facing officials in adopting internet-based ICT strategies (Milakovich, 2009).[1]

Democracy, Elitism and Citizen Participation

Theories of democracy date from the founding of the city-state in ancient Athens, Greece. The philosophical and theoretical origins of democracy can be traced back as far as Plato's *Republic* where concepts of freedom of assembly, equal representation, freedom of speech, electoral participation and collective action through voting formed the foundations upon which advanced post-monarchial democracies were founded. Although **Athenian Democracy** was an "elitist" form of citizenship with representatives who met weekly to decide legislative issues after consulting with citizens, nascent concepts of citizen participation and representative democracy evolved with democratic principles as societies became more complex. Democratic principles are embedded in the constitutions of most Western representative democracies and include, at a minimum:

1) Freedom of assembly, speech, religion, press and other mass media outlets to criticize the government in power.
2) Other "expressed" freedoms *from* government action such as those embodied in the Bill of Rights, the first 10 amendments to the U.S. Constitution.
3) Periodic free and open elections among competing political groups based on principles of equal representation (i.e. one person = one vote).
4) An independent judicial branch with the authority to review the actions of the executive and legislative branches of government.
5) Written and enforceable procedures for limiting the powers of government, resolving conflicts and protecting minority rights (Milakovich, 2010).

Citizen participation in public decision making is encouraged and expected, but neither guaranteed nor required in most democracies. Citizens are just as free *not* to participate as well. According to prevailing theories of **pluralism**, public opinion and policy formulation reflect competition among partisan group interests, professional associations and political parties. Decisions resulting from such deliberations (at least in theory) are responsive and accountable to broad-based citizen preferences, rather than narrow-focused private interests. On the contrary, **elitism** (similar to **oligarchy**) implies that powerful individuals or groups with special connections, interests, family ties or wealth anoint themselves with privileges and the authority to lead. These two opposing political theories are continuously reflected in contemporary political dialogue and debate.

Compared with the Platonic ideal of individual citizen action and participation, the nearly universal access provided by the internet is a new and potentially revolutionary phenomenon. According to one observer, e-government has the potential to become "an institution that helps to ensure reasoned reflection about political issues and active participation in **deliberative democracy** by citizens and by members of the government" (Jaeger, 2005: 1). Moreover, ICTs increasingly influence the cultural, economic, political and social lives of millions of people throughout the world. National, state and local governments are establishing a strong, albeit uneven, presence on the World Wide Web, with portals designed to disseminate information as well as receive feedback from the public. The U.S. State Department distributes a monthly online publication called *eJournalUSA*, also available on social networking websites such as *Facebook*—which communicates with 500 million people worldwide.[2]

What is citizen participation and how is it defined? Traditionally, citizen participation concerns many facets of voluntary or *coerced* participation in local, state and national issues requiring governmental decision making. The term "coercion" does not imply the use of force or violence to gain political power. Rather, it is used in the same sense that Theodore J. Lowi describes "forced compliance" with government policies and regulations (Lowi, 1964). An example of this option used in several democratic countries—but not in the United States—is the imposition of small civil fines for not voting to "coerce" individuals to cast a vote. Citizen participation implies a readiness on the part of both citizens and government officials to accept certain pre-determined civic obligations and roles; each contribution is accepted, valued and potentially used in decision making. The inclusion of citizen representatives as co-equal partners in decision-making processes contributes to successful citizen participation. In some form, citizen participation has played a significant role in the evolution of democratic forms of government since the founding of organized societies.

In modern high-tech democratic systems with multiple and competing information channels and communications systems, it is often difficult to persuade citizens—especially those lacking access to resources for expressing varying political opinions—to band together to discuss options and decide complex political issues. Socio-demographic factors such as level of education and income often determine who participates as well as outcomes of deliberations. The democratic image of an idyllic New England **town meeting**, an early American institution that combined citizen participation with deliberative democracy, is now all but a quaint memory. Technology and the mass media, especially television, have substituted for direct citizen-to-government deliberation and assumed a pre-eminent role in articulating interests and defining public opinion upon which citizen attitudes are based. The relative advantages of the internet as a medium for enhancing citizen participation have been touted for various purposes; however, prior to the 2004 U.S. presidential campaign the technology was unavailable and there was no comprehensive strategy to apply ICTs to electoral processes (Heeks, 1999). Barack Obama's 2008 run for the presidency was the first national political campaign to successfully apply new information technologies to garner political contributions and generate new voters (Hendricks and Denton, 2010; Todd and Gawiser, 2009).

Additional breakthroughs in political communication similar to the direct candidate-to-citizen dialogue used in Obama's 2008 high-tech campaign are being made in newly emerging and rapidly expanding polispheres (Chapter 1). Whether or not participatory strategies can be sustained or replicated by other candidates or successfully converted to the administration of public programs remains to be seen. The Obama administration has been far less effective in communicating administrative changes via New Media technology. Nonetheless, ICTs have become a permanent part of American political processes offering a greater number of citizens the option to exercise new forms of civic participation (Klofstad, 2011).

The Importance of Citizen Participation

Previous forms of citizen participation, not unlike their high-speed descendant, may be viewed from the perspective of benefits to be gained versus the costs to be borne. Implicit in this strategy for involving greater numbers of citizens in public affairs is the notion of reciprocal obligations and new relationships between individuals and society facilitated by communication channels such as the print media, radio, television and the internet (Lips, 2010). The potential benefits of participation to citizens versus the possible costs to society are perennial subjects for debate during political campaigns. In democratic societies, media sources become partisan and questions are premised on several related assumptions about citizenship and democracy.

First, individual citizens are able to bring about desired change through collective actions by expressing opinions, either individually or in concert with others through blogs, interest groups or **community organizations**; second, individuals have the opportunity to "practice democracy" by learning how to organize interests and implement desired changes; third, as citizens learn about politics and government through civic participation they are better able to appreciate the unique needs and interests of all community groups; fourth, as citizens learn how to resolve conflicting interests, the general welfare of the community benefits; and last, the widespread use of New Media helps individuals understand group dynamics as applied to mixed multi-racial and multi-ethnic groups.

Making government data available online in universally accessible formats allows citizens to comment, derive value and take action in their own communities. This includes providing greater access to environmental data to help citizens learn about the effects of pollution in their communities, communicate information about local conditions back to government agencies and protect themselves against hazardous environmental factors. For example, among the most popular features on the Commonwealth of Virginia's website are instructions on how to report dangerous road conditions, including potholes, to state highway authorities.[3]

It is not always possible to measure with precision *how much* value is added by investments in ICTs because government websites are becoming more than information super-highways flanked by billboards and a series of service stops along the way. Based on the availability of government-related information, such sites offer interactive online tools that can "extend public space [promoting] consultation and dialogue between citizens and their governments" (Lenihan, 2005: 274). The internet can strengthen democratic values because it "includes such democratic governance issues as government openness, active citizen participation and digital [online] voting" (Rho, 2007: 203). Just as the delivery of online services by government requires two-way communication, an informed citizenry is essential to discuss politics and cast votes via the internet. Opinions about the merits of combining e-democracy with pluralism are mixed.

Advocates generally stress e-democracy and online voting as extensions of digital governance, while others perceive its implementation as running counter to the values of liberal democracy (Clift, 2004; Knowles, 2005). The e-democracy optimists argue that the internet can be used to "enhance our democratic processes and provide increased opportunities for individuals and communities to interact with government and for the government to seek input from the community" (Clift cited in Riley and Riley, 2003: 11). Similar to the argument made by Robert Putnam (2000) a decade ago about the relationship between mass media and the loss of social connectedness, critics claim that the impersonal dialogue encouraged by the use of computers, e-government and the changing cultural values associated with social networking undermine the participatory nature of a democratic citizenship (Box, *et al.*, 2001; Denhardt and Denhardt, 2007). Nonetheless, increased opportunities for participation make it more difficult for public officials to ignore public opinion during deliberative processes. If voter turn out in the 2008 U.S. presidential election (the highest since 1968) is an indication of future trends, then the pro-e-democracy argument would prevail, at least in the short term.

According to pluralist democratic theories (above) increased citizen participation results in better governmental decisions. By opening greater numbers of access channels and encouraging new forms of civic participation, decisions become more acceptable and legitimate to the majority. Better government decisions, by definition, are more beneficial to greater numbers of "average" citizens. Citizen participation provides a source of special insight, information, knowledge and experience which contributes to the soundness of government solutions to public problems, especially in modern American politics, where the lines between campaigning and governing have become increasingly blurred. Information and communication technologies have also contributed to the lengthening of political campaigns and enabled candidates to solicit funds year round (Ornstein and Mann, 2000).

Active involvement in politics and decision making serves as a check and balance to other less visible forms of political activities, thereby increasing transparency and reducing the temptations for public officials to make corrupt or self-serving decisions. Citizen input can legitimize a program, its purposes, implementation and leadership. Unsupported leaders often become discouraged and drop activities that are potentially beneficial to average citizens, but are too difficult to implement in contentious political environments. Voluntary participation can also reduce the cost of paid personnel needed to carry out many of the duties associated with community actions as extensions of political campaigns or governmental policy. In all forms of government, there are various preconditions which either encourage or discourage active participation.

Prerequisites for Participation

Arguments in favor of various degrees of citizen participation have existed for centuries but, when examined empirically, the allegiance to genuine participation by public officials remains verbal in many instances (Milakovich, 1979). When it comes to actual implementation, however, many government officials advance numerous reasons why participation is not feasible or has to be restricted to selective forms of consultation with potential beneficiaries. Preconceived "elitist" notions that citizens lack interest or knowledge breeds neglect and mutual distrust. Arcane codes and by-laws also limit the mutual trust necessary for genuine participation. Past experiences with citizen participation show that such a commitment does not just happen, nor can it be taken for granted. There are several preconditions which encourage and sustain participation in particular situations. These include:

1) **An Appropriate Organization**: Participation is facilitated by appropriate organizational structures, such as volunteer **non-government organizations (NGOs)**. Citizens will voluntarily participate in a community activity when they have reasons to express their interests. If they view the organization as cumbersome, time consuming, dictatorial or grossly inefficient, they will not join, withdraw after joining or express their dissatisfaction by high levels of absenteeism or a general unwillingness to be supportive or cooperative.

2) **Benefits Gained Outweigh the Costs**: Citizens will voluntarily participate in various public activities when they see positive benefits to be gained. The benefits range from the internal satisfaction of

personal wants to the achievement of desired ends sought by a group. Goals can be economic in nature or include activities and projects to improve community conditions or standards. The key point is that people must view an activity, a proposed change or an issue as beneficial to them or their families. Benefits, however, seldom come without costs, and citizens participate when the benefits outweigh the costs. Costs involve such things as time, money, skills and prestige. Using their own scale of values, citizens determine whether or not they will participate (Homans, 1974). Often, there are costs or trade-offs for *not* participating, as well as for being active. This, too, is a part of the calculation each citizen must consider in deciding when and how to participate in governmental decisions.

3) **Way-of-Life Threatened**: Situations that may threaten people's economic status or lifestyles elicit citizen participation—often in a negative way. Whether people's perceptions are accurate or inaccurate makes little difference. If they perceive a threat, as many did during the health care reform debates, then they will organize volunteer groups to counter efforts to change. This is a reactionary form of citizen participation, and it is often spontaneous and extensive, such as the anti-Obama Tea Party movement in the United States. Citizen participation can be on either or both sides of an issue. Threatening issues are often viewed morally, socially, economically or religiously unacceptable to a group. When all or some of these issues are perceived as threatening by local citizens, participation can be extensive.

4) **Civic Obligation**: Citizens are more likely to voluntarily participate in a government activity when they feel obligated to support that activity. Traditionally, Americans have always wanted to be part of decisions affecting their lives. In recent years, however, fewer citizens have actively participated in social activities and community decision making (Putnam, 2000). Attempts to use electronic government and information technology to increase participation have been made to address this dilemma. The expanded reach of social networking has the potential to reverse the downward trend in cynicism and inspire more participation.

5) **Better Knowledge**: People are reluctant to participate in government activity when they do not have enough information to act responsibly. They are more likely to participate responsibly in public affairs if they understand the issue. When they do not understand, citizens act on limited information and opposition based on fear of change. If the public is knowledgeable and motivated to search for the information needed to participate in informed decisions on public issues, the internet could become a powerful tool for mass political literacy.

In summary, civic involvement takes place in a variety of different forms and at different levels, from having no voice at all in political deliberations to that of advisory roles to full representation at all stages. For participation to be truly effective, it is necessary for those affected by decisions to be involved in all stages of the decision-making process. According to the above preconditions for civic participation, the degree of citizen involvement can be enhanced by: 1) stressing the individual and group benefits of participation; 2) identifying and organizing appropriate groups receptive to citizen input; 3) helping citizens find positive ways to respond to threatening situations; 4) stressing the obligations each citizen has toward community improvement; and 5) providing citizens with better knowledge of issues and opportunities for participation.

Encouraging Civic Participation

The internet is ideally suited for "democratizing" politics and stimulating multiple forms of citizen input to government through all of the above methods and more. Participation occurs through browsing the World Wide Web for specific information, transmitting electronic publications and letters through e-mail, and using blogs to discuss issues, form coalitions and plan and coordinate activities (Feld and Wilcox, 2008). Blogging strategies will not be successful if they operate in a vacuum. The **blogosphere** is interconnected, and participants will be most successful if fully engaged in the wider world. It is possible to have a blog outreach strategy without having one's own blog. In so doing, many are learning how to participate in a democracy and actually see how actions could make a difference on specific political issues.

Political blogs succeed because they are interconnected networks in support of or opposed to a candidate or cluster of issues. Their sponsors are prepared to hold conference calls with allies in the blogosphere and willing to write guest entries for other popular blog networks such as the *Daily Beast, DailyKos, Huffington Post, Power Line* and *TechPresident*,[4] among millions of others. Committed, usually volunteer, staff must have the time to monitor what is being said about a candidate or issues in their respective polispheres and respond accordingly. In this "Brave New World" of technology, ICTs serve as electronic "webinars" for teaching skills necessary for informed citizens to participate responsibly in democratic processes and digital governance. The following section briefly describes how the internet developed and the specific roles that technology plays in encouraging citizen participation.

Development of the Internet and Political Participation

New channels of political communication requiring more demanding forms of political action have always arisen as information technology has changed. Three centuries ago the first stirrings of democracy found outlets through print media. Three generations ago, new ideologies and new forms of totalitarianism combined to use film and radio broadcasting as political propaganda. Today, the internet is being widely recognized for its potential to forge new linkages encouraging (as well as possibly discouraging) new forms of **political participation** in all advanced societies.

The mass acceptance of technological inventions such as the telegraph, radio, television and computers set the stage for this unprecedented integration of capabilities under the umbrella of the "internet." In much the same way the printing press radically transformed communication in 16th century Europe, the internet has revolutionized 21st century information distribution processes. The internet has revolutionized uses of the computer, cellular communications, smart phones and software as well. The adoption and saturation rates for new communication technologies have accelerated at an astounding rate. For example, it took 75 years for the telephone to reach 50 million people and 38 years for radio to reach 50 million listeners. Television took only 13 years to achieve the same number of viewers, personal computers just 16 years and the internet *only four years* to connect with 50 million users.[5] Rapid assimilation is due in part to the internet's low cost, ease of connectivity, wide reach and remote accessibility. Moreover, none of the previous forms of **mass media** were simultaneously worldwide broadcasting networks, mechanisms for information dissemination or tools for two-way collaboration and interaction between individuals without regard for geographic boundaries or time zones. This type of extended democratic information society was envisioned in the abstract as a global unifying force several decades ago (McLuhan, 1964). Since then, there has been substantial public support for additional government research on information technology and its impacts on society.[6]

The internet is one of the most successful examples of the benefits of sustained public investment and commitment to research and development of any information infrastructure. Beginning with early research in the 1960s and 1970s, government, industry and academia cooperated in developing and deploying the new medium. By 1971, the year the first e-mail was sent, the U.S. government made significant advances through the **Advanced Research Projects Administration (ARPA)**. That year, the institute developed **ARPANET** in an effort to connect military bases around the country to give them the same information capability as Central Command in Washington. The **National Science Foundation (NSF)** began using nascent internet technology in the mid-1970s to interconnect institutions of higher education. Soon thereafter, most university systems became interconnected to five major super computers. With the advent of more powerful personal computers, **linked area networks (LANs)** and internet browsers such as **Netscape** in the 1980s, individuals soon had access to the same central super-computing power as institutions. Technological innovation continues with the advent of broadband connectivity, digital internet multi-media, mobile computing, cellular telephone interface and multi-media systems integration.

Why is the Internet Different?

The internet is not just a revolutionary new technology, but an entirely different way of connecting and organizing human activity. It is not merely a means for linking individuals with existing commercial, governmental and political institutions, but a new way of redefining relationships altogether. The internet is an interconnected, multi-use worldwide open market which emphasizes communication, decentralization, information and specialization to achieve commercial and political goals. It is also an advanced information technology with the potential to change the way citizens interact with government. Previous technological applications such as the telegraph, telephone, radio, as well as broadcast, cable and satellite television all had similar potentials. Each of these pre-internet technologies can be compared with each other and with the World Wide Web to draw inferences about whether the internet may have greater—or at least different—potential to increase citizen participation. Its applications are much wider: the internet is being used as an "electronic ballot" for conducting elections, an "electronic town hall" to resolve conflicts and an "electronic courthouse" to settle disputes. The openness of the internet also has the potential to challenge authoritarian regimes as witnessed by the chaos following the Iranian election during the summer of 2009, the overthrow of the Tunisian government and the so-called "internet insurrection" in Egypt during late 2010 and early 2011 as well as the Chinese government crackdown on Google, among many other examples.

The internet is very well known, although its history and infrastructure are frequently misunderstood. In reality, the internet is an interconnected network of computers linked together by a common name and address or **domain space.** Using an **internet browser,** anyone with a PDA, computer or wireless device can communicate with anyone else on the internet simply by establishing a connection. The internet's private, cooperative, virtual and highly decentralized character makes it a tantalizing model for organizing multiple forms of human activity through technology. The internet has both the one-to-one characteristics of telephone and telegraph and the one-to-many characteristics of television and radio. It is both an individual communication device and a mass medium. Because of its packet switching rather than circuit switching character, it is far more difficult to impose physical borders on the internet than on other terrestrial wire-based, frequency modulation (FM) or microwave-based technologies. The internet is not a corporation or administrative arrangement: rather, it is a method for connecting computers and mobile communication devices.

The World Wide Web is a digital framework for organizing and storing information distributed across the internet. It facilitates "unbundling" and saves on storage costs because editors or publishers interested in collecting resources related to a particular subject matter need not obtain or maintain actual copies of the resource content. Information is available digitally simply by writing a web document (in HTML language) that contains pointers (known as **Uniform Resource Locators or URLs**) to the identified references and knowledge about available resources. The internet does not have the economic asymmetry of radio broadcasting or television, where it is cheap to receive information, but very expensive to broadcast it. In recent years, newspaper, television and radio networks have realized the potential of the new medium and integrated internet content with entertainment, news and commercial broadcast content.

Whom Do You Trust: Big Business or Big Government?

The most important characteristic differentiating the internet from other forms of mass media is its extremely low barriers to entry. Because it uses other existing physical communications infrastructures, a new internet enterprise need not build a radio transmitter, string wire or lay cable. All it takes to be an internet publisher (on the citizen side) is a personal computer, which can now be purchased for less than $200, and a $5 per month subscription to an internet service provider. Most of the large software internet servers such as Google, Microsoft and Yahoo! offer free e-mail service and also maintain huge databases containing billions of "micro-bits" of information about users. All it takes to become an internet service provider (on the business or government side) is about $25,000, most of which goes for labor costs and a high bandwidth connection between the terminal server and router into the larger internet. This is far less expensive than becoming a radio broadcaster, a print publisher or a telephone service provider even when there are no regulatory barriers to entry into those industries. Moreover, each internet user is also a *potential* supplier of content, although a much smaller number of users are also **content providers** or **critical analysts**. Active participation is limited to a relatively small number of bloggers and subject matter producers. Figure 2.1 illustrates four different levels related to the rise and use of New Media technology, showing that less than 15% of all internet users are also content producers or critical analysts.

The internet developed its own independent culture, which mistrusts traditional geographic, legal authority and political institutions. Its culture is quick to embrace new ideas for governance as long as they do not suggest intrusion, regulation or taxation by traditional political authorities or institutions (Bygrave and Bing, 2009). Nothing like this existed in the early days of telephony, radio or television broadcasting, which from the beginning were regulated by government. The net culture

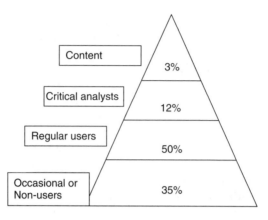

Figure 2.1 Internet Content Production

exerts a powerful influence of its own by including greater numbers of citizens in more locations and by shaping political and legal institutions. Although there is no president or board of directors or even an organizational chart for the internet, the medium is heavily influenced by powerful corporate hierarchies such as Google, Mozilla, Microsoft, Oracle and Yahoo! which maintain extensive databases containing information about users (Hindman, 2009). In more authoritarian political cultures, providers of information technology are obligated to respond to rules set by host governments—some of which conflict with Western values such as freedom of assembly, expression, press and speech. At this writing, Google has challenged the control of its search engine by the Chinese government authorities by refusing to turn over the names of websites critical of the regime.

How Do We Connect?

In most democratic systems of government, citizens are free to voice grievances against government and allowed to participate by voting every few years or when elections are called by ruling governments. The Platonic ideal that all members of a community should be able to participate in reaching common consensus on decisions has often been dismissed as impractical. However, with modern technology it is technically (and theoretically) possible for nearly all citizens to inform themselves about public issues. This was a dream since the early days of telecommunication and has been proposed in theory for decades by many influential futurists (Etzioni, 1972; Hiltz and Turoff, 1978; McLuhan, Fiore and Agel, 1967). For the citizen, the internet vastly increases the speed and volume of communication, as well as the ease of access to information.

The internet (and its earlier version known as Usenet) discussion forums and the World Wide Web contain huge quantities of political analysis and partisan commentary. There is much talk "on- and off-line" about the potential for the internet to improve citizen participation in government, which has assumed new and surprising forms such as: 1) targeted electronic mail; 2) electronic discussion forums, newsgroups or blogs; 3) mailing list servers, bulletin boards and similar systems; 4) WWW and similar forms of publication; 5) chatting, conferencing, text messaging on *Twitter* and related systems, unscripted video captures (citizens publishing speeches by politicians or officials making comments about them on numerous social networking websites such as *Facebook, MySpace, Twitter* and *YouTube*); 6) mass meetings, electronic town halls, surveys, opinion gathering, publication and dissemination; and 7) integration of digital media with mobile smart-phone access systems.

Facebook proved its political value during the presidential primaries in January 2008 when it offered live feedback from the Republican and Democratic debates moderated by ABC newsperson Charles Gibson at Saint Anselm College in New Hampshire. *Facebook* users participated in debate groups organized around specific topics such as candidate positions on issues and voter registration. Over a million people installed the *Facebook* application "US politics" in order to participate and comment on issues raised by the debating candidates. This debate informed the broader voting community that social networking could be an extremely powerful new way to become familiar with issues, interact with candidates and offer opinions. As Marshall McLuhan said several decades ago "the medium is the message" and the political process discovered a new medium for reaching a broader audience.

Online Citizen Participation Model

Discussion of the **online citizen participation model** requires knowledge of the participants and how various sources connect to the internet and application of the concept of **information continuum**. The fate of each of these components—separately and in solidarity—will determine the legitimacy of the internet as a source of reliable political news and opinion and, ultimately, as an alternative for information, elections, voting and a trustworthy medium for public service delivery. Who are the stakeholders comprising the internet?

1) Citizens and government institutions as users—connected to the net and interacting with it.
2) Governments as content producers and information providers.
3) Intermediaries (such as access providers).
4) Hardware manufacturers.

5) Software authors and manufacturers (browsers, site development tools, specific applications, smart agents, search engines and others).
6) The so-called "Hitchhikers" (knowledge managers, search engines, smart agents, artificial intelligence (AI) tools and more).
7) Financial backers (currently—corporate and institutional cash gradually being replaced by advertising money).
8) Other advocacy organizations.

Information on the Web is delivered to the user (either to government or to the citizens), and then processed and fed back to the information generator. The three important steps in the information continuum are:

1) Information delivery, that is, the means by which it is delivered.
2) Information processing or the "decoding" of information to be matched against institutional and personal needs.
3) Information feedback, how citizens respond to information (Srinivas, 2002).

The model in Figure 2.2 illustrates the give-and-take nature of information that is facilitated by the internet and the communication modes that it enables.

Not only is public information given out via the internet (facilities and services, city planning and zoning information, hearings and meetings, public projects by governments, opinions, individual business plans, lifestyle choices etc.) to citizens, but information is received, processed and used to modify values, behaviors and norms. This is one of the reasons why the internet is different than other forms of mass media. As support institutions on a second tier, business and industry, research organizations, universities, other local governments and prefectural/national governments also facilitate and support this interaction. The extent that different groups in various regions participate in civic and community activities varies with the type of businesses, information infrastructures, networks, public management systems and universities within communities and how they are integrated with information technology.[7]

Many "smart communities" are also in the early stages of facilitating citizen participation and especially online deliberation via the new technology. Through enabled links, numerous municipalities across the United States and elsewhere allow residents to learn about and get involved in civic organizations, such as churches, youth organizations, sports clubs and other volunteer organizations. This pattern is also apparent with respect to local websites. Another common citizen participation feature in the United States is the availability of e-comment forms to ascertain input from residents, a feature that is much less common in Europe. On the other hand, the opportunity for residents to provide input on local government services through online polling remains rare in the United States.

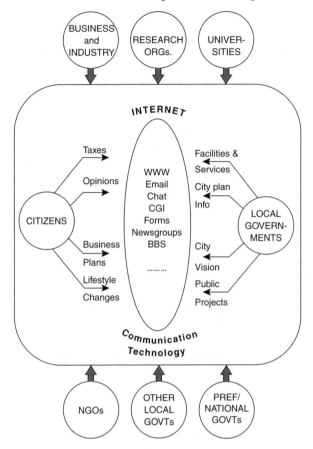

Figure 2.2 Online Citizens' Participation Model

Source: Adapted From Online Citizens' Participation Model of H. Srinivas (2002: 6)

Using the Internet to Increase Citizen Participation

The key commodity underlying effective online participation among citizens and governments is information (Mayer-Schonberger and Lazer, 2007). The World Wide Web has experienced explosive growth in activity, data, traffic, servers as well as general information in the last decade. However, its ability to produce accurate, high-quality, meaningful information, with low noise levels and without redundancy is still in its adolescence. Noise is generally defined as **information overload** making it difficult for individuals to focus on a particular issue. More difficult still for government efforts is the capacity of analysts to produce quality information and then use it to: 1) urge citizens to take a more active role in their government; 2) improve planning, policy analysis and decision making in government operations; and 3) evaluate the outcomes of service delivery. In a few instances, internet technology and web-based surveys are being used to overcome citizen reticence to face difficult budgetary problems (Robbins, Simonsen and Feldman, 2008).

Information Quality and the Internet

In the same way that one manufacturer's product is more attractive to customers because it has features that are better suited to their specific requirements, so too information has characteristics that add value, depending upon the purposes for which it is used. The critical aspects of value-added data are to provide the right information at the right time to the right user. Some of the information attributes are:

- **Quality**. The internet enables large amounts of information to be made available to end users, properly and sufficiently packaged to be useful.
- **Suitability, Scope and Relevance**. With feedback loops and communication possibilities widely incorporated in blogs, URLs, websites and homepages, it is also possible to tailor to the specific information needs of users. This also includes dynamic information that is "bundled" or packaged to suit different needs.
- **Accuracy**. While fraudulent information is indeed published on the internet, there is a larger question of information processing and management that has to be kept in mind when disseminating it online. In politics, accuracy is frequently in the "eye of the beholder" as conflicting ideologies are expressed online.
- **Timeliness**. Unlike a book or a brochure that cannot be easily modified after it has been printed, online information can be added to, changed, edited, deleted or updated easily and frequently. This ensures that the information can be kept current and timely but also presents problems of ensuring accuracy and validity.
- **Compatibility**. Easy access and updating of online information as well as the simplicity and cross-platform compatibility of internet information enables data and information to be disseminated, analyzed and compared (thereby, also avoiding duplication).
- **Presentation**. Common information formatting standards across computer platforms and operating systems enable appropriate presentation styles to be used (Srinivas, 2002).

Projects to Improve Citizen Participation

How do citizens access government programs that claim to improve citizens' participation in public decision making? How are citizens confronted with issues and asked to decide upon them? How do citizens put forward ideas and issues for discussion/debate/decision? Do decisions taken/recommendations made by citizen groups have any effect in the "real" political system or are they merely token in nature? Are any subjects or topics "off-limits" for citizen discussion groups? Using the internet to involve more citizens in deliberation and decision-making processes should be guided by principles such as: 1) providing basic information to citizens about rights and responsibilities of citizenship; 2) informing and educating about politics and issues of public concern; 3) helping voters to make up their mind about candidates, parties and issues in elections; 4) promoting opportunities for citizens to deliberate public issues, draft laws and deal with social problems (experience of analyzing complicated issues); 5) facilitating participation in reaching a decision included in the formal decision-making process; 6) opening communication channels between citizens and politicians; 7) guiding citizens through the growing jungle of publicly available information from government and other sources; and 8) offering incentives for participation by citizens in real decision making.

At a minimum, the following information and links should be provided by government cyber-participation projects:

1) Political information and issues for public debate, including:

   a) type of electoral system (local, regional, national, supranational);
   b) background of political candidates (biography, policy support, campaign finance, political literacy test);
   c) process of parliamentary legislation revealed in its various steps (committee resolutions and much other procedural detail, draft laws);
   d) broader issues such as social violence, commerce and finance, work and general debate on various aspects of international, environmental, military and economic policy, ethics and moral issues. also, when parliaments have debates, inquiries and commissions on various issues, then the public can be better informed with assistance of the internet;
   e) how to access government agencies and ministries as well as staff activities;
   f) where other administration and public offices display their documents;
   g) aids to political action and contact with delegates, public bodies and public officials.

2) Access to links:

   a) to mass media (press, local radio and citizens' television);
   b) lobbying groups (pro-environment groups, NGOs, specialist groups, trade unions, political parties, political and social reform groups);
   c) reference sources (institutes of learning, critical centers such as *World Watch* and *Oxfam* international).[8]

Internet Use to Increase Participation

In the United States, most federal, state and local governments have established a strong if uneven presence on the internet. Agencies provide public information online and many can be reached via comprehensive websites such as USA.gov, a web portal containing over 50 million websites with information about all U.S. federal, state and local government agencies. The U.S. Office of the Assistant Secretary of Defense for Public Affairs implemented a World Wide Web service, called DefenseLINK, containing current and historical news releases, daily summaries, press advisories, transcripts and contracts.

Local governments and other public and non-profit organizations established Freenets, online information services open to the public. These services provided local government services, documents and news, and acted as a medium for discussions among users about local issues. Similar to the "stages" of internet development discussed in Chapter 1, there are five levels for the government's use of the internet for political discussion and participation:

1) **First Level—Raw Information Provision.** Many local authorities now have websites presenting information about services on a departmental basis and giving contact phone numbers and (less often) e-mail addresses. Most local government still present information organized according to existing hierarchical structures rather than citizen needs.

2) **Second Level—Interaction.** One of the main issues at this level is the need to be assured of the identities of the persons interacting with public websites. Using the President's e-mail address (www.whitehouse.gov/) anyone with access to the internet can send a message to the President's staff. At least 5,000 messages arrive digitally at the White House every week. Interns read every message, track and tally them by issue and by opinion expressed and send a standard response. This was part of the political strategy first promoted by the Clinton administration and also adopted by the Obama administration (Chapter 5). Many governors and mayors have established similar websites.

3) **Third Level—Informal Discussion.** Local government officials and politicians participate in "grassroots" discussions with the public. No attempt is made to reach closure on issues, but deliberation could possibly influence the outcome of decisions. Discussion groups involve employees, elected members and the public. One of the best examples of this is provided by the Minnesota e-Democracy project that regularly involves participation by 400 people and politicians in regular discussions with the public and hosts online debates between candidates before elections (Stubbs, 1998).

4) **Fourth Level—Formal Consultation.** At this level, local government uses online technologies to consult with citizens on their views of proposed policy changes through questionnaires, structured discussion and voting. Some impressive work has been carried out in the planning area enabling people to explore 3D virtual reality representations of proposed building projects and highway projects. At this level it is almost impossible to avoid discussing direct online voting.

5) **Fifth Level—Democratic Community.** This represents a mapping of real space onto cyberspace. Key local organizations must agree to create a cross-sector local strategy to provide a coherent interface of information for a public online environment in which the whole community can share information, communicate, do business, learn and have fun. With the technology currently available, it is possible to build a shared vision in cyberspace and work to create it in the real world (Stubbs, 1998).

To summarize, at the first two levels, government tells its citizens what it thinks they need to know. The New Media, to quote a French expression, is used to demonstrate "old wine in new bottles." The next two levels involve dialogue between citizen and official and the final level is full collaboration with the community in its own re-creation. The levels represent a hierarchy not just in terms of technological complexity but in government's willingness to use ICTs to engage with citizens and citizens' willingness to trust government institutions. Each level shows an increasing respect for the citizen's right to be involved in governance in an ongoing manner, not simply at election time. The levels should be developed simultaneously not sequentially. The following cases illustrate various state and local government efforts to foster democratic or "e-democratic" communities.

Successful Environment and Electoral Project from The Netherlands

Decision-Maker/Teledemocracy is a large-scale project, ultimately designed—after 10 years—to connect all of the Dutch citizens (about 9.5 million voters) to the internet for the purpose of digital debate and voting. A small-scale experiment in the province of Noord-Brabant (Holland) in 1996 was very successful. One problem was that many citizens for one reason or another did not wish or were unable to participate fully. To allow "opting out" a new form of delegation was proposed. "Decision-Maker/Teledemocracy" used a general trusted **third-party intermediary model**, in which citizens could select any organization or person they like to submit their vote. This trusted party could be anyone: an individual person with a public opinion about the topic, a government, an interest group—or even a political party. These trusted parties can do what they want with the votes that are thus entrusted (given) to them. The five elements of the Dutch project were: 1) information; 2) debate; 3) individual advice; 4) collective advice; and 5) voting.

Electronic Community Networks, Digital Cities

The term "community network" is not easily defined. Anne Beamish offers the following definition: "a community network is ... a network of computers [connected by] modems ... via telephone lines to a central computer which provides community information and a means for the community to communicate electronically" (Beamish, 1995). A resident of a town or city uses the system by logging into a central computer with their personal computer. A series of menus appears on the screen and the user selects the information or communication services they would like. Participants can access information provided by city hall, a business or social service provider, participate in a public discussion on a local issue with others in the community or communicate via e-mail with others in the community.

Unlike the similarly named "online communities" or "virtual communities" community networks are based in a physical place. What participants have in common are their cities and neighborhoods. Community network projects commonly aim to provide improved access to information for citizens about their locality, city, town or neighborhood. Some are presented in an "electronic town hall" format which allows users to meet political representatives, and to visit administrative agencies offering basic services such as education, transportation, health and policing and find more specialized services such as legal advice, sports facilities, cultural sites and events. Other community networks enable and encourage citizens to contact local officials and politicians and a few provide a framework for electronic exchange "horizontally" among citizens, usually on topics of local significance. **Digital cities** and municipalities projects attempt an ambitious presentation of "virtually" all aspects of city life. Organizers and promoters of these projects often show awareness of inequality in citizens' ability or financial means to participate in electronic community networks (Holzer and Kim, 2003; Ishida and Isbister, 2000). **Electronic community networks** could offer one way to close the digital divide through multiple access points, including libraries, post offices, schools and other public places. Another approach to community networking is to promote universal access for all citizens of a region, using satellite networks or fiber optic cable. The Bill and Melinda Gates Foundation established by Microsoft's co-founder provides billions of dollars in funding for local schools to become "wired" to the internet.[9]

Community network projects include a variety of independent citizens' associations, initiatives or groups receiving official or private funding (e.g. U.S. government, European Union, private foundations) or they may be initiatives of (usually local) governments. Differences between various models sometimes become blurred, such as lobbying a local council to set up a project funded by federal stimulus funds. Community networks may emphasize particular aims, for example creating local jobs, historical preservation or reviving culture or ethnic identification with a region or locality. The features described above, and other effects of community networks, may influence national political processes, leading to increases in direct participation or involvement of citizens in more advanced forms of digital governance.

Online Participation and the Obama Administration

President Barack Obama was the first candidate for national office to successfully merge information and communication technologies (ICTs) and employ the internet to generate new voters as well as garner increased campaign contributions. During the 2008 presidential campaign, Obama recruited nearly 14 million online supporters (many of them first-time voters), and communicated directly with them by e-mail and cellular phones—as no previous candidate had—and via social networking websites such as *Facebook*, *MySpace*, *YouTube* and *Twitter*. During the campaign, Obama constantly placed advertisements in the side columns of the *Facebook* website, 52% of whose users are between the ages of 18 and 25. There were also pictures either of him individually, or of him with his wife and daughters in a pleasant family photo. The caption usually read either: "Register to Vote" or "Election Day is November 4th" or "Vote Early." He also had a "Support Obama" *Facebook* group which would periodically send messages to members that had information about polling sites, early voting information and updates on his campaign.[10] During the 2008 presidential campaign, candidate Obama even announced his vice presidential selection at 3:00 a.m. via an internet and an "alarming" cell phone message to supporters. His ubiquitous BlackBerry cellular telephone became a symbol of his administration's high-tech communication style. "By the end of the campaign, my.BarackObama.com website chalked up some 1.5 million accounts. And Obama raised a record-breaking $600 million in contributions from more than three million people, many of whom donated through the web."[11] How did Obama use ICTs to recruit so many new voters and generate millions of dollars in campaign contributions?

Obama's victory in the **Electoral College** was impressive, but not radically different from previous presidential campaigns (Todd and Gawiser, 2009). Several factors explain this extraordinary, yet ordinary, outcome. First, Obama's campaign obviously benefitted from anti-war sentiment, the Bush administration's inept handling of the economy and the sub-prime "mortgage meltdown" in the months immediately before the election. Second, the massive federal debt created by the wars in Iraq and Afghanistan and the collapse of property values and financial markets mobilized millions of anti-Republican voters, especially Independents, who turned out in large numbers for Obama and other Democrats. Third, his opponent, Sen. John McCain (R-AZ), admitted he had little understanding of either computers or the interconnections being created in a modern technology-driven political campaign. And last, Obama's use of electronic media struck a responsive chord with millions of younger, tech-savvy new voters who grew up with ICTs and were motivated to participate by direct and instant contact, collaboration and information sharing with the candidate (Milakovich, 2009). Table 2.1 indicates the success of the Obama campaign in reaching voters through social networking sites.

The internet played a significant role in promoting additional citizen participation in the 2008 presidential election. The ultimate impact that the Obama campaign may have had on the (online and offline) polispheres in the United States and elsewhere will be determined by his administration's success in achieving policy changes, especially in the areas of job creation, environmental regulation and universal health care coverage. As the first U.S. president to successfully employ ICTs for electoral success, Obama is now attempting to convert these new information and communication technologies to further his administration's ambitious public policy goals. The Obama administration is applying this strategy as a blueprint for communicating directly with citizens and further reforming administrative procedures in a wide variety of policy areas (Connelly, 2009). His apparent successes in reforming consumer protection, health care and financial regulation were overshadowed by the weak economic recovery and uncertainty over U.S. policy in Afghanistan—resulting in significant Republican gains during the 2010 midterm elections.

Organizing for the Presidency

Experience matters in politics as in life. Before being elected to the U.S. Senate as a Democrat from the state of Illinois in 2004 and later to the presidency, Barack Obama served as a community organizer on the South Side of Chicago. This early experience helping communities

Table 2.1 2008 Presidential Campaign and Social Networks: Obama vs. McCain

	Obama	*McCain*
Facebook	3,279,102 "Friends"	620,359 "Friends"
MySpace	1,043,850 "Friends"	218,172 "Friends"
YouTube	1,824 Videos uploaded	330 Videos uploaded
	20,024,491 "Channel Views"	2,221,268 "Channel Views"
Twitter	137,206 "Followers"	4,848 "Followers"

Source: Parycek and Sachs (2009: 34)

promote self-government reflects many of the benefits of participation (Obama, 2006: 327). Following his election, President Obama pledged to use the most current ICT tools available to make government less dependent on special interest groups and lobbyists and promote citizen participation in government decision making. Obama also committed to integrate citizens' opinions into the actual administration of government programs by:

- Establishing pilot programs to open up government decision making and involve citizens in the work of agencies, not simply by soliciting opinions, but by tapping into the vast expertise of the American citizenry to help government make more informed decisions.
- Requiring appointees who lead federal executive departments (State, Defense, Treasury, etc.) and rulemaking agencies (such as the FDA, FTC and SEC) to conduct significant business of the agency in public, so that any interested citizen can watch a live feed on the internet as agencies debate and deliberate issues that affect American society. These proceedings will be archived for all Americans to review, discuss and respond. Presidential appointees will employ all the technological tools available to allow citizens not just to observe, but also to participate and be heard in these meetings.
- Restoring the basic principle that government decisions should be based on the best-available, scientifically valid evidence and not on the ideological predispositions of agency officials.
- Increasing transparency by lifting the veil from "secret deals" in Washington with a website, a search engine and other web tools that enable citizens to easily track online federal grants, contracts, earmarks and lobbyist contacts with government officials.
- Giving the American public an opportunity to review and comment on the White House website for five days before signing any non-emergency legislation. (This proposal has at this writing proven to be too difficult to administer.)

The Obama administration began to act on most of these recommendations shortly after inauguration in early 2009 by sponsoring Community Town Hall meetings and asking for citizen input on a variety of issues facing the federal government. Participants were encouraged to submit video links asking questions of the president via the social networking website *YouTube*. In one of several public meetings held on March 26, 2009, President Obama answered some of the over 100,000 video questions submitted as well as responding to questions directly from a live audience. This type of direct democratic strategy for discussing contentious public issues can be risky. In many respects, it was a continuation of bitter partisan political campaign debates rather than a reflective discussion of issues by informed participants. During later public gatherings focusing on more contentious issues such as health care reform, opposition groups attempted to disrupt proceedings and many participants used the opportunity to criticize government in general. Some viewed these tactics as reminiscent of non-violent protest used by civil rights groups in the 1960s to oppose segregationist policies in Southern states; others described them as deliberate attempts by political opponents such as the Tea Party to disrupt community gatherings.

Another of Obama's early actions was to upgrade technology management positions to report directly to the White House. In addition, many of Obama's supporters continue to work toward his administration's policy agenda in groups such as *Organizing for America*, led by former Virginia Governor and Democratic National Committee Chair Tim Keane.[12] Despite such intentions, the public bureaucracy (the so-called "action" side of government) often lacks the capacity, competence as well as the motivation to break through ingrained administrative processes and initiate innovative reforms aimed at removing barriers to admission, collaboration and participation. According to Jonathan Bruel, Executive Director of the IBM Center for the Business of Government, "The [federal] workforce and the tools it is using are not up to the challenge, [creating] a disconnect between the tech-savvy Obama administration ... and the federal bureaucracy, which hasn't fully embraced those technologies" (Carlstrom, 2008). This perceptive statement is even more accurate when applied to the "crazy quilt" to overlapping and redundant state and local jurisdictions which comprise the federal system of government in the United States. This potential disconnect, combined with the constitutional separation between federal, state and local governments, as well as remnants of the Bush administration occupying key high-level policy-making positions, suggests that there may be more resistance to digital change than first imagined.

Further delays in the fulfilling of promises made during the campaign gave opposition Republican candidates and local elected officials time to use the new technology to resist Obama administration policies and dominate the 2010 Congressional elections. Moreover, any new president's appointment powers are limited to a few thousand high-level senior cabinet-level jobs out of approximately five million federal civilian and military employees, leaving many appointees from previous administrations in positions to influence implementation of key policy decisions. Thus, even if skilled specialists are available in sufficient numbers to facilitate the use of technology to reform bureaucracy, they may not share the same policy goals as the current administration.

Citizen participation was a key phrase in Obama's technological policy vocabulary since the start of his presidential campaign. In his campaign literature, Obama went even further and pledged to use ICT tools to make government less beholden to special interest groups and lobbyists and to promote more citizen involvement in governmental decision making. Part of this approach included the development of the Technology, Innovation and Government Reform (TIGR) Working Group, a team of more than 30 tech industry professionals whose mission was to create a 21st century government that is more open and effective, and leverages technology to grow the economy, create jobs and solve most pressing national problems.[13] In addition, federal agencies were encouraged to respect the integrity of and renew the historic commitment to science and technology to catalyze active citizenship and partnerships in shared governance with civic societal institutions.

Conclusions and Future Directions

Citizen participation in democratic political processes has been recognized as important to foster greater governmental accountability, responsiveness, trust and transparency. Tools provided by information technologies can be used as cost-effective measures to develop a more participatory democracy. This idea is generally considered wider and more inclusive than e-government because of the way citizens relate to governments and to each other. Its objective, according to the **United Nations Education, Scientific and Cultural Organization (UNESCO)**, is to strengthen public trust in government and to improve relations between government and its citizens. Derived from e-democracy are specific types of applications such as e-activism, e-participation and e-voting. E-activism is the use of electronic means to mobilize volunteers, raise funds, disseminate information and otherwise pursue the various functions of interest groups that seek to influence public policy. E-participation refers to the use of electronic means to encourage public participation in governmental decision making or agency rulemaking. E-voting promotes the use of electronic means to provide citizens access to electoral or polling processes.

According to democratic theories, efforts to increase citizen participation result in better governmental decisions that involve larger numbers of people and are, therefore, more acceptable and legitimate to the majority of citizens. Better government decisions, by definition, are more beneficial to greater numbers of so-called average citizens. Citizen participation provides a source of special insight, information, knowledge and experience, which contributes to the soundness of government solutions to public problems. Active involvement in public affairs and in decision-making processes also serves to check and balance political activities, thereby increasing accountability and reducing the likelihood of public officials making self-serving decisions. Citizen input can legitimize a program, its purposes, implementation and leadership. Unsupported leaders often become discouraged and drop activities that are potentially beneficial to average citizens, but too difficult to implement in divisive political environments. Voluntary participation can also reduce the cost of paid personnel needed to carry out many of the duties associated with community actions as extensions of governmental policy.

What may be predicted about the future impact of ICTs on participation of citizens in governance based on recent U.S. elections?

Information and communication technologies can contribute to democratic literacy in many respects: citizens can become better informed about public issues and associated law making; this should facilitate more informed debate (e.g. citizens can be better informed before approaching their legislator or Member of Parliament (MP) about a bill coming to a vote). Information prepares voters during and between elections to cast ballots in a more informed and critical way. Improved knowledge can inform voters about candidates, their qualifications for office, ideologies, political knowledge, previous performance on election promises, campaign finance, interest groups they support (e.g. business, religion, worthy causes such as environmental protection or labor law).

The ease of information provided by the internet and creation of new polispheres enables more citizens to join in a public debate more easily, to monitor election promises, to intervene by writing on blogs or to newspapers or even to start campaigns aimed at influencing public opinion and parliamentary decisions. This encourages and empowers citizens to be proactive and allows members of political parties to better judge the performance of their own delegates and candidates for public office. Forms of expression may further consist of lobbying MPs, public officials and commercial enterprises; informing and educating others, publishing on the internet; moral appeals; protest and social movements, non-governmental organizing; starting referenda or citizens' law making; promoting the renewal of democracy itself. As a result, more public organizations are being pressured to designate chief information officers (CIOs) to make sure that information planning and policy formulation are carried out effectively by the administration in power.

The ease of communication and access to information offered by the internet has led some observers to predict that a new public arena for open discussion or *agora* will emerge to aid collaborative decision making. During the coming few decades, future developments may also include: 1) closer guidance for MPs and governments by public will, especially in the legislative periods between elections to achieve political party policies guided by constituents; or 2) discovery that direct decision making by citizens on a greater number of issues may be an illusory promise of e-government. At this writing, few candidates for the U.S. Congress or the EU Parliament have followed the Dean-Obama approach to campaigning. There have been some weak attempts by the European Commission to stimulate electoral participation, but voter turnouts have not increased, especially among the youngest Europeans. Despite Obama's appeal, voting turnout among those under 25 in the U.S. presidential election also remained consistent with earlier years. Gradual transformation of representative democracy into a more deliberative process involving more citizens will take time. Nonetheless, electronic voting to select candidates and issues and definitive votes (plebiscites) on laws and public issues, with direct decision making by constituents on some issues, remain major challenges for both citizens and governments.

The potential benefits of improved citizen participation may be regarded by some as *idealistic*, others as *opportunistic* and some as even *unrealistic*. For those currently occupying high-level jobs it may represent a threat to their economic and political positions. Critics of **direct democracy** cite cases where citizens have acquired increased rights to legislate and failed to use those powers. Or instances such as the anti-immigrant legislation passed in Arizona and challenged by the federal government as unconstitutional. Other critics become even more alarmed, fearing a "dictatorship" of the majority, in modern terms projected as "an electronic mob." The majority may become highly selfish, act to reduce personal taxation or to avoid any disturbance to their own comfort (e.g. refusing to accept any personal or local environmental risks and displacing these onto other citizens, the **NIMBY** "not in my backyard" philosophy).

The challenge for citizens is to acquire the best available knowledge and learn how to apply democratic tools responsibly in the best interest of their local communities, states, or nation. Future political support for effective information management systems linking citizen to government cannot be assumed. Government must increase the number and improve the security of inter- and intra-governmental communication channels, provide clear information strategies on issues such as goals, means/modes, time-space and evaluation for effective development of citizen partnerships. As the use of the internet for two-way political communication and participation increases, the incorporation and synthesis of large volumes of comments, e-mail messages and opinions received and stored online may become increasingly difficult. The challenge for public managers and policy analysts is to interpret the significance of these data and present decision options to citizens and political decision makers in a comprehensible and understandable format.

Key Terms

citizen participation, 29
Athenian Democracy, 30
pluralism, 30
elitism, 30
oligarchy, 30
deliberative democracy, 31
town meetings, 31
community organizations, 32
non-governmental organizations (NGOs), 34
civic obligation, 35

blogosphere, 36
political participation, 37
mass media, 37
Advanced Research Projects Administration (ARPA), 37
ARPANET, 37
National Science Foundation (NSF), 37
linked area networks (LANs), 37
Netscape, 37
domain space, 38

3 Managing Citizen-Centric Digital Governance

The slowdown in the deployment and use of government portals suggests that some countries are finally realizing that portals alone won't achieve the promise of what technology can do for them. Moving forward, governments should focus on a coherent multi-channel strategy in which services should be citizen-centric, rather than program- or agency-centric.

John Kost, Managing Vice President for Government
Research Worldwide, Gartner, Inc.

Recent ICT-enabled policy initiatives promote expanded multi-channel strategies such as blogs, digital town halls, community forums and the expanded use of social media to promote **citizen-centric** governance and wider civic participation. This chapter focuses on four issues related to making public administration more citizen-centric and customer-focused. First, it addresses the origins of **customer relationship management (CRM)** and how the concept evolved from **total quality management (TQM)** and was subsequently applied in the public sector as **citizen relationship management (CzRM)**; second, it emphasizes the importance of CzRM when paired with ICTs to facilitate digital governance; third, the chapter cites specific cases describing how CRM and CzRM have been used by leading countries to implement electronic government; and last, the discussion focuses on practical applications which influence the value of future citizen-centric digital public services. Proposed changes to governmental communication and information systems should be guided by an awareness of the overall values and *raison d'être* of the public sector—with an explicit public commitment to securing both the *equality* and *quality* of services.

Total Quality Management and Customer Relationship Management (CRM)

Competing models have been proposed and deployed to increase the competence, managerial capability and productivity of government. Prior to the Information Age, most of the attempted reforms deployed top-down command-and-control strategies to improve bureaucratic performance and responsiveness. Since the early 1990s, many federal, state and local agencies have applied performance management strategies based on variations of market-driven concepts such as **business process reengineering** (BPR), customer relationship management (CRM), continuous quality improvement (CQI), or **Six Sigma** statistical process control systems. These approaches share a common origin: they were originally developed as private sector business strategies, part of the market-based **entrepreneurial paradigm** aggressively applied to the public sector from the mid-1990s until the mid-2000s. For policy makers, the challenge was to apply the correct model to the right problem and to do so consistently. In many instances, the facile notion that "what works in business works in government" proved to be illusory.

To better understand the evolution of citizen-centric information technology applied to government, it is necessary to briefly trace attempts—successes and failures—to develop and reform administrative systems during the past three decades of reinvention, results-orientation and retrenchment.

The 1990s witnessed a major restructuring of many basic productive enterprises, first in manufacturing and later in service industries, resulting in acquisitions, downsizing and global mergers. In the United States, this reawakening was caused initially by the increased awareness of competitive challenges from Europe and Japan and, in more recent years, from China and India. Around the same time, a more aggressive BPR movement emerged in the United States, urging radical changes to "reengineer" corporations in order to compete globally (Hammer and Champy, 1993). Many large multi-national firms quite literally reengineered themselves from the inside out using variations of quality improvement tools, theories and strategies. The extended use of electronic and digital commerce accelerated these trends. In addition, leading commercial firms mandated that *their suppliers* demonstrate commitment to customer service by meeting stricter quality procurement standards. Suppliers also had to show enhanced responsiveness to customer requirements, a process subsequently known as **supply-chain management** and perfected by large retailers such as Wal-Mart (Chapter 7).

During this era, many multi-national firms literally "broke-up" into smaller, more flexible, decentralized and interconnected units designed to establish closer working relationships with customers and suppliers. Management changes were paralleled by the expansion of ICTs to connect geographically distant suppliers with manufacturers and customers. Countries such as China and India benefitted from **outsourcing** and supply-chain management in part because of lower labor costs. **Downsizing** of labor forces in more developed countries was inevitable as many firms found they could be just as profitable with a smaller workforce. This grim capitalist reality has now reached deeply into all levels of the U.S. public service sector as well.

Until the beginning of the Great Recession (2007–?), business-oriented strategies in public administration championed entrepreneurism, outsourcing and **privatization** of public services. Such strategies were often ideologically driven, failing to recognize that public services are a dynamic and continually changing mix of functions, goals, personalities, structures and visions. Consequently, public sector administrative reform has been buffeted by contradictory changes, ranging from quality management in the 1980s to reengineering and results-orientation in 1990s, to resizing and reregulation in the 2000s. Reform efforts were supported by e-government initiatives intended to apply new and emerging technologies to fundamentally transform many facets of government operations. Many of these reforms were overly optimistic and failed to recognize the structural complexities inherent in American bureaucracy. It is now apparent that the application of information technology *by itself* will not stimulate behavioral or structural change to occur. The challenges for public administration are to create electronic and now digital governance systems capable of supporting and sustaining long-term changes (Fang, 2002: 2).

The Evolution of Quality Management

E-commerce and digital technology have been a major focus of interest for numerous customer service quality management studies (Beam, 2001; Camp, 1989; Douglas and Judge, 2001; Senge, *et al.*, 2008; Zbaracki, 1998). Many ICT concepts parallel Total Quality Management (TQM) theories and emphasize **quality management guidelines** such as participatory management, responsiveness to both internal and external customers and continuous improvement of internal processes (see Box 3.1). For example, TQM's emphasis on participative management has been incorporated into digital

---

Box 3.1: Summary of Quality Management Guidelines

1) Customer Orientation
2) Top Management Commitment
3) Education and Self-Improvement
4) Process Orientation
5) Continuous Process Improvement
6) Freedom from Fear
7) Teamwork
8) Communication rather than Inspection
9) Statistical and Systemic Thinking
10) Personal Commitment

Source: Milakovich (2006: 111–127)

governance through its support of citizen-oriented participatory democracy (Chapter 2). Fully integrated online digital technology allows more people to become more involved in public decision-making processes and provides "early warning" signals for citizens potentially affected by governmental actions. In addition, ICTs can be used to: 1) notify those affected in advance of public hearings; 2) access public records; 3) comment on legislation; and 4) monitor public hearings. Direct participation promotes active citizens' public spirit, develops moral character, protects citizens' freedoms and provides citizens with a voice to challenge the existing power structures (Robbins, Simonsen and Feldman, 2008: 564–565).

Past attempts to change internal operations of organizations suffered from political controversies, inconsistent applications and uneven results. In nascent citizen-centric ICT-enabled environments, the workforce is motivated by incentives to participate and encouraged to collaborate with broader cross-functional organizational improvement efforts. Management facilitates the transformation by empowering workers with the knowledge and skills necessary to meet constantly changing customer service demands and requirements (Chapter 5). This sharply contrasts with traditional Weberian top-down command and control Theory X structures which actively discourage worker participation. Online government also allows more citizens to become active "participative workers" and to voice suggestions to their civic "organization" (government). Many public managers, however, are still wedded to rigid command and control structures. This, among other factors, has slowed the conversion from hierarchical to networked citizen-centric governance.

Following the lead of the private market sector, scores of federal, state and local governments implemented quality management programs during the 1980s and 1990s. Given the sheer size, scope and visibility of the efforts, mistakes were inevitable. In some instances, variations of quality improvement theories were misunderstood and misapplied in both the public and private sectors (Douglas and Judge, 2001; Zbaracki, 1998). Unrealistic expectations, employee resistance and controversial "quality bureaucracies" plagued many otherwise well-intended organizational change efforts. For these and other reasons, a quality management backlash contributed to widespread cynicism and dampened enthusiasm for further non-manufacturing applications by the late 1990s. Reforms were also hampered when applied in the public service sector by:

1   The perceived negative experiences of other organizations.
2) The long-term time frames of many quality management programs compared to the short-term perspectives of most politicians.
3) Inflexible public sector management structures.
4) The lack of theory-driven research showing how to empower, motivate and reward public employees for customer service quality efforts (Chapter 5).

According to former Federal Reserve Board Chair Allan Greenspan, another major contributing factor was the "irrational exuberance" of the period—excessive expenditure of tax revenues generated by rising incomes and property values in the late 1990s and early 2000s. Like many consumers, governments at all levels borrowed and spent beyond sustainable levels. The fiscal crisis which subsequently enveloped the public and much of the private sector since the "mortgage meltdown" in late 2007 required massive federal intervention and increased public debt. Nonetheless, it is highly unlikely that full implementation of customer-oriented quality management would have forestalled the negative consequences of fiscal and monetary policies which led to the recession.

Digital Governance and Customer Relationship Management (CRM)

Digital governance incorporates ICT applications to meet the specific needs of employees and customers of public agencies as well as businesses, citizen groups, departments and non-profit organizations (Chapter 1). Digital technology is malleable enough to adapt applications, software and websites to reflect changes in the demands of constituents. Similarly, parallel quality management theories emphasize the incorporation of continuous improvement in organizational processes. Digital technology significantly improves government's ability to assess processes to determine which are operating efficiently and which are not—this is possible because of the ability of online databases to capture enormous amounts of information from applications, online surveys and public records. One of the major differences between current and past applications is that such data capture and storage systems were unavailable for decision making and process improvement in the 1980s (Milakovich, 1995).

Customer relationship management (CRM) is a familiar term in business circles which has attracted increasing interest in government (King, 2007). CRM is defined generally as a built-in capability to reorganize service delivery around customer intentions allowing an integrated view of customer needs. The information collected is used to coordinate and incorporate service delivery across multiple channels. Many governments have realized that managing relationships with customers is a powerful tool that can significantly improve relationships with citizens. There are many definitions, but James R. Evans and William M. Lindsay define customer relationship management succinctly as follows:

> Understanding customer needs, both current and future, and keeping pace with changing markets requires effective strategies for listening to and learning from customers, measuring their satisfaction relative to competitors and building relationships. Customer needs—particularly differences among key customer groups—must be linked

closely to an organization's strategic planning, product design, process improvement and workforce training activities. Satisfaction and dissatisfaction information are important because understanding them leads to the right improvements that can create satisfied customers who reward the company with loyalty, repeat business and positive referrals. Creating satisfied customers includes prompt and effective response and solutions to their needs and desires as well as building and maintaining good relationships.

(Evans and Lindsay, 2008: 24–25)

Barton J. Goldenberg defines CRM and its relationship with the internet as follows:

CRM success requires the seamless integration of every aspect of business that touches the customer—including people, process, and technology—revolutionized by the internet. Each component presents significant challenges, but it is the ability to integrate all three that makes or breaks a CRM system.

(Goldenberg, 2008: 13)

These definitions suggest that one of the most important aspects of digital governance is its seamless use—in combination with other ICTs—to provide citizens with information and deliver less expensive, higher quality services. Public managers expend considerable effort, energy, resources and time exchanging best practices, finding best value and rethinking government. The entrepreneurial government movement also provided citizens with greater opportunities to compare service quality in the public and private sectors (see Morgeson and Mithas, 2009).

What is the future of digital technology to enhance the customer service quality in government? The two approaches are parallel and mutually supportive. So long as concepts of CzRM and TQM are applied equitably to support organizational reform efforts, the adoption of e-commerce and digital technology will continue to play a significant role in ongoing efforts to improve government systems and services. Citizen relationship management (CzRM) promises higher levels of service quality through multi-channel interactions with governments organized around the expressed needs of citizens.

Defining Customer Relationship Management and Digital Government

Digital government is a growth industry, not just in economically developed regions of Asia, Europe and the United States but worldwide. In 2001, prior to the common use of the term, an AltaVista search on the related term "Electronic Government" found only 44,979 html documents

(Grönlund, 2002: 1). By 2004, a similar Google search yielded 12 million "hits" (Larsen and Milakovich, 2005: 57); in 2009, the same search yielded 53 million results. Another Google search on the term "digital government" in late 2010 yielded 107 million hits—an enormous exponential increase reflecting the global growth in government-to-citizen internet links. Digital government differs from traditional "in office" public service delivery in the following ways:

1) It is digital and becoming mobile and wireless, rather than paper-based and wired.
2) It is available to citizens/customers 24 hours a day, seven days a week.
3) It provides information and service delivery of various types and degrees of complexity not found in other mass media (Holden, Norris and Fletcher, 2003: 327).

Nearly a decade ago, Åke Grönlund (2002) offered a dual conceptualization of electronic government: how it affects changes in both internal and external government operations.[1]

Internal and External Operations

Internal operations refer to the use of information technology (IT) for automation, cooperation, infrastructure development and integration among agencies as a decision-making tool; e-government in this sense has existed for several decades. The application of ICTs for **external** operations is newer and occurs when government agencies use the internet to conduct transactions, provide and receive information and deliver services to citizens. Ideally, external changes reinforce internal process improvements that enhance effectiveness, efficiency, service quality or transformation (U.S. House of Representatives, 2002: 4). Definitions are consistent with newer digital governance concepts in the sense that they underscore one of the important aspects of online government: the use of the World Wide Web and digital devices to provide citizens with additional information and enhanced online services. They also diverge because they encompass less accessible internal activities of agencies and other units of government. Digital governance is generally viewed as the external use of web-based internet applications and other information technologies, combined with management processes which enhance access to and delivery of government information and services to the public agencies and other government entities.

When examining digital governance from a CRM perspective it is generally assumed that governments are capable of maintaining citizen relationships with established internal processes necessary to manage advanced digital systems. Obviously, this assumption is selective and does not apply to all governments in all nations: a multi-channel strategy is a necessary but an insufficient condition by itself to transform existing organizational arrangements.

Transformation of CRM into CzRM

In the private sector, an evolution and transformation of the customer service relationships changed how organizations provide information, deliver services and interact with current and future customers. Previously, customers were regarded as passive buyers with predetermined consumption habits and purchasing patterns. The concept of "one-size-fits-all" dominated advertising and product marketing prior to the information revolution in the mid-20th century. Since the advent of television, radio and internet advertising, the view of customers has changed dramatically. They are no longer seen as passive buyers, but as partners, co-creators of business value, collaborators and co-developers of personalized experiences (Prahalad and Ramaswamy, 2001: 4). Expansion of two-way communication on the internet has further accelerated innovations in marketing strategy.

From the CRM perspective, customers are seen as unique individuals with distinct interests and needs; they have a right to color-coded, customized, quick and convenient service at market costs (Nasif, 2004: 1). In addition, self-service technologies give customers the ability to have their needs met whenever they want by using online banking, electronic account statements and e-commerce. Firms such as Amazon.com, eBay and Dell Computer pioneered the direct supplier-to-customer model to eliminate inventory and overhead expenses of retail outlets. As customers experienced increasing access to a wider range of private sector services, many began to expect the same level of service from the public sector (Xavier, 2002: 3). Despite growing demand for reform, many CRM projects failed because of lack of data processing capability, availability and quality.

Because of the size and scope of many CRM initiatives, significant pre-planning is essential. This step involves a technical evaluation of the data and the availability of technology employed in existing systems to determine the level of effort needed to clean and integrate data. If a company's CRM strategy is to track life-cycle revenues, expenses, margins and interactions between individual customers, this must be reflected in all its business processes. Data must be extracted from multiple sources (e.g., departmental/divisional databases such as sales, manufacturing, supply chain, logistics, finance, service etc.), which require comprehensive integrated systems with well-defined structures and high speed data processing capability. **Data cleaning** is an important and time-consuming component. Data from other systems can be transferred to CRM systems using appropriate interfaces. Equally critical are the human resources needed for successful implementation. This requires an understanding of the expectations and perceptions of all stakeholders involved in distinct processes.

The same basic principles apply to public sector applications. Governments all over the world are pressured by the need to gather data on population growth and demographic changes, tempered by the technological and knowledge explosions, citizens' expectations and reluctance to raise taxes. Consequently, governments are adopting CRM practices in order to respond to the demands of citizens, and referring to them as Citizen Relationship Management or CzRM (Coleman, 2004: 4).

Why Digital Governance Needs to be Paired with CzRM

Digital governance influences the quality of relationships between public administrators and citizens by providing information and delivering a wider range of public services more efficiently. Technological changes need to be paired with a customer-focused strategy such as CzRM to facilitate citizen-focused service. According to Ramon Barquin (2004: 20), the core of CzRM is *government for the people* that provides much more effective, efficient and simplified service to citizens. As online self-government experiences increase in use, they can be examined from a CzRM perspective to identify value-added gains or problems when used by individual citizens and government agencies. CzRM focuses on providing citizens timely, consistent and responsive access to information and services using channels *that the citizen prefers*. CzRM focuses on strengthening cooperative links between government and citizens, realizing operational and financial efficiencies, and building supportive environments which encourage innovation and responsiveness. Accordingly, CzRM strategies are multi-channel, developed from a 360° view of the citizen and oriented around the citizen's needs, not just those of the organization. Governments should be proactive in predicting all possible services needed by citizens and offering integrated solutions, for example websites, call-centers or one-stop shops.

Most governments now recognize the advantages of having a single contact number or website as a portal where citizens can find information about services, contact public offices, e-mail questions and receive answers quickly. Several public call-centers now provide single "311" **non-emergency telephone numbers** to contact public offices for non-emergency services, thus making it easier for citizens to know how to contact responsible officials in government agencies and freeing up "911" channels for true emergencies. In Miami-Dade County, Florida, citizens seeking information or filing complaints against public agencies or private companies are directed to the appropriate agency through a 311 call-center. In New York City, residents may contact either 911 or 311, and also submit photos or videos to a call-center to record their complaint. Bicyclists for example can summon police directly by taking pictures and sending them over their cellular phones if a motorist is blocking a bike lane. The 311 system in Baltimore, Maryland, is linked to the **CitiStat** database and allows managers to better track the performance of city services such as responses to calls for assistance, trash pick-up, street repairs or snow removal. The program also records and plots data from residents' service calls so public officials can identify trends and respond appropriately (Perez and Rushing, 2007). One-stop portals also provide citizens a single point-of-contact to reach public officials when initiating routine actions such as moving, paying taxes or applying for a driver's license, passport or social security number.

In what may be a precursor for the future, residents in Los Angeles' 13th legislative district can download a free iPhone application to snap and submit photos of potholes, graffiti and even dead animals for the city to fix or clean up. The phone's **Global Positioning System (GPS)** will automatically provide the city with a location, eliminating the time needed to report 311 issues over the phone, in person or via e-mail.

Different modes of access are available with today's technology: appearing in person face-to-face, using a cellular mobile phone, writing a letter, sending a fax, sending an e-mail, sending a short mobile communication text message or using the internet. If a citizen fills out a form on a website, then that transaction does not take up time of a public servant and a considerable reduction in costs is possible, for both citizen and public official. The multi-channel integrated service approach further increases the possibility that tech-savvy citizens will select the most cost-effective alternative. Services provided by the public sector should be oriented toward meeting citizens' needs, not reinforcing administrative and bureaucratic hierarchies.

In sum, CzRM facilitates government becoming citizen-centric. Implementing CzRM requires a shift in culture and a reorientation by public authorities. The technology needed to make this change is widely available but, more importantly, it requires attitudinal changes among public servants which are generally more difficult to achieve (Milakovich and Gordon, 2009: 500). When accompanied by performance management strategies, self-service *by* citizens and *for* citizens reduces costs and improves the level of public confidence in the quality of service received.

Citizen Relationship Management (CzRM) and Digital Governance

There are distinct differences between the missions of public and private sectors which make it more difficult to apply market-driven techniques to public sector operations. The latter can offer goods and services at lower prices and earn greater profits from serving greater numbers of customers more efficiently, typically without having to negotiate or engage in **collective bargaining** with unions. Conflicts between unionized public sector and non-unionized private sector workers have increased with the downturn in the economy and complicated already tense labor negotiations since the economic recession. Despite tense labor-management issues, modern citizens want choice, convenience and control over their relationships with public agencies. With a few exceptions, the primary drivers for implementing CRM in the private sector—customer retention and increased profit per customer—are absent in the public sector. However, CzRM principles hold intriguing possibilities for governments, which have much to gain from better understanding of their customers. Not only are government agencies among the largest service providers in the world, but they are subject to democratic political processes which may force them to quickly move in different directions. CzRM has the potential to cope with some of the most pressing service quality challenges (see Box 3.2). Among other benefits, CzRM can assist in streamlining government processes, improve inter-agency data sharing and provide enhanced self-service options to the public.

Delivering online services requires governments to customize citizen services based upon a broader range of user characteristics (Larsen and

---

Box 3.2: Government-to-Citizen Case Study—The Development of South Dakota's Service Direct Portal

This case illustrates the quality improvements made by the state of South Dakota with regard to the state's development of a one-stop "Service Direct" web portal. The establishment of South Dakota's Service Direct portal is also a prime example of government utilizing digital technology to enhance CzRM because the ultimate goal for customers is to have successful interactions with South Dakota state government. Prior to Service Direct Government-to-Citizen (G2C) services were of questionable quality. In fact, citizens and businesses were often confused and unsure of which state agency to contact to get things done. Citizens had to make several phone calls or visits to state agencies during regular office hours to find the right agency for help or to get one of their forms. However, that all changed after the online Service Direct portal was initiated; users could now: access and download state forms from the comfort of their own home; access information about all state forms; access many state publications; search for forms by category, agency or keyword. Thanks to Service Direct, all state forms, now numbering over 1,300, are only three clicks away on the internet. South Dakota's Service Direct portal has also been ranked high on quality by the citizens that use it. In fact, based on customer satisfaction surveys administered by the state of South Dakota, users rated the site a 2.0 out of 4, with 1 being excellent.

Source: Blackstone *et al.* (2005: 188–195). See: www.sd.gov/servicedirect/

Milakovich, 2005: 59). Government must become more responsive to citizens seeking differentiated services based on individual customer requirements and budgetary constraints. Knowledge about how to access public service channels is critical. If governments expect citizens to use the internet as an end-to-end self-service channel then they must provide citizens with detailed guidance on how to access the service.

Public administration in many communities is battered by deep-seated conflicts over policy preferences reflecting ideological disagreements about how to best achieve public policy goals. For many public officials, responsive customer service quality is often viewed as an expensive "add-on" rather than a built-in feature to satisfy customers. Powerful bureaucratic and legislative interests also resist regulatory reforms in order to placate well-heeled special interests. These create divisions among citizens which, in turn, affect the delivery of public services—especially those required for non-routine emergency responses to homeland security threats, natural disasters and other contingencies.

Identifying the Customer/Stakeholder, Defining Goals and Measuring Progress

As part of a broader effort to reach out to all citizens, many governments acknowledge a wider set of citizens as customers and other stakeholders. Mission statements recognize the impact of technology not just on citizens, but also on government employees, non-profit agencies and private sector organizations as well. For example, the Asian country of Singapore has developed a strategic framework that includes a government-to-employee (G2E) component, recognizing that to be successful both in service delivery and in policy implementation, there needs to be an emphasis on employees to ensure they perform at their best and meet the challenges of the new global economy.[2] Programs emphasizing intergovernmental coordination and collaboration stress that there can be no development or expansion of online resources without a coordinated approach to both information technology and human resources management (Chapter 7).

Key performance indicators must accompany online government transformations to determine effectiveness. Open and transparent status reporting and the use of **benchmarking** and best practices have increased (Camp, 1989) and are gradually becoming embedded in public sector management practices. Consulting with citizens, businesses and interest groups is key to online initiatives.

The Canadian government has undertaken extensive public opinion polling to ensure that programs continue to meet client needs and expectations. For the past decade, the Canadian government has also relied on various international benchmarking initiatives to measure progress. The Treasury Board of Canada launched a public reporting process involving both departmental and government-wide reporting.[3] In addition, an online Citizens' Panel enables the national government to collect valuable information to help better understand current perceptions and future expectations for online government.

Expanding Collaboration with the Private Sector?

Since the economic collapse in 2007 and the American presidential election of 2008, there has been a growing debate about the private sector's capacity to invest and to innovate without direction and regulation from a leaner, more efficient *and* accountable central government. French President Nicolas Sarkozy, among other world leaders, welcomed "the return of the state" to public policy making. Others shrink from the idea of government management of complex social systems such as financial services, health care and environmental protection. Nonetheless, **collaboration** with the private sector is more common, with government entering into a vast array of sophisticated new business arrangements, contracts and **cooperative agreements** with non-governmental providers where risks and rewards are shared and the focus of both parties is less on partisan politics and more on delivery of positive outcomes. Far removed from the simple outsourcing models of the past, these arrangements are designed to achieve genuine partnerships that go beyond merely installing information technology—rather they encompass all activities necessary to provide needed assets and services. Too often, such efforts are viewed as crisis interventions rather than collaboration. For example, the federal government under President George W. Bush implemented the **Troubled Asset Relief Program (TARP)** fund in October 2008 to forestall a national financial collapse. Since then, many large banks, financial institutions and manufacturers and their corporate officials have, in effect, become legally indebted partners with federal agencies for loans they are obligated to pay back in the future.

In many cases, these new **transformational outsourcing** projects are funded by cost savings or revenue collections generated by downsizing and hiring non-union workers. Effective transformational outsourcing requires an environment which is supported by good management practices and positive employee relationships; some governments have worked for several decades to put these in place. In many regions, however, controversial strategies such as contracting-out and downsizing have led to confrontations between unionized and non-unionized workers, especially in states and local governments coping with severe budget deficits. The service cuts have also created additional risks for citizens. The city of Los Angeles was forced to make deep cuts in highway maintenance, prompting city workers to warn motorists of the increased dangers of road hazards. The city of Oakland, California, laid off police officers and warned citizens that they would no longer respond to certain crimes, such as household burglaries. Citizens must either protect themselves or hire private security. In Broward County, Florida, even *unionized* sheriff's deputies responsible for jail intake and control were fired and offered the option to be rehired at substantially reduced salaries.

Private sector companies differ substantially from public agencies in numerous respects, particularly in their use of non-unionized workers. In addition, the private-sector approach to applying ICTs is primarily profit-driven, rather than service-driven. These and other fundamental differences have created intense controversy between business and government, particularly surrounding collectively bargained contracts for salaries and benefits. The business community is not subject to the same degree of public accountability, and is substantially less concerned with equality and redistribution of resources. Although future directions remain uncertain, enthusiasm for various forms of unregulated **contracting out** has diminished considerably with the Democratic sweeps of both the U.S. House and Senate in 2006 and the election of Barack Obama as President in 2008. Although currently driving public policy in the United States, this sentiment may change in the future as the basis for government revenues shifts and expenditures either increase or decrease with the expansion or contraction of the economy.

Coordinating Multiple Tiers of Bureaucracy and Government

Information and communications technologies can be instrumental in overcoming governmental specialization and intergovernmental divisions. In the early phases of adopting e-government, progress in many countries was hindered by governmental processes and structures that were largely powerless to overcome well-entrenched bureaucratic, corporate and political sub-governments of influence and power (Chapter 7). While CzRM and **networked government** are ultimately the keys to successfully transforming attitudes and behaviors in public service, securing necessary cross-functional cooperation is often difficult. In taking a citizen-centric approach, governments must build bridges, not only between agencies on the same tier of government, but among different divisions and levels of government as well. Considerable progress has been made in solving G2G intergovernmental problems since the tragic events of 9/11 and Hurricane Katrina in 2005. Still, private sector cooperation has been uneven. Corporate executives often view closer governmental relations and regulations as a threat to their independence and make investments in the form of campaign contributions and lobbying fees to pressure groups and politicians committed to protecting and preserving the status quo. (Questionable relationships between oil companies and politicians were exposed and became the subject of U.S. Congressional investigations following the BP oil disaster in the Gulf of Mexico during the spring and summer 2010.)

The United States federal government has focused on a stated goal of scrutinizing all federal IT investments to ensure maximum efficiency, interoperability and minimal redundancy. With the passage of various information technology laws and regulations, governments recognize the lost opportunity and sunk costs of fragmented systems and processes that duplicate data collection and information gathering efforts (Chapters 1 and 6). In addition, the costs to business of multiple compliance reviews by separate federal agencies is a disincentive for collaboration, but one that can be significantly reduced through **cross-agency cooperation**. As discussed in later chapters, cross-agency projects and interoperability are especially important to ICT applications and partnerships. Current funding practices in which appropriations are made on an agency-by-agency line-item basis, however, actively discourage this approach. The U.S. federal government proposed overcoming this barrier by creating an e-government fund to support inter-agency projects to improve citizen access to federal services. Unfortunately, this fund fell victim to budget cuts. This approach has also been considered by other countries, all of which face similar barriers to citizen-centric government to varying degrees.

Ranking Countries According to E-Government Maturity and CRM

Accenture is a global management consulting, technology services and outsourcing firm that also conducts surveys on the extent of electronic government and information technology in numerous countries.[4] The majority of those countries surveyed by *Accenture* also recognized that intergovernmental **fragmentation** was a significant barrier to progress, but few had strategies to deal with the issue. Countries with stronger central governments such as Italy, Canada, Australia and Ireland have created a vision to deal with this problem.[5] *Accenture* not only conducts global studies but ranks countries by **e-government maturity** and overall customer service maturity on a regular basis. In the two studies mentioned below, the company also studied and ranked the countries according to their implementation of customer relationship management (CRM).

In a 2002 study, *Accenture* researchers selected 22 countries that used the internet in an attempt to evaluate 169 common service needs that might typically be provided by a national government.[6] Researchers accessed and evaluated the websites of national government agencies in these countries to judge the quality and maturity of services and the level at which business was conducted electronically with government. Services were assessed in 12 major sectors: agriculture; defense; eDemocracy; education; human services; immigration, justice and security; postal delivery; procurement; regulation; participation; revenue and customs; and transportation. Among the leading nations, Ireland implemented a single portal to centralize government procurement and a one-stop shop for businesses to work together with the Irish Government. This portal handles tender submissions and vendor registration. The portal provides businesses with a simple two-page set of instructions in its "Suppliers—Getting Started" page. Subscribers to this website receive e-mail alerts as new opportunities are published, access to business opportunities with the public sector as well as clear and concise information on working with government agencies.[7]

In 2004, *Accenture* conducted both quantitative and qualitative research to study attitudes and practices regarding e-government among 5,000 regular internet users in 12 countries in North America, Europe and Asia, as well as a quantitative assessment of the maturity of public services. The study also revealed gaps between the online services that governments provide for citizens and the ways citizens view and actually use these programs, pointing to an historical problem that all governments have in accurately assessing the value added by ICT strategies. In response to this need, the study discusses *Accenture's* **Public Sector Value Model**, an analytical tool designed to help government agencies deliver increased value at a time when budgets are shrinking. While not focused exclusively on digital governance, the model's principles can be applied to help governments better manage online programs. From 2000 to 2004, Canada ranked first out of the 22 countries evaluated in terms of e-government maturity, or the level to which a government has developed an online presence. Singapore and the United States shared the second-place ranking, followed closely by Australia, Denmark, Finland and Sweden, which were tied for the fourth place. France ranked eighth, the Netherlands and the United Kingdom tied for ninth, and Belgium, Ireland and Japan jointly held the eleventh position.

Accenture researchers in each of the selected countries utilized the internet in an attempt to fulfill service needs that might typically be provided to businesses and citizens by a national government. In the majority of the countries surveyed, participation of private organizations was actively encouraged. Despite Singapore closing the gap, Canada maintained its position in first place. In the top category, Innovative Leaders, Canada and Singapore joined the United States as the three countries recording Overall CRM Maturity scores of greater than 50%.

The followers of the Innovative Leaders are called Visionary Challengers and countries such as Australia, Denmark, the UK, Finland, Hong Kong, Germany, Ireland, the Netherlands, France and Norway were included in that category. In the 2002 study, *Accenture* also ranked these countries according to CRM maturity (see Figure 3.1).

Although CRM rankings were not identical to the e-government rankings, there is an obvious correlation between the countries ranking high on both indices. Canada led in both categories and the two other innovative leaders from the e-government ranking also scored high in the CRM ranking. The United States was in third place in both rankings and Singapore in

Overall maturity by country - 2002

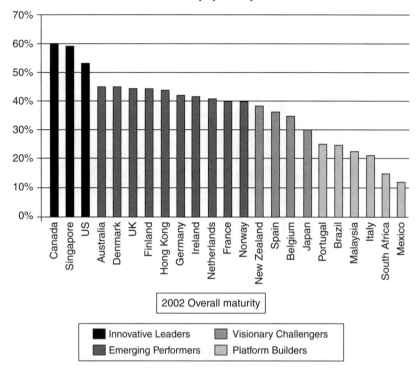

Figure 3.1 Overall CRM Maturity Rankings, by Country

Source: Jupp (2003: 133)

seventh place in the CRM ranking but in second place in the e-government ranking (see Figure 3.2). (These rankings can also be compared with more general e-government readiness and transaction rankings presented in Chapter 8.)

According to *Accenture*, governments which adopted customer relationship management (CRM) principles early in their e-government initiatives were improving at a much faster pace. Portals were becoming far more prevalent, but their true potential continued to be unrealized because of the barriers to cross-agency cooperation. The global fiscal crisis may yet be the catalyst for dismantling these barriers, as governments, businesses and citizens acknowledge that the benefits of common platforms and information sharing outweigh the perceived costs associated with disrupting the status quo.

As governments have placed more services online, they are asked what value has been added. According to *Accenture*, their conclusions were that e-government had delivered substantial value and demonstrated dramatic

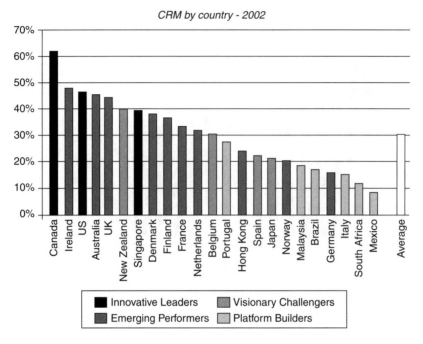

Figure 3.2 CRM Maturity, by Country

Source: Jupp (2003: 144)

improvements in the expansion of services, ease of interaction and costs of service delivery. What it cannot do, however, is lead to the sweeping transformation of government service that will lead to higher performance—consistently generating the outcomes citizens want and that governments need to deliver. Transformation requires an entirely new vision of leadership for customer service—one that is proactive and embraces the concepts of cross-functional government, citizen-centered and multi-channel interactions. While e-government is a catalyst for this change, it is also only one (albeit important) component of the transformation. Because of this, their report, *Leadership in Customer Service: New Expectations, New Experiences* analyzes "the many facets of future leadership in service delivery. As their methodology changed, many of their rankings changed as a result" (Accenture, 2005: 2).

As seen in Figure 3.3, Canada again led and the United States moved to second place, ahead of Singapore. Denmark has reached the third place but Singapore has now dropped to the fourth place. Overall we can see that most of the top countries in the 2002 study still are in the top range of the 2005 study.

In other studies, *Accenture* also ranked countries by CRM maturity. Their methodology changed in the 2005 study and countries were ranked by

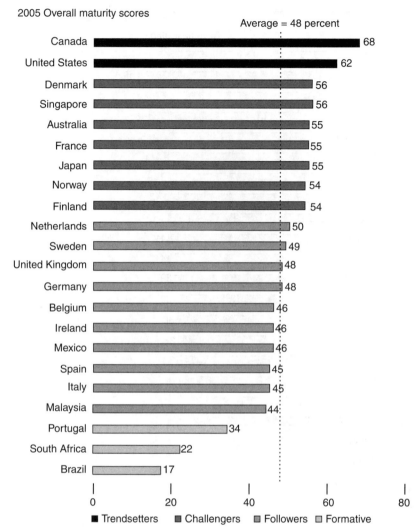

2005 Overall maturity scores

Average = 48 percent

Canada is the leader in service delivery maturity, followed closely by the United States. Differences in scores of 2 percent or less generated joint rankings.

Figure 3.3 Overall E-Government Maturity Rankings, by Country

Source: Accenture (2005: 9)

overall customer service maturity (see Figure 3.4). This was a new indicator of how far countries had reached in their customer-focused approach. Because of this change in methodology, it is impossible to compare the 2005 CRM ranking with earlier studies, but the later study measures the same trends as well as the customer-focused approach of countries.

Overall customer service maturity

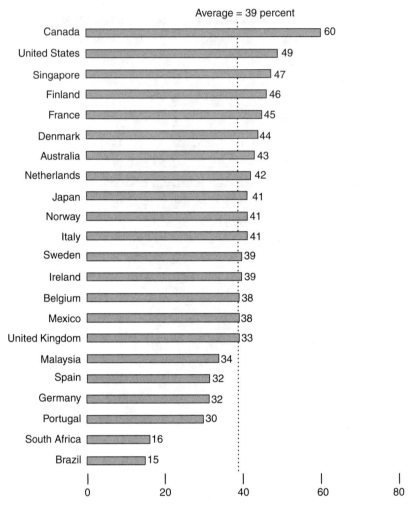

Customer service maturity was the most influential factor in how countries fared in our overall rankings this year.

Figure 3.4 Overall Customer Service Maturity, by Country

Source: Accenture (2005: 14)

The same pattern appears here as in the 2002 study. Countries which scored highest on the customer service index also scored well in the e-government maturity index. The striking similarity of these findings indicates how important the customer-focused approach is in the process of implementing digital governance.

Current Situation: How CRM is Used to Implement Digital Governance

Globally, many governments have reached the upper limits of services that can be provided online without transforming internal information management and human resource systems. Likewise, many are approaching the limits of what can be done with online services in their current form. The question for decision makers then becomes: have ICTs generated real value for the citizens? For all of the investments, is there evidence that governments are delivering truly better outcomes? According to one observer, public-sector value gains from e-government during the early 2000s were primarily incremental and limited (West, 2005). This conclusion pre-dates advanced applications and the exponential growth of social networking, but may still reflect the operational reality of most subnational units. Government information is now more readily available to more individuals and this may have reduced costs of information dissemination as well as some citizen frustration. Progress is difficult to measure with precision, but there are some clear examples of successful implementation.

There are numerous examples of service delivery innovation that have led to increases in convenience for citizens. **Tallinn, Estonia**, is one of **Intelligent Community Forum**'s top seven technologically advanced cities. The government has provided computerized schools and a large-scale digital skills training program and has developed a smart ID card. WiFi connections are available throughout the city via over 700 public access kiosks as well.[8]

Another example of the application of ICTs by Intelligent Cities is the small French city of **Issy-les-Moulineaux**, an industrial suburb of Paris. With only 63,000 inhabitants, the city's government decided in the mid-1990s to fully embrace what they saw as the reality that e-government and e-democracy would be the trend in 21st century governance. This decision was not that different from risks taken by other local and state governments in the hope of attracting new businesses or other niche expertise to their cities. Some towns might give tax incentives, essentially gambling that large corporations would come and employ large numbers of their constituents. Issy-les-Moulineaux gambled that ICTs would become an emerging field and, if they could be at the forefront, one day they may have an importance that vastly exceeded most cities with similar populations. Their speculation was correct, and their investment paid off. In 1997, the Interactive City Council was launched, providing all of the residents with a free broadcast of town meetings via either cable television or the internet. In order to fully grasp how audacious an initiative this was at the time, think back to the status of the internet in 1997. Without doubt, very few citizens were anywhere near as familiar with navigating the internet as today, while the residents of this small town bordering

Paris' 15th *arrondissement* were already watching their government deliberations on projection computer screens. This is not the full extent of the
Interactive City Council, however; if citizens wished to have their say, they
could also pose questions or comments to lawmakers via e-mail or a toll-
free phone number, and then presumably watch live as those whom had
been voted in by citizens responded immediately and directly to such
citizens. The impact of the Interactive City Council was noted by ICT
specialists around the world, and additional benefits started to flow the
city's way. Today, nearly 60% of businesses that are headquartered in Issy-
les-Moulineaux are ICT-related because technological companies saw a
government that was willing to invest in their products (Shark and
Toporkoff, 2008: 332). An example of one such company that was born
here is *France 24*, France's first network news channel, similar to CNN in
the United States. The population has been undeniably bolstered economically by this infusion of industry, and Issy-les-Moulineaux has become a
"recognized Cyber-City."

Citizen-centric governments must focus on all facets of leadership for
customer service to cope with challenges facing the public sector. In the
process, public agencies will develop many of the characteristics that are key
to becoming intelligent **high-performance governments**: they will adopt
measures to accommodate the needs, expectations and perceptions of citizens; they will work collaboratively within and across agencies; they will
offer multiple channels of interaction, using innovative technologies and
unprecedented flexibility to citizens; and they will reach out to their citizens
proactively, teaching them the tools they need to make full use of the newly
enhanced service offerings and deliver maximum public-sector value.

Implications for Citizens and Citizenship

The previous sections traced the evolution and provided examples of
citizen-centric networked ICT strategies in the United States and in
several other countries. The following section deals with the future challenges facing governments to permit citizens to seamlessly interact with
public administrators.[9]

Accountability to Citizens or Customers?

One of the core values within public administration has always been **accountability**. The concept is complex and multi-faceted. In its most narrow sense,
accountability means holding politicians and bureaucrats responsible for their
actions by some kind of external review standard. As government becomes
more complex, the issue of accountability becomes so as well.

The idea that public servants should serve individual citizen interests
originates from vastly different understandings of the relationship between
the political and the administrative systems, their values and the issue of

accountability. The thorny question becomes: to whom are public officials accountable and for what results?

Public accountability to citizens in their role as customers reflects the dilemma faced by many governments which are, by necessity, becoming more fee-for-service based. At the same time, citizens are demanding improved levels of service quality as they experience lower wages and higher user fees *and* taxes. Adopting the "entrepreneurial" paradigm in favor of the "administrative management" model that had prevailed in the public sector since the late 1800s may have had long-term negative consequences. The feasibility of these approaches has been reconsidered in the light of the growing frustration with the weakness of the private economy since 2007. The conventional view of bureaucracy was that it produces poor service quality, impersonal treatment and in some cases incompetence. As the world's fiscal crisis worsened, however, governments were viewed more favorably as "safety nets" to protect citizens and institutions against the worst effects of deepening recession. Accountability is and has always been an important concept in the public sector. At the same time, government is also becoming more and more reliant on external expertise and knowledge. Cooperation with private sector companies as intermediaries can have great benefits for government, but at the same time public officials must be acutely aware of the different drivers present in the private and public sectors.

Use of Intermediaries and Changing Citizen Demands on Government

In the private sector, thousands of consultants claim to have developed expertise in customer relationship management. The 2009 Google search on "CRM" yielded 26 million hits, most of them private consultants or intermediaries. While the private sector today is influenced by CRM practices, a whole new market is developing for consultants to disseminate practices to the public sector. Consulting companies have the specialized knowledge that government entities now find useful in order to deal with present challenges. However, most consultants are experts in CRM, not CzRM. Private consultants are familiar with implementing CRM strategies to enhance commercial drivers, not government drivers. Commercial drivers are: 1) increasing top line revenue by increasing sales; 2) increasing bottom line (net profits) by downsizing; 3) reducing overheads and service; and 4) improving customer satisfaction to increase customer retention. By contrast, government drivers are: 1) meeting performance and service goals at the lowest cost to taxpayers; 2) improving quality of service within shrinking budgets; and 3) increasing citizen satisfaction at the lowest cost. Differences in drivers for the private and the public sector reflect the significant influence of private consultants in the adoption of CRM practices.

The initial reason for implementing CzRM in public administration was in response to citizens who wanted to change government practices. Citizens still want more services but are reluctant to pay more in taxes. Furthermore, so-called "entrepreneurial" strategies tend to respond to the ego-centric interests of individual citizens rather than the broader public interest. The rise of the customer-centric concept with increased attention to individual rights might therefore occur at the expense of collective responsibilities. Changes in citizens' demands and views of government may occur as a result of more fundamental and complex changes with interactive technology. Private consulting companies play a role as intermediaries at this level, because they may be seen as stakeholders, due to their interest in the opening of a new and huge market for their services. Politicians are affected by the public opinion, because it reflects the interests of a majority of the citizens. The service demands of citizens, however, may not reflect the harsh financial and political constraints facing political decision makers (Robbins, Simonson and Feldman, 2008: 574).

Improved Service Delivery at Lower Costs

According to the Deputy Associate Administrator of the U.S. federal General Services Administration (GSA) Office of Citizen Services and Communications, the cost and quality of service are not proportional. The integrated multi-channel service approach within CRM provides higher service quality at lower cost (Coleman, 2004: 6–7). Public services which require personal assistance, face-to-face contact, telephone, mail and fax are expensive in time and effort, whereas self-service on a website, e-mail and interactive voice response systems are less expensive. Thus, the best and least expensive quality of service is provided by a combination of face-to-face, telephone, fax, website self-service, e-mail and interactive voice response systems. This relationship is illustrated in Figure 3.5.

The lower productivity of the private economy since the beginning of the worldwide recession has complicated citizen–government relationships. It has resulted in shrinking tax bases which, combined with citizens' reluctance to pay higher taxes, has placed greater fiscal stress on governments, especially states, counties and municipalities. This has muted somewhat the knowledge and technological explosion which gave rise to the use of ICTs in government, especially in industrial nations. At the same time, many people have developed a "where's my bailout?" attitude towards government services. They want government to satisfy their individual demands and expect protection from economic perils, but they do not have confidence in the execution of service delivery and even regard government itself with hostility. These contradictory trends reflect general anxiety about the economy and pervasive negative attitudes towards government institutions in general.

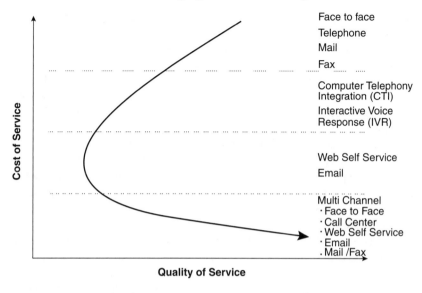

Figure 3.5 Relationship between Cost, Quality and Type of Service

Source: Larsen and Milakovich (2005: 62)

Nonetheless, the argument for improving online service is strengthened in a recessionary economy because internet transactions can be as much as ten times less expensive than face-to-face or telephone transactions (Grönlund, 2002: 31). In addition to the expanded use of the internet for transactions, CzRM also encourages the possibility of citizen self-service. It is critical to remember, however, that implementing a CzRM system is not without expenditures. CzRM systems demand initial investments in computers, communication infrastructure, software, web design, expert staff and training of employees. Reduced costs will not be achieved overnight and the benefits will tend to occur in a different fiscal year from the year the investment was made.

Using ICTs to Overcome Digital Divides

When examining the implementation of CzRM in the public sector, a persistent problem is the existence of the digital divide. Concern about digital divides is widely shared and underscores the fact that unequal access to technology and the internet may further exacerbate divisions among existing social groups (Grönlund, 2002: 39). Poor, uneducated and elderly citizens are particularly vulnerable because of the risk that government services will be accessible to some rather than others, based on the existing economic and knowledge inequalities in society. The USA.gov website is an example of how only those citizens with computers and access to the internet are able to benefit from the improvements in the quality of service that portals and websites provide, even though *all* taxpayers are contributing to its budget. (The same criticism applies to other public services such as libraries and schools for special needs children.) In some instances, digital initiatives as well as other public services result in a type of "negative redistribution." This is especially true if the new forms of technological interaction become fee-based, as many citizens would prefer them to be (Chen and Thurmaier, 2008). Citizens would have to "pay and go online, or get in line." This dual system did not exist in the "old" type of pre-internet service delivery era when everyone had to stand in line to receive Medicare, social welfare, Social Security and unemployment benefits.

The existence of the digital divide stems from a recognition that there are information "haves" and "have-nots" in the Internet Age, and that the basis for such divisions includes demographic characteristics such as age, gender, income, education, ethnicity, race, region and locality. From a public policy perspective, questions about digital divides include: 1) Where do they exist? 2) Why do they exist? 3) To what extent can they be corrected by changes in public policy? Government officials at all levels in Canada and the United States and many other developed countries such as the United Kingdom, Australia, New Zealand as well as several European Union (EU) countries, recognize the existence of digital divides within their populations. Attempts have been made by public agencies to equalize the distribution of online services—with mixed results.[10] Digital divides between economically developed democratic countries and poorer, less democratic nations also have important implications for globalization and the delivery of government services (Chapter 8).

Because they lack the money, skills and equipment necessary to access the internet, the poor, undereducated, elderly and other disadvantaged citizens do not have the same opportunity to benefit from improved service via the World Wide Web.[11] There are gender differences as well. Males use the internet more often than females, worldwide, reflecting continued discrimination and subjugation of women in certain regions (Chapter 5). In the United Kingdom, United States, Australia, Canada and the Scandinavian countries, however, women's internet use equals or exceeds that of men. Younger people were originally more frequent users of the internet than older ones, but the number of older users, male and female, is rapidly catching up. Recent studies suggest that minority males are more likely to use social media to access governmental websites. Predictably, those with larger personal or family incomes are far more likely to have internet access than those lacking financial resources. In the United States, limited access to computers and the internet, among other factors, has resulted in lower educational achievement scores and the re-segregation of public school districts. Making government more internet-based, 24/7 accessible and convenient to all citizens should be combined with increasing educational opportunities for ensuring self-service skills, enhancing the abilities and possibilities for all citizens to go online.

Age, ethnicity, income and racial differences regarding internet access are sensitive subjects. Racial differences among white users (a much higher percentage) and black and Hispanic users (a lower percentage) were clearly revealed by survey data in the United States (see Fairlie, 2005). Surveys from other economies, more and less developed, have also shown similar differences, but the specific distributions depend upon the ethnic and racial mix within each country. Some of these gaps have also closed as access to assistance programs is more widely available in certain communities—alleviation of this disparity is difficult because it depends on the availability of educational opportunities and redistribution of scarce public resources.

If one believes that social responsibility is more than merely responding to the aggregative interests of citizens, the problem of digital divides shows that making government more internet-based, 24/7 accessible and convenient to citizens should be combined with a concern for ensuring that all citizens possess the skills, abilities and ICT literacy necessary to go online.

Conclusions and Final Remarks

There is a broad recognition in the world of digital governance research that if governments are to successfully implement changes they need to adopt customer-focused strategies. This chapter has explored the importance of using principles of customer relationship management (CRM) when implementing digital government. According to the *Accenture* studies cited above, there is a strong relationship between countries scoring high on the CRM maturity scale and the use of e-government. If governments are unaware of the importance of CRM when implementing digital governance then they are much more likely to fail.

Citizen relationship management is one among many models which provide a strategic vision for more effective service quality. Critical service quality improvements—by and for citizens—demonstrate the importance of CzRM in the public sector. From a strictly functional, service delivery focus, the adoption of more responsive customer service practices is an opportunity to improve accessibility and level of satisfaction with government services. But from an academic and theoretical perspective, this transition raises more fundamental implications for the overall understanding of complex government–citizen relationships.

This chapter has discussed both the possible advantages as well as disadvantages of applying CzRM in the public sector. Four concerns are present when introducing this private sector strategy into the public sector.

First, public administrators have to keep in mind that those they deal with are citizens first and not just customers. Second, improved service quality must not happen at the expense of the fundamental values and drivers of the public sector. Third, the adoption of CzRM practices and the use of the internet in general must recognize and correct for the existence of digital divides. Last, making government more internet-based and accessible and convenient to citizens should be combined with an explicit concern for ensuring the abilities and possibilities for all citizens to go online.

Actions by public administrators and politicians to set in motion multichannel CzRM practices are taking place as a response to structural changes in the American society in recent years. Although it is difficult to predict the exact contours of future development, nothing signifies a decrease in CzRM initiatives—the opposite seems more likely. No matter what direction development takes in future, there is a pressing need for a discussion of government's role, more specifically the role of public administration in stimulating both the quality and equality of government services.

The economic downturn has further limited the ability of many otherwise receptive governments to expand online services. For those who have begun the process, however, many have developed characteristics which are key to becoming high-performance governments: they assume a citizen-centered perspective to deliver service in terms of the needs, expectations and perceptions of their citizens; they work collaboratively within and across agencies; they offer multiple channels of interaction, using innovative technologies to offer unprecedented flexibility to citizens; and they reach out to citizens proactively, giving them the tools they need to make full use of the newly enhanced service offerings and deliver maximum public-sector value.

The trend toward customer-focused, decentralized, flexible, performance-based and results-driven government is accelerating worldwide as more attention is being paid to recommendations for change and to success stories from an expanding number of public agencies. Lessons from other countries are also accessible online and applicable to different localities, as many governments have implemented customer-oriented changes using similar processes (Chapter 8). These include the expanded use of "citizens' charters" that guarantee specific levels of service, quality "marks" which recognize agencies for exemplary service, "secret shopper" programs which use public employees to evaluate levels of service in other agencies, "311" non-emergency telephone systems and the publication of compliance procedures to be followed by citizens when agencies do not meet their own service standards. Most of these reforms are relatively inexpensive and yield impressing results when skillfully executed.

Most importantly, governments need to learn from the mistakes of the past to fully use a customer-focused approach when deciding issues in the future. What we have *not* seen yet is the wholesale reinvention of service delivery in the government sector, using innovative practices, processes and technology as enablers. The agenda for progressive governments is now moving from implementing ICTs for their own sake to transforming public-sector value through multi-channel internet service delivery. In the future, governments must be ready for a tsunami of new and more demanding customers: ones that are familiar and at ease with multiple technologies and always-on service, ready whenever they need to connect. The next generation of tech-savvy citizens is already surrounded by the internet, social networks and text messaging. They are not running governments today, nor are they the people that public administration currently serves. They will soon be, however, and governments need to be ready for them. That is the challenge. It is time for governments to again reinvent themselves to prepare for a new wave of more demanding citizens/customers.

Key Terms

citizen-centric, 57

customer relationship management (CRM), 57

total quality management (TQM), 57

citizen relationship management (CzRM), 57

business process reengineering (BPR), 58

Six Sigma, 58

entrepreneurial paradigm, 58

supply-chain management, 58

outsourcing, 58

downsizing, 58

privatization, 59

quality management guidelines, 59

digital government, 62

internal and external operations, 63

data cleaning, 64

"311" non-emergency telephone numbers, 65

CitiStat, 66

Global Positioning System (GPS), 66

collective bargaining, 66

benchmarking, 68

collaboration, 69

cooperative agreements, 69

Troubled Asset Relief Program (TARP), 69

transformational outsourcing, 69

contracting out, 70

networked government, 70

cross-agency cooperation, 71

fragmentation, 71

e-government maturity, 71

Public Sector Value Model, 72

Tallinn, Estonia, 77

Intelligent Community Forums, 77

Issy-les-Moulineaux, France, 77

high-performance governments, 78

accountability, 78

4 Virtual Learning

Using the Internet for Education, Training and Quality Improvement

Export anything to a friendly country except our management system.
W. Edwards Deming (referring to the United States)

In the highly competitive and mobile 21st century global economy, all organizations seek better ways to innovate, improve productivity, measure results, motivate employees, serve customers and raise quality standards. Reforms are also accelerating at all levels and in all functions of government, including the armed services, education, intelligence and security agencies, revenue collection, state departments of health and human services and military reserve units. It can be especially challenging for the public sector to integrate new technology, upgrade equipment and provide advanced training to meet extraordinary administrative, financial and institutional challenges. In order to initiate, implement and sustain these changes, public agencies must devote considerable time and resources to maintaining and improving customer service and security systems, all under the watchful eye of opposition political leaders whose ideologies often conflict with current policy directions.

Financially beleaguered and politically vulnerable units of state and local government are integrating the human, physical and technical resources necessary to improve customer service and strengthen cross-functional (interdepartmental) communication across jurisdictional (geographic) boundaries. To achieve horizontally linked and networked system reforms, public agencies must develop enhanced capacities for inter- and intra-organizational coordination, knowledge management, organizational learning and performance assessment (Milakovich, 2006a; Kahler, 2009). Public and non-profit managers must understand and apply New Media methodologies to compare results, exchange information about best practices, combine human assets with information technologies and standardize performance measurement processes. Common ICT frameworks are necessary to determine whether goals are being achieved within the revenue parameters set by private markets or public budgets.

Public education and training are among the largest and most controversial public sector and corporate expenditures in the world. Over one-half of all public budgets are used for teachers' salaries, classroom facilities and educational materials. Recently developed web-based education, or **virtual learning,** is an advanced ICT-enabled model which allows online access to faculty, classrooms and websites from anywhere on the globe, at any time, at significantly lower costs. Virtual learning encompasses the overall use of the internet and information technology for education and training and is viewed by many as a cost-effective alternative to traditional lecture-discussion classroom delivery methods.

Maintaining open government customer service quality improvement requires periodically updating or reinforcing core values of the effort. Quality awards or prizes provide a way to sustain such changes; they are an under-utilized resource that can serve as catalysts for change, help identify areas needing improvement, support internal collaboration, motivate everyone to achieve specific goals and provide learning tools to retain expertise. The competitive challenge and distinction that accompany pursuit of an award, charter mark or prize can be a source of employee motivation and pride (Milakovich, 2004). Perhaps most importantly, the data generated by various performance recognition techniques can help to develop and test applications to assist managers in determining which practices are best suited for their organizations. This chapter shows how recognition programs enhance public administration education and training; describes various international quality awards; and highlights successful case studies of award-winning schools from several American states. Hundreds of quality award programs have been created during the past three decades. Recipients of these awards are a largely untapped reservoir of detailed information about how various organizations successfully changed internal processes to measure and meet performance goals. The full global description of international quality award programs is too extensive to cover completely, but the evolution of several countries' awards has been described elsewhere (Chuan and Soon, 2000; Flynn and Saladin, 2001; Hui and Chaun, 2002).

Regardless of the type of organization or its mission, employees need to be motivated and recognized for supporting organizational goals. The questions raised in this chapter are: 1) Is online virtual learning a viable alternative to traditional educational and training strategies? 2) How will the transition from traditional to virtual learning take place without leaving vulnerable groups behind? 3) Will the organized teaching profession accept alternative teaching methods? 4) How is success measured and what lessons can be publicized and transferred? 5) What choices are available to managers in selecting the most appropriate recognition programs? 6) What organizational values are recognized by quality awards or prizes? 7) Does applying for an award or prize provide the comparative standards, objective assessment and the outside perspective needed to evaluate the performance of internal systems and results? If so, do other organizations regard winners as models for improved performance? These are long-term empirical questions which can only be answered fully by examining integrated knowledge management systems linking diverse databases across many micro-organizational functions (Agor, 1997; Senge, 1994, 1996; Wimmer, 2002).

Improving the Quality of Web-Based Education and Training

Globalization has spread information and communication technologies (ICTs) that have not only flattened the world, but permeated nearly every aspect of life, especially education, job training and social relationships. The global recession combined with a continuous evolution of learning technologies pressures businesses and schools to take on new forms—changes that challenge traditional classroom delivery systems and learning strategies. New ways of communicating, working and "virtual traveling" beyond existing geographic boundaries of time and distance are constantly developing. As a result, "educational institutions everywhere find themselves forced to cope with the knowledge explosion and new information brought by the growth of the internet, a shift in the roles of public and private educational systems ... and a growing emphasis on new content delivery approaches" (Zabriskie and McNabb, 2007: 226). Still, most public education is delivered by a "bricks-and-mortar" bureaucracy that generally ignores or resists changes needed to adopt ICTs required by the knowledge revolution. In addition, budgetary constraints and organized group interests form barriers to the adoption of web-based virtual learning. Education and training are among the public policies most directly impacted by global mega-trends and, paradoxically, among those most resistant to change.

Public Investment in Education

Public investment in educational infrastructure, teacher salaries, textbooks and training is an enormous global expenditure—one that has not returned the value expected in many communities. In the United States alone, nearly one-half of all state and local budgets (and almost an equal proportion of personnel) are dedicated to public elementary and secondary (K-12), higher education, libraries and specialized educational services. Parents expect their children's public schools to accurately reflect local community values. Most educational internal processes such as **curriculum, testing, fiscal control, resource management, teacher certification** and **textbook selection** are controlled by independently elected state and local school boards, administrators and faculty. If dissatisfied with the services provided by their local school, the only options for most parents are either home schooling or enrolling their children in private schools, an expensive alternative generally available only to affluent families.

State-level policy makers have more influence when it comes to educational concerns because most educational funding is provided by states and local governments (93%) rather than the federal government. State-level policy makers are better able to keep themselves updated on educational and quality issues. California, Florida and Indiana require students pass graduation qualifying exams—variously known as California's Standardized Testing and Reporting (STAR) program, Florida Comprehensive Achievement Tests (FCAT) and the Indiana Statewide Test of Educational Progress Plus (ISTEP+)—to be awarded a high school diploma. The effectiveness of standardized testing is still subject to political interpretation. To overcome the disparities among states tests, 31 states are designing a standardized high school graduation test, similar to the SATs for college-bound students, which would be administered to all graduates.[1]

Numerous church-affiliated elementary and secondary schools and nearly one-third of all institutions of higher education in the United States are privately operated. The advent of **charter schools** and educational **vouchers** parallels the entrepreneurial movement and they are designed to circumvent the power of public school lobbies. Many state initiatives have floundered or been tied up in court as a result of constitutional due process and equal protection issues based on school choice. According to proponents, exposing schools to "market forces" allows parents to choose the type of school their children will attend, stimulates competition, increases efficiency and quality of schools or forces low performing schools to improve or close. Such Social Darwinian measures may or may not be the suitable response to the quality problems in education—exposing schools to quality reward systems used in business, government and health care may help breed learning environments which best match students' needs. The 2010 documentary film *Waiting for Superman* questions the quality of public schools and blames teachers' unions for poor quality student performance while advocating non-unionized charter schools as an option.

Concern for the future of public K-12 education extends all the way from local neighborhoods to the Office of the President of the United States; reforms have been the subject of contentious rhetoric and debate for decades. Yet, the rancor has done little to ensure long-term improvement. Politicians tend to be more concerned with incremental "quick fixes" than long-term solutions to difficult quality improvement problems. Unfortunately, instituting programs that are capable of evaluation is difficult, and many are subject to high levels of debate and controversy. Stakeholders involved in the debate over educational reform advocate a wide variety of alternatives to the public schools such as charter schools, **International Baccalaureate (IB)** programs, magnet schools and school vouchers.

Educators increasingly recognize that students reflect multiple learning backgrounds and goals and stress flexibility and choice in the adoption of learning materials. The textbook industry is being impacted by evolving internet technologies, increased availability of online "open source" content and curricula, active used textbook markets and numerous textbook rental start-ups. Publishers are now shifting content to websites and charging less money for the "e-versions" of textbooks. Barnes and Noble booksellers has implemented an e-textbook program in conjunction with marketing its Nook© reader. **Open Educational Resources (OERs)**— materials distributed for no or minimal cost—have become commonplace and faculty are accepting online alternatives to printed textbooks (Harley, Lawrence, Acord and Dixson, 2010).

American educational systems suffer from multiple quality problems, among the most severe being an extraordinary drop-out (or defect) rate in secondary schools, over 50% in some rural and urban districts. Not only are the resulting "system failures" unprepared for careers and civic responsibilities, but scarce resources are wasted on the need for rework. No industry in the world could survive such abysmal failure rates. Nonetheless, political subsidies, state laws mandating educational levels and egalitarian ideology support many otherwise failing systems. In addition, less than half of the students entering college are adequately prepared for college-level courses. Worse, low-income students are systematically discriminated against by extreme variations in local property tax valuations, the primary basis for funding school districts in most states.

President Obama has addressed the drop-out crisis with a **Race to the Top** program which includes austere measures that enforce sanctions on so-called "non-performing schools," including firing teachers and closing failing schools. Federal government efforts affect only about 1% of all schools, but they are being reinforced at the local level by the downsizing of many underperforming districts, especially those in already vulnerable urban areas suffering from high drop-out rates: in many communities the fiscal crisis has brought many of these underlying issues to the boiling point. Virtual delivery of online academic services is emerging as an alternative to traditional educational systems because of its lower costs, flexibility in achieving learning goals and its potential to close the digital divide.

Virtual Learning as an Alternative

Increasing numbers of organizations and educational institutions are implementing **virtual learning communities (VLCs)** to encourage cost-effective knowledge sharing. An explosion of web-based technology has led to an increasing volume and complexity of knowledge, stimulating the proliferation of VLCs, defined as: "information technology based cyberspaces in which individuals and groups of geographically dispersed learners accomplish their e-learning goals" (Chen, Chen and Kinshuk, 2009: 136). Such communities have grown during the past decade as businesses, educational institutions and a few general purpose governments have realized the expanded potential for use of internet resources. The objective of VLCs is to enhance individual performance by encouraging participants to become independent learners. How learners share knowledge by providing ideas and helping others resolve problems online is critical for enhancing learning performance. Consequently, participants in virtual learning activities need to understand precisely what knowledge will fulfill their needs.

Virtual learning promises to close existing knowledge gaps among educational institutions in many regions around the world. If obstacles such as the digital divide are overcome, New Media further promises customized learning, personalized teaching and a unique environment for targeting educational processes and curricular materials to individual student needs. Students have the opportunity to focus on subjects of interest and the flexibility to study them at their own pace. With a more flexible schedule and interactive learning processes presented on existing technology used by students for social networking, the capacity for individualized learning increases. Moreover, VLCs have the potential to impact individual goals, careers and professional identities by supporting **lifelong learning**. Virtual schooling expands educational access, provides high-quality learning opportunities, improves student achievement and skills, allows for greater educational choice and achieves administrative efficiencies. However, it is not without opposition, especially from the organized teaching profession.

Advocates for traditional learning methods argue that virtual alternatives fail to motivate students, result in loss of human contact and reduce job opportunities in the educational profession. Social isolation, lack of social skills and higher unemployment may result. In addition, the digital divide brought about by socioeconomic disparities between rich and poor families makes virtual learning inaccessible for those who cannot afford it. Corporate sponsorships, grants, projects and other programs intended to provide resources for individuals and educational institutions that cannot afford computers and other technological devices are crucial for ICT accessibility. Lack of national graduation standards is a significant problem in the United States; standardization of processes must occur to connect students with learning centers. Governments will play a major role in overcoming resistance from the teaching profession and supporting further development of **e-learning** methods and standards. In the debates over the future of education, many are asking how the transition from traditional to virtual learning will take place without leaving vulnerable groups of children behind.

Virtual schools can be classified in different ways, but the two most common methods of delivery are 1) asynchronous and 2) synchronous. Discussion boards, e-mail exchanges and social networking facilitate the **asynchronous** or passive method and support relationships among learners and teachers, even when participants cannot be online at the same time. The asynchronous method is a key component of flexible e-learning. **Synchronous**, active or simultaneous e-learning is supported by media such as chat groups, teaching modules and videoconferencing to help teachers and learners develop learning communities. Both these delivery models allow teachers to assume the role of facilitators to encourage students to develop and achieve self-directed learning goals. Instructors are among the class which is structured more along the lines of a round-table. Thus, content delivery is transformed from a hierarchical structure to a flatter, more interactive and networked one.

Regardless of the method of delivery, curricula should be consistent with traditional teaching methods, but delivered in a more personalized, self-directed and interactive manner. Virtual curricula are increasing for several reasons, including: 1) greater involvement in open and distance education; 2) potential increases in quality, productivity and flexibility which have attracted more students and revenue; 3) the widespread use of technology to increase learning opportunities for anyone who wants to extend their knowledge; and 4) significant cost reductions and improvements in delivery methods (Farrell, 1999). In many schools, e-learning already supplements the existing lecture-discussion teaching format. There is, however, continuing political resistance to New Media technology applied to traditional learning environments.

Defining and Funding High-Quality Virtual Education

Public education is funded primarily by property and sales tax revenues, so nearly everyone who purchases goods or services or owns or rents property has some financial stake in assuring the quality of public education. Perhaps more importantly, it is through K-12 education that the nation's future workers and leaders are prepared for productive lives. Primary and secondary K-12 education focuses on career training, civic education, college preparation and producing qualified workers and responsible citizens for business and government. Without quality educational results, societies fail.

Producing knowledgeable individuals is a major goal, but publicly funded K-12 education has a much broader social mission: to produce a competent, well-educated population capable of independent thinking and resolving the problems of society. Rather than merely serving as an inexpensive recruiting service for business and industry, schools should also teach students to be critical thinkers, so they will become men and women of independent mind, distanced from the conventional wisdom of their own time and with strength and skill to change what they see as wrong with society (Postman, 1995: 59–60). Investment in schools provides society with a means to continuously reexamine dreams, hopes and values for the future. Simply put, assuring quality educational systems ensures the future of society. Understanding this concept leads to an inevitable understanding of the importance of providing quality education at all levels.

Quality Education and Lifelong Learning

Defining quality in education is more difficult than merely supporting it. Today's students are tomorrow's leaders and without quality education, a nation loses its competitive edge and lags even further behind in the rapidly globalizing world. Society expects educational systems to achieve lofty goals, and assuring quality is the only way to guarantee that those goals are met in ways that reflect its values and culture. Inevitably, quality is subject to multiple interpretations in diversified societies. Quality definitions are also a function of people, processes and public policy. In education, quality must be improved in many different processes, but politicians and policy makers have made it difficult to measure quality accurately because of the narrow focus on standardized testing and minimum standards. This emphasis may have actually diminished quality; there must be more attention to how students learn as well as developing alternative learning processes.

Why it is vital to assure quality in K-12 education is often overlooked because the answer seems either too simplistic or self-evident. Quality in education is often viewed as a static notion, an adjective describing a final product. "He is an A student" or "She scored high on her Scholastic Aptitude Test (SAT) test" becomes the operational goal of the system. Indeed, ranking students is the final product of many components of the system. There is much, much more to improving public and private service quality than this one-dimensional view. Successful service firms recognize the complexity and multi-faceted nature of customer service quality improvement. The multi-dimensional nature of quality is clearly evident in education. With all of the different processes and components that go into delivering educational services, it is impossible to measure quality of education based solely on the final product. In fact, in the true essence of lifelong learning, there is no final product.

Education has become a continuous, lifelong pursuit. One of the realities of the 21st century global knowledge society is that everyone will be required to relearn numerous times throughout their working lives. The average person now changes jobs *seven times* during his or her career. For many, it may take decades to realize a satisfactory return on the investment of time and resources devoted to learning. In many ways, these are "sunk costs" that can never be recovered (Chapter 1). With the globalization of the U.S. economy and its negative impact on job security, more workers are assuming mobile overseas assignments requiring technical skills, a second (or third) language as well as geographic knowledge and cultural sensitivity not generally possessed by today's graduates. Quality virtual education must focus on continuous improvement, evaluation of processes and public policies to deliver the knowledge, skills and resources necessary to empower students to become lifelong learners. This includes current and future customers of virtual courses and degrees delivered via the internet. The number of such programs is multiplying rapidly as more individuals and institutions recognize the need for **just-in-time learning** for new career assignments. Most colleges and many high schools are now "wired" to the internet and World Wide Web. Students expect courses to utilize information technology and many now conduct research and access libraries and other research databases via computers and **distance learning** systems available to students via computer linkages.

Since computers and other electronic software (such as **two-way video imaging**) are also used, distance learning "involves replacing some or a majority of traditional classroom instruction with technology-enhanced e-learning that takes place outside of the classroom" (Zabriskie and McNabb, 2007: 226). Therefore, most forms of asynchronous distance learning do not require students to be in the same location or complete coursework at the same time. Numerous studies applaud the fact that online access to courses increases flexibility and access for students. Many high achievers, especially in small or geographically isolated communities, are taking advantage of specialized online courses that their local schools do not offer (Nitkin, 2005: 30). The flexible time schedule also offers students who work or have disabilities or difficult work schedules to accomplish their academic goals when they would not be able to do so in a traditional institution. In some American states, students must take distance learning courses if they want to study subjects, such as languages, where budget cuts have limited the availability of such courses.

What was formerly known as distance learning—and is now described as virtual learning—has both positive and negative aspects which can potentially further accessment, accessibility and quality of education. However, the lack of in-person interaction and computer software, technical difficulties and the possibility of distractions could hinder learning delivered via the Web.

Acceptance of Virtual Learning Environments

The high cost of traditional classroom education is prompting interest in virtual learning communities. Virtual learning implementation in the current school or corporate training environment can only occur if there is commitment and trust between the many stakeholders involved in educational processes. Most importantly, there is a need for change in present educational methods so students are treated fairly with the same opportunities to benefit from ICTs. Although the promises of virtual learning are infinite, there is opposition to it. Barriers include poor quality of educational websites, students' lack of relationship ties within social networks, students' lack of capabilities in using community websites involved in knowledge sharing and the failure of cognitive processes such as negative attitudes toward sharing knowledge online. Among the teaching profession, three related issues limit the acceptance of virtual learning: 1) fear of job losses; 2) inadequate or outdated technologies; and 3) questions about the quality of instruction.

Not everyone regards virtual learning as a high-quality alternative to traditional education and training. According to a 2002 policy statement by the **National Education Association (NEA)**, a national organization representing teachers, face-to-face opportunities with teachers and socialization opportunities with other children are critical to foster learning. The NEA's statement warned against arrangements where students received all or most of their education at home and rarely convened in a classroom. Other aspects of virtual learning could also undermine the quality of education provided online. Students could easily be distracted from academic learning and become involved in non-academic interaction (games or pornography). This is a risk in any online learning setting, as isolation in the virtual world could allow some students to become less focused on their educational materials.

In addition to teachers, many parents and some students express concerns about the lack of face-to-face interaction in the online environment. However, students' general perceptions of the quality of instruction differ widely. If someone is social and interactive, the lack of face-to-face interaction could be unfavorable. On the other hand, students who are less interactive and lack social assertiveness may not communicate with teachers as much as an online facilitator. As more virtual courses are offered as alternatives to traditional instruction, there are sharp debates about the quality of online learning and teaching. While some believe that online education shows promise as an innovative and creative pedagogical method offering flexibility and convenience by providing learning opportunities to anyone, at anytime and anywhere, others hold more skeptical views, perceiving distance learning, especially "for-profit" institutions, as inadequate and inappropriate substitutes for on-campus and face-to-face instruction (Shin and Lee, 2009: 32). Congress has conducted hearings focusing on for-profit online educational institutions and their access to federal assistance funds.

Regardless of the differing opinions about its effectiveness, the teaching profession has already been impacted by social networking and virtual learning. Teachers themselves will have to return to school to learn new technologies to improve the learning process for students. Learning technologies such as **Blackboard, Moodle** and **Sakai** can offer faculty more effective ways to deliver courses online. However, as in any profession, many are afraid that computers and other learning technologies will become the main source of providing education to students. Job security may be threatened. If teachers do not overcome this fear, online learning will be impeded. Instructional technology must be seen as a means rather than an end in itself. The effectiveness of online instruction is not determined solely by the technology, but rather by the instructor who is truly devoted to the success of the learner and understands the dynamics of virtual learning. State governments can also help instructors overcome apprehension by working with the teachers' unions to adapt the new technology to assure those who do change will be rewarded. Workshops and information technology classes can be provided for educators to learn and instruct students how to use virtual tools. With additional training and inevitable budget cuts by states, both teachers and learning communities will advance positively in an expanded and more cost-effective virtual learning environment.

The second major issue plaguing distance learning is the possibility of technical difficulties and the lack of up-to-date equipment impeding class time and coursework. Unequal access to computers means some students as well as instructors in online classrooms may experience technical problems with the delivery of courses, especially those who are novices with the application of computer technology. Teaching courses exclusively over the internet, using a variety of components including digital media, opens up uncharted pedagogical and technological territory. Technical problems may frustrate students, impede their learning and severely decrease the quality of education provided. If such problems are overcome, then results can be stunningly positive. E-learning could actually help overcome digital divides as disadvantaged students could have access to high-quality instruction without having to be physically present in classrooms.[2]

The third issue is assessing the quality of instruction provided via the internet. In 2009, a systematic study by SRI International for the **U.S. Department of Education** analyzed online learning research literature from 1996 through July 2008 (Means, Toyoma, Murphy, Bakia and Jones, 2009). Analysts screened more than a thousand empirical studies to determine those which 1) used a rigorous research design, 2) contrasted an online to a face-to-face condition, 3) measured student learning outcomes and 4) provided adequate information to calculate an effect size. As a result of this screening, 51 independent effects were identified. The analysis found that, on average, students in online learning conditions performed better than those receiving face-to-face instruction. The difference between student outcomes for online and face-to-face classes—measured as the variation between mean scores of treatment and control groups—was larger in those studies contrasting conditions that combined elements of online and face-to-face instruction with conditions taught entirely by face-to-face instruction. Researchers noted that these **blended learning** conditions often included additional learning time and instructional elements not received by students in control conditions. This finding suggested that the positive effects associated with blended learning may not be attributed solely to the delivery media. There were only a small number of rigorous published studies contrasting online and face-to-face learning conditions for K-12 students. In light of this small sample, the authors cautioned against generalizing to the K-12 population because most of the results were derived from studies in other settings (e.g., medical training, higher education). Nonetheless, findings such as these further question the viability of the heavy public sector investment in traditional bricks-and-mortar education, when alternative, less expensive delivery methods could generate equal or better results.

Rather than defending the current flawed system, educators should focus on finding a mission and delivery system for all types of schools to make sure that every stakeholder understands and believes in its mission. Stakeholders' opinions reflect the common goal of quality education and a sense of commitment and **ownership of educational processes**. This definition is multi-faceted and highly complex, emphasizing evaluation processes, identifying common goals and providing motivation and ownership. Applying new definitions of virtual quality has not been without controversy, especially when it comes to adopting and measuring results of educational achievement.

Adopting E-learning Strategies

Once a school decides to offer e-learning options it has to take into account the initial costs of the transition from traditional to virtual learning. Virtual delivery uses not only instruction technology, but e-mail, online chat rooms, internet resources and archived resources to teach students. Virtual classes are offered to meet the needs of all grade levels as well as continuing students. Like traditional schools, virtual learning requires curriculum, faculty, students and technological expertise. Most virtual education programs require heavy investment in the initial phases and the technology start-up and maintenance costs can run as high as $10,000 to $100,000. As more private firms provide virtual learning services, these costs are expected to decrease. Governments will play a major role in guaranteeing fair information technology implementation processes in public schools so that adequate adaptation and technical support are available. Not only must governments assure students and teachers the means and resources for adopting learning technology, they must also guarantee that those teaching have knowledge of how to use it effectively. Therefore, it is crucial for e-learning programs and processes to be constantly updated for virtual learning to be both efficient and effective.

State approval or regional accreditation is important with respect to the ways that the public views virtual schools' credibility. Parents and students will be able to identify online courses that are state accredited and certified. This will guarantee to all educational stakeholders that the curriculum taught by virtual methods offers equal or better results than the educational status quo. Governments can advertise virtual learning especially for those who cannot afford a private school or are located in remote areas. Rural residents and those who live too far from the nearest school or university will benefit from having internet access and taking courses online. Accountability for course certification will remain a major governmental responsibility.

As virtual educational systems develop and expand, they should be accompanied by quality assurance, significant improvements in delivery methods and cost reductions. A good quality virtual learning environment will contain skillfully crafted and carefully designed courses that provide learners with valuable learning experiences. Simply reproducing existing material in electronic format will not enhance effective learning. Creating online courses demands rigorous planning as well as imagination to capture its true potential. With any teaching and learning activity, a critical evaluation of the effectiveness of existing practice provides insights into what works and what does not. Adopting this strategy will ensure that courses within the virtual learning environment will improve access and enhance the quality of learning. Assessments are the key tools for improving e-learning effectiveness, identifying what online students learned during the school year and informing students and parents of remaining knowledge gaps. Assessments could eventually replace grades, since they provide precise information about students' performance.

Students who take courses from a virtual school with an independent method of delivery are similar to students who take traditional distance learning courses. The virtual experience creates independent students because they are responsible for developing their own learning plans. Encouraging students to become more independent prompts them to think more critically. Independent students are already teaching themselves or being taught by a parent, with only minimum involvement from a teacher. The virtual school provides the curriculum materials that will be used by the student throughout the course.

Although virtual learning appears to exclude human contact, it may actually promote a more comfortable learning environment for students to share thoughts with their classroom peers. Even in traditional classroom environments, online discussions are becoming more frequent as a means to encourage communication and engagement. Discussions among students have great potential for fostering literacy skills, strengthening communication and building a sense of community. Rather than engaging in traditional reading and lecture-discussions and responding to tests, students read e-books on notebook computers, submit discussion questions and respond to the readings in electronic journals. The virtual classroom can be a more independent environment for students and, at the same time, instructional technology fosters a comfort zone for sharing ideas. Such efforts must be encouraged and rewarded.

Rewarding Quality Improvement

One of the most cost-effective (and generally apolitical) ways to overcome resistance, provide objective feedback and guide the transition is the use of quality and productivity awards as benchmarks, incentives and prizes for achieving organizational changes. Competition for an award can help interested agencies accomplish the following goals, among others:

1) Identify processes needing improvement.
2) Conduct internal self-assessments.
3) Receive objective feedback from outside examiners.
4) Identify appropriate benchmarks for process improvements.
5) Establish procedures and motivate employees to meet higher performance goals.

In addition, externally judged awards assist managers in determining which strategies are most efficient for resource utilization, recruiting, training and improved organizational performance. Numerous award programs now evaluate, recognize and transfer information about processes, methods and systems to achieve results. Awards can be used to advance knowledge about learning theory, standardize processes and assist managers in determining which among many e-learning and training strategies are best suited for their organizations. Agencies should not seek awards as an end in itself, but rather a means to promote a broader strategy for spurring private innovation and change. Moreover, agencies are encouraged by the highest political circles to select the right award for the appropriate goal and "consider partnering with other entities that might administer, support or catalyze the prize" (Executive Office of the President, 2010: 3).

Failures to continuously improve internal processes, human resources and information technologies are pervasive problems for many different types of service organizations. Government agencies are especially vulnerable because it is difficult, even under the most favorable circumstances, to improve performance with limited or often declining resources—with decisions always subject to changing external political forces. Moreover, computers, software and new technologies change so rapidly that equipment, systems and training protocols become obsolete after just a few months of service. (The public sector is even more vulnerable to ICT obsolescence because of its dependence on procurement systems that are influenced by political as much as cost-effective and quality considerations.) Other public sector infrastructure potentially vulnerable to human and material failure include airports, schools, state and local electoral voting systems, roads, security systems and public utilities. Governments are complex service organizations which face unique challenges that may inhibit the adoption of new equipment, systems, training and technologies. Improving performance is more challenging because:

1) Individual agencies exhibit uneven capacity (and willingness) to measure performance.
2) Political interests conflict with multiple pre-existing problems of defining citizen and customer needs.
3) Private interest groups compete with each other and with government agencies for limited resources, more privatization and less regulation.
4) Public agencies often find service quality standards difficult to set and enforce.
5) Outcomes, performance and results are less tangible and more difficult to measure (deLancer Julnes and Holzer, 2001; Donaldson, 1999; Milakovich, 1998, 2003, 2006; Sanderson, 2001).

In addition to these factors, a dearth of relevant examples of successful models in *specific* functions contributes to a pervasive need for "hands-on," operational and practical models to guide management changes. The absence of benchmarks and performance measures exposes public agencies to political opponents who argue for more privatization, less government and lower taxes.

Despite the anti-government rhetoric that often accompanies political debates about improving (or replacing) public services, not all bureaucrats are incompetent nor are all government programs inefficient or ineffective. On the contrary, there is substantial evidence that citizens are satisfied with the majority of government programs they receive (Goodsell, 2003; Neiman, 2000); as noted earlier, many federal agencies receive **customer service quality ratings** equal to or higher than private companies. Political leadership is necessary to merge divergent interests, redesign management systems and convert to online service quality improvement (Executive Office of the President, 2010; Rago, 1994; Sensenbrenner, 1991).[3]

Private businesses have several advantages over public agencies. Among them is the luxury of choosing customers and target markets; another is focusing on selected demographics. Government agencies must cater to an entire population, or at least a large sub-set of an eligible population, generally without regard for individual ability to pay. Governments attempt to meet a wide range of citizen expectations with limited resources provided from a variety of external sources—many of which they do not control. Rather than raising revenues directly from paying customers in a competitive market, public agencies are dependent upon tax revenues, user fees and intergovernmental transfer funds for their operating revenues. Their primary customers are also their political sponsors and often their harshest critics: elected representatives serving on local boards and commissions, members of state legislatures and the U.S. Congress, many of whom find it convenient—if not advantageous—to criticize "bloated" bureaucracy. There are fewer incentives for legislators to acquire the detailed knowledge necessary to evaluate programs on their merits than there are temptations to criticize policies that a majority of their constituents oppose.

Government agencies oversee or provide a variety of services to recipients or users who expect courtesy, empathy, fair treatment and responsiveness *without* paying for the service directly. Customers may also be suppliers who wish to develop an efficient, effective (and profitable) business relationship, overseers who want accountability, or simply concerned taxpayers who seek accountability for "their" scarce resources. Sometimes they are adversaries who hold diametrically opposed views regarding "the best way" to allocate public resources. Still others are reluctant regulatees who must comply with government regulators (or at least meet minimum reporting standards) or suffer civil fines or criminal penalties. Unlike most businesses, governments must sometimes form awkward **partnerships** with "customers" who may be recipients *as well as* co-producers of services (Alford, 2002; Hodge and Greve, 2005). For instance, a physician could be a taxpayer, recipient of services, political activist, as well as a front-line manager for the Medicare or Medicaid program.

Public agencies generally do not select or recruit their customers and must serve those who either cannot or will not purchase services from private providers; others form **natural monopolies** that provide services to particular groups in confined geographic regions or defined industries without competition. Most public school students, for example, are obligated to attend schools with their age cohorts in geographically designated local districts, rather than choose from among various alternatives. In many instances, governments must negotiate expectations with customers as direct service providers or co-producers, and then seek to meet co-determined standards. Forming this type of "uncooperative partnership" is more challenging than dealing with customers who have choices of suppliers and pay market price for goods or service in a commercial transaction.

Legal obligations restrict the range of discretionary actions that public agencies can take to satisfy customers and blur lines of political control and accountability. Furthermore, there is always the danger that government officials are granted "too much" discretion to please their customers. The National Academy of Public Administration (NAPA) criticized the U.S. Government Accountability Office (GAO), one of the most respected agencies in the federal government, for "over responding" to one of its primary customers, the U.S. Congress, and losing its traditional role as impartial and objective evaluator of federal programs (Pegnato, 1997).[4] When Oracle Corporation, the nation's largest developer of commercial software, was negotiating the U.S. General Services Administration, the close relationship which developed between the two entities was viewed by many as a conflict of interest. Oracle had once partnered with the California Department of Information Technology when suspect contracts led the state legislature to abolish the entire department, leaving the nation's largest state temporarily without an IT division.[5]

Availability of new information technologies prompts public service organizations to adopt new performance management systems designed to decentralize decision-making authority, empower employees, streamline internal management processes and measure results. Certain management styles and techniques encourage higher levels of performance, internal organizational changes and responsiveness to customers; others do not. Applying for an award, a grant, an audit certificate or a prize reinforces positive incentives for employees to improve their processes and services. Awards can also serve as a cost-effective way to disseminate knowledge about best practices for managing personnel and technology. This eliminates much of the guesswork from a "trial and error" approach to different improvement strategies and allows less experienced organizations to participate sooner and avoid *ad hoc* approaches to decision making.

International Quality Awards, Charters, Prizes and Standards

The movement towards more citizen-centric, decentralized, flexible and results-driven information management systems is accelerating worldwide as more attention is being paid to successful models for reform. Many private companies have undertaken actions to implement customer-oriented and performance-based changes (Kettl, 2002b; Sanderson, 2001). Widely used in Asia, Australia, Canada and Europe, variations of methodologies such as awards, citizens' charters, charter marks, prizes and audit standards help spread success stories from an expanding number of private companies and governments (Chuan and Soon, 2000; Hui and Chaun, 2002; Tummala and Tang, 1996). Globalization of the reform effort, with heavy emphasis on communication and information technology, encourages citizen access to information, adoption of knowledge management processes and wider participation in public decision making (Fountain, 2001; West, 2001; Wimmer, 2002).

The leading international **quality awards** and standards for quality include: the **Deming Prize** in Japan, the **European Quality Awards** and the **ISO 9000–14000** series, and the **Malcolm Baldrige National Quality Award** (BNQA) in the United States.[6] These prizes, awards and audit accreditation programs influenced the creation of numerous state-sponsored "**mini-Baldrige**" programs in the United States and elsewhere that recognize success at the sub-national state and local level. Forty-five of the 50 U.S. states, and many local communities, now share similar goals using the BNQA criteria to advance service quality initiatives. In the United States alone, over 1,800 private, non-profit, manufacturing and service organizations have received recognition by states and local awards for service quality and productivity improvements in the past decade. In addition, over 80 countries, including Canada, Ireland, Mauritius, Israel,

New Zealand, South Africa, Slovenia, Singapore, Sweden and Taiwan have established national quality awards. Over half those award programs are based on criteria similar to Malcolm Baldrige Awards.

The Deming Prize is the oldest of the major awards (established in 1950) and it is considered by many Japanese to be as prestigious as the Academy Awards and the Nobel Prize for quality recognition.[7] Although less well known in Europe and North America, the Deming Prize influences the development of quality management practices throughout Asia. The **Union of Japanese Scientists and Engineers** awards the prizes for individuals and applicant companies as well as divisions within companies, including non-Japanese companies and service organizations, for their total quality control. In recent years, companies from India, Malaysia and Thailand have won several Deming Prizes.[8]

The ISO 9000–14000 certification is the fastest growing **quality assurance** system in the world and is applicable to most types of organizations. The International Organization for Standards (ISO) audit certification—commonly known as the ISO 9000 through 14000 series—is neither a prize nor quality award *per se*, but requires the application of many of the same objective criteria and review by outside examiners. (*ISO* is not an acronym, but the shortened Greek word for equal.) To date, only a few governments are ISO certified and more research is needed on its effectiveness in improving the management capacity of service organizations (Chu and Wang, 2001; Lowery, 1999). Nonetheless, the ISO series maintains a commitment to customer service quality improvement and shares many of the same criteria as the Baldrige, Deming and European quality awards. Together, the criteria used by each of these methodologies form a standard multi-national definition of quality processes applicable to most types of organizations. (See Box 4.1 for a composite of the European awards and seven Baldrige award criteria.)

Box 4.1: Global Criteria for European and American Quality Awards

1) **Leadership:** how senior executives guide the organization and how the organization addresses its responsibilities to the public and practice good citizenship.
2) **Strategic Planning:** how organizations set strategic directions and determine key action plans.
3) **Human Resource Management:** how organizations enable workforces to develop full potential and how they are aligned with the organization's objectives.
4) **Information Analysis and Technology:** the management, effective use and analysis of data and information to support key organization processes and performance management systems.

5) **Quality Systems and Processes:** how key production/delivery and support processes are designed, managed and improved.

6) **Customer/Market Focus:** how the organization determines requirements and expectations of customers and markets.

7) **Customer/User Satisfaction:** how the organization meets customers' requirements.

8) **Corporate Governance and Social Responsibility:** responds to post-Enron concerns about corporate corruption and social responsibility.

9) **Supplier/Partner Relationships:** just-in-time delivery and supply chain management.

10) **Results:** the organization's performance and improvement in its key business areas: customer satisfaction, financial and marketplace performance, human resources, supplier and partner performance, and operational performance. For private businesses, this category also examines how the organization performs relative to competition.

Source: Adapted from European Foundation for Quality Management Awards at www.efqm.org/en and Malcolm Baldrige National Quality Awards at www.quality.nist.gov/BusinessCriteria.htm

The European Quality Awards, created in 1990 and now referred to as the European Foundation for Quality Management (EFQM) awards, spawned many national and regional quality awards throughout Europe and influenced the development of ISO 9000 standards. The newest categories for the award were added in 1994: the Public Sector Award and the Small and Medium-size Enterprises Award. Each applicant is reviewed by a team of Award Assessors, which determines a total score for the application. Based on the final report of the team of assessors, the jury selects the most outstanding organizations for the award.[9]

National Digital Governance Awards

The **National Digital Governance Awards** recognize outstanding agency and departmental websites and projects at the application and infrastructure level.[10] All United States and international government levels may enter their actively functioning, fully operational applications and projects. The contest is held concurrently with the Best of the Web Awards (BOW) contest which has recognized excellence of official Web portals of United States cities, counties and states for the past 15 years.[11] In addition, private companies, such as Granicus, Inc. also sponsor awards specifically recognizing digital implementation by state and local governments.[12] Awards honor government agencies that leverage streaming media technologies to improve efficiency in public services, enhance public communication, improve community engagement and facilitate transparency.

The Malcolm Baldrige National Quality Award (BNQA)

Organizations which demonstrate productivity, results and the highest levels of customer service are eligible to apply for the BNQA, but the number of awards per year is strictly limited. Although federal agencies are ineligible and there is no specific category for government agencies, the BNQA has accepted applications (since 1995) from educational and health care organizations (Box 4.2) and from non-profit organizations (since 2000). Each year, the BNQA gives a *maximum* of two awards in six categories (manufacturing, service, health care, education, non-profit and small business), in contrast to other award programs which do not restrict the number of winners. As a result, several government agencies have been recognized by the BNQA.[13]

The original purpose of the BNQA was to answer the challenge of global economic competition by improving the quality of American manufactured goods, productivity (and profits) through the use of quality initiatives. Public recognition of improvements and achievements provided examples for others to emulate. Winners are required to publicly share

---

Box 4.2: The Malcolm Baldrige and State Quality Awards

The Malcolm Baldrige and **State Quality Awards** promote quality in education. Additionally, the awards focus on process evaluation and satisfaction of relationships between stakeholders as well as on results measured with a comprehensive method, which allows schools a chance to compare how they are performing with the goals society has set for them (creating lifelong learners with the ability to be responsible, productive citizens who will be able to solve our social problems). Awards such as these foster the adaptation and application of service quality philosophies in business to education. There are now hundreds of "benchmarks" or models of state and local governments in a wide range of services. Total Quality Service concepts and theories are being used in a number of schools, colleges and universities with a new generation of students learning with an environment of teamwork, shared decision making responsibility and accountability for results.

Source: U.S. Department of Commerce, National Institute of Standards and Technology, Malcolm Baldrige National Quality Awards available at www.nist.gov. Website: www.mcb.unco.edu/

information about quality strategies at a national conference to assist other organizations and to encourage them to become part of the national quality improvement effort. This requirement is important because learning from the experience of others can stimulate organizations to become part of a broader quality process and find more effective ways to improve their performance. Many state and local organizations also have their own awards and encourage recipients to share their success formulas (Box 4.2). Three-quarters of the states also require winners to showcase their procedures with potential applicants.

As a public–private partnership designed to reward exemplary and innovative management processes, the BNQA recognizes successful innovation strategies and acknowledges the importance of results. Winners are required to show how their processes have positively affected the quality of outputs. Although awards still reinforce the need for private sector international competitiveness in manufacturing, they now emphasize the equally important need to raise the quality of domestic services, especially in education, government and health care.

In addition to awards, benchmarking and e-gov initiatives, **citizen charters** guarantee specific levels of service and **charter marks** to recognize agencies for exemplary service (Davison and Grieves, 1996; Van Thiel and Leeuw, 2002). Citizen charters, similar to a "bill of rights" (for airline passengers, consumers, health care patients, taxpayers, travelers, etc.) have been enacted during the past two decades in nearly 20 countries, including Australia, Belgium, Canada, Denmark, Finland, France, India, Ireland, Italy, the Netherlands (See Box 4.3), Norway, Portugal, Spain, Singapore, Sweden, as well as governments in the United Kingdom.[14] At the organizational

---

Box 4.3: The Netherlands e-Citizen Charter

1) **Choice of Channel** As a citizen I can choose myself in which way to deal with the government. Governments ensure multi channel service delivery, i.e. the availability of all communication channels: visit, letter, phone, e-mail and Internet.
2) **Transparent Public Sector** As a citizen I know where to apply for official information and public services. Government guarantees one-stop-shop service delivery and acts as one seamless entity with no wrong doors.
3) **Overview of Rights and Duties** As a citizen I know which services I am entitled to under which conditions. Government ensures that my rights and duties are at all times transparent.
4) **Personalized Information** As a citizen I am entitled to information that is complete, up to date and consistent. Government supplies appropriate information tailored to my needs.

5) **Convenient Services** As a citizen I can choose to provide personal data once and expect to be served in a proactive way. Government makes clear what records it keeps about me and does not use data without my consent.

6) **Comprehensive Procedures** As a citizen I can easily get to know how government works and monitor progress. Government keeps me informed of procedures I am involved in by way of tracking and tracing.

7) **Trust and Reliability** As a citizen I presume government to be electronically competent. Government guarantees secure identity management and reliable storage of electronic documents.

8) **Considerate Administration** As a citizen I can file ideas for improvement and lodge complaints. Government compensates mistakes and uses feedback information to improve its products and procedures.

9) **Accountability and Benchmarking** As a citizen I am able to compare, check and measure government outcomes. Government actively supplies benchmark information about its performance.

10) **Engagement and Empowerment** As a citizen, I am invited to participate in decision-making and to promote my interest. Government supports empowerment and ensures that the necessary information and instruments are available.

Source: www.govtech.com/gt/articles/104894

(micro) level, several steps are being taken to maximize a charter's effectiveness. Charters are bolstered by well-developed systems and procedures; providers must make sure that all employees understand the terms and standards stated in a charter. Charter marks reward excellence, reinforce standards and raise the level of public service provided. They also improve public service via feedback to applicants.

The Obama administration developed a *Strategy for American Innovation* calling for federal agencies to create more transparent, participatory and collaborative government using prizes and challenges (Executive Office of the President, 2010). Federal agencies are encouraged to use awards, certificates, charters and prizes to motivate and reward employees and as internal self-assessment tools for refining and updating service quality initiatives.[15] An outsider's unbiased view can help identify a type of customer who is being neglected, a process that is failing, or purpose that is unfulfilled. Furthermore, applying for an award or quality certificate such as the International Organization for Standards (ISO) 9000–14000 series (described above) reinforces core values and provides an objective framework for making necessary management changes (Lowery, 1998). Even for successful organizations, an annual strategic process review is a valuable learning experience to sustain results-driven high performance.

Summary and Conclusions

The virtual learning experience is a promise to overcome gaps in educational systems. It offers an array of positive opportunities to educational institutions to improve processes, reduce costs and offer time flexibility to students. There are several barriers to full implementation of e-learning including computer literacy, digital divides and teachers' resistance to change. Governments have to ensure that information technology systems are distributed fairly for those who cannot afford them and help teachers overcome the fear of technology replacing them as educators. Also, there has to be rigorous assessment of virtual learning effectiveness to assure quality, significant improvements and cost reduction so students and educators do not pursue yet another failed educational experiment. Several steps must be taken to establish high-quality virtual learning schools. The general approach to virtual learning will be acceptance, adoption and adaptation. If these are accomplished, the infinite positive effects that e-learning will have in forming learning communities will be worth the hard work.

The importance of quality education is undeniable. Today's students are tomorrow's leaders and without quality education, any nation will lose its competitive edge and lag even further behind the rest of the globalizing world at a time when it can least afford to fail. Society expects its education systems to achieve lofty goals, and assuring quality is the only way to guarantee that goals are met. Unfortunately, quality is difficult to define and subject to multiple interpretations in a diverse society. Quality is a function of people, processes and policy and awards are a generally under-utilized resource for organizations committed to improving service quality and performance. In education, quality must be improved in many different processes including teacher education and training, resource management and curriculum. Unfortunately, politicians and policy makers have made it difficult to measure quality accurately because they have focused too much on standardized test results and minimum standards.

Rewarding customer service and performance management is a cost-effective way to share best practices, measure results, add value and achieve quality and productivity goals. Quality awards can serve as catalysts for change, identify areas needing improvement, support internal collaboration, motivate everyone to achieve specific goals and provide learning tools to retain expertise. The competitive challenge and distinction that accompany pursuit of an award, charter mark, or ISO certification can be a significant source of employee motivation and pride. Perhaps most importantly, the data generated by various performance recognition techniques can help to develop theories to assist managers in determining which practices are best suited for their organizations. Awards, benchmarks, citizen charters and audit standards will never entirely eliminate the differences between the missions of non-profit, public, or private organizations, nor should they. They can, however, provide a rich database for assisting businesses and governments in implementing change strategies, developing successful performance measures and reaching out to all customers being served.

The Malcolm Baldrige Award criteria are among the best performance indicators and available free to any school applying for this award, or a comparable state quality award; both have the obvious benefit of providing immediate feedback and suggestions for improvement. The national award as well as many of the state and local awards recognize and promote quality and productivity in American education. These awards achieve the goal of improving and recognizing quality by objectively evaluating applicants and making recommendations to those who do not meet the high standards to be able to improve. At the very least, the BNQA competition provides a rich reservoir of in-depth case studies and models for public agencies to follow.

As quality recognition becomes *the* primary factor in judging an organization's performance, those who fail to accept the new demands of an increasingly competitive global economy will be less likely to survive. Customer satisfaction is already an obsession for many global service organizations, and most companies go beyond merely "satisfying" customers to *exceeding* their expectations. Consequently, awards, benchmarks, charter marks and international audit standards will most likely play a more significant role by offering credibility in the eyes of citizens, customers and employees alike. This will be especially important for corporations and governments seeking to regain public confidence and trust. The critical question for future micro-organizational research is: do quality awards change internal organizational processes and systems to provide incentives for individual employees to become more responsive to citizens, students and supervisors?

All stakeholders interested in preserving the future—educators, parents, students, teachers, public officials and taxpayers—must be willing to set aside previous notions of how education should be delivered and results measured. Doing so would force stakeholders to analyze processes involved in educational quality improvement and experiment with alternative learning methods. Full utilization of virtual learning technology may be thwarted by existing (and highly politicized) processes that resist experimentation with alternative delivery methods. If changes do not occur, standards will continue to be raised without providing students with the means to reach those standards and it will not be the students who fail, it will be our institutions.

Key Terms

Part III

Administration

Implementing Online Digital Governance

Both the Clinton-Gore and Bush-Cheney administrations (1993–2009) used ICTs to initiate top-down management reforms, including the expanded use of electronic government, to achieve very different policy goals. Their respective policy agendas addressed many of the issues discussed in previous chapters, including customer service quality, online participation, privatization and results-driven management of federal programs. Attempts to make such profound organizational transitions in the operations of federal agencies required significant changes in administrative, legislative, technological and socio-cultural infrastructures as well as linkages to other civic institutions—most of which generally failed to result in lasting reforms. ICTs were also used to promote other public policies, such as gender and racial equality, while reinforcing pre-existing commercial and governmental interests. Major conflicts erupted over the most effective methods to reform administrative and political systems. Whether success can be achieved through greater regulation or more private sector involvement is a contentious political issue that continues to divide the electorate, executives and legislators. As a result of these efforts, many bureaucrats have become more defensive and greater numbers of citizens are less tolerant of inefficiencies, mismanagement and lack of responsiveness in both the public and private sectors (Chapter 5).

Improving public productivity via the expanded use of ICTs continues with a new urgency resulting from the depth of the economic recession and fiscal stresses plaguing both business and government. Managing performance isn't a new challenge for federal government; it has also been the goal of many states and local governments for decades. From the passage of the Government Performance and Results Act (GPRA) in 1993 through the deployment of the Bush administration's Performance Assessment Rating Tool (PART) in 2003 to the passage of the American Recovery and Reinvestment Act (ARRA) in 2009 and Health Care Affordability Act of 2010, there have been numerous attempts to improve program evaluation and performance management. The ultimate effectiveness of many of these policies depends upon public acceptance of New Media by citizens exercising democratic freedoms and responsibilities (Chapter 6).

The Information Age has stimulated the application of ICTs to deliver government services—at all levels and in most functions. Digital governance has become a primary area of interest and study for numerous public policy specialists. Chapter 7 describes representative examples of how governments are applying ICTs to improve interoperability among agencies and enhance government-to-government (G2G), government-to-employee (G2E), government-to-business (G2B) and government-to-citizen (G2C) services. Co-production is increasing as more citizens are making online choices involving tax returns, health insurance, investments, mortgage loans, student loans and retirement savings plans. The chapter also questions the results of some of these efforts and the future of digital governance as a means to enhance availability, lower cost and improve the quality of co-produced public services. Without enhanced citizen access to the internet and additional knowledge of how to utilize new technology, further efforts may be limited.

5 Accountability and Equality of Access

Balancing Political Responsiveness with Administrative Effectiveness

Governments have the opportunity to make life easier for their constituents by recognizing how the role of "consumer" and "citizen" are complementary.

Steve Ballmer, CEO, Microsoft

Citizens are using ICTs to demand more accountability for their tax dollars and greater value for services they receive from public agencies. Current and potential users are frustrated: they are asking why governments cannot or will not provide the same level of direct or virtual service as private for-profit service companies. Previous chapters have shown how the two sectors differ and why citizens now expect greater efficiency and **political responsiveness** as well as lower taxes (or at least better value), especially from fee-based and tax-supported public institutions. Elected political leaders and appointed managers must become more actively engaged in the details of managing information technology to change organizational processes, essential for the conversion to networked digital governance. Specific guidelines for managers and politicians to empower employees and respond to citizens as customers are presented below and referred to as "point-of-contact" accountability on page 130.) Different motivators can and should be used to encourage public managers, particularly state and local officials, to reorient existing bureaucratic hierarchies to become more flexible and customer-focused within networked management systems. Many bureaucrats and their bureaucracies are still locked into Information Age or even Industrial Age systems which fail to meet 21st century requirements for governance (see Table 5.1).

Although more citizens are communicating directly with governments instantaneously using computers and wireless devices, the expansion of virtual government services has not kept pace with global exponential growth of the internet (Chapter 8). Most public agencies still offer call-center or face-to-face service, albeit accompanied by improved customer service standards and enhanced information technology. Questions about the costs and benefits of online delivery remain unanswered. Anecdotal evidence about the value of ICTs is widely available from

Table 5.1 The Evolution of Governance Models

	Old Public Management	*New Public Management*	*Leveraged Governance*
Era	Industrial Age	Information Age	Networked Age
Accountability Strategy	Hierarchy	Output	Blended contributions to shared outcomes
Challenge	Rise of non-hierarchical strategies, tactics	Inability of managers to control outcomes for which they are responsible	Mixed systems of accountability; agile dynamic, effective

Source: Kettl (2009: 223, Table 7.1)

private consultants, intermediaries eager to obtain government contracts. But such counsel often comes at a high price: it is contradictory, ideologically biased, industry-specific and self-serving. For example, IBM commissioned a book by one of its senior consultants on the "Greening of IT" which was little more than a sales-pitch for its energy efficient servers (Lamb, 2009). The former chair of George W. Bush's Texas Government Reform Committee wrote a polemic extolling the virtues of Web 2.0 which (coincidentally) recommended Bush policies such as privatization, cutting "red tape," installing market-driven government and promoting educational vouchers (Eggers, 2005). Citizens are rightfully suspicious about partisan prescriptions from both the public and private sectors. Most notably, they are concerned about fraud perpetrated by banking, commercial, financial and real estate interests, revealing a callous disregard for the public interest, even *after* bankrupt corporations and their executives received large government "bailouts" or private consultants benefitted from large taxpayer subsidies.

Elected officials are passing laws and public managers are enacting regulations to meet citizen demands for more accessible, efficient and responsive government (Chapter 6). Partially as a result of the digital revolution, more citizens demand greater civic accountability and officials are challenged to balance **administrative values** (efficiency, ethics, professionalism and productivity) with **political values** (accountability, democracy, participation and responsiveness). Although these goals need not conflict, it is difficult to reconcile them, especially in the downsized and deficit-conscious fiscal environments currently enveloping most public sector decision making processes (Milakovich and Gordon, 2009: Chapter 2). Political conflicts inevitably lead to questions about spending priorities, filtered through an antiquated system of federalism, to achieve economic improvement goals. For example, estimates are that at least one-half of the Obama administration's $787 *billion* **economic stimulus** money, appropriated by Congress in 2009 under the **American Recovery and Reinvestment Act (ARRA)**, was used by state and local governments to meet budget deficits, only indirectly providing jobs and stimulating private sector economic development. This appears to be a global trend as by October 2009, more than 50 countries had committed over $2.5 trillion to fiscal stimulus and pledged another $18 trillion in public funds to underwrite the financial sector and other industries. Nonetheless, critics legitimately ask: what are the results of the billions already spent? Prior to the fall 2010 U.S. elections, Republicans offered a "pledge to voters" which, among other promises, redirects the unspent billions in stimulus funds towards deficit reduction and other fiscally conservative priorities.

Although substantial progress has been made to integrate politics and information technology, several important questions remain unanswered: 1) Are private sector models, methods and service standards applicable to the public sector? 2) If so, which of the many available approaches deliver the best results to varied recipients of government services? 3) What administrative and political barriers limit the application of technological solutions to public problems? 4) How do governments or private contractors reconcile political considerations with improved customer service? 5) Have information and communication technologies been used to advance the interests of women and minorities? 6) What new roles should appointed and elected officials assume in guiding change processes and resolving disputes among administrators and citizens? These questions are always more difficult to resolve because of the complex intergovernmental substructure of federalism and the often stressful customer–supplier relationships that exist within the public sector.[1] The following section describes how these inherent conflicts thwart rational solutions and traces past efforts by public agencies to establish customer service standards for delivering higher quality customer-centric services.

Applying Customer Service Standards to Government

Public managers are continuously challenged to measure and fill "gaps" between citizen/customer expectations and the level of service provided. Public agencies are expected to meet **balanced performance standards** with citizens, interests and elected officials to accommodate preferences of diverse individuals and groups—many of whom believe that contracting out or privatization are preferable for government to "run like a business" (Beckett, 2000; Zeithaml, Parasuraman and Berry, 1990). Privatization of public services has been widely touted as a policy option by many politicians, especially during periods of financial scarcity. This cliché carries with it a very different meaning after the traumatic failures of banks and financial institutions and the scandals surrounding large corporations such as American International Group (AIG), Enron, Goldman Sachs, Lehman Brothers and Tyco International. Nonetheless, partisan divisions of opinion are widening between Democrats who espouse government solutions and Republicans who are adamant about applying business know-how to reconfigure (or replace) the operations of public agencies.

Debate continues over such fundamental political issues as 1) who should receive how much of which valued public resources in society, and 2) who delivers which services to whom at what costs. These questions cannot and *should not* be separated from multiple forms of delivering public services, whether online, by mail, telephone or in person. Many public employees and their professional associations continue to promote digital management practices and virtual government aimed at responding to citizens as valued customers. However, when compared to for-profit private businesses, it is nearly always more challenging for governments to balance conflicting interests, set performance standards and motivate employees to respond to citizens as valued customers. Still, citizen expectations about the quality of services provided by governments are likely to rise even higher in the future (Kettl, 2002b; U.S. General Services Administration, 2005). Predictably, offering customer-centric services may also conflict with partisan political agendas, bureaucratic processes and deeply rooted vested interests.

Innovative governmental actions are often limited by outdated organizational structures. Rather than encouraging and rewarding employees for serving customers well within a decentralized, networked **bottom-up management** of a customer-responsive full-service system, many public agencies are still unable (or unwilling) to abandon existing systems which restrict employee responsiveness and emphasize routine protocols for all demands, processes and systems. Consequently, there is often more talk about improving customer service than there are actual efforts to apply quality improvement methods, service standards and theories (Douglas and Judge, 2001; Gaster and Squires, 2003; Kettl, 2009). Additional **barriers to acceptance** of customer-responsive governance include:

1) Resistance to change and adherence to rules-driven management systems instead of networked, customer-focused work cultures.
2) Lack of experience with (and some trepidation about) the use of output or results measures for allocating resources, especially at the state and local government level.
3) Personnel systems which reward individuals but lack incentives for rewarding team performance, also characteristic of the private sector.
4) Fear of the budgetary and political consequences of *not* meeting customer standards.
5) Failure of elected and appointed officials to cooperate with efforts to adopt performance initiatives and standards.

6) Divided accountability for achieving results, especially in regulatory compliance agencies, such as the much-maligned U.S. federal Securities and Exchange Commission (SEC) and many state agencies with similar "regulatory" responsibilities.

Another harsh reality of public sector innovation (or lack thereof) is that advocates for more online alternatives must convince appointed officials (specialists) while at the same time persuading elected representatives (generalists) and competing with others (the mass media and private interests) who typically are more interested in eliminating or replacing government than improving its services. Numerous sources advocate contracting out, lowering taxes, higher productivity, less government, pay for performance, reduced budgets, termination or privatization (Eggers, 2005; Greene, 2002; Grimshaw, Vincent and Willmont, 2002; Hodge and Greve, 2005). Elected officials, including New Jersey Republican Governor Chris Christie, have found it politically advantageous to blame public employees and their unions and advocate policies which go well beyond downsizing by reducing public employee health and retirement benefits to balance state budgets.

Conflict regarding standards and strategies for achieving goals is expected in a democratic society. One of the major achievements of the Clinton administration was to minimize disagreements by creating explicit written standards for federal agencies to identify their customers, find out what they wanted and develop objective **customer service standards** to measure agency performance. Federal executive agencies first published customer service standards in September 1995 and have since developed performance indicators and integrated them with budgetary requests.[2] Standards were derived from customer surveys, data analysis, employee input and feedback from customers and suppliers to make everyone aware of mutual expectations. Although these standards generated visible baseline data on relative agency performance, the Bush administration shelved many of the initiatives, changed priorities and stalled the momentum for reforms in the Republican dominated White House and Congress from 2001 to 2006.

Despite persistent political conflicts and ideological differences among businesses, governments and non-profit agencies, many public agencies have succeeded in changing their image (of unresponsiveness) by applying various customer service, information technology and quality improvement strategies to a wide range of federal, state and local public services (Berman, West and Milakovich, 1994; Carr, Kehoe, Barker and Littman, 1999; Hellein and Bowman, 2002: Milakovich, 2006a; Osborne and Plastrik, 2000). Still, basic conflicts over who should deliver public services persist.

Business vs. Government Strategies

Unlike many quasi-monopolistic government agencies, commercial firms must pay close attention to customers because of ever-present competition from other providers who offer the same product or service faster and cheaper. The consequences of market failure in the private sector often mean bankruptcy. (Consider the recent plight of two out of three of America's largest automobile manufacturers and their struggle to compete with Chinese, German, Italian, Japanese and other "foreign" producers as one among several examples of this capitalist reality.) As customer expectations rise, private firms must respond with better products and services at lower prices or lose market share: for many, increasing customer satisfaction, attracting new customers and retaining the old ones is a life or death struggle. (In some cases, "death" may be only a temporary condition under U.S. bankruptcy laws.) Moreover, loss of revenue and reputation that accompany failure to satisfy customers are driving forces for internal systems improvement as well as a competitive strategy for allocating resources. Private firms remain viable by offering goods and services at lower prices in open markets. In addition, they gain financially from serving greater numbers of customers more efficiently and maintaining longer term relationships with them. Typically, customers pay market price for a product or service and do not conflict with each other over who should offer what types of services or how they should be offered. Competition occurs between producers to offer lower prices and better product and service quality.

Governments on the other hand are not as responsive to market constraints as private businesses, yet they are responsible for the delivery of major public assistance, education, emergency management, immigration, law enforcement, national security, public safety and military services; in addition, they directly purchase, oversee and regulate the quality of goods and services produced by millions of private contractors. With few exceptions, most public agencies do not gain financially from providing better service to customers, nor are employees recognized for contributing to such efforts. The opposite is often true: budgets are usually determined in advance of expenditures, so more customers may mean *fewer resources* available to spend on those being served. This *post hoc* approach can be especially damaging for collaborative processes, such as contracting and purchasing which depend on public and private sector cooperation. According to consensus estimates, the federal government alone could save as much as 20% of the over $600 billion spent annually on equipment and service purchases merely by expanding its e-procurement systems. Unfortunately, there have been few incentives for Congress or state legislatures to enact such changes. In the past, public agencies received much of their operating revenues from elected representative legislative bodies, such as cities, counties, states, other governments and special districts within designated quasi-monopolistic geographic jurisdictions.

The economic downturn has permanently changed traditional sources of revenue for governments and forced many to increasingly draw funds from proprietary services, designated trust funds or user fees collected *directly* from recipients. These funds are restricted to specific services such as airport or highway operations, cable television, utility franchises, water and sewer, or solid waste disposal. Turnpike tolls, for example, can only be used for the construction and maintenance of highways. The proprietary fee-based and intergovernmental shares of the operating budgets of many large state and local governments now *exceed* the amount collected from general revenue sources (taxes). Simply put, local governments are *literally* closer to the people and must treat citizens as valued customers, especially when fines, license fees, service charges and tolls are paid directly by service recipients and "earmarked" for the operation of specific public purposes.

Whatever the sources of revenue or the nature of the relationship between citizen, employee, manager and elected official, there is general agreement among all parties that public agencies should provide the best quality service at the lowest costs. Especially since increasing numbers of citizens now pay governments' bills directly (as fees, service charges and tolls) they demand accountable, efficient, fair and effective *value* for their scarce resources. Public managers and front-line employees apply online tools and techniques to narrow the "gaps" between perceptions and expectations of service quality to establish customer-focused accountability and responsiveness (Zeithaml, Parasuraman and Berry, 1990). Still, innovative public sector decision making and resource allocation are constrained by: 1) deeply held and often conflicting ideological (political) beliefs about the purposes of government; 2) private interest group access to elected officials and competition for limited public resources; 3) difficulties in setting and enforcing service standards (for both public and private sectors); and 4) resistance to developing multiple measures of outcomes, performance and results.

Fragmented distribution networks, multiple overlapping services (too many local school districts, police and fire departments, for example), political pressures and conflicting community values also affect relationships among various stakeholders (i.e. clients, customers, taxpayers, students, recipients, voters or users). In addition to extensive federal reform efforts, many states and local governments have attempted to de-layer traditional bureaucratic hierarchies, empower employees and redesign performance management systems to provide better service to citizens/customers (Berman, West and Milakovich, 1994; Hellein and Bowman, 2002; Milakovich, 1998). Political trade-offs are frequently made between optimal allocation of critical resources and those available for public needs. For example, state and local public school budgets are passed in advance of revenue collection and, despite the best efforts to predict enrollments, many taxation authorities in fast-growing geographic districts are underfunded when the actual number of students exceeds budget estimates. In addition, many school districts are downsizing or cutting resources due to sharply lower property tax values (Chapter 3).

Under such fiscal constraints, improving customer service or information technology by itself would not resolve massive budget shortfalls.

Often, the goals and purposes of some public organizations reflect inherently divisive relationships with customers. Banking regulation, building and zoning code enforcement, tax collection, law enforcement and corrections, for instance, must be responsive to segments of the community which often adamantly reject being "served." In addition, unlike most of their counterparts in the private sector, governments are obligated by law to be as concerned with equity and fairness of resource distribution as they are with efficiency and effectiveness of resource utilization. This often places government agencies in direct conflict with private business interests which view only the "bottom-line" and ignore critical community needs. Although market-based public–private partnerships have increased in recent decades, there will always be an underlying conflict between the missions of the two sectors.

Competing management strategies are not always compatible, but they need not be mutually exclusive. There are numerous examples of intelligent cities which have succeeded in forming creative partnerships with public and private providers to enhance public sector enterprises. One such area which has overcome such divisiveness is **Moncton, New Brunswick** in Atlantic Canada, which has grown from a small railroad hub to an impressive Canadian customer contact center through the Canadian government's partnership with other municipalities and private corporations. The city has built an IT outsourcing industry by partnering with private sector carriers and grown into a telecom-centric economy with tens of thousands of jobs for its citizens. The city is now focusing on its **Vision 2010** plan which calls for collaboration with regional universities to promote tech-based entrepreneurship and diversify its IT economy.[3]

Policy implementation at nearly all levels of government will always be enmeshed with conflicting political ideologies, interests and leaders. The U.S. federal government has stressed customer service and results management as cornerstones of reinvention and results-oriented efforts since the early 1990s. Prior to the Bush-Cheney administration, there was an established national strategy for applying customer service quality principles to improve operations of all types of government agencies (Gore, 1995; Milakovich, 2006b). These strategies encouraged the expansion of ICTs to more efficiently deliver public services. Most of the models used to guide public officials in their new customer service roles and responsibilities were superseded by ideological considerations (i.e. privatization) during the Bush-Cheney years.

Whether in the name of efficiency or political expediency, nearly every president in the past 120 years has attempted to "reform" the federal bureaucracy—Barack Obama is no exception. The following section takes a brief retrospective view of modern reform attempts by the U.S. federal executive branch.

Reinvention, Reform and Results

For nearly the first hundred years of American political history, expectations for improved government performance were minimal because there was no distinction between politics and administration. Indeed, politics *was* administration and vice versa. There was little concern with "performance" because all government jobs were filled by **patronage** for the loyal campaign workers supporting successful politicians. After President James Garfield was assassinated in 1883 by an embittered lawyer rejected for federal service, Congress passed the Pendleton Act to insulate administrative decision making from political influences. The Act created the Federal Civil Service and provided for neutral (that is, less politicized) federal public administration and sought to increase government productivity by raising the competency levels of U.S. federal employees.

The Brownlow Committee of 1937 and the Reorganization Act of 1939 further committed the federal government to efficiency, economy, reduction of separate agencies and staffing, as well as the elimination of duplication between agencies.[4] The first and second Hoover Commissions in the 1950s recommended the establishment of a senior executive service (SES), a reform which was not accomplished until Jimmy Carter's administration (1977–1981). Some state and a few local governments followed the federal government's lead. In 1982, the Reagan Administration's Grace Commission offered over 400 specific recommendations for increasing the efficiency of federal government operations.[5] Many of the most controversial recommendations, including closing obsolete military bases, also took several years to achieve.

Modern reform efforts began in 1993 with the **National Performance Review (NPR)** which lasted until the end of the Clinton administration in January 2001.[6] This was generally viewed as the most comprehensive and successful of 11 previous attempts during the 20th century (Arnold, 1995; Kettl, 1998). The NPR challenged federal agencies to cut red tape, downsize, deregulate and offer customer service equal to "the best in business."[7] Specific, and often contradictory, recommendations included putting customers first, decentralizing decisions, empowering front-line employees and reducing administrative costs by focusing on results. The NPR was a high level initiative endorsed by former president Clinton and vice president Al Gore, who personally led the initial six-month review of all federal government agencies and identified targets for waste reduction and opportunities for management improvement (Gore, 1995). The NPR managed to avoid extreme politicization and received generally positive reviews for achieving most of its major goals (Kettl, 1998).[8] Many basic NPR precepts, however, conflicted with long-held views of accountability and the role of public service. In addition, fiscal and monetary policies during the era contributed to employment growth, lessening the urgency for reform.

New Public Management, Public Service and Reinventing Government (REGO)

Opposing political theories reflect different concepts about the role of government in an increasingly globalized and "wired" society. Clinton's National Performance Review (NPR) was integral to pre-fiscal crisis trends in public administration, as well as its European counterpart, **New Public Management (NPM)**. The theoretical foundations of the Clinton-Gore reinventing government (REGO) movement were derived from the New Public Management movement and stressed the economic rationalist perspectives of public choice and principal agent theories (Chapter 1). NPM surfaced in Great Britain and New Zealand in the 1990s and influenced the movement toward entrepreneurial, market-based and customer service quality principles. NPM and the NPR presumed that all human beings were self-interested with ego-centric goals and that public servants possessed an "entrepreneurial spirit" coupled with a desire to reduce the size of government. Public interest was seen as the *aggregation* of the individual interests of each citizen making choices on narrow individual interests.

Reforms were opposed by those who believed that public administration should represent values of **New Public Service (NPS)** which asserts that the public interest should be first and foremost a result of dialogue and deliberation about shared values. Among the contemporary criticisms of the New Public Management entrepreneurial paradigm was that "Public servants do not deliver customer service; they deliver democracy" (Denhardt and Denhardt, 2007: ix). Accordingly, public administration should focus on democracy, **citizenship** and pride when talking about governmental actions, instead of keywords such as market-based, competitive and customer-oriented. Public servants' motivation is a desire to contribute to society and be guided by law, community values, political norms, professional standards and citizen interests. The interest of citizens should be *integrative*, whereas the interests of private customers tend to be more *disintegrative*.

There is and always has been a distinction between customers and citizens, because the former chooses between products in the market, whereas the latter decides what actions are important enough for government to accomplish at public expense. "Citizens are described as bearers of rights and duties within the context of a wider community. Customers are different in that they do not share common purposes but rather seek to optimize their own individual benefits" (Denhardt and Denhardt, 2007: 60). Citizens are an integral part of a governmental system, not merely consumers of government services, but *co-producers* of representative democratic values. In their role as customers, citizens need not think about the interests of others. Public interest may be compromised when citizens are transformed into customers with damaging effects on democratic governance and public administration (Bekkers, Dijkstra, Edwards and Fenger, 2007).

NPS focuses more attention to policy, process and agencies where officials are accountable to citizens, not customers. According to the NPS, political and administrative systems should not be separated with completely distinct values:

> Ultimately, those in government must recognize that public service is not an economic construct, but a political one. That means that issues of service improvement need to be attentive to not only the demands of "customers" but also to the distribution of power in society. Ultimately, in the New Public Service, providing quality service is a first step in the direction of widening public involvement and extending democratic citizenship.
>
> (Denhardt and Denhardt, 2007: 62)

One of the public sector's original *raisons-d'être* was to correct imperfections in private markets. REGO/NPR and the New Public Service represent opposing views of accountability—different aspects are emphasized. This is due to various perceptions of the relationship between political and administrative systems. Discussing the differences between these two systems is as relevant today as it was more than a century ago, when then political science professor Woodrow Wilson defined the relationship between policy making and implementation, and consequences for the overall actions of government are just as significant (Wilson, 1886).

Reinventing government gave administrators and executives more discretion to be creative, innovative and discretionary in carrying out government policies. Accountability was defined as satisfying the preferences of individual customers of governmental services. By imposing the entrepreneurial paradigm on public administration practices, REGO emphasized administrative values and represented a clear distinction, as Wilson did, between political and administrative systems.[9] ICTs were used to gather public comments, communicate with citizens and distribute reports from agencies on their progress towards reaching goals. During the 2000 presidential campaign, then Texas Governor Bush signaled a change in policy and stated his intention, if elected, to eliminate waste and inefficiency by making government more "results-driven."

The use of performance data to make budgetary and programmatic decisions became the foundation of Bush's **President's Management Agenda (PMA)**, the ideological blueprint for management during his administration (Executive Office of the President, 2002). Bush distinguished the PMA from earlier reforms by infusing the report with political rhetoric and a general lack of specifics. During the presidential campaign, he avoided acknowledging that the federal workforce had been reduced under the NPR, doing so only *after* winning the election. As a conservative, he was skeptical about past efforts to increase citizen access and expand the use of information technology, but later rethought this strategy and adopted an electronic government initiative as part of the PMA. Under the Bush administration's aggressive **competitive sourcing** initiative, also part of the PMA, federal agencies were evaluated less on the quality of customer service than the extent of their privatization efforts (Chapter 6). The global financial crisis and mortgage meltdown beginning in 2007 largely halted further privatization efforts. At different rates and to various degrees, New Public Management and New Public Service have been gradually abandoned in developed countries in favor of digital era governance (Dunleavy, Margetts, Bastow and Tinkler, 2006).

As U.S. industry faces the likelihood of more intense international competition, lower profits, further job losses and shrinking global market share, business and political leaders are responding by reconfiguring their internal work environments. Even the most disciplined firms, however, discover that demand for better customer service nearly always exceeds the management capacity of employees to consistently "meet or exceed" customer expectations (U.S. General Services Administration, 2005). Although many firms embraced new management paradigms, others underestimated the discipline, time and training effort required to change procedures and apply customer service standards to public agencies. As economic conditions worsened, many companies responded by relearning how to simultaneously become more competitive, quality-focused and customer-driven. Others simply outsourced jobs, downsized workers, and cut healthcare and retirement benefits. In many instances, the economic and social empowerment of women and minorities was negatively affected by these responses.

ICTs and the Empowerment of Women and Minorities

Since the beginning of the women's liberation movement in the 1960s, there has been a struggle between the two genders to contribute to the economy and be rewarded equally by society. With the surge in ICT usage, this field has come under scrutiny for its lack of equal opportunities for ethnic and racial minorities and women (Hafkin and Huyer, 2006; Mehra, Merkel and Bishop, 2004). According to Nancy Hafkin and Sophia Huyer, every woman wants to become a "cyberella," fluent in the uses of technology, comfortable with computer technology and capable of working in virtual spaces. **Cyberellas** are confident in their use of ICTs and fully able to master the skills needed to work with all different types of technologies. In contrast, "cinderellas" are identified as the majority of women who work in the basement of the information society with little opportunity to reap benefits. They are caught between low-paying "sticky floor" jobs and the "glass ceiling," an invisible upper-limit on earning power and promotions due to gender. Although there have significant improvements in recent years, on average, women in the same jobs in the United States still earn just 76 cents for every dollar earned by their male counterparts. Disparities are even greater in developing nations.

Gender and racial mainstreaming are longer-term approaches that attempt to equalize ethnic, gender and racial disparities. They are public policies designed to make equality of opportunity part of all aspects of society, including university admissions, scholarships, public programs, projects and jobs. However, mainstreaming has resulted in a negative backlash prompting allegations of reverse discrimination that may limit its use as an appropriate strategy for alleviating problems faced by women and minorities. In recent years, there has been a lack of enforcement due to a dismantling of governmental equality enforcement units, such as the U.S. federal Equal Employment Opportunity Commission (EEOC). Under the Bush administration, the budget and staff of the EEOC were cut nearly 20%, resulting in a huge backlog of uninvestigated complaints of racial and gender discrimination.[10]

Where gender and racial mainstreaming may be lacking, the United Nations **Millennium Development Goals (MDG)** initiative offers a substitute. The MDGs focus on life issues facing women and minorities in many developing nations. The goals go far beyond ICTs themselves, offering a broader view of what should happen for gender equality and women's empowerment to exist on all economic levels, including use of technology.[11]

How can ICTs contribute to the empowerment of women and minorities? Different areas of empowerment include economic, educational, socio-cultural, psychological, political and legal. However, within each of these areas, more governmental action is needed to expand the empowerment and economic opportunities of women. Women are often overlooked when it comes to ICT employment opportunities and other high-tech jobs because of the misconception that societies are "gender neutral" and that women do not need extra assistance. This way of thinking is detrimental because everyone dismisses what women have to offer and they are not given the opportunities to show their talents and skills (Hafkin and Huyer, 2002: 41). One of the biggest problems facing women in developing nations is not being able to provide for their families. When gains are made by women that improve their livelihood, men with superior physical and political power often take them away. Women are missing opportunities to better their lives through lack of access to ICTs. Poor women are most affected and have the most difficult time gaining empowerment with or without the help of ICTs. Because of this, many ICT initiatives are being used as intervention measures to help prevent continued mistreatment of women and minorities. Intervention-driven ICT initiatives have improved the lives of many women. However, they often fall short of providing greater benefits to all women.

There is very little comparative data about women's use of ICTs. Few national databases are collected so available statistics are rather limited in scope. Countries with the most data are nations that already have high concentrations of internet usage and greater indicators of gender issues, such as the U.S. and Canada. There is a need for more data from developing countries where women are systematically discriminated against. Without increased awareness of the scope of the problems and without action to fulfill the need, women in these countries will continue to be ignored. Most countries that provide data are wealthier nations in the Western hemisphere. Only five countries in Latin America even provided data on wage discrepancies (Argentina, Brazil, Chile, Mexico and Venezuela); these are also among the richest and more politically progressive nations in that region. South Africa was the only country providing data on the African continent and no data were available from the Middle East.

Education is vital for gender and racial equality. Studies have shown that boys have greater access to education than girls in many developing nations, and that even if girls do gain access to education, they are less likely to participate in higher-level science and technology classes. There are some indications that girls in developing countries are beginning to close the gender gap in the classroom, but boys are still perceived by teachers to be more confident in using mathematics and technologies. SchoolNetAfrica raises awareness about the gender related issues in education and encourages the use of the internet for virtual learning.[12] Although not specifically promoting the empowerment of women and ICTs in education, SchoolNetAfrica focuses on the overall improvement of education for African children. Despite an undeniable awareness of the problems facing the entire African continent, there is little action being taken to address the problem.

Despite the grim statistics, there is considerable optimism that ICTs can be used to achieve gender and racial gains, or at least equalize opportunities for women and minorities.[13] It is difficult to determine if the gains are real or token: progress with regard to providing equal opportunity for both men and women of all races and ethnic backgrounds is difficult to measure. There is little doubt that the lives of many women around the world have been changed by ICTs. Their introduction, combined with outsourcing, provides women in developing nations with opportunities they would never have received without globalization (Friedman, 2005). Merely introducing ICTs into a society, however, will not automatically mean that women or ethnic minorities benefit equally. Studies have shown that increased access does little for women's empowerment (Hafkin and Huyer, 2002: 57). Added legal measures and strict enforcement are still needed for minorities to be protected and women to be treated equally with men. ICT policies and regulations are important in promoting **racial and gender equality**. At each level—international, regional, national and local—equal opportunity ICT policies and regulations are fundamental to the success of minority and women's empowerment in both the public and private sectors.

Lessons from the Private Sector: Do They Apply to the Public Sector?

For over two decades, private industry has focused on improving customer service as part of a broad performance management and profit-motivated effort. As businesses focused on changing internal management processes to respond to customers, non-value-added costs were eliminated, systems became more efficient, product and service costs decreased and, in most instances, consumers benefited. In other cases, opportunities for corruption also increased. Cynicism and skepticism resulting from distrust of public and non-profit officials are also partially explained by high-level scandals, official misconduct and mismanagement of trust funds (Berman, 1997; Herzlinger, 1996; Kamarck and Nye, 2002). Rebuilding faith and trust in government as well as improving the management capacity and competence of career civil servants have been prominent themes of many national reform efforts.[14] As bank failures and the mortgage meltdown spread throughout the U.S. and global economies, millions of citizens questioned the integrity, leadership and motives of private business leaders, especially in banking, insurance and financial institutions.

Improvements in government services may have lagged behind those made by businesses in the 1990s, but many more individuals were harmed by the deregulated economic climate of the "Lost Decade" from 2000 to 2010. Many Americans suffered heavy losses because they entrusted their careers, investments and retirement funds to private Wall Street firms such as American International Group (AIG), Bear Sterns, Goldman Sachs, Lehman Brothers and Merrill-Lynch. Still others lost their jobs or received modest pay increases which failed to keep up with inflation. Nonetheless, ideological battles continue as many voters still favor political candidates who advocate the use of business "know-how" to deliver government services; others would like to see the abdication of public agencies altogether and contracting out or privatization of government services (Hodge and Greve, 2005; Raffel, 1999; Savas, 2000).

Regardless of the means and methods selected, the public sector faces serious managerial challenges to genuinely motivate, empower and reward employees. Elements critical to the successful delivery of quality customer service initiatives both in office, by telephone or online are: 1) employee commitment and empowerment; 2) responsiveness to citizens as valued customers; and 3) political support.

Empowering Public Employees

Teaching employees to think differently about customers, managers, suppliers and themselves is critical to the success of any organizational change effort. Motivating employees to improve customer service results from: 1) a sense of common purpose; 2) the desire to succeed resulting from employee empowerment; 3) training for new methods of responding to customers; and 4) the need for reward and recognition. In citizen-centric, quality-managed and ICT-enabled organizations, everyone develops a shared sense of common purpose by respecting the rights of customers and making their satisfaction a primary goal. **Empowerment** is the devolution of authority and freedom to do what is necessary *within pre-established limits* to satisfy customers (Block, 1991). Empowerment gives front-line employees— with the motivation to change—a voice in decision-making processes, a stake in the success of the organization, tangible rewards, training opportunities and process-ownership. Rather than a set of rigid rules or procedures, empowerment is a common attitude shared by all members of the organization. Rewards may be used to change employee behavior: they can be *intrinsic* in the form of peer recognition and better working conditions, or they can be *extrinsic* with bonuses, charter marks, incentives or recognition by competitive quality awards and prizes (Chapter 4). Regardless of the form of the recognition, empowered public employees, managers and elected officials share the goal of providing the best services to all those they serve.

Changing the collective mindset of any organization requires delegating authority and responsibility to those who are in direct contact with recipients of the services. Accountable and empowered front-line employees with specialized knowledge and expertise are trained to perform their tasks without close supervision. Managers must carefully select front-line workers, provide them with a strong organizational foundation and culture in which to work, offer them strategic guidance and give them the technological support necessary to perform their jobs. Empowered employees are more likely to respond to customers' demands in the same manner that management responds to their own needs. Empowered front-line employees can then be granted the authority to make decisions *within prescribed limits* at the point of customer contact (below). Public employees become more accountable to those they serve as well as to their bosses in the organization. This transformation in thinking can be very challenging for some public service organizations, especially for managers of regulatory agencies (e.g. intelligence, judicial, law enforcement, tax collection and building and zoning code enforcement) who believe they are exempt because of the evaluative and regulatory judgments that they exercise over their customers.[15]

One reason rule-driven management is so pervasive (in both the public and private sectors) is that many managers still believe it is essential to standardize service among different employees and service units (Barry and Parasuraman, 1991). This translates into the type of universally despised "bureaucratic impersonality" that is more often found in the public sector because of its tradition of formal Weberian organizational structure, a vestige of Industrial Age bureaucracy (Chapter 1). Excessive dependence on impersonal and inflexible rules contradicts the entire concept of employee empowerment. Advanced ICTs which merge face-to-face with **virtual services** utilizing internet systems such as **Skype.com**—software using two-way cameras built into most personal computers to link citizens directly to public administrators—are capable of overcoming impersonality of citizen-service contacts. Although computer video technology is still developing, nearly one in five (20%) of all U.S. adults have already participated in an internet video conference call using their computers. Broad-scale use of such systems would be of special benefit to elderly, home-bound and disabled individuals. Many local governments also offer **telenetworking** at-home work options for employees wanting to save commuting time and parking expenses. These systems are modeled after "virtual teller" options offered by many commercial banks which provide secure face-to-face banking services and also promote reductions in energy consumption and environmental conservation. Using ICTs to enhance face-to-face contacts helps to resolve service quality disputes when they occur, rather than waiting for a supervisor to intervene.[16]

Bureaucratic delays, excuses for inaction and unnecessary transfers between departments fail to utilize the advantages that empowerment and decentralization contribute to improving customer service and satisfaction (Milakovich, 2003). The fastest and most immediate way to solve a customer's problem is to do so instantly *at the point of initial contact*, rather than waiting for approval from higher management (see Box 5.1). Changing control-oriented managerial mindsets, developing trust relationships and balancing service delivery and regulatory enforcement responsibilities are among the most serious challenges facing those who see the potential value in digital governance (Nyhan, 2000). With the proper training, empowered employees recognize the limits of their authority, can be held accountable when they exceed that authority and know when to delegate decisions to someone else. Above all else, they can be able to distinguish between routine and non-routine problems and initiate corrective actions to effectively deal with different situations. Empowering employees to apply those techniques at critical points in service transactions improves both **citizen responsiveness** and utilization of resources (see guidelines in Box 5.1).

Despite the general absence of internal processes responsive to customer demands, managers must assume the difficult (and politically sensitive) task of balancing and prioritizing preferences among diverse individuals and groups who all expect higher levels of service. Absent incentives to bolster the "bottom line," public managers must identify customer expectations and establish performance standards that satisfy multiple users of services. Regardless of the type of transaction, everyone benefits from the knowledge gained from objective customer surveys which evaluate the level of service expected versus that provided by agencies. Adjustments can and should be made for the nature of the service provided: for example, recognize that customer service principles *are* inherently more difficult to apply to public functions such as the courts, policing, building and zoning code enforcement, corrections, environmental protection and tax collection.

Box 5.1: Guidelines for Point-of-Contact Accountability

1) Empower public employees to respond to customer concerns as they occur. Advanced training is required.
2) Conduct online surveys and assemble focus groups to evaluate the level of service expected by citizens and provided by administrators.
3) Prioritize customer expectations and establish performance standards for routine and non-routine situations.
4) Analyze gaps between expectations and perceptions of service.
5) Recognize that non-routine and regulatory services present unique measurement and enforcement problems.
6) Separate regulatory from distributive and redistributive services.
7) Apply customer service measures in agencies on the basis of function and impact.
8) Define specific guidelines for responding to citizens in both extreme and routine situations (using Six Sigma and Pareto statistical techniques).

Source: Adapted from Milakovich (2003)

Satisfactory customer service outcomes are less likely to be achieved when services are mandatory, paid for indirectly, and involuntary. (For instance, paying a stiff fine and court costs for a traffic citation is a fee-based and *very* involuntary transaction that most citizens would prefer not to have in the first place.) In other instances, when services are distributive, voluntary and fee-for-service based, managers and politicians have fewer reasons (or excuses?) for not applying a networked customer service model because citizens are paying for the service directly—satisfaction is easier to measure and results can be used to make adjustments in delivery processes.

Regulatory compliance and rule enforcement activities often reflect hostile relationships between citizen and government and should be differentiated from routine general service delivery issues. It is infinitely easier to distribute Social Security checks to the addresses or bank accounts of nearly 50 million eligible Americans than it is to protect roughly the same number of consumers from identity theft, mortgage loan fraud or deceptive real estate sales practices. Separating non-routine governmental *regulatory* functions from more routine ***distributive*** and ***redistributive*** service delivery activities permits managers to maintain **point-of-contact accountability** by defining parameters for responding to citizen demands in conflict situations. Developing decision systems to guide elected officials and managers in distinguishing policy actions based on *function* (e.g. education, courts, police, welfare, water and sewer, etc.) and *impact* (i.e. regulatory, deregulatory, distributive, redistributive) facilitates the difficult task of segmenting routine governmental activities suitable for application of customer service models from those which may not be.

Responding to Citizens as Valued Customers in the Networked Age

Organizations that systematically define who their customers are, analyze what they want and how their expectations can be met, increase the probability of success by customizing responses and more precisely targeting limited organizational resources. Developing successful customer-service strategies requires identifying various existing and potential customers in the public marketplace. Citizen responsiveness, together with reliability, assurance, empathy and measurable outcomes, are the principle dimensions used to judge an organization's customer service quality (Zeithaml, Parasuraman and Berry, 1990). In addition to redefining the needs of different types of customers, empowered employees must recognize the importance of responding promptly when conflicts do occur (Milakovich, 2003). Responding to customer problems at the initial point-of-contact, problem resolution and **secondary recovery techniques** (procedures to correct errors after they have occurred) must be taught to all employees, not just to managers. An effective customer service management system rewards employees for quality service—managers are responsible for designing and maintaining that system.

As public service organizations become more ICT-driven, governments respond to citizens as valued service recipients who want issues resolved quickly without unnecessary bureaucratic delay or unreasonable excuses for inaction. (How much delay is "necessary" and which excuses are "reasonable" can be analyzed by comparing customer input with established performance standards.) Governments can adopt a "marketing" orientation, in the sense that each person in the organization can be trained to empathize with a customer and help resolve the problem—no matter how trivial or openly hostile the question (Coffman, 1986). When disputes occur, most people need a reassuring statement from a public official that he/she understands the problem and is trying to resolve it as soon as possible. Too often, public agencies are so consumed with bureaucratic control that the emotional support needs of citizens are neglected. This results in part from the top-down **command-and-control** type of management structure more commonly found in rules-driven (rather than customer-driven) public bureaucracies.

Rather than maintaining strict Weberian hierarchies for all types of services, empowered and trained public employees can distinguish which strategies are most appropriate for particular situations. The challenge for modern governance is to balance mixed systems of accountability with the introduction of virtual alternatives to become, in Donald Kettl's words, "more agile, dynamic and effective" (2009: 223). Table 5.1 on page 114 traces the **evolution of governance models** from past and present eras.

Historical patterns of governmental accountability, public administration tradition and practice, budget deficits and **crisis management** require the maintenance of top-down command-and-control systems.

Balancing top-down and bottom-up pressures has been identified as a problem for public agencies (Kettl, 1998). Nonetheless, most elected officials prefer to delegate authority to agencies that implement rules from the top. At the same time, they realize that rigid control systems waste resources, stifle individual service, restrict flexibility and impede immediate responsiveness to customers. The networked customer service approach of granting bottom-up, as well as top-down, accountability encourages entrepreneurship by modifying the traditional relationship between citizens, managers, suppliers and elected officials (Sarbaugh-Thompson, 1998). Front-line workers assume the authority to resolve the problem *and* accept the accountability for the results of decisions within pre-determined limits established for routine decisions.

In New Media public service delivery environments, public managers have to balance the two potentially conflicting perspectives: the traditional top-down legal-rational approach *and* the empowered citizen responsive bottom-up process. Without comprehensive employee training, shifting to the bottom-up networked approach too quickly could pose challenges to the rule of law and administrative regulation upon which American government is based. Conversely, not focusing on networked delivery systems and customer needs within a reasonable timeframe increases frustration levels and inhibits accountability, empowerment and responsiveness.

New Roles for Elected Officials

Resolving online customer service disputes may require the occasional intervention of elected officials who provide most of the operating revenue, rules and strategic goals for public managers. As leaders of public service organizations, elected officials play an active role in redesigning processes to accommodate citizen demands. Elected officials can use digital tools to enhance their ability to represent constituents. This could overcome citizens' distrust of public officials and encourage ICT implementation. Citizens, however, are neither elected representatives nor experts in the technical functions of governments. Therefore, they must rely on public managers and other experts to understand the complexity of situations and problems and communicate with them about solutions. Citizens can advance public policy goals and learn self-governance by participating in government activities that affect their interests (Chapter 2). Conversely, public managers can enhance closer collaboration by using digital management systems. As a result, citizens in many governments may now expect more information and a greater range of choices about the types of services available and who will provide and receive them. This places a burden on public managers to select from among the available alternatives those which best respond to citizen preferences in a cost-effective manner. The presence of competing interests creates a problem to be resolved by elected and appointed officials—not a barrier to implementation—when defining customer expectations and closing gaps between expectations, perceptions and performance (U.S. General Services Administration, 2005).

In many public school districts, for example, academies, charter schools and magnet programs are being used to promote parental choice, local control, student achievement and diversity (Chapter 4). Students with special competencies, needs and talents are no longer confined to a one-size-fits-all education delivered within the borders of their residential district. Similarly, corporations have adapted to the new internet-driven world of electronic commerce by realizing that they no longer *own* their customers. Likewise, governments in customer-focused "borderless" and technology-driven public agencies must recognize that they don't *control* their citizens merely because they live in certain geographic jurisdictions. Commitment to enhanced customer service builds confidence and mutual trust, encourages participation in decision making and reinforces democratic political values such as accountability, community control, decentralization, equal access to information and open government.

Unlike the private sector, public agencies must be concerned with a broader set of *non-economic* demands for equality, equity and fairness in the distribution of resources. As legitimate spokespersons for their constituents, elected representatives are responsible for resolving disputes between government officials and individuals who feel they have been unfairly treated. Many local elected officials are eager to perform this **electoral activist** role as representatives and spokespersons for those who elected them (Svara, 1999a). Politicians who try to "selectively" influence individual transactions between front-line workers and citizens, however, make it more difficult for managers to improve an organization's overall customer service (Box, 1999; U.S. General Services Administration, 2005). Without point-of-contact accountability granted to public employees, elected officials who play the *ombudsman* role may also find themselves squeezed between top-down pressures (citizens as voters) and bottom-up demands (citizens as customers). Satisfying the collective needs of these very different constituents' interests could conflict with other pressing public policy goals, such as fiscal control and austerity. Elected officials must be involved as co-partners and mediators with public employees and managers to improve the level of ICT-enabled customer service. With proper theory to guide decisions and ICT tools to engage citizens, there is nothing inherently inconsistent about maintaining political accountability, resolving disputes among varied interests *and* improving customer service.

Conclusion: Balancing Administrative Effectiveness with Political Accountability

The architecture of digital governance makes it ideally suited as a substitute for traditional Weberian command-and-control bureaucracy, discussed in Chapter 1. Unlike traditional agencies, digital delivery systems are continuously interactive, non-hierarchical and available to citizens 24 hours a day, seven days a week. Moreover, the internet's open-source structure permits citizens to access information at their own pace and for their own purposes. Whether or not either party acts on the new sources of communication remains uncertain and depends on the level of confidence and trust between individuals and their governments.

Rather than extending the capacities of government using existing structures, enhanced communication and information technology is viewed as an alternative for improving long-term **administrative effectiveness**. The transactional aspect of digital governance allows citizens, bureaucrats and politicians to learn how to become co-producers of services, sending as well as receiving information and conducting complex transactions online. Inevitably, conflicts among the various stakeholders involved in decision making will occur during the transition; the ultimate test of the viability of digital governance is its ability to change relationships and resolve disputes among affected individuals and institutions.

Public officials know that merely placing more information online does not guarantee that citizens will be satisfied with service provided by public agencies. Governments must empower employees *and* reorient management systems to monitor performance to ensure standards are met. Everyone has new responsibilities, including citizens, politicians and bureaucrats. New Media ICTs provide valuable feedback in determining whether progress is being made. There are now many global success stories available to guide the effort; numerous public agencies have generated tangible performance measures, changed administrative systems to achieve results and delivered on promises of improved service to their customers (Chapter 7). Federal, state and local agencies now have explicit written customer service standards in specific service arenas. These successes can be used to help citizens, elected representatives and public officials perform the difficult task of improving performance. In many jurisdictions, the traditional top-down model of public administration is being supplemented by more flexible, networked and customer-responsive strategies. Benchmarking, best practices, ISO certification, charter marks and quality awards can also be used to compare results, achieve policy goals, highlight successes and define customer service reorientation efforts (Camp, 1989; Coplin and Dwyer, 2000; Keehley, *et al.*, 1997).

There is a pervasive need for empirical research to help guide officials to find successful models or relevant case studies (or any data-based studies at all) for improving public sector performance. When combined with relevant theory, such studies could inform public managers in the continuous struggle to reduce costs, provide better service and increase productivity. The absence of empirical case studies, combined with the need for representation of broader *citizenship* interests and greater **political accountability,** may account for much of the past conflict between service providers and individual recipients of services (DeLeon and DeLeon, 2002; DeLeon and

Denhardt, 2000; Kettl, 1998; Sanderson, 2001; Swiss, 1992; Wilson and Durant, 1994). Research findings generated by successful applications offer public administrators a clearer understanding of customers' needs and how management systems and empowered employees can meet them.

While acknowledging the importance of citizenship, civic engagement and partisanship to maintain accountability, democratic values, equity and pluralist democracy, it is equally important to respect citizens' rights to receive full value for their tax dollars. Public managers cannot excuse inefficient, incompetent or unacceptable employee behavior or failure to meet service standards because some citizens fail to participate as actively as others in all aspects of governance. Public services (even those relating to law enforcement and regulatory compliance actions) can respect customer service standards set by accrediting associations, community associations, other governments or the private sector. If this means drawing from successful cases, methods or techniques of other governments or private providers, then public officials should welcome the challenge and the *opportunity* to show how they, too, can meet citizen demands for improved online customer service while maintaining full service alternatives for special needs citizens.

Key Terms

political responsiveness, 113
administrative values, 114
political values, 114
economic stimulus, 115
American Recovery and
  Reinvestment Act (ARRA), 115
balanced performance standards, 115
bottom-up management, 116
barriers to acceptance, 116
customer service standards, 117
business vs. government
  strategies, 117
Moncton, New Brunswick, 120
Vision 2010, 120
patronage, 121
National Performance Review
  (NPR), 121
New Public Management
  (NPM), 122
New Public Service (NPS), 122
citizenship, 122
President's Management Agenda
  (PMA), 123

competitive sourcing, 124
cyberellas, 124
gender and racial
  mainstreaming, 125
Millennium Development
  Goals, 125
racial and gender equality, 126
empowerment, 128
virtual services, 128
Skype.com, 128
telenetworking, 129
citizen responsiveness, 129
point-of-contact accountability, 130
regulatory compliance, 130
distributive and redistributive
  services, 130
secondary recovery techniques, 131
command-and-control, 131
evolution of governance models, 131
crisis management, 131
electoral activist, 133
administrative effectiveness, 134
political accountability, 134

6 Advancing Digital Governance and Performance Management

e-Government is not about putting thousands of government forms or reams of information online. Rather, it is about government making better use of technology to better serve citizens and improve government efficiency, cutting government's time to make decisions from weeks or months to hours or days.

The President's Management Agenda

The transition from Industrial Age administration to Networked Age digital governance is an ongoing public policy initiative that is changing long-standing behaviors and relationships among bureaucrats, citizens and politicians. If 24/7 availability and convenience, interactivity, customer focus and customization become the norm in the public sector, access will become easier and interactions with government agencies will fundamentally change. Networked digital governance offers significant advantages for those who receive faster and user-friendly services, enhanced opportunities to co-produce results and better value for their taxes or user fees.

In addition to extending the reach of ICTs, digital governance provides a mutual opportunity for both citizens and government to lower costs of transactions, shorten lines and eliminate burdensome paperwork. This, in turn, increases productivity through the merging of human resources and information technology. However, in too many instances, traditional bureaucratic practices prevail: citizens are frustrated with the shoddy service, not just from government, but also from intermediaries and poorly supervised "outsourced" contractors who fail in their basic oversight responsibilities. Making organizational changes permanent is only as effective as leaders' abilities to articulate program goals, obtain accurate information about program performance and overcome barriers to efficient and reliable evaluation and oversight. New leaders of this initiative may not be identifiable in advance, but they are more likely to emerge from the bottom-up in the newly reconfigured networked digital age.

Since the early 1990s, **accountability for performance** has been recognized, among other problems, as one of many dilemmas facing all governments (Behn, 1999; Lamb, 2008; Powner, 2006). Even under the best of circumstances, managing performance is difficult to achieve because demands for services *always* exceed resources and revenue available to meet them. This conundrum has only worsened during the Great Recession as more governments exhaust reserve funds, increase deficit spending and are forced to raise taxes and make program cuts. Managing the performance of individual sub-units of public agencies (budgeting, IT, emergency services, operations, personnel, etc.) is especially difficult during periods of economic slowdown because stakeholders want more, feel justified in requesting more and organize special interest groups or lobbies to pressure politicians to get more. Today, everyone wants a personal "stimulus package" from government. Despite such unrealistic expectations, **performance management** strategies can and should be used to reinforce core values (i.e. collaboration, cost reduction, efficiency, participation, results-measurement, satisfying external customers, teamwork, etc.), measure results and make necessary program adjustments.

This chapter concentrates on the evolution of federal legislative and regulatory authority to improve government performance, public agencies' responsiveness to such efforts and the impact of digital technology on citizens' attitudes towards the advent of online government. Among other issues, the chapter addresses how past policy decisions impact current conditions, whether investments in ICTs have been favorably received by the public and to what extent enhanced internet use has resulted in better government performance.

Legislation and Regulations to Improve Performance and Security

Public administrators must understand how laws, policies and rules govern both traditional and online interactions. Planning and policy decisions are based on collection, interpretation and analysis of accurate objective data from reliable sources, often referred to as **data points**. Gathering and cleaning data is challenging for most organizations and decisions based on such data are only as good as its quality (Milakovich, 2006a; Peters, 2010; Thompson and Strickland, 2002). Increasing reliance on multiple sources of electronic data reinforce the need for accurate and reliable data collection systems. When combined with databases such as CitiStat priority resource allocation system discussed in Chapter 3, public information and communication technologies can enhance privacy, security and performance management capabilities.

Major policy changes have occurred as ICTs have become embedded in daily social interactions and work lives of all stakeholders who must identify, interpret and understand laws and regulations impacting government operations. Among the many laws that have been enacted are the: 1) Administrative Procedure Act (APA) of 1946; 2) Housing Act of 1949; 3) Freedom of Information Act (FOIA) of 1966; 4) Privacy Act of 1974;

5) Paperwork Reduction Act (PRA) of 1980; 6) Computer Security Act of 1987; 7) Government Performance and Results Act of 1993; 8) Clinger-Cohen Act of 1995; 9) Electronic Government Act of 2002; 10) Performance Assessment Rating Tool (PART); 11) the American Recovery and Reinvestment Act of 2009; and 12) the Patient Protection and Affordable Care Act (PPACA) and the Health Care and Education Reconciliation Act of 2010. This is far from a complete list of applicable legislation and regulation, but it is representative of continuing efforts in the United States to improve administrative and ICT performance as well as achieve other substantive public policy goals. Each is discussed briefly below.

The **Administrative Procedure Act (APA) of 1946** recognized the importance of strengthening relationships between accountability, public participation and rulemaking in the post-World War II pre-internet era over six decades ago. The APA still governs how administrative agencies of the U.S. federal government propose and establish regulations and guides federal courts in reviewing agency decisions. Federal agencies proposing new regulations are required to publish them in advance for review and comment by affected businesses in the *Federal Register* (www.gpoaccess.gov/fr/about.html). The APA was Congress' first attempt to make bureaucracy more transparent by encouraging distribution of information to the public on a **need-to-know basis**. Under that principle, the burden rested with the inquiring citizen to demonstrate why information was needed; the presumption was that information was safeguarded unless a strong case could be made to the contrary. So long as public trust in bureaucracy remained high, as it did during the post-World War II era, and no major interests were harmed or threatened, that arrangement was satisfactory. Bureaucratic secrecy went largely unchallenged until the Vietnam War era in the late 1960s, and little information filtered out when agency personnel decided to restrict it.[1]

Significant expansion of federal authority occurred with the passage of the **Housing Act of 1949**, authorizing the issuance of federal mortgage insurance and the construction of public housing. The legislation was part of President Harry Truman's **Fair Deal** program which also mandated citizen participation in a variety of decisions involving federal housing assistance programs, low-rent public housing, slum clearance, rural housing and housing research. The federal government tried, but failed, to induce segments of the private building industry to concentrate on the production of lower priced housing. The Act shaped the growth of American cities and suburbs and affected other public policies in the post-war era. According to one survey, the **Federal Housing Administration (FHA)** mortgage financing program ranks second and urban renewal programs rank fourth on the list of top influences on the post-war American metropolis (Lane and Sohmer, 2000: 292). These laws and programs facilitated the rise in suburban homeownership, destroyed rail transportation systems, spurred the growth of interstate highways and promoted the construction of huge inner-city public housing projects (commonly referred to as urban "ghettos"). The resulting air pollution, clogged highways, suburban sprawl and urban decay still plague many American cities.[2]

Freedom of Information, Open Government and Privacy

The **Freedom of Information Act (FOIA) of 1966** (5 U.S.C. § 552, as amended by Public Law 104-231, 110 Stat. 3048) holds government officials accountable for their actions and those of others. The rationale for this statute is crucial for open government and representative democracy; even more so when substantial responsibility is entrusted to non-elected (administrative) personnel. The statute also responds to the need for transparency in government decision making and operations. Public scrutiny and **sunshine (open government)** and **sunset (closure) laws** increase the public's ability to inquire successfully into the activities of bureaucracy. Publicity is one means of enforcing accountability by encouraging a better-informed citizenry to act more intelligently and purposefully. Sunset laws automatically expire after a set number of years and add another dimension to oversight. By requiring positive legislative action to renew agency authority, some examination of agency performance is more likely to occur. Cursory reviews or near-universal renewals of agency authorizations by legislatures do not serve the purposes of sunshine or sunset legislation. Open government statutes are used as a performance management instruments as part of broader legislative efforts to hold public executives accountable for their actions.

At both state and national level, increasing numbers of legislators respond positively to public pressures and, in some cases, lead public opinion as well as follow it. Furthermore, designated federal oversight entities (such as the **U.S. Congressional Budget Office (CBO)** and **U.S. Government Accountability Office (GAO)**) have been granted increasing authority by Congress to analyze budget requests, conduct oversight investigations, discipline administrative agencies and issue reports critical of program implementation. Executive agencies such as the **U.S. Office of Management and Budget (OMB)** and state bureaus of the budget ("mini-OMBs") are increasingly active in holding operating bureaucracies accountable for performance. Although the focus of most legislatures is on budgeting rather than program management, the exposure provided by the FOIA and its amendments have made it more difficult for bureaucracies to hide wasteful expenditures or avoid the consequences of poor decision making. Unlike the APA, the FOIA and related legislation were based on the principle that the timely provision of information to the American people, upon their request, was a necessary and proper duty of government. The Vietnam War era law presumed a citizen's right to know, with some limitations on the kind of information to be made available (mostly related to national security).

Debates over withholding information intensified during the administration of Lyndon B. Johnson (1963–1969) and were overshadowed by revelations about government cover-ups contained in publications such as the *Pentagon Papers* (Ellsberg, 2002). The effect of the FOIA was to increase the *potential* for citizen access to government briefings, files and records. This statute is increasingly recognized as a means to expose bribery, corruption and mismanagement. In most instances, agency accountability was enhanced because information was brought to light by advocacy interest groups or the mass media. Despite such efforts, trust in government in the United States steadily eroded from the end of the Vietnam War in 1974 until the present (Chapter 10). The FOIA allows agencies broad discretion in the release of information upon request from individuals, interest groups or the media. If an agency declares that releasing data would harm national security, the information remains secret.

President Bill Clinton pledged during the 1992 presidential campaign to open government and, in October 1993, took major steps to fulfill that promise by formally reversing a 12-year policy under presidents George H. W. Bush and Ronald Reagan to withhold government information from the press and the public. Clinton's attorney general, Janet Reno, issued new procedures governing U.S. Justice Department responses to FOIA requests for some departmental documents. The OMB created a new policy requiring executive-branch agencies to make government information, in electronic form, accessible to scholars and librarians, among others. By contrast, the George W. Bush administration virtually suspended the Act under a self-serving national security exception preventing the release of information about decisions leading up to the wars in Afghanistan and Iraq. Bush's suspension of the full implementation of the FOIA, allegedly in the interests of national security, limited access to sensitive information about the activities of armed forces and intelligence agencies in the war on terrorism. (Not surprisingly, requests for information dramatically increased, creating a huge backlog of unprocessed FOIA applications by the end of the Bush presidency in 2009.) Other issues relating to electronic transfer of documents have emerged that will demand attention in the future (Milakovich and Gordon, 2009: 67).

First, access to online electronic data is thought by most observers, including many members of Congress, to be protected under the FOIA, but other troubling questions remain unanswered, some with privacy and security implications.[3] Second, there is growing unease that the wholesale privatization of government services which also took place during the Bush-Cheney administration greatly diminished public access to information about those contracts, primarily because FOIA provisions do not automatically extend to private-sector entities. Nearly 40 states have also passed similar statutes since the revision of FOIA, with varying degrees of enforcement. Free and open exchange of information is crucial for access, accountability and transparency. Clearly, freedom of information continues to have substantial importance, in the eyes of both government officials and citizens who, for myriad reasons, wish to monitor what government does. Without unrestricted access to information, government performance can be neither debated nor improved.

The Obama administration pledged to maintain open and transparent decision making, but has struggled with specific cases. During his first few days in office, Obama issued executive orders tightening ethical rules, enhancing FOIA rules and freezing salaries of White House officials earning more than $100,000 per year. For certain other controversial issues, however, such as those related to allegations of mistreatment and torture of detainees at the infamous *Abu Ghraib* prison in Iraq, the administration has been reluctant to release un-redacted documents and photographs of alleged prisoner abuse, even though grotesque pictures of abuses are widely available on the internet. Recently, New Media technologies have been used to expose tactical and strategic planning for the wars in Afghanistan and Iraq as well as U.S. State Department communiqués. The website **WikiLeaks** was founded in 2006 and claims to have a database of more than one million leaked diplomatic and military documents. In July 2010, WikiLeaks released a compilation of more than 76,900 documents about the war in Afghanistan not previously available for public review. This set off a firestorm of protests from the Obama administration that such sensitive records may jeopardize the lives of U.S. and coalition soldiers serving in the region.[4]

Numerous other laws have been enacted to protect individuals at both the national and state government levels and better safeguard an individual's rights to fair treatment and privacy (Garson, 2006: 156–157). The **Privacy Act of 1974** prohibits federal agencies from accessing personal records unless they are formally investigating an individual. (In mid-1993, the U.S. Supreme Court ruled in **U.S. v. Landano (508 U.S. 165)** that FBI records were not automatically confidential, especially if a criminal defendant was seeking access to relevant information to establish his or her own innocence.)

The **Paperwork Reduction Act (PRA) of 1980** (44 U.S.C. 3501 *et. seq.*) replaced the Federal Reports Act of 1942 and was enacted to relieve businesses from mounting federal information collection and reporting requirements and minimize the paperwork burden for individuals, small businesses, educational and non-profit institutions and other governments resulting from data collection by or for federal agencies. Its purpose was to ensure the greatest possible public benefit from information created, collected, maintained, used, shared and disseminated by or for government. This provision included the reduction of information collection burdens and the improvement of service delivery to the public. It ensured that the collection and disposition of information by or for the federal government is consistent with applicable laws, including laws relating to privacy and confidentiality as well as security of information such as the **Computer Security Act of 1987** (Public Law 100-235) and access to information, including section 552, Title 5 of the legislation. The Act ensures that "communication and information technology is acquired, used and managed for *no other reason* than to improve the success of agency missions" (italics added). Moreover, it strengthened the accountability and responsibility of the Office of Management and Budget (OMB) and all other federal agencies to Congress and to the public for implementing information collection review process, information resources management and related policies and guidelines. The Act was amended in 1986 and 1995 to make **information resources management (IRM)** a tool for managing the contribution of information activities to program performance, and for managing related resources, such as personnel, equipment, funds and technology (U.S. Government Accountability Office, 2000).

The 1987 Computer Security Act was prompted by increasing access to information and use of computers by federal agencies and the vulnerability of confidential data contained in files. This statute required federal agencies to develop security plans for computer systems containing sensitive information. Those plans are subject to review by the **National Institute of Standards and Technology (NIST)** of the **U.S. Department of Commerce**.[5] The law also mandated the creation of a Computer Systems Security and Privacy Advisory Board within the Department of Commerce to identify emerging managerial, technical, administrative and physical safeguard issues relative to computer systems security and privacy. The Board's authority is restricted and does not extend to private sector systems or federal systems which process classified information.

Consumer protection legislation at the national level includes the **Fair Credit Reporting Act**, the **Family Educational Rights and Privacy Act** and the **Fair Credit Billing Act**, also known as the Truth in Lending Act. Congress also established the **Privacy Protection Study Commission** to develop information policies and practices and to look into intrusions on individual privacy by agencies outside the national executive branch.[6] Over half a dozen states have enacted privacy laws, and an even larger number have adopted their own versions of the Fair Credit Reporting Act. In short, there has been considerable government activity in this area, but concern persists that corporate Big Brother may still have too much access to personal records. There are also persistent concerns that "hackers" in *both* the public and private sectors may invade individual privacy, mine data and steal identities to a far greater extent than ever before.[7]

The private sector learned the importance of guaranteeing privacy in the early days of the evolution of the World Wide Web. The growth of online marketing and e-commerce brought with it major copyright, ethical, intellectual property, privacy and security issues. For citizens whose online requests for government information are rejected, the issue immediately becomes: what are the reasons why? Others whose privacy has been compromised by corporate or government surveillance ask why such unwanted intrusions occurred and how can they be prevented. Public agencies and departments decide on a case-to-case basis what information can be made public, based on their respective laws and policies. Federal open government laws are aimed at balancing privacy rights with an individual's right to access public records; government agencies are responsible for enforcing internet privacy and security laws to protect individuals.

Improving Performance, Standards and Results

The **Government Performance and Results Act of 1993** (P.L. 103-62, 107 Stat. 28) was one of the major laws passed during the Clinton-Gore reinvention era which mandated the measurement of performance, productivity and results in all federal executive agencies. The Government Performance and Results Act (GPRA) shifted the focus of government officials from program "inputs" to program execution and measurement of results. The Results Act (as it is known) sets out specific requirements for defining long-term goals, annual performance targets and reporting of actual performance compared to targets. Agencies are required to adopt a strategic planning process based on measurable results related to the agency's mission and objectives. Federal managers are held accountable for achieving public sector results and are also given more discretion to manage programs for optimum performance. The legislation embedded various budgeting and performance management concepts in all federal agencies. In general, the performance management capacities of federal agencies exceed those of all but the largest states and local governments; however, the size and scope of federal programs present additional performance management challenges.

In carrying out the provisions of the GPRA, the OMB Director requires each agency to prepare an annual performance plan covering each program activity set forth in the agency's budget. The plan establishes performance goals and defines the expected level of performance to be achieved by a program's activity. Goals must be expressed in objective, quantifiable and measurable form. Also, there must be a budgetary request to provide specific assets and resources necessary to meet those goals. Performance indicators are used to measure and assess relevant outputs, service levels and outcomes of each program activity. OMB strongly encourages the use of information technology to achieve open government most efficiently.[8] In essence, managers are encouraged to be creative and may even earn bonus compensation in cases of savings. Finally, and with greater frequency, public managers realize that demands to "do more with less" by improving service quality can best be achieved through the enhanced use of IT and digital governance. Attempts to improve performance reflect a long history of partisan bickering over legislative and regulatory attempts to reform bureaucracy.

As the GPRA moved to its implementation stages in the late 1990s, political battles erupted as agencies began submitting departmental management plans to Congress. Republicans sought to cut what they defined as "excess" expenditures and portray Democrats as supporters of "unnecessary and wasteful" spending. Following electoral losses in 1994, President Clinton was no longer working with a Democratic House or Senate. Many feared that the GPRA evaluations would become partisan exercises, with Republicans then in the majority grading unpopular agencies rigorously on criteria unrelated to the requirements of the law. Although President Clinton was opposed to congressional oversight and there were no legislative requirements to do so, various congressional committees reviewed the first performance plans. Indeed, low grades enabled Republicans to gain political support and further criticize the "bloated" federal bureaucracy for wasteful spending and "big government" programs. During its first year under a Republican-led Congress, only 45% of the programs received "effective," "moderately effective" or "adequate" scores; in contrast, by June 30, 2006, 72% of all federal programs were rated as effective or adequate. Citizens can access archived performance ratings for over 1,000 federal executive agencies on the website **www.ExpectMore.gov**.

The **Clinger-Cohen Act of 1996**, formally known as the **Information Technology Management Reform Act (ITMRA)** and co-sponsored by former Representative William F. Clinger, Jr. (R-PA) and Senator William S. Cohen (R-ME), was designed to improve the way that federal agencies acquire, use and dispose of information technology (IT) equipment and software. The Act was the first to make each agency responsible for its own IT acquisition, a strong signal to the bureaucracy that information technology management was going to be legislated and decisions to purchase the best and most effective technology would be required. The Act called upon agencies to implement results-oriented IT planning and emphasized an integrated framework of technology aimed at efficiently performing the business of government. All facets of capital planning are taken into consideration just as they would be in private industry, including cost/benefit ratios, expected life cycles of the technology, flexibility and possibilities for multiple uses.[9]

The **Electronic Government Act of 2002** (P.L. 107-347) was signed by then President George W. Bush on December 17, 2002 and was the first major revision of federal privacy policies since the Privacy Act of 1974. The Act amended the Clinger-Cohen Act and established an Administrator of a new **Office of Electronic Government** within the U.S. Office of Management and Budget.[10] The Administrator is appointed by the president, confirmed by the Senate and assists the OMB Director in implementing electronic government initiatives, including new programs provided for under the Act (U.S. General Accounting Office, 2004). The legislation included efforts to expand the use of ICTs and computer resources to deliver government services more efficiently, making government more citizen-centered, result-oriented and market-based. The overall goals of e-government initiatives were to provide high-quality customer service regardless of whether the citizen contacts an agency by telephone, in person or on the Web, cut operating costs, provide citizens with easy access to government services and make government more transparent and accountable. The E-Government Act served as a model and the primary legislative vehicle to guide federal IT initiatives and strategies to make government information and services more available online. E-government was defined in the Act as:

> the use by the government of Web-based Internet applications and other information technologies, combined with processes that implement these technologies, to—(A) enhance the access to and delivery of government information and services to the public, other agencies and other government entities; or (B) bring about improvements in government to operations that may include effectiveness, efficiency, service quality, or transformation.[11]

The stated purposes of the Act were to: 1) provide effective leadership for federal information technology projects; 2) require the use of internet based IT initiatives to reduce costs and increase opportunities for citizen participation in government; 3) transform agency operations, promoting interagency collaboration for e-government processes; and 4) to make the federal government more transparent and accountable. The 72 page law was divided into five titles and incorporated the language from at least four other bills that were introduced separately in Congress. The five titles of the bill also amended different parts of the United States Code in the areas of federal information policy and security.

Title I defined the job of the administrator as assisting the Director of OMB and the agency's Director of Management, in coordinating the efforts of the administrator of the **Office of Information and Regulatory Affairs**, another OMB unit, to carry out relevant responsibilities for prescribing guidelines and regulations for agency implementation of the Privacy Act, the Clinger-Cohen Act, IT acquisition pilot programs and the Government Paperwork Elimination Act. The Act also required the General Service Administration (GSA) to consult with the Administrator of the Office of Electronic Government on any efforts to promote e-government. Title I established the **Chief Information Officer (CIO) Council**, with the OMB Deputy Director of Management as chair, and detailed its organizational structure and mandate; it also established an E-Government Fund for integrity of information technology projects. Title II focused on enhancing e-government services, establishing performance measures and clarifying OMB's role as the leader and coordinator of federal e-government services. It required agencies to participate in the CIO Council and submit annual agency e-government status reports. Executive agencies are required to adopt electronic signature methods and the federal courts and regulatory agencies must establish websites containing information useful to citizens. The measure also established privacy requirements for agency use of personally identifiable information and required privacy guidelines be established for federal websites. The U.S. Code was amended by adding a new section facilitating procedures to encourage agencies to use and share in savings for procurement and allowing state or local governments to use federal supply procurement procedures for IT purchases. Importantly, the title also mandated the development of common protocols for geographic information systems (GIS).

Title III is known as the **Federal Information Security Management Act (FISMA) of 2002**, and superseded similar language in the Homeland Security Reform Act of 2002. It also amended a sub-chapter of U.S. Code stipulating the general authority, functions and responsibilities of the OMB Director and individual agencies to develop and maintain federal information security policies and practices. Agencies operating or controlling national security systems must preserve appropriate levels of information security and are required to conduct annual independent evaluations. FISMA amended the Clinger-Cohen Act by requiring the Secretary of Commerce to promulgate security standards for federal information systems. The role of the National Institute of Standards and Technology (NIST) was defined to develop standards, guidelines and minimum requirements for information systems used by federal agencies or contractors as well as replacing the existing Computer System Security and Privacy Advisory Board with the Information Security and Privacy Advisory Board. Title IV authorized appropriations for the bill and Title V specified the Confidential Information Protection and Statistical Efficiency Act of 2002, establishing limits on the disclosure of data and information by government agencies and designating the OMB Director as responsible for overseeing confidentiality and disclosure policies. It also identified the Bureau of the Census, the Bureau of Economic Analysis and the Bureau of Labor Statistics as "designated statistical agencies" and outlined their responsibilities regarding the use, handling and sharing of data (Herdon, Cullen and Relyea, 2006: 39–42).

Former President George W. Bush's emphasis on performance management was evident in the **Performance Assessment Rating Tool (PART)** which incorporated five government-wide initiatives from the President's Management Agenda (PMA): 1) strategic management of human capital; 2) competitive sourcing (i.e. privatization); 3) improved financial performance; 4) budget and performance integration; and 5) expanded electronic government (Chapter 5). Government officials as well as the American people can follow how well different departments and agencies are implementing those initiatives by using an executive-branch management scorecard.[12]

The PART identified department or agency performance goals on each of the five initiatives listed above by using the basic (and perhaps oversimplified) principle of a traffic light to determine a program's ranking by giving three scores: red for failing, yellow for progress, green for success. The pilot effort began in FY 2003 with scores given after agencies filled out yes/no questionnaires composed of 25 questions related to 1) program purpose and design, 2) strategic planning, 3) program management and 4) program results. Twice a year, scorecards are distributed, one for management and the other for general program performance. (These are separate because even if agencies are efficiently managed, the PART ranking may be irrelevant when agencies' missions have changed or been achieved.) Initially, the Departments of Defense, State, Health and Human Services, and Justice all received red lights. A year and a half after the release of the PMA, 26 federal agencies received red scores on *competitive outsourcing* and only six made progress on *strategic management of human capital*. The simple scorecard reflected a measurement system then used in businesses, which President Bush wanted to apply to give him greater leverage over what he called the federal government's "vast empire" of programs, agencies and bureaucrats. Updated performance ratings of individual agencies were accessible on the OMB website.

OMB developed the PART to assess and improve program performance via a formal review process that identified a program's strengths and weaknesses. OMB considered completing a PART review to constitute compliance with the GPRA (above). There was concern that performance management initiatives were a passing fad, but most organizations agreed that the Bush agenda deserved consideration and gave PART generally positive reviews. Despite some methodological reservations, the GAO was generally supportive of PART and OMB evaluations. The methodology was recognized in July 2005 by the independent and prestigious Harvard University Kennedy School of Government *Innovations in American Government* Awards, administered by the Council for Excellence in Government. The awards recognize innovative government programs that take a creative approach to solving significant public problems.[13] Despite its apparent success, PART remained controversial because of its ideological bias toward contracting out and privatization as well as its limited integration with agency budgeting processes. Program reporting requirements largely disappeared after the Bush administration left office. President Obama initiated major policy initiatives which superseded the limited scope of the PART process.

The **Patient Protection and Affordable Care Act of 2010 (PPACA)** was signed into law by President Obama on March 23, 2010. Along with the **Health Care and Education Reconciliation Act of 2010** (signed a few days later), this legislation was a compromise version of the health care reform agenda of the Democratic Congress and the Obama administration. The PPACA includes numerous health-related provisions which take effect over a four-year period, including expanding Medicaid eligibility, incentives for businesses to provide health care benefits, prohibiting denial of coverage/claims based on pre-existing conditions, establishing health insurance exchanges, subsidizing insurance premiums and support for medical research. The Act authorizes $20 billion for technological applications for improving health care delivery and medical records systems. The CBO estimates that the net effect (including the reconciliation act) will expand coverage and reduce the federal deficit by $143 billion over the first decade, but the accuracy of this projected figure is hotly debated. The costs of these provisions are projected to be offset by a variety of taxes, fees and cost-saving measures, such as new Medicare taxes for high-income brackets and fees on medical devices and pharmaceutical companies; there is also a controversial tax penalty for citizens who do not obtain health insurance (unless they are exempt due to low income or other reasons). This and other provisions of the act have been challenged by 20 states in the federal courts as violations of the separation of powers clause. As of this writing, two lawsuits brought by states have been overturned and two others (Florida, Virginia) have been upheld. The future status of the Act remains uncertain.

Politics and Performance Management

Developing and enforcing reliable performance measures which are *both* outcome-oriented and consistent with public expectations is a major challenge for legislatures and chief executives. Designing effective **performance measurement** and policy management tools is much more difficult in the public sector than in private business where the "bottom-line" profits and return on investment (ROI) serve as visible yardsticks for success. No comparable comparative measures exist for government programs.

Laws and regulations define goals and significantly impact what public administrators can and cannot accomplish. Issues of communication, privacy, procurement, security and management, as well as oversight responsibilities and responses to emergencies are all guided by legislative rules and regulations governing how governments conduct business. (This is not to be confused with government oversight of private communications and e-commerce, but rather relates to government officials and private citizens using portals and websites to access information and conduct transactions online.)

Since the 1990s, federal program effectiveness and public accountability have been impacted by New Media communications and a renewed focus on results, service quality and customer satisfaction. Nonetheless, rational efforts to improve performance are nearly always subject to partisan politics, as both political parties view with suspicion legislation proposed by the other; many regard such proposals merely as political attempts to win elections rather than genuine efforts to reform public management processes. For example, the Results Act directed federal agencies to develop performance measures ultimately aimed at delivering better services with fewer resources. This led to numerous pilot projects in federal agencies, as well as in some state and local governments. They were designed to increase the potential for more effective (or perhaps selective) use of expenditures to improve or terminate ineffective (or politically unpopular) programs. Sponsors argued that government performance should not be judged solely on the basis of amounts of money spent or activities conducted, but rather on whether ideas and approaches produce real, tangible results for the taxpayer's dollar. The pragmatic approach implied in such a strategy may be a long-term goal, but does not necessarily reflect the political realities of fragmented congressional budgeting processes.

Productivity and results measurement will continue to grow in importance, if for no other reason than public awareness of the limited resources available to successfully implement public policies. Reforms may be delayed by electioneering and congressional control of the federal budget. For example, it wasn't until November 2007, 14 years *after* the passage of the Results Act, that President Bush signed an executive order directing all federal agencies to designate agency performance improvement officers as a central point of contact and accountability. Each agency has now created a government-wide system for tracking and reporting performance and results. The order embeds into the machinery of government performance management reforms begun under both Presidents Clinton and Bush, such as strategic planning, regular program assessments and the evaluation of employees based on the performance of their agencies' programs. So long as future presidents maintain the structure created by GPRA, new political administrations will inherit a network of skilled senior career executives capable of improving performance and making results of agency programs publicly accessible. Future administrations not committed to performance improvement, results-driven management, or transparency of results would have to justify decisive reasons for changing course.

While each of the initiatives described above have particular strengths and weaknesses, problems with design and implementation often limited their impact. There are two fundamental problems with the way government currently approaches performance management. First, many measures used to assess performance are not operationally useful. Federal managers tend to view performance measures as a paperwork exercise to keep them from getting into trouble with the GAO or the Office of Management and Budget. Even though PART is the federal government's primary performance management tool, only 23% of federal managers report having knowledge of its details, and just one in four members of this small sub-set say they use PART data when making decisions (Kettl, 2009: 172–173). Perhaps they don't use it because they often aren't measuring the right things. What does a yellow light mean? The second major problem with the measurements currently being used is that they are not meaningful to the public or external constituencies.

Government focuses on counting and reporting the activities of particular agencies, such as how many inspections of slaughterhouses were conducted by the Department of Agriculture last year or how many food companies were inspected by the Food and Drug Administration (FDA). Performance evaluation should instead emphasize public outcomes and results—whether there were spikes in food-borne illness—rather than keeping track of programmatic activities only tangentially related to results. The best way to avoid such problems in the future is to establish a system of effective, operational indicators to identify those government programs which are and are not working, and determine what needs to be fixed. In other words, performance management systems need "leading indicators," not lagging ones. There are some guidelines for the current administration and its chief performance officers to follow to enhance the chances of success.

1) **Define goals up front.** Create useful measurements by identifying what it is you seek to accomplish. Once you have a clear objective or standard of performance, you can work backwards to create effective measures to judge performance.
2) **Keep it simple.** The key to effective oversight is looking at the right measures, not the most measures. Focusing on a limited number of items, which are directly linked to your goals, will also make measurements useful to managers and ensure they do not place an undue collection and analysis burden on an organization.
3) **Make data transparent and accessible.** Releasing information publicly will help engage the general public in the work of government, as well as allowing measurement experts in academia and business to analyze data and offer ideas to improve federal management. Transparency also creates an incentive for agencies to do a better job of collecting and using data.
4) **Release data in real time.** Old information reveals how well an agency did. Managers need up-to-the-minute data to help improve how they are going to do.
5) **Listen to the people who know best.** There is no better source of information on the health of federal organizations than the people who work in them. Look at the 2008 Best Places to Work in the Federal Government (bestplacestowork.org) rankings, which measure employee engagement at federal agencies.
6) **Don't try and "Reinvent."** Build on what already exists. The Obama administration should reexamine the Performance Assessment Rating

Tool (PART) and the Government Performance and Results Act (GPRA) and highlight information that is relevant to managers and salient to the public.

7) *Make performance management a top presidential priority.* Establishing a Chief Performance Officer (CPO) is a step in the right direction and an encouraging sign. Moving forward, the question is whether or not the president's whole leadership team, including Cabinet secretaries, will prioritize this issue and hold managers accountable for measuring performance.

(Steir, 2009)

Governments generally fall behind in managing performance because they rely on "lagging indicators" to evaluate agency performance. In other words, future decisions are based on data collected in the past. This often results in a "too little too late" abdication of oversight responsibilities. When **Bernard Madoff's** massive **Ponzi scheme** was uncovered, it was evident that the **U.S. Securities and Exchange Commission (SEC)** under the Bush administration was aware of his activities years earlier but unable (or unwilling) to intervene. Worse, the SEC failed to take action in a number of other cases because of its "hands-off" ideology regarding financial regulation of any sort. Former SEC Chairman Christopher Cox (2005–2009), a former Republican Congressman from Newport Beach, California, was adamantly opposed to federal regulation of business and applied that ideology to agency management. The same *laissez-faire* attitudes prevailed in other life-threatening incidents, natural disasters exacerbated by human errors. It wasn't until the dikes failed in New Orleans and thousands of people were stranded on rooftops by Hurricane Katrina that it became apparent that the Federal Emergency Management Agency (FEMA) was broken and unable to respond. Years before the massive oil spill despoiled the pristine environment in the Gulf of Mexico in the summer of 2010, federal watchdog agencies warned about the hazards of deep-water drilling operations. Oil companies, such as BP, countered that environmental "regulations" covering on-shore and shallow-water operations forced them to utilize the riskier deep-water drilling procedures.

In another embarrassing case, the **Consumer Product Safety Commission (CPSC)** became a target for overhaul only *after* toxic toys manufactured in China were recalled. President Obama addressed these issues and elevated the responsibilities of protecting consumers by creating a new executive bureau that will consolidate employees and responsibilities from a host of other regulatory bodies, including the Federal Reserve, the Federal Trade Commission, the Federal Deposit Insurance Corporation and even the Department of Housing and Urban Development. When fully operational, the new **Consumer Financial Protection Bureau** in the U.S. Department of Treasury is expected to have hundreds of employees and a budget of up to $500 million. In all these cases and many others, negative early warning signals were ignored.

Performance Management and the Obama Administration

In April 2009, President Obama named a Washington-area entrepreneur and management consultant Jeffery Zients as the federal government's first **Chief Performance Officer (CPO)**. Zients replaced Nancy Killefer, who awkwardly withdrew as Obama's first pick for the top federal management position earlier in February to avoid controversy over issues related to her personal income taxes. Zients also serves as deputy director for management at the Office of Management and Budget. Anything but an outsider, Zients is a multi-millionaire who made his fortune as a management consultant who ran *Portfolio Logic*, a consulting firm that invests in business services and health care companies. Zients is a connected Washington insider who served as chief executive officer and chairman of the Washington-based Advisory Board Company and as head of the Corporate Executive Board. Zients also launched an unsuccessful bid with other Washington-area investors in 2005 to buy the Washington Nationals baseball team (Lunney, 2009).

President Obama focused attention on government accountability and program efficiency early in his administration. He asked department heads during their first cabinet meeting for specific proposals to cut their budgets. Obama proposed the elimination of dozens of government programs shown to be wasteful or ineffective, adding that there will be "no sacred cows, and no pet projects." Obama's Six Themes for deciding which programs to cut look remarkably similar to the principles applied by Clinton and Bush:

1) Put performance first.
2) Ensure responsible spending of American Recovery and Reinvestment Act (ARRA).
3) Transform the federal workforce.
4) Manage across sectors by partnering with the private and non-profit sectors and collaborating across levels of government.
5) Reform federal contracting and acquisition.
6) Install transparency, technology and participatory democracy.[14]

Assessing the Impact of Technology

Public attitudes toward the internet and use of government websites and social media are inconsistent. Today, at least two-thirds of all adults regularly use the internet, including one-third who log-on at work. Utilization rates are even higher among minorities, teenagers and young adults.

Internet use varies along age, economic, gender, generational and racial lines, being very prevalent among people under age 50 but not nearly as widespread among those over 65. Although the internet promises increased civic participation for some, minorities and less-educated individuals are being left behind. Controlling for education level and income, some studies suggest that whites are more likely than either African Americans or Hispanics to seek information about politics online (Alvarez and Nadler, 2001). Whites, blacks and Latinos are equally likely to access government information using digital technologies, but blacks and Latinos are *more* likely than whites to view government use of social media as helpful and informative (Pew Internet and American Life Project, 2010: 5–6). More than one-third of all those who access the internet can be classified as frequent users (Figure 6.1).

What do citizens want most from online government? The research firm of Peter D. Hart and Robert M. Teeter investigated experiences and expectations among 1,003 citizens, 150 government officials in federal, state and local government, and 155 institutional customers of government in the business and non-profit sectors.[15] The findings considered potential uses of online services, benefits of use, how quickly the technology should develop and concerns about the digital divide. There are still signs of an expanding knowledge gap in terms of education and income, as internet use is nearly universal among college graduates, but remains a less common experience for those without high school diplomas (Pew Internet and American Life Project, 2010: 12). Technical skills and sufficient funds to own a computer and connect to a browser service are required; the economic recession has amplified differences between the internet "haves" and "have-nots."

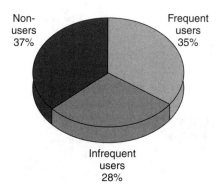

Figure 6.1 Americans' Internet Use
  Source: Hart-Teeter (2003)

While the public expresses a generally positive view of the internet, many still have deeply held concerns about privacy and question online security for higher level transactions. Three-quarters of all internet users say that ICTs have had a positive effect on their lives. Most users, however, do not completely trust the Web for financial transactions: over one-half say that making banking or credit card transactions over the internet is "just somewhat" or "not at all safe." The combination of attitudes—very positive, but not entirely trusting—extends to how people think about government presence on the internet as well. Despite such reservations, a majority of internet users in the United States take advantage of what government has made available online: fully two-thirds report having visited at least one of numerous federal, state and local government websites. This represents about half of the general public. Among those most likely to have visited government websites, nearly three-quarters are "frequent internet users" who go online several times a day compared with slightly more than one-half who are "infrequent users" (Figure 6.2). Americans use ICTs more commonly at the federal level than at state and local levels, but that pattern is changing as more governments shift to digital service provision.

Americans seem generally satisfied with their virtual government encounters. Among internet users who have visited a government website, seven of 10 rate the quality of the sites as "excellent" or "good." Over 60% said that it is "very" or "fairly easy" to find the information needed on government websites; only 36% found this to be a "fairly" or "very hard" task. In addition, frequent internet users were more likely than less frequent users to say it is easy to find what they need. Businesses and non-profits also are accessing the internet at higher rates. A large majority of the business and non-profit leaders interviewed say they have used government websites, and those who have visited these sites rate them favorably.

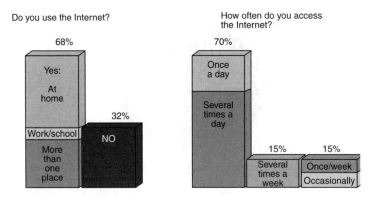

Figure 6.2 Online America
Source: Hart-Teeter (2003)

Many also indicate that these sites have helped their organization. The survey did not evaluate the extent of internet use for more advanced searches for political information on blogs, portals or social networks. Among those who report that their business or organization interacts at least "sometimes" with the federal government, three-quarters say that being able to find information or conduct transactions over the internet has made it easier to find information or conduct business with federal agencies. In addition, a majority of business and non-profit leaders say that the ability to find government information on the internet has made it easier for them to comply with government regulations.

In the surveys conducted by states, and in the studies conducted by international research organizations, the most common services which respondents say they want to be provided online were: 1) renewing a driver's license; 2) voter registration; 3) state park information and reservations; 4) voting on the internet; 5) access to one-stop shopping (one portal for all government services); 6) ordering birth, death and marriage certificates; 7) filing state taxes; 8) obtaining hunting and fishing licenses; and 9) accessing medical information. Some local governments now permit licensing and permit renewal online.[16] Desirable features were followed most often by voter registration, obtaining state park information and making park reservations. Another common theme is the notion of one-stop shopping for government services, or the ability to access specific government information, such as medical or health care data. (For an expanded list of services available online see Appendix A.)

Citizens' Attitudes towards E-Government Services

What do citizens expect from online services? Although the public in general sees the potential for better government, they also see technology as making an important contribution to a more participatory democracy. Nearly three-quarters of adults (including two in three who do not use the internet) believe that people's ability to communicate with their elected representatives is enhanced with e-government (Chapter 2). African Americans and Latinos are more likely than whites to view government use of social media as helpful and informative (Pew Internet, 2010: 39). That the public evaluates government not only as consumers of public services, but also as participatory citizens, is confirmed by data comparing public attitudes towards government with government officials'. Figure 6.3 shows that citizens consider accountability to be the most important benefit, whereas public officials recognize greater access to information and more convenient services as most important.

When asked to name the most important outcome of internet engagement, most adults choose greater participation and a more informed citizenry, compared with a smaller number who opt for more efficient, cost-effective and convenient government services. Nearly three in four

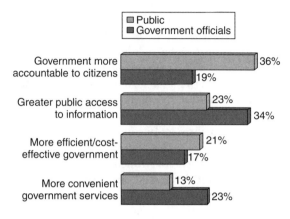

Figure 6.3 Most Important Benefits of E-Government
Source: Hart-Teeter (2003)

Americans believe that their ability to communicate with elected representatives will improve with time and greater access to ICTs. Predictably, government officials are also likely to see greater public involvement as an outcome—almost 80% say that people's ability to communicate with their elected officials will get much or somewhat better, and 75% believe that the government as a whole will be more accountable to its citizens—although they are more likely to believe that digital access will result in easy-to-use and convenient services and improved coordination among all governments. This appears to be reinforced by the meteoric rise of social networking, as a recent study found that 91 of 100 United States Senators have a *YouTube* channel and 87 have a *Facebook* page (Perera, 2010).

Business and non-profit leaders are also more optimistic than the general public that internet access will result in better services, but they are more skeptical that accountability will improve. Strong majorities believe that people's ability to get information from government will improve and that government will be able to offer more convenient services. Cynicism remains high. Although a solid majority of respondents expect that their ability to communicate with elected officials will improve, only about one-half think that government accountability will get better (34% saying that it will not change, only 12% saying that it will actually get worse). Perhaps this is due to a perception that greater communication does not always equal more accountability. Americans see the benefits of online government as more than better or cost-efficient services, regarding ICTs as a way for citizens to become more involved.

Despite these generally optimistic opinions, government has suffered for the last several decades from an increasing lack of public confidence and trust. Many analysts, observers and practitioners believe that this trend can be reversed by the successful implementation of ICTs. Newer research takes into account the public's perception of online risk and deals with privacy and security concerns. Growing public awareness has been brought about partially by the media attention regarding high-profile security breaches. Additionally, the public is becoming increasingly aware of how pervasively data is used by internet marketeers for "spamming." Three critical variables in an attempt to rebuild public trust are 1) the establishment of a privacy policy for personal and proprietary information, 2) information misuse safeguards and 3) online security, particularly for financial transactions and online payments. Only about one in five non-e-commerce users trust that the government will keep records confidential. One issue of concern is that governments share too much data; although customers believe that will result in better service, they are concerned with the ability to maintain data integrity. These concerns must be addressed to insure the restoration of trust in government as well as increase the rate of adoption of e-gov.

Does the availability of online options improve customer satisfaction with the services they receive? Despite reservations, most Americans say they accomplish most of what they want to do on government websites (Pew Internet, 2010: 16). Ultimately, the value added by expanded use of ICTs is essentially a function of perceived value to the user. Because government provides so many different channels of service delivery in order to meet the needs of all users and carry out its sovereign duties, the success of ICTs will be contingent upon the ability to provide superior multi-channel service in a rapid and efficient manner. By a slim margin, more citizens still prefer the use of telephone rather than online contact with government officials. Satisfaction is measured in terms of expectation vs. actual experience. Users expect that information will be easier to find, access and use. Their experience and techno-savvy behavior will be a major indicator of how much government is committed to improving services to citizens and businesses. According to citizen surveys, some of the benefits of participating in e-gov that would be satisfying are speed of transactions, convenience (no standing in line), no hours, more accurate information by eliminating human error, off-site transacting (home or work), cost effectiveness and better accessibility. Concerns among business users that influence their satisfaction are the lack of person-to-person contact, poor quality of information, privacy, security and the difficulty or impossibility to ask questions. Despite the concerns and lack of familiarity with ICTs, businesses and citizens are generally more satisfied with the e-gov experience than with traditional government.[17]

Notwithstanding shared concerns about security, privacy and access, all stakeholders want to be better informed about ongoing public policy initiatives (especially those affecting them personally) and the full range of benefits that government agencies have realized from investments in internet technology, including enhanced internal administration and better coordination across federal, state and local levels of government. Fully three-quarters of government officials report that their agency or division has increased its resources devoted to information technologies such as the internet; 84% believe that these technologies have contributed to better public outreach; 75% say that this has helped their internal administration; but only 29% of the public (including 49% of frequent internet users and 26% of infrequent users) and 37% of business leaders are at all familiar with e-gov.[18]

Despite general support for technology, opinion polls consistently show that Americans believe that as much as 48% of every federal tax dollar is wasted. Plainly, the public does not believe that it is getting its money's worth from wide range of government services it pays for. The more familiar that people become with digital governance and the more importance they place on expanding it, the more they will prefer using tax dollars to pay for it. Nearly two-thirds of all adults who put a high priority on investing in digital government believe it should be paid for through tax dollars, compared with only one-quarter who place a low priority on ICTs and feel the same. In addition, 60% of people who are "very" or "fairly familiar" with ICTs favor paying for digital government through tax dollars, compared with only one-third of those "not at all familiar" with ICT initiatives who say the same.

As more governments pursue goals of providing public services that work better and cost less, more public agencies will enter into different types of creative public–private partnerships to implement innovative communication and information technologies to more efficiently deliver services to citizens. All stakeholders in this process must relearn basic and (sometimes) advanced skills to meet citizen requirements. Public officials will inevitably be called upon to facilitate the transition (Svara, 2009).

Conclusions: Has D-Gov Improved Public Sector Results?

Despite earnest attempts by the American Congress and recent presidents to achieve program results, communicate with constituents, improve government performance and infuse the public sector with the spirit of competition and free-enterprise entrepreneurship, the divisive environment in which politics, policy making and program implementation take place cannot be ignored. Political reforms, often recycled from the past, can contribute to positive results, but they may also isolate certain groups of citizens and pressure public administrators to respond defensively. Campaign rhetoric always stresses the aim of more effective government and better value for tax dollars. After being elected, however, chief executives are often frustrated in their attempts to push through their own political agendas. President Obama's impatience with Congress was clearly evident during the consumer protection, health care and financial reform debates in Congress during 2009–2010. Although elected on promises, politicians are ultimately judged by the electorate by results; success of administrative policies is inextricably linked to the international, state and local politics that surround them. President Obama's leadership will be challenged to find policy agreement with the Republican-dominated 2011–2012 House of Representatives.

Progress and innovation in pluralist democracy results from good laws imposed through power struggles to develop policies and regulations with lasting effects. Circumstances and priorities shift, however, as they did in November 2010, reflecting the unpredictable nature of politics which ultimately governs the course of administrative reforms. Management decisions in government are not simply choices to better utilize resources; they are rarely motivated by economic determinants alone, but by political forces as well. Both the Clinton and George W. Bush management reform agendas (as well as those of presidents before them) offered visions to achieve important procedural and substantive goals of their administrations. Just as Bill Clinton could not escape the personal scandal surrounding and eventually enveloping his administration, the broader environment had a significant impact on the outcome of Bush's Presidential Management Agenda.

When George W. Bush ran for office in 2000, almost no one foresaw the dramatic events of 9/11 or Hurricane Katrina or how his administration would react to them. His consequent actions, especially the decision to aggressively pursue the war on terrorism on Iraqi soil, overshadowed much of his overall reform agenda. Management decisions came into play with the creation of massive government bureaucracies with new 24/7 missions, the Department of Homeland Security (DHS) and the Office of the Director of National Intelligence (DNI). Issues of particular importance involved executive branch expansion and reorganization, contracting out, faith-based initiatives and personnel reallocations. Ironically, despite Bush's campaign rhetoric about more efficient management of smaller government, his tactical decisions to pursue an increasingly costly and unpopular war in Iraq, cut domestic programs and increase the size of bureaucracy reversed all of the progress on budgetary, deficit reduction, jobs growth and regulatory reform achieved under Clinton.

Controversy over the best strategies for managing performance in the Networked Digital Age reflects the centuries-old debate about the "proper" relationship among politics, policy and private management of public-sector functions (Chapter 5). Public administrators are responsible for analyzing options and recommending policies to elected political leaders who, in turn, decide which alternatives to adopt. Rather than assuming the ideological superiority of one model over another (as did many Bush appointees), public managers need to be more informed about fact-based strategic options that best achieve the goals of specific public policy areas. Is the customer-centered entrepreneurial approach applicable to all sectors of public management? For example, which model, or combination of approaches, best achieves immigration reform while overseeing day-to-day operations of airports, border patrol and customs enforcement and also maintains responsibility for public expenditures? Is privatization of public functions a practical alternative or an abdication of political accountability? The ongoing challenge for public administrators is to remain as neutral and detached as possible from the politics of administration and to better understand the results of policy decisions.

Senior public administrators are cross-pressured by conflicting ideological demands and must understand the theoretical as well as practical foundations of alternative performance management strategies. Compared to the early 1990s, greater numbers of administrators now possess the authority, as well as the knowledge and management tools, to improve performance. During the reinvention era (1993–2001), critics accused the Clinton-Gore administration of changing government management practices to run operations "too much" like a business. On the other hand, many bureaucrats resisted reform attempts because they believed their positions were threatened by a reinvented (and downsized) federal government. For many, the worst was yet to come.

The George W. Bush administration (2001–2009) selectively endorsed some of the Clinton reforms but actively promoted shifting federal program responsibility away from government entities to faith-based, non-governmental or private contractors through a controversial strategy of privatization to achieve partisan policy goals. This attempt failed to yield positive results. Without objective research-based data, political forces nearly always restrict decision-making options and thwart management reforms (Milakovich, 2006b). Administrators and policy makers need objective data to decide whether to support the incremental public-oriented reforms of the past, encourage the greater use of private-market-driven options (such as charter schools, contracting out, privatization or vouchers), or form cooperative partnerships with non-governmental organizations. Such decisions require solid theory-based research findings in the areas identified above to bolster support for recommended policy changes and to provide reliable advice to elected officials. Ultimately, citizens exercising democratic freedoms and responsibilities are the final judges of the success or failure of such efforts.

The proving ground for performance management reforms has dramatically changed since President Obama's election in 2008; the success of many U.S. public agencies, and the leaders who direct them, is now measured in practical terms by assisting citizens whose lives have been disrupted by downsizing, unemployment, floods, hurricanes, fires, tornados and snow storms, as well as protecting domestic security and fighting the war against terrorism. Too many citizens have lost their homes, jobs or retirement accounts and are being gouged by profit-driven health care institutions. President Obama succeeded in fulfilling many of his campaign promises to correct these conditions, but millions of Americans are still suffering from slow economic recovery.

The Obama-Biden administration encountered monumental economic problems which dictated many of its initial policy decisions. The use (or misuse) of massive government spending initiated by Bush to directly subsidize large corporations and financial institutions and by Obama to subsidize state and local government only heightened the "where's my bailout?" mentality, increased debt and placed greater pressures on public budgets and regulators. Better program management, information technology, performance measurement and changes in budgetary processes won't alter that reality until the economy improves——thereby accelerating tax revenues. Nor will audits, evaluations or efficiency measures alone close the gap between existing revenues and insatiable demands for greater spending to stimulate the economy. Budgeting requires prioritizing spending decisions to overcome the impacts of scarcity—something that governments have never been well equipped to do. Changes in budgetary processes can make the elusive solutions more obvious and (perhaps) easier to implement. This creates a focus on achieving results, the yield of technology.

All governments face difficult choices in the future. Those who advocate more investments in ICTs must compete with other powerful interests who benefit from the status quo. This is not to say that digital government cannot and should not be parcelled out and pursued in more precise segments. It is likely that successful implementation of ICTs will heavily depend on the ability to build support from the "bottom-up" given the practical complexities of implementation described in this and earlier chapters. Rather it is to say that any such segmentation should be situated within a broader and more holistic perspective of connected governance. That local and national solutions should be framed within this wider systems perspective enables better recognition of the interrelated dimensions of change both inside and outside of the public sector.

As important as are the questions raised in this chapter, the ultimate success of digital governance goes beyond merely viewing the public as a "customer" or as a service recipient—ICT performance management strategies must also facilitate strengthening democratic and corporate accountability and more socially inclusive and responsible governance. The resulting amalgam of social and technology policy should be based on the best available, timely and accurate decision making from new sources of information. Improvements in the relevance and transparency of public policy decisions serve as a vehicle for rebuilding trust in government. Digital governance demands that technology becomes not only a driver of more diverse service channels for more sophisticated users (a critically important group often spurring innovation and service improvement), but also a platform for expanding participative capacities for all citizens.

Key Terms

accountability for
performance,136
performance management, 137
data points, 137
Administrative Procedure Act
(APA) of 1946, 138
need-to-know basis, 138
Housing Act of 1949, 138
Fair Deal, 138
Federal Housing Administration
(FHA), 138
Freedom of Information Act
(FOIA) of 1966, 139
sunshine (open government)
laws, 139
sunset (closure) laws, 139
U.S. Congressional Budget Office
(CBO), 139
U.S. Government Accountability
Office (GAO), 139
U.S. Office of Management and
Budget (OMB),139
WikiLeaks, 141
Privacy Act of 1974, 141
U.S. v. Landano (508 U.S. 165), 141
Paperwork Reduction Act (PRA)
of 1980, 141
Computer Security Act
of 1987, 142
information resources management
(IRM), 142
U.S. Department of Commerce, 142
National Institute of Standards
and Technology (NIST), 142
Fair Credit Reporting Act, 142
Family Educational Rights and
Privacy Act, 142
Fair Credit Billing Act, 142

Privacy Protection Study
Commission, 142
Government Performance and
Results Act of 1993, 143
www.ExpectMore.gov, 144
Clinger-Cohen Act of 1995, 144
Information Technology
Management Reform Act
(ITMRA), 144
Electronic Government Act of
2002, 144
Office of Electronic
Government, 144
Office of Information and
Regulatory Affairs, 145
Chief Information Officer (CIO)
Council, 145
Federal Information Security
Management Act (FISMA) of
2002, 146
Performance Assessment Rating
Tool (PART), 146
Patient Protection and Affordable
Care Act (PPACA) of 2010, 147
Health Care and Education
Reconciliation Act of 2010, 147
performance measurement, 148
Bernard Madoff, 151
Ponzi scheme, 151
U.S. Securities and Exchange
Commission (SEC), 151
Consumer Product Safety
Commission (CPSC), 151
Consumer Financial Protection
Bureau, 151
Chief Performance Officer
(CPO), 151
internet use, 153

7 Applying Digital Technologies to Improve Public Services

More organizations understand that it is critical to collaborate across boundaries that previously divided them from others within and outside ... because as the complexity of issues grows, people are beginning to understand that any one organization can only do so much.

Peter Senge *et al.*, *The Necessary Revolution*

Since the emergence of the Information Age a generation ago, e-commerce and digital technologies have been applied to enhance nearly every business process as well as many aspects of government operations. Expanded availability and new forms of communication, information transfer, education and training are driving forces behind the push for citizen-centric virtual government, detailed in Chapters 3 and 4. The benefits of collaborative business–government–citizen connections are becoming more apparent with faster **broadband internet connectivity** leading to higher levels of convenience in dealing with commercial and governmental enterprises. Even during the economic recession, sales grew steadily by more than 10% per year in the technology sector, suggesting that further expansion of ICTs will improve productivity in the post-recessionary era. As more people use the internet to connect with government agencies—and more agencies link with each other, employees and businesses—society as a whole experiences a positive transformational effect.

Widespread application of ICTs opens new multi-channel interactions between stakeholders in entirely different ways. Rising public expectations encourage political candidates, interest groups and government service providers to create more customized online experiences. The integration of knowledge management (KM) systems with ICTs is widely regarded as a vehicle for increasing governmental efficiency at all levels and within all functions (Blackstone, Bognanno and Hakim, 2005; Kumar, Mukerji, Butt and Persaud, 2007; Tolbert, Mossberger and McNeal, 2008: 558). Adoption of digital technologies facilitates infrastructure development and organizational change through the application of cross-functional horizontal management, improved **information quality management**, flattening of command-and-control hierarchies, decentralization of organizational structures and the creation of new behavioral norms—all essential elements detailed in Chapters 5 and 6 to improve customer service quality and develop high performance workforces.

What follows is a discussion of *how* governments are using digital governance concepts to connect with institutions, employees, citizens, customers, clients, patients, taxpayers and other stakeholders. Examples of federal and state government websites show how public agencies are responding to demands for greater connectivity, interoperability and responsiveness from citizens who themselves are learning how to navigate the web.

In the United States and elsewhere, governments at all levels are applying e-commerce and digital technology to improve government-to-government (G2G) services, government-to-employee (G2E) relationships, government-to-business (G2B) interactions and government-to-citizen (G2C) transactions. Legal, political and regulatory constraints that arise when attempting to apply e-commerce and digital technology within government infrastructures are also discussed, as well as the future of digital governance as a means to improve the quality and productivity of public services.

Applying E-Commerce and Digital Technology to Improve Government-to-Government (G2G) Services

G2G interactions involve all forms of communications, data exchanges and other transactions among government agencies, branches and departments at different levels within public administrative systems. ICTs enable government to communicate faster and share data on a larger scale. G2G includes intra- and inter-agency networks as well as interoperable linkages between federal, state and local agencies. Legislative actions focus on developing general government-wide policies as well as promoting paperless transfers, especially among "tree-cutting" agencies such as the **U.S. Internal Revenue Service (IRS)**, which now distributes tax forms and provides other services online. As previously mentioned, past bureaucracy reforms have resulted from: 1) public pressures from well-organized (and well-funded) lobbies and political action groups; 2) the need to cope with man-made crises or natural disasters as well as manage complex social systems; and 3) public acceptance of the need for more regulations to protect consumers, clients or patients of banks, insurance companies, and financial and health care services. Digital governance differs from previous reforms in its focus on intergovernmental collaboration and information sharing.

Knowledge is power—and many past crisis-based "coping" actions managed by traditional bureaucracies have discouraged collaboration, communication or sharing of information. To the contrary, multi-channel G2G improvements target the elimination of barriers preventing exchange of information between government agencies, thereby reducing cumbersome bureaucratic overhead structures and allowing greater free-flow of information on a wider range of public issues. Among the areas most recently addressed: emergency management procedures, financial services, consumer product recalls, health care information technology and grants-in-aid applications. Better coordination also reduces duplication, unifies individual websites and increases cyber security and citizen trust. Several government agencies have undergone extensive reorganizations during the past decade aimed at facilitating closer ICT linkages, among other purposes.

One of the most prominent and visible reforms was the creation of the **U.S. Department of Homeland Security (DHS)** in 2002. Its mission is to better coordinate diverse functions such as customs, immigration, transportation security and emergency management (formerly located in other federal agencies) into one central federal executive department for more concerted responses to border security and prevention of terrorist attacks. These and similar reorganizations mandated intra- and inter-agency exchanges at all levels to overcome communication deficiencies in homeland security and intelligence operations following the tragic events of 9/11. In 2005, Congress created the **Office of the Director of National Intelligence (DNI)** by merging 15 disparate agencies located in other bureaus and departments—including the CIA and various defense intelligence agencies—to encourage greater interoperability among federal, state and local agencies and functions. Intelligence agencies are charged with collecting, analyzing and disseminating information on potential threats to national security, as well as providing warnings of surprise attacks against U.S. citizens and institutions. More sophisticated information technology has improved the capacity to recognize newer types of threats and how intelligence agencies respond to them. ICT-enabled government departments and agencies share data and conduct digital exchanges between key governmental officials.

Existing bureaucratic cultures, histories, legal restrictions, leadership changes and oversight by specialized Congressional committees continue to pose major challenges for effective coordination and policy implementation. Federal legislation described in Chapter 6 supports policies and regulations promoting accountability, better access to information and transparency. Other laws and rules were aimed at specific agencies, primarily federal and state taxation authorities, to promote electronic rather than paper transfer of data, especially business and tax forms. Such cumulative top-down vertical reforms have become increasingly successful as measured by accuracy rates, increased productivity and public acceptance (West, 2005: 82–100).

Emphasis on more targeted government operations and measurable performance outcomes—as well as benchmarks and "best practices" in the public sector—are important parallel driving forces behind the implementation of G2G services. In addition to reorganizations of national government functions, several state and local governments have passed laws, ordinances and regulations encouraging the expansion of digital exchanges, cost savings and productivity improvement measures. Most of these efforts have been incremental and piecemeal, initiated by individual states and local governments without a comprehensive national strategy.

Less visible, but no less important, are regulatory and structural changes which mandate cross-functional *horizontal* ICTs aimed at reducing and eventually eliminating vertical bureaucratic "silos" dominated by powerful sub-governments, especially at the state and local levels. Reducing the influence of powerful interlocking sets of interest groups, legislative committees and bureaucracies (often referred to as **iron triangles**) is a challenging task which is resisted because it disrupts power relationships and the status quo (Peters, 2010: 31–37). Attempts to break up these cozy triangles of influence, money and politics are often met with resistance from both the political left and right. Opposition to President Obama's health care reform efforts, for example, was and still is led by numerous lobbying groups, **Political Action Committees (PACs)** and other special interest groups representing drug companies, **Health Maintenance Organizations (HMOs)**, hospitals and health insurers who aggressively lobbied against changes by Congress or state legislatures (until they received concessions). In Washington, over 11,000 registered lobbyists outnumber senators and congressmen and exert pressure at every level of government. Campaign finance incentives to resist change or to modify legislation to accommodate special interests are especially intense at the sub-national level, where the content and enforcement of regulations varies greatly from state to state. Among many other regulatory responsibilities, state and local governments perform vital functions such as licensing teachers, lawyers and physicians, inspecting hospitals, issuing building permits and regulating banks, realtors and insurance companies.

Most citizens think of bureaucracies as massive faceless organizations with hundreds of thousands of bureaucrats and multi-billion dollar budgets. With the exception of federal executive mega-agencies such as the U.S. Departments of Defense or Health and Human Services and a small number of large urban metropolitan city and county bureaucracies (Chicago, Los Angeles, New York, Miami-Dade County, for example), most state and local government agencies are relatively small service organizations comprised of fewer than 50 employees. They are "owned" by 511,039 separately elected local and state officials who wield nearly absolute power in many small communities and are skeptical—if not actively resistant—to "efficiency experts" who might usurp their constitutional powers. They are "operated" by a larger professional cadre of about 20 million public administrators who are under intense external pressures from outside political sources described above. One of the major challenges facing governments implementing ICTs is to persuade local administrators and political officials that such changes would be in their best interests when in many instances, they initially may not be. This is a tough sell in many cash-strapped local communities.

Federalism vs. Standardization

The antiquated U.S. system of federalism is a complex maze of intergovernmental relationships—compounded by loose (or often non-existent) campaign financing rules, local control of elections and powerful special interest influence. Federalism exists today as a major encumbrance to the full implementation of integrated online citizen services in an efficient, rational and standardized manner.

In addition to the 50 state and five territorial governments (American Samoa, Guam, Northern Mariana Islands, Puerto Rico and the U.S. Virgin Islands) there are nearly *88,000* separately elected local governments, including cities, special districts, townships and school districts. Included in this crazy quilt of overlapping jurisdictions are over 3,000 counties, quaint vestiges of 19th century political structure where "county seats" are literally a day's horseback ride from each other. Each of these local fiefdoms is controlled by a "board of directors" consisting of six to 12 elected officials who act as commissars and often blur the line between politics and administration.

Corruption is an all too common occurrence repeated again and again in states and local governments. In what has become a mind-numbing media circus, local officials are regularly investigated for misuse of public funds. In July 2009, the mayors of Hoboken and Secaucus, New Jersey, were among 44 people arrested on charges of bribery, public corruption and money laundering. In September 2009 three Broward County, Florida, officials (a school board member, a current county commissioner and a former city commissioner) were charged in an FBI investigation with bribery for payoffs to support special interest legislation. Federal investigators made additional arrests of contractors and other appointed and elected officials for fixing lucrative building contracts.[1] The mayor and entire city council of Bell, California, were arrested and indicted in 2010 for corruption and misappropriation of public funds. These investigations—and the media coverage they generate—increase cynicism and further weaken public trust in government.

The U.S. political system of **fragmented federalism** is highly vulnerable to financial downturns as well as extra-legal influence. As a result, many governments are unable to utilize public resources unless or until a highly publicized political scandal, major crisis or natural disaster disrupts the status quo. Competition between levels of government creates further delays. Almost five years passed before a Federal District Court concluded that the U.S. Army Corps of Engineers was liable for damages caused by weak levies and recommended compensation for victims of Hurricane

Katrina in New Orleans. The federal government is appealing that judgment, further delaying settlements with affected residents. Such a disaster may again be occurring as a result of the compounding effects of numerous banking and financial institution failures (also regulated by the states), foreclosure fraud and the disappearance of local property tax bases resulting from declining real estate property values. In addition to these long-term structural problems, most local governments are facing budget-busting employee and retiree health care costs. According to a national survey, half of the nation's cities, counties and townships expected less revenue in 2010, 26% forecasted increased consolidation of local services and 21% said they needed fewer employees.[2] Higher salary and benefit costs are shrinking budgets, forcing state and local officials to take drastic actions (hiring freezes and layoffs) to contain long-term employee benefit and health care costs. In the future, public agencies may be even less prepared to deal with extreme emergencies.

Few advanced industrial democratic governmental systems are *less* standardized than the American federal democratic republic. Imagine what could happen to our antiquated, fragmented, decentralized and locally controlled system of governance if a Technology Czar (or Czarina) could press a button and convert all governments from their present "analogue" state to the Digital State? Problems with the conversion to High Definition TV originally scheduled for February 17, 2009 but postponed until June 12, 2009 pale in comparison to the administrative and organizational changes needed to reform the fractured framework of federalism. Nevertheless, many organizations are embracing ICTs to integrate new skills and change traditional bureaucratic behaviors and regulatory environments to positively impact the level of service provided to citizens. In response to these forces, federal executive agencies and many state governments deploy ICTs to improve communication and collaboration in specific policy areas. Examples of several of these initiatives follow.

Government-to-Government ICT Applications

The tragic events of 9/11, Hurricane Katrina and the Gulf of Mexico oil spill—as well as numerous other less publicized natural and man-made disasters—highlight the magnitude and urgency of problems facing first responders in their attempts to effectively coordinate emergency efforts. The **Disaster Management Interoperability Services (DMIS)** initiative applies ICTs to enhance the ability of public, private and non-profit agencies to respond to emergencies. DMIS offers federal, state and local emergency managers open online access to disaster-management information, planning and response tools. DMIS provides participating agencies with the resources and capability for enhanced cost-effective situational awareness, disaster response, resource requests and access to collaborative environments for training and preparedness exercises. Open DMIS uses cutting-edge information technology to improve the delivery of disaster assistance information and services by creating single internet-based portals to coordinate agencies and provide disaster information and services.[3] A growing number of similar initiatives and programs at all levels are designed to improve coordination and communication among geographically diverse units of government. Some 60 programs spread throughout federal, state, regional and local agencies and public safety associations now utilize various aspects of DMIS communications.

The Department of Homeland Security (DHS) emphasizes interoperability, as well as tools "to move data between municipal departments, communities and other agencies and entities, such as hospitals, blood banks, and human and animal shelters" (Skinner, 2008: 1). Since August 2005, DMIS has been deployed in more than 94 actual emergencies and in over 530 disaster preparedness exercises involving more than 1,400 DMIS user groups in all 50 states. This has led to a number of procedural and infrastructure improvements with G2G emergency management systems. Emergency managers can now more easily monitor major disaster and national security events, coordinate state, federal and private responses, and collaborate on damage assessments and summaries. Incident management software also improves the response time of emergency personnel contributing to significant decreases in the loss of life and property.

In an effort to coordinate various federal initiatives, the Office of Management and Budget (OMB) and the **President's Management Council (PMC)** approved **SAFECOM** as a high priority digital government initiative in 2004. The Office of Emergency Communications (OEC) develops guidance, tools and templates and the Office for Interoperability and Compatibility (OIC) supports SAFECOM-related research, testing, evaluation and standards. OEC is managed by the Directorate for National Protection and Programs and OIC is managed by the Science and Technology Directorate. SAFECOM was developed from the bottom up working with existing communications initiatives and key emergency responders to heighten multi-jurisdictional and cross-disciplinary coordination.[4] Comprehensive information on topics related to emergency response communications are featured along with best practices that have evolved from real-world situations. While several government programs address this issue, much of this work has been disconnected, fragmented and often conflicting. The horrific events of 9/11 and the inept response to Hurricane Katrina as well as other natural disasters highlight inadequacies of traditional emergency response interoperability.[5]

SAFECOM has resulted in numerous improvements including: conducting a digital, national interoperability baseline survey; creating a digital grant guidance document that is used by the Federal Emergency Management Agency (FEMA), Community Oriented Policing Services (COPS) and Open Directory Program (ODP) state block grant programs to promote interoperability improvement efforts; and the development of a Statewide Communications Interoperability Planning (SCIP) methodology, which involves the use of digital technology to enhance information gathering and the development of project plan roadmaps.[6] Several projects developed **standard operating procedures (SOPs)** for the design, manufacture and evaluation of interoperable two-way digital wireless communications products created by and for public safety professionals.[7]

There have also been several applications of SAFECOM to enhance G2G services and operations at the state and local level. The **Clark County Nevada Urban Area Working Group (UAWG)** in Las Vegas sought to improve the quality of communications interoperability between urban areas within the state of Nevada. SAFECOM was applied and used to facilitate a major action planning session organized to review various data from interviews and exercises involving the communication project at hand. This resulted in the development of a number of strategic initiatives that outlined the action steps necessary to improve communications interoperability between urban areas in Nevada.[8]

Grants.gov is the U.S. government's primary online service portal to assist potential recipients to find and apply for government-wide competitive grants-in-aid. The website improves the efficiency of online grant search and application processes by enabling applicants to electronically interact with federal grant making agencies. This portal enhances G2G services, including: avoiding applicant system development, redundancies and operations costs; eliminating **Federal Register** posting requirements; increasing data accuracy and integrity of grant applications; providing customer support, including a state-of-the-art help desk; allowing grant programs to reach a broader, more diverse applicant/grantee pool; eliminating the need for multi-agency forms clearance; creating opportunities to consolidate agency vendor file(s); and supporting agencies' compliance with the **Federal Financial Assistance Management Act (Public Law 106–107)** requirements for a common electronic grant system.[9] Grants. gov also enhances G2B and G2C services because some federal grants are also available to non-governmental entities (e.g. businesses and non-profit organizations); however, most of the discussion in this section focuses on how Web portals improve G2G services.

There have been numerous attempts to improve the quality of relationships between governments in the United States. In Washington, D.C., the Mayor's Office of Partnerships and Grants Development (OPGD) sought to improve its ability to find grant opportunities for citizens. OPGD had previously utilized a manual paper-based method of locating grant opportunities—specifically a newsletter-type document with grant opportunities that was faxed to various eligible government agencies. Unfortunately but predictably, the OPGD team was never able to confirm that the lengthy faxes were received by the intended recipient—or read at all. Utilizing Grants.gov, OPGD enhanced process efficiency by notifying, searching for and alerting agencies to potential grant opportunities.[10]

Everything that happens occurs somewhere. Consequently, "geographic location is an important attribute of [almost all] activities, policies, strategies, and plans" (Longley *et al.*, 2001: 4). For example, health care managers deal with geographic issues when deciding where to locate new hospitals; law enforcement officers use Global Positioning Systems (GPS) to track suspects and locate stolen merchandise or property; transportation authorities use it when choosing routes for new highways; and government emergency management agencies can better cope with space issues when responding to disaster situations. GPS has become a key component for improving G2G services. GPS links computer software to geographical databases and creates digital maps tailored for specific purposes. Firefighters, for example, can utilize systems to view the interior features of buildings before entering them. Private sector applications include the much sought after commercial portable GPS systems available for airplanes, cars and boats. Viewers can obtain visual or statistical associations among variables such as addresses or landmarks and also retrieve and manipulate information to provide new information capabilities based on spatial relationships between available data sets.

Application of GPS strengthens G2G services and operations for most governments and many citizens. In particular, state departments of transportation, public safety, social services, planning and environmental protection benefit from increased efficiency, productivity and service delivery. Government agencies have incorporated geospatial data, information and technologies as emergency management tools and homeland security applications. The State of New York integrated its Accident Location Information System (ALIS) with a statewide GPS system linking New York's Department of Motor Vehicles, Department of Transportation and Office of Cyber Security and Critical Infrastructure Coordination. ALIS has improved "emergency response time by providing police and other emergency services personnel with more accurate location-based data. The system also collaborates with local and county governments to ensure more complete data collection" (Cassidy, 2008: 1). The State of Connecticut implemented a coordinated emergency response system among all of its public safety departments including local police and fire departments. Connecticut documented a significant reduction in emergency response times and a 99% accuracy level in locating addresses and geometry, ensuring that no time was wasted by emergency services searching for an address. At the federal level, GPS has been used by several homeland security agencies to enhance emergency response efforts for emergency preparedness, first responders and mitigation for rapid access to the most accurate, up-to-date geospatial content. For example, FEMA established a number of GPS solutions with the goal of enhancing collaboration and interoperability with state agencies and departments to more effectively deploy resources during emergency situations. Regardless of the methods by which it is employed, GPS is a key application of digital technology to enhance G2G services and operations. Unfortunately, federalism again interferes with standardization as most state and local GPS systems are incompatible and based on proprietary standards.

As with all new social innovations throughout history, every change that moves a society forward contains contradictions of an equal proportion which could have negative long-term effects (Rogers, 2003). Global cultural changes are occurring because of the increasing volume of new ICTs entering the marketplace; technologies are dramatically altering the way we communicate and interact within public spaces (Chapters 8 and 9). Authoritarian regimes use new technologies to increase surveillance of dissidents and political opponents. The evolution of GPS, social networks, mobile and wireless technologies creates even deeper problems, often without sufficient "firewalls" or security enhancements to protect individual privacy and security. New technologies threaten personal privacy and increase the desire to remain anonymous in a wired world. It is possible for an outside user to obtain access by using someone else's computer address for themselves or, the worst case scenario, stealing data, personal information or even identities. The possibilities of harm being inflicted are extensive because of the rise of the problem of **identity theft**, although it is widely recognized that most of the stolen information is obtained offline. The best defense against unwanted intrusions on personal privacy is a well-trained cadre of public officials.

Improving Government-to-Employee (G2E) Services

G2E refers to virtual relationships between government agencies and their employees as well as how government workers serve citizens. Through the use of the internet, governments provide employees with detailed information about pay dates, changes in personnel rules, holiday information and employee benefit and training programs. G2E relationships can also enhance the management of civil service recruiting, procurement and internal communications among government employees and non-government contractors serving as consultants, intermediaries and principal agents.

The **Central Personnel Data File (CPDF)** and the new **Enterprise Human Resources Integration (EHRI)** warehouse are first and second generation human resources reporting systems used by the federal government. Both HR systems store workforce information sent from the Office of Management and Budget (OMB), but EHRI has three sophisticated enhancements: 1) a central data repository for all executive branch employee records; 2) an electronic Official Employee Record (OER); and 3) a set of analytical tools for human capital forecasting and trend analysis.[11] Human resource departments complete their employee training protocols online for its ease and considerable cost savings. E-learning can automatically track and record an employee's development and allow managers and supervisors to check progress. E-learning can also take place at the employee's convenience. Furthermore, such programs offer the advantage of consistency of training procedures as virtual learning courses become standardized.

The federal government began transmitting pay information for executive branch employees electronically in March 2010. The New Orleans-based National Finance Center, which processes payroll statements for more than 140 offices across the three branches of government, began sending leave and earnings statements to workers electronically, although workers can still choose to receive paper versions. The change will save taxpayers about $4 million annually. The Department of Homeland Security was the first to see the changes, followed later by employees at other executive branch departments, including Agriculture, Housing and Urban Development, Justice, Labor, Treasury and Veterans Affairs. The move stems from an OMB contest that sought cost-cutting ideas from federal workers. Former OMB Director Peter R. Orszag describes this as an example of how federal employees can use their experience and unique knowledge to streamline what works in the federal government saving taxpayer dollars and improving performance.[12]

Privacy and Security Issues

Digital government services cannot be delivered at the expense of established expectations of personal protection. Increased capabilities of ICTs to access personal information and public fears about privacy violations represent the twin horns of a dilemma facing governments embarked on d-government initiatives. Applications should be developed initially with privacy protection built-in upfront rather than retrofitted to accommodate privacy concerns *after* they have been exposed. This is very difficult to achieve, however, as technology changes and new security weaknesses are always being found and exploited. The standard of public (and legal) expectations with respect to privacy protection is generally higher for governments than for the private sector. One reason for this is that a citizen/client often has no choice but to deal with a government agency, given its monopolistic role in providing certain services. Accordingly, there is a higher need to trust government's information management practices than (perhaps) the private sector, where there is an option to switch to another competing firm if trust cannot be established and maintained. Citizen/client concerns over privacy and security protection still rank at the top of lists of issues associated with digital government (Culbertson, 2004: 72).

Balancing information access and privacy protection demanded by citizens and clients before using virtual government requires careful attention to information management and effective personnel training. Addressing privacy and security issues has significant implications for government employees and operations, especially since the aggregation of information about citizens and clients in common databanks represents a large part of expected efficiency gains from ICTs. The critical question for public agencies has been and always will be: At what point do the privacy concerns of those whose information is at issue outweigh the efficiency gains of broad-based access to and management of information (Culbertson, 2004: 72)? When quality assured, such strategies can increase the conviction among citizens that personal information entrusted to governments is protected, as well as ensure that the use of d-government will expand information access, not limit it.

Information management and training have implications across governments, as strategies must, by definition, be standardized. Citizens will not accept situations where different agencies of government apply different standards for privacy protection and information access. **Standardization** is essential for implementation. Corporate information management plans also demand a high level of central coordination across divisions as well as attention to new issues brought on by online access, such as electronic records management and data sharing. While these issues are not unique to government, they are closely associated with it in the public mind because of concerns about internet security, privacy and data aggregation. In order to meet high standards of public trust and to ensure compliance, many governments have chosen to go beyond simply improving policy measures and administrative practices by passing legislation in this area (Chapter 6). Meeting standards set in privacy protection and information access legislation and regulation has major organizational implications for governments. Several have chosen to create independent review boards and officers reporting directly to legislatures rather than government executives in order to better meet public expectations.

With the growth of globalization, outsourcing is commonplace in many large businesses, and even in some smaller ones. However, a new trend has emerged in government: outsourcing the management and procurement of contractors. Independent firms have taken over the managerial obligations of businesses at lower costs to run some of the basic functions of a company. Business–government relationships are becoming increasingly interconnected and difficult to manage.

Enhancing Government-to-Business (G2B) Relationships

Interaction between business and governments takes place in both the real and virtual worlds by exchanging information, commodities, products and services. The driving forces behind G2B relationships are interest from the businesses as "customers" of the public sector and the pervasive use of electronic means to perform activities such as contracting, purchasing and sales. One of the major purposes of G2B is to facilitate procurement decisions and develop an open and competitive marketplace for government purchases. G2B applications are growing in importance as they focus attention on cost reductions and increasing competition between companies bidding for government contracts. Depending on the type of relationship and transaction, contacts between government and business can take many forms: coercive, contractual, regulatory, redistributive or market-driven. G2B also involves "providing information [to the business community] on topics such as compliance, zoning, applications, and permits" (Blackstone *et al.*, 2005: 13). In addition and more importantly, G2B involves the notion of **electronic procurement** (i.e. purchasing or e-commerce) and electronic business resource centers.

Application of digital technology to e-procurement enables innovation and transforms how governments buy goods and services and oversee suppliers. E-procurement systems offer many more firms the information and opportunities needed to bid for contracts and provide services to government (Chen *et al.*, 2008: 540; Hardy and Williams, 2008: 155). One noticeable benefit of e-procurement is increased competition and lower costs for government–business transactions. "In the United States it was reported that e-procurement reduced the cost of transactions from US$120 to around $20 and reduced delay from around 40 days to less than 5 days" (Coulthard, Castleman and Batten, 2004: 2). Another benefit involves the role of government as an e-commerce initiator and supply-chain manager (Chapter 3). As major purchasers of goods and services, governments are requiring suppliers to adopt customer service quality and supply-chain management systems assuring higher quality goods and services at lower costs. This can assist in the modernization of public services by reducing existing transaction costs, providing better monitoring, seamless processes and coordination of purchasing across government agencies. Increased accountability and transparency also help resolve more difficult public policy issues such as minority set-asides and sole-source contracting. Closer G2B applications are also important because of their potential to produce savings by easing compliance costs, improving procurement practices and increasing transaction speed. This application of digital governance is receiving increasing interest from the business community as both customers and providers of goods and services and as a means to more efficiently perform contracting and purchasing activities.

Governments worldwide spend hundreds of billions of dollars to procure supplies and services from private companies. In the United States alone, the federal government spends over $600 billion and makes over 50 million purchases annually. The types of goods and services that governments purchase vary widely, from routine office supplies to sophisticated technology, new defense weapons systems and space satellites. According to a group of tech-industry CEOs, the federal government could save as much as $1 trillion over the next 10 years by moving to an e-procurement system.[13]

Many states apply e-procurement technology as well as e-commerce to improve G2B services. In Florida, e-procurement is applied through MyFloridaMarketPlace, an online central source exchange system for both buyers and vendors, serving state procurement activities, facilitating digital interactions between vendors and state government agencies/ departments and providing support tools for world-class procurement processes. The website offers a number of benefits for both buyers and vendors.[14] Among the benefits to vendors are: a single point of registration, state-of-the-art digital tools such as immediate internet-based transactions versus traditional paper-heavy methods, increased access to buying entities and enhanced opportunities for economic development, especially for small businesses who gain access to the entire state marketplace simply by registering on a website. For buyers, the system offers a one-stop shopping experience for accessing online catalogs with information about registered vendors in the state. Additional benefits include: more choice as a result of numerous registered vendors offering goods and services; reduced paperwork via online purchase requisitions and quoting/sourcing capabilities; faster order processing time via automated transactions and approvals; reduced costs of goods and services by enabling the State of Florida to act as a single standardized entity during contract and purchase negotiations. On the negative side, the state procurement system lacks government controls, is overly dependent on vendors and has little oversight by the state legislature. Centralized decision making allows vendors to reduce their own costs by influencing purchasing decisions. The Florida case demonstrates the importance of political demand for IT innovation, but also points to the need for professional management, a strong infrastructure and political leadership.[15]

The premise behind applying **Electronic Business Resource Centers (EBRC)** is that online government services are "easiest to use and most likely to gain acceptance if they are geared to the needs of the user, rather than organized hierarchically" (Blackstone *et al.*, 2005: 118). EBRCs are online gateways that guide businesses through all the steps necessary to start and operate in designated geographic districts. EBRCs offer access to information, guides, links, tools and downloads providing a number of advantages to businesses, including: one-stop shopping for business information needs; single vs. multiple information sources; broadband processing speed for online transactions; and risk reduction by providing all information for compliance and tax requirements. The federal government employs a number of EBRCs in association with the business community.

The U.S. Government's official EBRC is **Business.gov**, managed and operated by the U.S. Small Business Administration (SBA) in coordination with more than 21 other federal agencies and departments. The website was part of President George W. Bush's Presidential E-Government Initiative[16] and serves as a one-stop shop for businesses seeking access to government services and information on how to improve the quality of their own business operations. Its mission is to help the business community comply with government regulations, which can be an expensive and off-putting task for many organizations.[17] Utilizing EBRCs can save enormous amounts of time and financial resources with regard to administrative, record-keeping and regulatory compliance requirements and provide effective and efficient access to laws, regulations, forms and agency contacts. Business.gov is a prime example of how government can apply concepts of digital technology and e-commerce to improve its G2B services. The portal was recently awarded the Excellence.Gov award—recognizing successful programs that improve the delivery of government services to citizens, businesses and other government agencies through the application of information technology. The award was recognized by the American Council for Technology (ACT) and its Industry Advisory Council for demonstrating best practices in a federal e-government program and improving organizational performance using information technology.[18]

Regulatory and rule making processes are complex undertakings for over one hundred and fifty federal regulatory agencies and thousands of sub-national agencies issuing more than 4,500 new regulations each year at the federal level alone. Enforcing these regulations imposes significant accountability and information demands on government agencies as well as those they regulate. In addition "before adopting a new regulation, agencies ... are required to publish notice of proposed rulemaking in the *Federal Register* ... they also need to complete scientific, engineering, and economic analyses, as well as respond to comments submitted by outside organizations and individuals ... [In all] the demands of analysis and information process can strain limited agency staffs, as well as limit the public's capacity to review and comment upon major regulations as they are developed" (Coglianese, 2004: vii). Three decades ago, the U.S. government began responding to business demands for less paperwork and more mutual discussion of regulatory requirements; since the mid-1990s, regulatory agencies have applied e-rulemaking to improve the quality of G2B regulatory services.

E-rulemaking is the use of digital technology to "enable government agencies to manage the rulemaking process more productively; it could also expand and enhance the public's involvement in this process" (Coglianese, 2004: 13). The incorporation of e-rulemaking with digital technology provides a number of potential quality improvements, including: 1) increased democratic legitimacy; 2) improved regulatory procedures; 3) decreased administrative costs; and 4) increased regulatory compliance. In addition to these general service quality improvements, e-rulemaking improves data mining capabilities: writers can learn from various data sources available; web-publishing of rules enhances the ability to find supporting analysis for various aspects of regulations and/or provisions in an underlying statute; conflict identification tools help ensure consistency within and across rules; customizable, automatic alerts allow users to sign up for e-mail alerts of rules affecting them that have been added to an agency's regulatory agenda; rule-compliance wizards create simple programs such as TurboTax© for tax filing; plain language tools help to clarify jargon and aid agency staff with regard to drafting rule language; and analysis of public comments allows agencies to summarize and categorize feedback received from the public and business community.

Governments are implementing more features that enhance public accountability and transparency while at the same time protecting individual privacy and system security. Protections allow citizens to post comments or otherwise provide feedback about government performance; privacy must be guaranteed for reliable feedback. Agencies benefit from citizen complaints, suggestions and recommendations for change. Citizen comments provide diverse perspectives and experiences, although many agencies fail to encourage feedback. Without secure feedback mechanisms, managers are unable to correct flaws inherent in organizational communication and coordination processes. Something as simple as an opportunity to make a comment on *Twitter* empowers citizens by giving them an opportunity to voice their opinion about government policies and services.

Dozens of federal government websites have been consolidated into one comprehensive site.[19] Both the title and subject of regulatory action are clearly listed on the e-rulemaking website and anyone can review and comment on any of the new regulations issued by federal agencies. The website is searchable and shows a full complement of documents including proposed rules, regulatory proposals, final rules, cost-benefit analyses and many other facets of multi-agency regulatory processes. By its own estimates, the website saved over $70 million over five years by creating a central portal rather than having each agency operate its own.[20]

Government revenue collection processes are among the most arduous, burdensome and controversial, both for individuals and for large corporations. **Expanded Electronic Tax Products for Business (EETPB)** and **E-Verify** for businesses were also presidential E-Initiatives that have been applied successfully to reduce the paperwork and reporting burdens on businesses by providing accurate tax information, offering the option of electronic tax filing and even providing models of simplified state and federal tax laws.[21] EETPB has been one of the most effective applications as over 70% of all federal taxpayers filed electronically in 2010.

Not every G2B application has the full support of the business community. Applications which improve the efficiency of services involving sensitive issues such as employee verification, citizenship, immigration status and social security eligibility can interfere with established business practices (such as hiring undocumented aliens as laborers at below minimum wages) and are opposed on both practical and ideological grounds. This is evident with programs such as E-Verify which impose costs on businesses as well as stir-up intense political conflicts. Anti-immigrant laws such as those that passed by the State of Arizona in April 2010 strictly enforcing citizenship requirements, giving police greater arrest powers and targeting undocumented workers can also enflame emotions and exacerbate political conflicts.

National identification cards have been used in many other countries for decades. Cards are carried as positive identification verifying essential information such as who the holder is and where they reside. National ID cards have been proposed by various divisions of United States government for decades, but have not been approved. National ID cards raise civil liberties and privacy issues and are seen by many as means of tracking and profiling Americans. The **Real ID Act of 2005** (P.L. 109-13, 119 Stat. 302) was a U.S. federal law pertaining to authentication and standardization of procedures for issuing state driver's licenses and identification cards, as well as improving security for various immigration issues relating to terrorism. The law required verifiable state driver's licenses to be accepted by the federal government for "official purposes," defined by the Secretary of Homeland Security as documentation for boarding commercial airline flights, entering federal buildings and nuclear power plants. Not a single state has implemented all provisions the national ID card system and there remain unresolved intergovernmental, privacy, political and security issues, concerns about who has and does not have access to databases and complex issues relating to the costs and level of service provided online.[22]

E-Verify is a voluntary federal program originally established in 1997 for employers to check whether or not prospective employees are legally authorized to work in the United States. E-Verify has grown in use: on average, more than 1,400 employers sign up each week, and employment checks exceed 200,000 a week. In 2008, a total of 6.6 million checks were made, double the number of 2007. Halfway through 2009, 5.5 million worker checks had been made online and approximately 192,000 companies were using E-Verify. Since September 8, 2009 all federal contractors have been required to use the system under regulations issued by the Department of Homeland Security and the Social Security Administration, which jointly oversee the program. The **federal contractor rule** added an additional 150,000 to 180,000 employers representing about half a million businesses, still a tiny fraction of the approximately 6 million businesses employing more than 115 million people in the United States. During fiscal year 2008, as part of the crack-down on hiring illegal aliens, **Immigration and Customs Enforcement (ICE)** made more than 1,100 criminal arrests associated with workplace investigations. Of those arrests, only 100 were business owners, managers or supervisors. Employers who utilize so-called "seasonal workers" have few incentives to comply with E-Verify and some actively resist the registration procedures.

In addition to the federal contractor requirement, Congress has been pressing to require companies receiving economic stimulus funds from the Obama administration to use E-Verify to ensure employees are eligible to work in the United States. With the collapse of comprehensive immigration reform legislation and the acrimonious debate surrounding the actions by the State of Arizona, the only apparent way to deal with the problem is incrementally. Conservative Congressmen are pushing for an expansion of the rule, but the Obama administration is not comfortable with the proposal because of the administrative burdens imposed on businesses and the possibility of anti-Hispanic discrimination. Congress passed a short-term extension of the program's authorization in the fall 2008 after Sen. Robert Menendez, D-N.J., tried to block a bill reauthorizing the program for five years. Rep. Ken Calvert, R-Calif., who authored the original legislation, attached an amendment to the economic stimulus package that would have reauthorized the program for four years.[23] The Obama administration argued that a delay would provide an opportunity to review the impact of the rule before its wider application to the private sector.

The E-Verify system has been tested to handle up to 65 million inquiries a year. Lawmakers are further pressing for requirements that individual recipients of public health care, social welfare and unemployment benefits must be verified as U.S. citizens. The business community argued vehemently that E-Verify is the wrong solution at the wrong time and leads to cost increases. Controversy has dogged both the Real ID and E-Verify programs, as critics argue that they are too costly for companies and the results are unreliable. Although DHS officials say the E-Verify system is now 99.5% reliable, an inspector general report released in 2009 found the system's error rate to be above 4%; a 2010 study by the U.S. Immigration and Naturalization Service estimated error rates at above 50%.[24] Such variation does not inspire confidence in government.

Government-to-Citizen (G2C) Services

Citizen interaction within democratic processes creates more opportunities for e-learning and electoral participation. The pervasive use of cellular telephones, iPhones, personal computers and the internet is a driving force for the development of G2C linkages to meet citizen demands for more convenient and efficient services. G2C involves all forms of communications, transactions and other interactions which take place between governments and citizens. The concept of G2G reflects the use of ICTs to better serve citizens via strategic applications such as citizen relationship management (CzRM), electronic voting and other IT applications (Chapters 3 and 4). This facilitates citizen interaction with government and encourages participation, considered by many as the ultimate goal of digital governance.

Enhancing online G2C services makes government more accountable and allows citizens to look up voting records, comment on federal legislation, monitor public hearings and communicate directly with public officials. This is a major benefit because direct participation promotes active public spirit and moral character, protects freedoms and provides citizens with a voice to challenge existing power structures (Robbins *et al.*, 2008: 564). Also, through the application of digital technology "government would become more efficient and effective, and agencies would be more responsive to ordinary citizens. By taking advantage of the internet, digital government could narrow the gap between citizens and leaders, and make people feel more positive about the public sector" (West, 2005: 167–168). Although states and local governments receive mixed reviews for their online efforts, many have used ICTs to foster democratic participation and deliver services for several years (Tolbert *et al.*, 2008).

The Commonwealth of Virginia has one of the most advanced systems of digital communication of any government in the United States, allowing citizens to access the progress of bills being considered by the legislature and notifying citizens when any changes occur in the legislation which might affect them. The state has also applied digital technology and e-commerce to overcome one of the most difficult periods in its modern history, a revenue shortfall of more than $5 billion in 2000. The objective of eVA was to enhance the quality of processes by which the commonwealth and its private-sector suppliers conducted business; and it did just that. As one of the nation's premier public sector internet purchasing systems, eVA was recognized by the National Center for Digital Government as "Best of Breed" in the electronic-commerce and business-regulation category in its 2002 Digital State Survey; eVA represents a prime example of "the use of technology to improve government performance. Prior to eVA the quality of G2B services and operations in Virginia were below standard; before eVA selling and buying on behalf of government was a daunting task" (Blackstone *et al.*, 2005: 95–96). Reasons for this included: complex, decentralized hierarchies; use of time consuming paper-based processes; inconsistent format of purchase orders and other procurement documents; high rate of returns due to errors in products and pricing. Post-eVA created an entirely different situation.

The application of eVA was described as nothing short of a "fundamental innovation" in government–business relationships. Its use created a single electronic portal for all the state's purchasing needs, automated workflows, data capturing of essential procurement information and activity, and provided a means to securely transmit transactions and data. This offered a "single face" of government for the business community, reduced costs by eliminating the need for multiple procurement systems, provided self-service tools across multiple government agencies, facilitated information sharing and made it possible for the entire bid-evaluation process to be managed electronically. E-VA is a benchmark for e-procurement programs and an example of the potential for e-procurement to advance the goal of more efficient and effective governance (Blackstone *et al.*, 2005: 95–108).

The federal government also provides benefits for certain groups of citizens, known as **entitlements**. Over one-half of the total U.S. federal budget is distributed to citizens, mainly to the elderly as Social Security retirement or as Medicare payments. Many eligible recipients are unaware of benefits, where to find information about them, whether or not they qualify, who to contact, or even how to go about applying. Websites such as **Benefits.gov** are designed to enhance citizen information about and access to federal government assistance programs. Specifically, the website utilizes the internet to connect citizens to government benefit programs, increase access to information (especially for people with disabilities), reduce costs and inefficiencies and become the primary virtual source for all federal, state and local government benefit programs. By all accounts, the portal has succeeded in accomplishing these goals and significantly enhanced G2C services. Before it existed, information regarding government benefits and other assistance programs was spread across more than 31 million federal government web pages![25] Even if citizens knew what programs and/or benefits they were eligible for, the number of web pages alone undoubtedly caused major confusion and dissatisfaction with regard to the quality of G2C services. Fortunately, Benefits.gov allows citizens to access all of this information through an award-winning single online web page.[26]

The Department of Health and Human Services **Substance Abuse and Mental Health Services Administration (SAMHSA)** also has a website that is an invaluable resource for families, social service workers and individuals seeking mental health treatment centers in their localities.[27] SAMHSA was established in 1992 and directed by Congress to target substance abuse and mental health services to the people most in need and to translate research in these areas more effectively and more rapidly into the general health care system. Over the years SAMHSA has demonstrated that prevention works, treatment is effective, and people recover from mental and substance use disorders. Behavioral health services improve health status and reduce health care and other costs to society. Continued improvement in the delivery and financing of prevention, treatment and recovery support services provides a cost-effective opportunity to advance and protect individual health. The agency also provides grants and contracts to state and local community projects which aim to achieve the same goal as the agency itself.[28]

The United States is the largest consumer of goods and services in the world. Two-thirds of the U.S. economy is consumer driven and the U.S. imports far more than it exports. U.S. citizens are at the top of the list when it comes to consumption—whether it is food, clothing, cars, electronics or services. **Consumer.gov** is a website to enhance the G2C service and protect American consumers.[29] The website is also a work in progress, a single source of information on almost any goods and/or service available to American consumers. Aspects of Consumer.gov include "ScamAlert," which provides up-to-date and credible information regarding fraudulent and deceptive practices occurring in the marketplace; it features "In the Spotlight," which showcases new education and consumer awareness campaigns focused on protecting the American consumer. The Obama administration expanded consumer protection by creating a "Super-agency" to better coordinate and protect people from mortgage fraud, predatory lending practices and other forms of institutional corruption (Chapter 6).

Natural disasters such as earthquakes, floods, hurricanes, storms and tornados expose many Americans in need of government assistance and create an overwhelming demand for assistance to victims. Consequently, former president George W. Bush issued Executive Order 13411 in August of 2006 which called for the establishment of a task force headed by the Secretary of Homeland Security with the goal of improving the quality of federal assistance to disaster victims—the result of this task force was the **Disaster Assistance Improvement Plan (DAIP)**. The DAIP is an online application geared to improving the quality of G2C services via the creation of a one-stop disaster benefits portal. Through DAIP citizens can apply for disaster assistance across all programs that receive federal government assistance.[30] DAIP provides a number of improvements to U.S. citizens including: significantly reduced paperwork for victims of disasters who apply for government assistance; simplified searches regarding available benefits/assistance; speedier processing of assistance applications which increases receipt of aid; and DAIP frees up government resources that were traditionally burdened with the process-ing of applications to focus on more important services such as helping disaster victims.[31]

Constraints on Applying E-Commerce and Digital Technology to Government

The application of digital technology and e-commerce is an effective way to enhance the overall quality of government services in a wide variety of areas. However, there are always constraints and barriers to implementa-tion. With regard to digital governance, these constraints include, among others: bureaucratic fragmentation, digital illiteracy, industry co-optation, lack of citizen satisfaction measures, limited budgetary resources, political opposition, and privacy and security issues. We have seen examples of all of these in the above-referenced federal, state and local cases.

Traditional Weberian bureaucracy and federalism help ensure checks and balances to prevent the national government from obtaining too much power. However, when it comes to implementing customer-centric quality improvements within bureaucracies, fragmentation creates a number of obstacles. In general, federal administrative activities can be viewed as four primary functions:

1) policy making;
2) program implementation;

3) compliance, evaluation and enforcement; and
4) internal operations and infrastructure.

Policy evaluation attempts to determine the effectiveness of program operations and regulatory compliance efforts. Internal operations are administrative functions, such as financial management, that support day-to-day activities needed to carry out policy making, program administration and compliance activities. ICT-enabled government offers the opportunity to streamline these activities and improve productivity by enabling agencies to focus on their core competencies and mission requirements. Such initiatives eliminate unnecessary redundancy, while improving service quality by simplifying processes and unifying agency islands of automation.[32] Another challenge is to overcome parochialism in many government agencies and departments which still operate with "agency-centric" thinking instead of adopting a "big picture" mentality that incorporates increased responsiveness to government constituents (i.e. citizens and businesses).

There is a need for investment in resources, both financial and human, in any ICT-enabled service quality improvement initiative. The application of digital technology and e-commerce is not an inexpensive investment. It is not surprising that "one of the most formidable obstacles many public-sector leaders face is finding money to pay for digital government and modernization. The funding challenge is particularly acute for local governments, which had fewer IT dollars to dispense even before the state cutbacks of recent years" (Eggers, 2005: 233). Another important challenge is measuring citizen satisfaction. Reaction from citizens to internet-enabled reforms has been generally positive (Chapter 6). Most citizens believe that their ability to access information from government will get better and that government will be able to offer more convenient services; overall both businesses and citizens are generally more satisfied with the virtual experience than with traditional government. However, citizens who seek more responsive government services still have concerns related to techno-phobia, especially those with limited knowledge of computers and others who are rightfully concerned about personal privacy and security.

Information Technology Policies and the Obama Administration

Several laws have been enacted to accelerate the digitization of government documents, integration of websites and expansion of information and communication technologies (Chapters 5 and 6). Legislation and regulation have improved the management and promotion of electronic government services and processes. This provides a framework for performance measures using ICTs to improve citizen access to government information and services, as well as for other purposes. Upon assuming office in 2009, one of President Obama's first administrative actions was to appoint a federal Chief Information Officer (CIO) and create an Office for **Chief Technology Officer (CTO)** for the federal government.

In March 2009, President Obama appointed Vivek Kundra as federal CIO responsible for coordinating IT policy and operations across federal agencies. He was assigned the difficult task of saving federal government resources while helping to institute the president's vision for a Web 2.0 government. He reports directly to the White House, and is expected to not only economize with web-based approaches, but potentially encourage entirely new waves of economic development. Elevating the position to White House level helps ensure that the public will have access to information, and to rethink how citizens interact with government in an information economy. Kundra's office launched **Data.gov**, an innovative open-source portal that publishes vast arrays of government data and employs new technologies for public dissemination. Just as the Human Genome Project spurred new industry applications and research into DNA and genetics in the 1990s (eventually mapping the human genetic code by 2006)[33] the integration of open-source coding with government holds the potential to fundamentally change the political economy. Besides making data available for citizens, the federal government also hosts space online where citizens can turn to each other for solutions to social problems, much as they do now on social networking sites like *Facebook* and *Twitter*.

In April 2009, President Obama appointed Aneesh Chopra, formerly Virginia's Secretary of Technology, as the nation's first Chief Technology Officer (CTO). Chopra and Kundra met over a decade ago as entrepreneurs in Northern Virginia's Indian American business community. They worked together for Virginia Governor Timothy M. Kaine's administration and then as technology and innovation advisers on President Obama's transition team. The CTO focuses on overall technology policy and innovation strategies across departments while the CIO will oversee day-to-day information technology spending and operations within agencies. Chopra is in the Office of Science and Technology Policy and Kundra in the Office of Management and Budget. Both have established impressive track records for taking innovative approaches to using technology in government. Chopra created a social network for clinicians in remote health clinics, and also spearheaded a state-sponsored venture capital fund to let Virginia state agencies try out unconventional tools to improve their services. Kundra invited software developers to use the District of Columbia's government data to create internet and smart phone applications intended to give citizens easier access to city information. His efforts to let the public observe the city's contract-letting process helped spur the development of **Recovery.gov**, a website designed to track federal stimulus funding. Their jobs include modifying budgets, organizing federal employees and contractors, and reworking technology systems, all while stimulus money is being distributed to create jobs and support new projects. The jobs require a broad set of skills including both knowledge of technology and the ability to connect with the IT industry while operating within the confines of government.[34]

Conclusion: D-Government as a Means to Enhance Government Services

While it is impossible to fully cover all applications, this chapter has described representative examples of how governments are integrating e-commerce and digital technology to bolster G2G, G2E, G2B and G2C connections. The question still remains: what is the future of virtual government with respect to enhancing the overall quality of government services?

The majority of U.S. citizens view digital government positively as making an important contribution to a more participatory democracy, even though many do not yet regularly access the internet for public services (Chapter 6). The application of digital technology *by* government allows more people to become more involved *in* government and makes government more accountable. In an ICT-driven quality managed organization, the workforce is motivated by worker participation (where workers can actively contribute to the quality improvement efforts) versus an Industrial Age command and control organization where worker participation is neither encouraged nor rewarded. Activities such as accessing voting records, commenting on federal legislation, communicating directly with the chief executive or members of Congress, and monitoring public hearings promote greater citizen knowledge of democratic processes. Transforming citizens into valued customers and reconfiguring administrative systems to accommodate demands stem from structural changes in society, greater citizen participation and more direct linkages between citizens and government agencies. Managing customer service quality requires responsiveness to both internal and external customers; ICT applications respond to the specific needs of other government agencies and departments, businesses and citizens. In addition, digital technology is malleable, allowing government to more easily adapt programs and websites to reflect changes in the demands of its constituents.

All organizations need to commit additional resources to continuously update their websites; many governmental agencies are in the process of *becoming* their websites. Better website maintenance develops trust and encourages citizens and members of the business community to utilize government ICT resources. Governments have created links to a wide range of activities such as benefits, citizen complaints, educational institutions and investment opportunities for businesses. There has been some slippage as a result of the global financial stress as many sites have not been updated in several years and contain inaccurate information, disconnected links and incorrect e-mail contact information. The commercial advantages of delivering service via ICTs are obvious. In nations such as Australia, citizens can register government complaints through agency websites. Nations such as China, Estonia, Finland, the Netherlands and the Czech Republic are attracting overseas investors through their websites (Chapter 8). In 2000, Beijing's mayor launched an initiative to integrate and simplify the application process for starting new businesses in China. Rather than navigate through the layers of arcane rules and regulations of multiple agencies, investors can now conduct application, reporting and administration processes on a single website that shares information with several government agencies. The depth of the worldwide financial recession and the changes it has inspired make it less likely that governments will revert to traditional service delivery.

What is the forecast for the future of digital government with respect to enhancing the quality of government services? So long as proposed changes in technology are framed within a comprehensive strategy emphasizing collaboration, leadership, interoperable networks, information sharing, and standards, e-commerce and digital technology will continue to play a significant role in ongoing efforts to improve the quality of public services.

Key Terms

broadband internet connectivity, 163
information quality management, 163
U.S. Internal Revenue Service (IRS), 164
U.S. Department of Homeland Security (DHS), 165
Office of the Director of National Intelligence (DNI), 165
iron triangles, 166
Political Action Committees (PACs), 166
Health Maintenance Organizations (HMOs), 166
fragmented federalism, 167
Disaster Management Interoperability Service (DMIS), 168
President's Management Council (PMC), 169
SAFECOM, 169
standard operating procedures (SOPs), 170

Clark County Urban Area Working Group (UAWG), Las Vegas, NV, 170
Grants.gov, 170
Federal Register, 170
Federal Financial Assistance Management Act (Public Law 106–107), 170
identity theft, 172
government-to-employee (G2E) relationships, 172
Central Personnel Data File (CPDF), 172
Enterprise Human Resources Integration (EHRI), 172
standardization, 174
government-to-business (G2B) relationship, 174
electronic procurement, 175
Electronic Business Resource Centers (EBRC), 176
Business.gov, 176
e-rulemaking, 177

Part IV

Globalization and Interactive Citizenship

In many developed and developing regions of the world, public officials have overcome obstacles to the adoption of New Media technologies and implemented ICT-enabled breakthroughs in a wide range of public services. Governments in several countries now use digital technologies as strategies to encourage participation, enhance transparency, increase effectiveness and facilitate public sector reform; still others conduct elections online, collect more tax revenue and deliver public services more efficiently. Chapter 8 compares progress in selected world regions, highlights benchmarks and best practices (lessons from leading countries) and presents examples (such as the Brazilian parliament, Denmark e2012, Malaysia and Swedish Postal Service) of value-added public sector applications. Comparisons show how nations at different stages of economic development deploy ICTs to deal with financial and economic crises, overcome digital divides and respond to natural and made-made disasters. Realistically, even in the most advanced economies, obstacles to full implementation remain.

Chapter 9 expands the discussion of global trends identified in Chapter 1 and returns to the broader themes of how ICT-enabled innovations in technology, transportation and telecommunications are driving global trade and economic growth. Chapter sections trace the history and advantages of free trade; discuss how rapidly the use (and possible misuse) of ICTs has changed the practice of public administration; show how relationships among individuals, businesses and governments are being affected; and explain how U.S. foreign and military policy is influenced by dependence on foreign sources of energy. Cases demonstrate how ICTs are being used by public administration in several countries to mitigate the effects of global recession, reduce dependence on fossil fuels and convert Industrial Age legacy industries to less hierarchical future-oriented citizen-centric networked systems.

Chapter 10 summarizes lessons learned from the book, highlights recurring themes, discusses paradoxes and outlines future challenges.

8 Global Inventory of Digital Governance Practices

Interactive technologies offer governments a way to reap the benefits of inclusive policy-making on economic crisis issues at relatively low cost.

United Nations E-Government Survey, 2010

During the past two decades, New Media technologies have migrated from the most economically developed countries to emerging less developed nations. New forms of interaction, deliberation and decision making are being informed by ICTs and are informing citizens while simultaneously transforming relationships between businesses and governments. Public and private sector innovations are being driven by demand for internet access, new mobile cellular PDAs, hardware and software systems. The information-transformational use of ICTs has led to new forms of service delivery capable of providing citizens with additional means to access information and interact with and participate in government.

The total number of "wired" governments has steadily increased and now ranges from highly developed and wealthy nations in North America, Asia and Europe to very small island states such as Barbados and Mauritius.[1] Digital governance is becoming a pervasive global trend within all branches of public administration in nearly every country, as well as in numerous sub-national states and local governments within many nations. An increasing body of research analyzes the depth and breadth of electronic and digital government in industrialized democracies, in emerging nations and in large metropolitan areas within different nations (Chadwick and Howard, 2009; Chen *et al.*, 2008; Curtin, Sommer and Vis-Sommer, 2003; Hernon, Cullen and Relyea, 2006; Holzer, Manoharan and Van Ryzin, 2010; Nixon and Koutrakou, 2007; Roucheleau, 2007; Shea and Garson, 2010; Traunmüller, 2004; United Nations E-Government Survey, 2008, 2010; Wimmer, 2005; Wimmer *et al.*, 2005).

Despite technological advances, there have been few systematic comparative analyses of the current state of ICT-driven digital governance which take into account vast demographic, economic, political and structural differences among nations. Numerous internal and external factors affect information dissemination, service delivery, citizen participation and deliberation. Not all governments are prepared for high-tech changes, nor are their citizens regularly engaged in civic interactions. On the contrary, many developing nations are benefitting from not having to invest in obsolete technologies. This chapter compares progress in selected world regions, highlights benchmarks and lessons from leading countries, describes how governments in different nations use ICTs to accomplish their missions and presents case studies of public sector applications. Because of the depth and scope of global ICT applications, initiatives illustrating progress in selected parts of the world are highlighted. Endnotes and references direct readers to more detailed discussions of ICT applications, development and implementation in other advanced and emerging nations.

Global Differences by Region

Countries at varying levels of economic and political development have committed substantial resources to create both the infrastructure and supportive environment for linking with their citizens, businesses and other governmental entities. This is an ongoing process that has accelerated in recent years. Despite occasional anomalies (such as a rich nation failing to invest in ICTs), there is strong correlation between a nation's relative economic strength and available human resources—as measured by **per capita gross domestic product (GDP)** and level of literacy—and the extent of ICT implementation. Factors such as geographic location, access to health care, public debt, population size, educational system and form of government also influence the level of and return on investments in ICTs. The association between wealth, education and technological innovation is confirmed on several international surveys which review the current condition of electronic government and describe in detail strategies used by various governments for improving information and services online (Cap Gemini, 2007; Holzer and Kim, 2008; OECD, 2007; UN E-Government Survey, 2008, 2010; West, 2008).

Depending on the methodology and scope of the study, each of these analyses reveals a slightly different but highly correlated ranking of global ICT progress. Over 95% of the national governments of all nations now have websites or portals to access information. Despite this near global saturation level, the content of information on these portals is still controlled by central governments and not fully open to public view. This is especially salient in non-democratic forms of government. Looking in depth at websites alone may not reveal the full extent of digital integration, but it does provide an eye through which the technological advancement of a country can be viewed.

In a 2008 **Brookings Institution** study of 1,667 national government websites, the Nordic countries ranked highest among the sample (see Table 8.1). Using a detailed analysis of national government websites in 198 nations undertaken in summer 2008, the Brookings report studied the features available online, variation that exists across countries and how current e-government trends compare to previous years, as far back as 2001. The report concluded that just over 50% of government websites offer services that are fully executable online, up from 28% in the previous year. Ninety-six percent of websites provide access to publications and 75% have links to databases. More problematic was that only 30% show privacy policies and 17% publish security policies. Only 16% of government websites have any form of access for disabled persons, while 57% provide foreign language translation to non-native readers; 14% offer the ability to personalize government websites to a visitor's area of interest, while only 3% provide Personal Data Assistant (PDA) "smart-phone" accessibility. The remainder of the report reviewed these findings in greater detail and closed by making recommendations for more effective use of digital technology (West, 2008).

Using a more comprehensive and detailed methodology, the 2005, 2008 and 2010 **United Nations** (UN) E-Government Surveys indicate how rapidly ICTs are being assimilated and integrated into various cultures and present a very different line-up of leading countries. In the 2008 edition of the UN survey, Sweden and Denmark ranked number one and two, the United States third and Norway fourth among the nearly 192 UN member countries studied. In just two years, several other governments in middle-income countries made great strides in developing online services: the

Table 8.1 E-Government Ratings by Region (%)

	2001	2002	2003	2004	2005	2006	2007	2008
North America	51.0	60.4	40.2	39.2	47.3	43.1	45.3	53.1
Western Europe	34.1	47.6	33.1	30.0	29.6	35.2	36.8	37.2
Eastern Europe	43.5	32.0	28.0	27.1	29.2	31.7	30.1	30.1
Asia	34.0	48.7	34.3	31.6	37.3	35.9	39.5	39.7
Middle East	31.1	43.2	32.1	28.1	27.4	29.4	33.5	32.3
Russia/Central Asia	30.9	37.2	29.7	25.3	25.0	30.6	27.8	31.2
South America	30.7	42.0	29.5	24.3	25.9	28.0	32.1	33.3
Pacific Ocean Islands	30.6	39.5	32.1	29.9	27.9	32.4	33.8	39.0
Central America	27.7	41.4	28.6	24.1	24.1	25.0	29.2	31.2
Africa	23.5	36.8	27.6	22.0	22.0	24.3	26.0	26.3

Source: Compiled by author (D. West). Available at: www.brookings.edu/~/media/Files/rc/reports/2008/0 817_egovernment_west/0817_egovernment_west.pdf

Table 8.2 Top 20 Countries in E-Government Development Index

1. Republic of Korea 0.8785	11. Singapore 0.7476
2. United States 0.8510	12. Sweden 0.7474
3. Canada 0.8448	13. Bahrain 0.7363
4. United Kingdom 0.8147	14. New Zealand 0.7311
5. Netherlands 0.8097	15. Germany 0.7309
6. Norway 0.8020	16. Belgium 0.7225
7. Denmark 0.7872	17. Japan 0.7152
8. Australia 0.7863	18. Switzerland 0.7136
9. Spain 0.7516	19. Finland 0.6967
10. France 0.751	20. Estonia 0.6965

Source: UN E-Government Survey (2010: 114)

Republic of Korea, the Netherlands, Australia, Spain, Singapore, Bahrain, New Zealand, Finland and Estonia (Table 8.2). Comparing the 2010 results with 2008, the more recent survey gives more weight to advanced stages of online development such as 1) availability of transactional services and 2) promotion of a connected approach to e-government.[2] Nations leading the 2010 UN E-Government Survey are quite different from those ahead in either the Brookings study or the 2008 UN survey.

Not surprisingly, the results of the 2010 study are highly correlated with broader world internet adoption rates in various geographic regions. North America has the highest rate of internet dissemination, followed by Oceania/Australia, Europe, Latin America, the Middle East, Asia and Africa. Between 2000 and 2010, global access to the internet increased nearly 500%. In spite of the global economic recession, the estimated number of internet users worldwide reached 2 billion by the end of 2010, or nearly 30% of the entire global population (Figure 8.1). Of those, 1.2 billion reside in developing countries. Growth rates and other trend data suggest that those able to harness the potential for expanded broadband access and mobile cellular networks in developing countries have much to gain in the future. Some of the richest and most applicable lessons for the future application of ICTs to public services will be learned in the emerging economies in the less developed world.

There are several international organizations that promote civil interests, economic cooperation and trade among nations. The **Organization for Economic Cooperation and Development (OECD)** is a group of 34 advanced economically developed countries that accept principles of representative democracy and free-market economy. The OECD originated in 1948 as the Organization for European Economic Co-operation (OEEC) to help administer the Marshall Plan for the reconstruction of Europe after World War II. Its membership was later extended to non-European states. In 1961, it was reformed into the OECD by the Convention on the

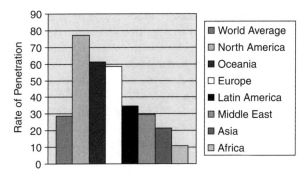

Figure 8.1 Internet Penetration Rates

Source: Internet World Stats: www.internetworldstats.com/stats.htm

Organization for Economic Co-operation and Development. Its mission is to help member countries achieve sustainable growth and full employment while raising the standard of living and maintaining financial stability.

Many OECD nations are included in a smaller **Group of 20 or G-20** countries established in 1999 to bring together globally important highly competitive industrialized *and* rapidly developing economies such as China and India to discuss key issues affecting the global economy. The inaugural meeting of Finance Ministers and Central Bank Governors of the G-20 took place in Berlin on December 15, 1999, hosted by German and Canadian finance ministers. Member countries represent about 90% of the world's wealth, 80% of global trade and two-thirds of the world's populations. More select still, but increasingly less influential, is the **Group of Eight or G-8** (formerly the G6 or Group of Six), a forum created by France in 1975 for governments of the then eight most powerful nations of the northern hemisphere: Canada, France, Germany, Italy, Japan, Russia, the United Kingdom and the United States; in addition, the European Union is represented within the G-8, but is prohibited by law from chairing the group. G8 ministers also meet throughout the year, such as the finance ministers (who meet four times a year), foreign ministers and environment ministers. The United States plays a leading role in all of these and other international organizations.

The G-20 will soon officially replace the G-8, which is dominated by the richest industrialized nations, as the preeminent forum for discussion of global economic policy. This is a major victory for emerging nations that have been demanding a "level playing field" for international recognition. The G-8 continues to meet twice a year to discuss specific policy issues, such as security, but the group is gradually relinquishing power to the G-20. President Obama has been a leading spokesperson for broadening the power bases to include rapidly developing countries such as such as China, India, Korea and Brazil. Trade issues, which are important to developing and developed nations alike, are being addressed in depth as individual economies begin to emerge from recession (see Chapter 9).

The G-20 nations are intent on preventing the excesses that precipitated global financial strains by supporting tougher sanctions to enforce **environmental protection,** energy sustainability, moderate executive compensation and the elimination of tax havens. There are still deep disagreements on issues such as **International Monetary Fund (IMF)** reforms, minimum capital requirements for financial institutions and limits on executive pay and bonuses. World leaders gathered in Pittsburgh, Pennsylvania, for the third G-20 summit in September of 2009 and agreed that member nations should submit their economic policies to a "peer review" process to ensure uniformity of regulatory procedures. No sanctions or other types of punitive measures would be imposed, but countries would be assessed as to whether their policies contribute to the strong and balanced growth of the global economy. This would require all countries, including China and the United States, to be open to criticism about how their internal economies are managed.[3] National interests notwithstanding, G-20 nations are incorporating ICTs to accomplish global economic as well as domestic societal goals.

The American Paradox

Even with its high level of economic development, accumulated wealth and historical advantage in technological research and development (R&D), the United States has fallen behind several less affluent industrialized democracies in the application of ICTs to public services. According to the Science, Technology and Industry Scoreboard of the OECD, the U.S. ranked 15th in broadband adoption, dropped to 11th place in broadband access and 10th place in affordability.[4] Using a weighted average of business, consumer and government indicators, a more recent Canadian study challenged the OECD data and ranked the United States in first place in broadband connectivity.[5]

Nonetheless, the United States may be losing its technological advantage as one of the leading industrialized nations of the world. America lags behind Korea, Japan, Iceland, the Netherlands, Sweden, France, Denmark, Norway, Canada and Belgium in **internet subscribers per household,** broadband access and customer service quality. Whereas 36% of all Swiss residents have access to internet subscription services, 31% of Americans have access to the internet at home. More worrisome is broadband access. Without faster internet transmission speeds, the application of newer G-3 and G-4 PDA applications is limited. In 2007, the United States dropped to 15th among 30 OECD nations, down sharply from fourth place in 2001. Thirty-five percent of Danes have access to high-speed broadband, compared to only 22% of Americans. Slower internet speeds limit the ability of Americans, especially those living in underserved areas, to take full advantage of newer media-rich G-3 and G-4 internet applications. Darrell West (2008) argues that the United States must invest more in research and development to maintain its technology edge in the 21st century. How new R&D funds will be generated during the current economic crisis without fundamental changes in business–government relations remains to be seen.

According to the 2008 UN Survey, the United States federal system of government (not federalism) was viewed the model for e-government worldwide. This may not be indicative of the real shortcomings of the U.S. government's information technology, but rather reflects the lack of trans- actional and e-commerce features found in other national and ministerial websites. The USA.gov web portal still remains one of the most compre- hensive government websites in existence. Its success is even more impres- sive because of the vast size of the U.S. federal, state and local bureaucracy and the enormous amount of information and services provided online. From a service delivery perspective, an increasing percentage of cities in the United States offer online services, including the payment of utility bills, parking tickets, building permits, taxes, applications for jobs, permits, licenses and property registration[6] (see Appendix A). Still, juris- dictional disputes and lack of resources among states and local govern- ments limit U.S. innovation.

Explanations for this American paradox differ, including the previously mentioned: 1) preference for "market-based" solutions to public problems; 2) weakened economy precipitated by deregulation and the sub-prime "mortgage meltdown"; 3) general public disregard for the profession of public administration (not uncommon in other regions as well); 4) absence of a centralized governmental structure to guide technological innovation; and 5) legislative and regulatory limits on the application of innovative changes. Despite these limitations, the United States is a leader in North America and ranks among the world's most technologically advanced and internet-ready nations.

Regional Differences in Participation

There are major **regional differences** among the five inhabited areas of the world in terms of e-government participation. The UN e-participation civic engagement index showed a modest aggregate upward improvement among 189 countries offering online services to citizens in 2008 as compared to 179 in 2005. Moreover, the survey indicated that a greater number of nations were in the middle to top one-third of the e-participation utilization, capable of using ICTs to broaden and deepen political participation by enabling citizens to connect with one another and with their elected representatives. The e-participation index assesses governmental implementation of products and services concerning e-information, e-consultation and e-decision making. **Germany.info** is a good example of a comprehensive portal for visitors.[7] However, 82% of the countries surveyed still remained in the lower one-third of the UN study. Although this amounts to an overall improvement over the 2005 assessment, the results still indicate that few countries have implemented fully integrated transactional policies and services. In terms of the *total* number of internet users in world geographic regions, Asia leads, followed by Europe, North America, Latin America, Africa, the Middle East and Oceania (Figure 8.2). China alone has more that 420 million internet users.

The Republic of Korea scored highest (1.000) on both the 2010 **e-participation index** and the aforementioned e-government development index. This was primarily due to its strength in e-information and e-consultation, which enabled citizens to be more interactive with their government agencies. Korea was followed in order by Australia (0.9143), Spain (0.8286), New Zealand (0.7714), UK and Northern Ireland (0.7714), Japan (0.7571), the United States (0.7571), Canada (0.7286), Estonia (0.6857), Singapore (0.6857), Bahrain (0.6714), Malaysia (0.6571), Denmark (0.6429), Germany (0.6143) and France (0.6000). Notable movers from 2008 to 2010 also included Chile, Colombia, Singapore and the United Kingdom, all of which joined the world's top performers in online service development. Not surprisingly, over 90% of all countries scoring highest on the e-participation index are concentrated in Europe, the Americas (North, Central and South) and Asia. (This may be less of an indication of e-government capacity and progress than the existence of free-market economies and democratic forms of government.) As indicated on Figure 8.3, participation is generally a function of industrialized democratic nations clustered in Asia, Europe and North America.

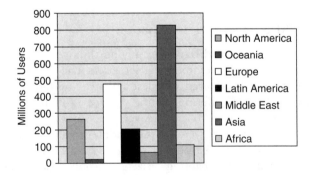

Figure 8.2 Internet Use by Region

Source: Internet World Stats: www.internetworldstats.com/stats.htm

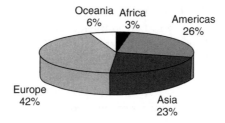

Figure 8.3 E-Participation Index: Top 35 Countries
Source: UN Study (2008: 78)

The leading countries possess the intellectual and financial resources necessary to support the development of ICT infrastructure and recognize the importance of centering program implementation on needs of customers, citizens, private enterprises and other stakeholders. European countries have sophisticated transactional platforms which can also facilitate digital governance. Governments using ICTs to empower each of their major stakeholders do so by building bridges, one citizen at a time, to access valuable databases and build a digital future. The UK's national government website contains valuable information about history and family ancestry (Box 8.1).

In all but a few cases, governments are moving forward, albeit more slowly due to recession, in infrastructure development around the world. Given the high fiscal demands for supporting pre-existing infrastructure (appropriate policies, capacity development, ICT applications, human resources, privacy, security concerns and relevant content) which must be in place to fully transact online government, it is not surprising that progress has slowed. Lack of technology, web development staff, financial resources and expertise has also hampered further growth in

---

Box 8.1: The United Kingdom's Direct.gov website

Provides a portal to the National Archives allowing access to multiple databases of digitized public documents such as government publications and historical documents dating from the 8th century. These include census records, immigration documents, family records and military service. These and other innovative applications not only provide valuable services, but also serve as a platform for delivering valuable e-learning, civics lessons as well as cultural and historical materials online.

Source: www.direct.gov.uk/en/index.htm

many hard-pressed local governments. As previously mentioned, smart communities around the world are implementing ICTs and offering citizens more advanced features on their websites (Holzer, Manoharan and Van Ryzin, 2010; Moulder, 2001; Holden, Norris and Fletcher 2002). As illustrated by studies that concentrate primarily on large metropolitan areas, perhaps neglecting the spread and potential achievements made by small and mid-sized communities, New Media has facilitated the retrieval of information about local government and the completion of various governmental service transactions online (Holzer and Kim, 2003; Rocheleau, 2007).

In developing countries with large urban/rural digital divides, governments are forced to adopt creative approaches to delivering services over ICT channels to communities with uneven access to networks. Community centers with operator-assisted online counters or internet cafes have been the most popular mode of delivering services in underserved regions (Bhatnagar, 2004: 34). Ongoing efforts to close the digital divide and increase participation can profoundly shape government–citizen relationships. For many developing countries, mobile technology is becoming a feasible way to reach out to the wider population, especially in rural areas (see Box 8.2).

Overcoming Global Digital Divides

Whether and to what extent the digital divide disrupts progress depends upon how a country or region's economic and political resources are distributed. Digital divides reflect how economic power is distributed in any society. The **global digital divide** is one manifestation of the unequal distribution of wealth and power in all societies. Regardless of geographic location, those with higher incomes have greater access to the computers and internet and are more likely to use technology to their advantage. Urban residents are typically better connected to broadband electronic

---

Box 8.2: Brazil—House of Representatives e-Participation

The Brazilian House of Representatives website allows citizens to talk to their representatives and to participate in debates directly through the internet. The Brazilian government also provides e-participation platforms that permit MPs and citizens to communicate through chat rooms, discussion forums and the service *Fale com Deputado* or Talk to an MP. In a country as vast as Brazil and with a geographically dispersed population, online participation has provided citizens with a greater voice in the creation of law and policies.

Source: www2.camara.gov.br/popular

media than rural dwellers. Those with more education have both higher incomes and better access to internet and wireless connectivity.

Many developing countries are beginning to take seriously the prospects for domestic reforms linking digital governance with broader participation and stronger democracy. The primary service orientation of developed countries with respect to their government agendas may influence their international assistance efforts aimed at recipient countries in the developing world. Organizations such as the **World Bank**, the International Monetary Fund (IMF) and the **World Trade Organization (WTO)** are instrumental in providing financial assistance to developing nations to, among other goals, invest in necessary ICT infrastructure. These organizations are often accused of favoring developing over less developed nations by requiring strict conditions for funding assistance projects. The results, according to some critical observers, can be catastrophic.

> Together these institutions encourage economic structural adjustment, privatization and market liberalization in emerging markets. Within the competitive global framework, developing countries are left with little choice other than to comply with the neoliberal agenda. As a result these countries are often left with crippling debt and a fragile economy. Meanwhile, foreign investors and multinational corporations gain control of a significant portion of the world's resources, finance, services, technology and knowledge. Whilst these multinationals report record profits, around 50,000 people die each day from poverty.[8]

Such a danger is compounded by findings stemming from a wider set of New Media initiatives involving project sponsors and knowledge transfers from developed to developing countries. An absence of sufficient cultural sensitivity in crafting projects within the contours of a localized setting is also a common source of failure (Bhagnagar, 2003).

For many techno-optimists, online government is a harbinger of good governance in a wireless broadband environment that promises unbounded progress in all realms of governance. Global parameters of information management, democratic freedoms and technological deployment have shifted considerably since the 9/11 terrorist attacks in 2001 and the global financial crisis beginning in 2007. An expanded focus on security and financial accountability and a movement toward bilateral relationships between developed and developing nations have been forged through traditional efforts at international assistance in numerous ways. For many Western countries, the exporting of democracy must now compete with the expansion of more technologically sophisticated security apparatus, with both domestic and international implications. Appendix C shows the countries least able to provide e-government services, most of which also depend on international assistance for financial resources. It is worth noting that most of the countries in the bottom 35 are clustered in Africa and Central and Southern Asia. Plainly, the global digital divide has significant implications for the future of international relations and developmental assistance strategies. Regional differences in internet access and use are also quite pronounced among different countries and *within* countries. Northern Europe has more internet users than Southern Europe, as does Western or Atlantic Canada as opposed to Central Canada.

The lack of ICT infrastructure constitutes a significant barrier to implementation of e-governance projects in Africa as well as other developing regions. If the goal is to improve interaction between public services and its stakeholders, all stakeholders including average citizens should be able to have access. Yet ICT infrastructures in government institutions are often technically inferior to those in private sectors and NGOs. The general public has limited access to basic tools such as radios and telephones. In addition, the costs involved in constructing a high bandwidth infrastructure as well as meeting universal access needs for the majority are very high.[9]

The ICT-enabled route alone, however, is insufficient *by itself* to achieve lasting changes. Enhanced use of ICTs makes new processes of coordination possible, but the governance challenge discussed in previous chapters cannot be met solely through the virtues of electronic information and communication devices alone. For example, both the American and Canadian federal public services have been criticized as wasteful; in Canada, the bureaucracy has four times more human resources personnel per employee than similar organizations in the private sector; and it takes twice as much time to fill positions than other organizations. Indeed, the decentralized nature of ICTs may also weaken nation-states, their institutional order, authority and legitimacy (Paquet, 2004).

Core industrial and business regions typically have more internet access and users, whereas peripheral geographic areas (agricultural, extractive, rural, underdeveloped, etc.) have fewer resources and opportunities to connect. In the broadest sense, the so-called **global north** has more internet access and users than the less economically developed **rural south**. Even in developed economies, rural areas are typically not as well served. Economics of network allocation reflect population density and even small distances can make a big difference. Small communities within commuting range of larger urban centers often find themselves forced to finance their own microwave transmission towers to assure wireless service because private telecom providers do not find the prospect profitable enough. Geography plays a major part as deserts, jungles and mountainous regions have lower internet access than plains, river valleys, or moderate climates. Much of this can be changed with the combination of newer technologies and investments such as O3b, but the global digital divide is still more noticeable in the Southern Hemisphere and threatens to increase if the global economy continues to slump.[10]

Satellite networks such as O3b designed to reach underdeveloped regions of the world are becoming viable alternatives, but they require considerable private funds or public subsidies, either by government, private investors or very generous corporate sponsors. Internet access and use within countries also vary with the demographic characteristics of the population. Income and education together account for more of the differences than all other variables combined. Connecting to and using the internet is relatively expensive, especially for those without reliable access to electrical power and only a small proportion of discretionary income. But since that is the classical definition of poverty, it is not surprising that the digital divide too is an economically and politically created barrier (Riley, 2004: 9).

Correcting the global digital gap requires an understanding of the breadth and depth of the cultural, racial, educational, knowledge and literacy divide that exists in any given jurisdiction. Conventional wisdom argues that expanded digital services may exacerbate these inequities. On the contrary, internet usage statistics show that the fastest growing regions in the world are Africa, the Middle East and Latin America. Wealthy countries in underserved regions are ahead of some nations in relatively more developed regions. For example, Dubai won the Best Middle East e-government portal in 2005 by offering over 300 online services. There are of course much higher numbers of internet users in more developed regions such as North America, Oceania and Europe so percentage increases in all forms of New Media are by definition likely to be lower (Figure 8.2). However, developing nations without the sunk costs of paying for obsolete technologies such as landlines for telephone service are better positioned to benefit from future dissemination of ICT systems.

Many national, provincial, state and local governments are seeking ways to close the digital divide and are doing so with newest technologies. Even with the latest ICTs, it is a continuing challenge to ensure successful delivery of digital services (Riley, 2004: 18–21). Like policies which aim to equalize opportunities and redistribute resources, the digital divide can only be corrected through providing expanded economic opportunities and improving the quality of education available to all citizens (Chapter 4). The spread of cellular technology facilitates the use of less expensive higher quality systems by extending the benefits of ICTs to emerging nations without the high costs of investing in obsolete infrastructure. Mobile phone systems have rapidly expanded, especially in Africa, as the number of fixed landlines worldwide is decreasing (see Figure 8.4). Compared to the growth rate of telephone lines, mobile phone subscriptions have increased four times as fast. In addition, capacities of mobile phones are rapidly expanding to include voice, text messages, e-mail and even full internet browsers, making mobile access the communication medium of the future. Full wireless broadband internet access via mobile phones is still restricted because of its added subscription costs.

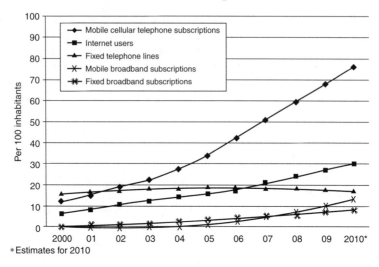

Figure 8.4 Global ICT Development, 2000–2010

Source: www.itu.int/ITU-D/ict/statistics/material/graphs/2010/Global_ICT_Dev_00-10.jpg

Nonetheless, the rapid development of ICT-mobile phone linkages offers unprecedented opportunities to improve the education and health for those living in underserved communities that lack schools or access to health care facilities. Information provided via mobile phones can help to diagnose and treat illness and assist in the early detection and containment of epidemics.

Regardless of the level of economic development, providing online government services in underserved areas, especially those offered by local governments, is more likely to positively affect levels of citizen trust and confidence in their governments (Nugent, 2001: 230; Tolbert and Mossberger, 2006). Few governments outside Asia, Europe and North America can presently afford to make the necessary infrastructure investments to move beyond basic informational applications to more advanced digital governance stages. There is evidence, however, that selected metropolitan areas and a few other countries have utilized ICTs to fully nourish citizen participation and build a foundation for enhancing participatory democracy. This is particularly true for democracies such as the United States, which, in contrast to its traditional European central government counterparts, has a political foundation that has always been "fascinate[ed] with direct democracy" (Elberse, Hale and Dutton, 2000: 131; deTocqueville, 1948). Given this positive association, greater accomplishments through information and communication technologies are possible as more citizens access the internet and learn about the advantages of democratic participation from other regions.

E-Government Readiness Rankings

There are major differences in economic capacity as well as internet readiness of nations in different regions of the world. **Internet readiness** reflects the ability, expertise, infrastructure and human resources necessary to fully implement online government. The UN e-government readiness index is a composite set of measures comprising the web measurement index, the telecommunication infrastructure index and a human capital index. The web measurement assessment looks at how governments develop e-government policies, applications and tools to meet the growing needs of citizens for more information, services and tools. It measures the online presence of national websites, along with those of the ministries of health, education, welfare, labor and finance of each United Nations member state. E-government readiness also places citizens at the forefront, by focusing on the governmental services and products that primarily affect them (UN E-Government Survey, 2008: 31). Again, Europe (0.6490) had a clear lead over the other regions, followed by the Americas (0.4936), Asia (0.4470), Oceania (0.4338) and Africa (0.2739). Asia and Oceania were slightly below the world average (0.4514), while Africa lagged far behind. Plainly, these indicators reflect huge variations in levels of economic development as well (Figure 8.5).

Not surprisingly, European countries made up 70% of the top 35 countries in the 2008 e-government readiness rankings; Asian countries 20% of the top 35; and North American and Oceania regions 5%.[11] With a few exceptions, these distributions remained the same in 2010. As a group, European countries have invested heavily in deploying broadband infrastructure, coupled with an increase in the implementation of e-government applications for their citizens. According to the International Telecommunication Union (ITU), European countries make up nine of the top 10 countries in broadband subscribers per hundred, with Denmark,

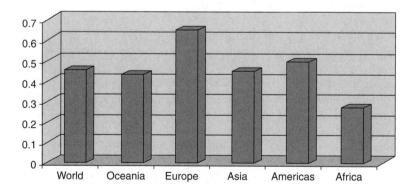

Figure 8.5 Regional Average of E-Government Readiness

Source: UN Survey (2008: 38)

the Netherlands and Iceland being the top three countries. The success of the European countries can be attributed to their investment in infrastructure and connectivity, most notably in broadband infrastructure.

Regarding connectivity, a robust broadband network is critical for adoption of advanced government applications and services. In the 2010 UN Survey, it was apparent that governments which invested in broadband infrastructure scored relatively high. A closer look at the infrastructure index reveals that investment in cellular infrastructure has also had a dramatic impact over the past three years in both developed and developing countries. This has also bolstered the pro-democracy movement, with some glaring exceptions.[12]

Another indicator of the strong correlation between wealth and technology is the fact that in 2008 there was only one developing country (Malaysia) in the top 35 from Africa, Central America, Central Asia, South America or Southern Asia in the UN survey. In 2010, Bahrain and Chile joined this advanced group (Appendix C). The high cost of deploying technological infrastructures capable of handling multiple applications is the primary reason for this discrepancy. In addition, many developing countries are unable to fully implement e-government infrastructure because of pressures to fund other competing social needs that must be met within the context of tight **budgetary constraints**; these include health care, highway construction, education and unemployment compensation. Public sector leaders from G-20 countries have begun to champion various African and Latin American initiatives such as debt relief, a dot-com task force aimed at bridging the digital divide and trade policy reforms. Expansion of digital media coverage both online and through other electronic channels increases opportunities for citizens in the developed world to be exposed to the plight of poorer countries (while also creating pressure from within developing countries for more openness and better governance). This was illustrated by the global relief efforts following the devastating earthquakes in Haiti on January 12, 2010 and in Chile on February 27, 2010.

Much of the focus in developing countries has been on leveraging technology to bring about transparency and overcome traditional governmental weaknesses, notably elimination of bribery, excessive corruption and weak accountability to citizens. Such an approach has been the hallmark of digital government efforts in rapidly developing countries such as China and India, where lack of transparency, corruption and poverty are persistent concerns.

In sharp contrast, Northern European countries were standouts on all types of web measures, with the United Kingdom, the Netherlands, Norway, Denmark, Spain and France in the global top 10. Most of the Nordic countries employed similar web development strategies. Each has a primary site that is informational and tightly integrated with gateway sites to provide services. Using this approach, the Scandinavian countries scored very high on the availability of services and transactions, where they excelled compared to most other countries. Compared to previous years, Denmark, Finland, Norway and Sweden still have a large amount of content available in other languages, but not nearly as large a percentage as in the past. This is mainly due to the enormous growth of the information and content available on the Swedish, Norwegian and Danish websites[13]. The UN Survey focused mainly on the G2C and G2G aspects of e-government and on access to web-based public services. Although the survey captured some elements of government-to-business linkages, this dimension was a relatively small segment of the annual survey.

Compared to other European nations, Spain improved since 2005 and assumed the lead in the Western European region by moving up 19 positions to the number 20 spot in 2008 and number 9 in 2010. Spain has improved immensely on the web measurement index, as well as on the infrastructure index. The deployment of broadband increased the number of personal computers per 100 from 19 to 28 and internet users per 100 went from 24 to 43. On the web measurement side, Spain has a separate e-government portal that strongly encourages e-participation and provides online transactions on a secure link and communication via mobile phones with citizens, providing security alerts. Spain has also enhanced its national sites through better multi-media tools (video and audio clips). The Spanish Ministry of Finance allows e-mail sign-up and the creation of online personal accounts on secure links with its Ministry of Education, a one-stop shop. All these improvements increased Spain's total web measure index. The *Madrid Participa* project has been used to increase citizen participation in the decision-making process in Spain's capital city of Madrid, offering a more dynamic and continuous dialogue between political representatives and citizens. *Madrid Participa* uses secure eVoting technology together with the paper channel to carry out more convenient and user-friendly consultations while avoiding the costs of a traditional vote. To date, the eConsultations platform has been used regularly in 22 formal citizen consultations involving more than 3.5 million Spanish citizens.[14]

France's national website is among the highest ranking in the Western European region.[15] The website has a strong e-participation presence and expanded features for online consultation, including a separate e-government portal with a time frame to respond to citizens' queries and e-mails. The site also contains a number of news feeds and RSS to continuously update citizens with information from media and blogs. Another interesting feature is a section on "major projects," which keeps citizens aware of major policy proposals and priorities of the government. The French Government also decided to share digital-dividend broadcasting spectrum between both electronic communications and audiovisual services, following the recommendation of the Digital Dividend Parliamentary Commission published in July 2008.[16] This decision is an important contribution to achieving a critical mass of mobile broadband users. If similar actions are undertaken by other member states, it will also be a key step in reaching fully integrated decisions across the EU. This decision was presented as part of the "France numérique 2012" plan unveiled to help achieve the French Government's long-term objective of ensuring that 100% of the French population has access to high-speed fixed/mobile broadband anywhere in the country.

Conducting Transactions Online

In addition to the e-government maturity research covered in Chapter 3, *Accenture* consulting group conducted quantitative research on citizens' perceptions and practices related to online government in the 12 countries, including the United Kingdom and the United States. Four hundred regular internet users were surveyed in each country (with the exception of the United States, where 600 regular internet users were surveyed. Regular users were defined as individuals who used the internet at least once a week from any location). Saving time and money are the primary reasons that citizens said they conducted transactions with governments online. In every country except Sweden, at least 75% of the survey respondents said that they would make greater use of the technology if it saved them time and 70% said they would do so if it saved them money. Among respondents in Sweden, the figures were 60% and 48%, respectively. However, despite such interest in online government services, the study found that citizens rarely take advantage of them. The top reasons given by internet users for rarely or never visiting government websites included difficulty finding the correct site (up to 26%), ease of conducting business by telephone (up to 20%) or in person (up to 34%), online privacy concerns (up to 18%) and internet security issues (up to 17%). Actual percentages varied depending on whether the country had low, medium or high internet penetration rates. The study identified five emerging trends:

1) After a period of rapid expansion, the pace of expansion is slowing and many countries have hit a plateau of e-government maturity.
2) Leaders in e-government are reaping tangible savings by being able to deliver enhanced government services while making operations more cost effective.
3) Promoting e-government is becoming a growing priority in order to drive up usage.
4) As countries reach higher levels of maturity, they face new challenges in integrating services. While some governments seek to integrate services across their own agencies and departments (horizontal integration), leaders are tackling the more complex challenge of integrating local, state, federal and even international services (vertical integration).

5) There is growing interest in offering personalized services to the individual citizen. By identifying and segmenting their citizen/user base, governments are able to provide citizens with more relevant services and information—quicker and more cost-effectively (Accenture, 2004).

In many **high-tech countries**, such as Canada, Denmark, Estonia, Finland, Japan, Korea, Sweden and Switzerland, as well as less affluent developing nations, information technologies have been used to overcome many of these financial and political obstacles to development, resulting in a leap-frog approach—integrating multiple media sources such as cable television, cell phones, computers and PDAs to connect individuals, governments, multi-national corporations, international organizations and financial institutions. Estonia, Finland and Spain have declared internet access to be a legal right of citizenship. In the Republic of Korea, the Netherlands and Sweden, more than 80% of all households have internet access. Switzerland was a relatively late adopter but has since established a central administrative body to develop policies, including data sharing protocols, based on agreements between the federal government and the cantons (states) which signed the cooperative agreement.[17] Since 1998, Switzerland has implemented e-voting in elections in three cantons— Geneva, Neuchatek and Zurich.[18] Several studies have confirmed that the results of e-voting have the same levels of accuracy and reliability as mail-in (postal) ballots.

All of these are impressive examples, but perhaps no country demonstrates how interrelating information technologies can enhance development better than the Republic of Estonia, which liberated itself from the confines of the previous Soviet era in the early 1990s to become a Baltic powerhouse for digital adoption and innovation.[19] An important factor in Estonia's emergence as a global leader has been the commitment by its politicians and administrators to focus comprehensively on a national e-government strategy for the development of democratic institutions and public operations as well as supporting the commercial marketplace and civil society. Early investments by government generated both results and recognition: the country was the first to experiment with electronic voting on a nationwide basis and, by 2009, Estonians completed 91% of all tax declarations online.[20] Estonia pioneered the development of an internet voting system to increase turnout in domestic elections; the nation also had the highest voter turnout among all European nations in both the 2007 and 2009 European Union (EU) Parliamentary elections.[21] In addition, the software for immensely popular free global computer audio-video communication system, *Skype*, was first invented and developed in Estonia. One of the most successful video conferencing applications yet developed, the company was acquired by eBay in September 2005 for $2.6 billion.[22]

Scandinavian countries still hold the lead in providing **transactional services** (the opportunity for online financial transactions and citizen e-consultation and e-decision making). This is one of the primary reasons why these countries have soared to the top of many other measures, such as the e-government participation and readiness indices, discussed above (see Figure 8.6).

While these early (and relatively unique) successes can be attributed to determined national efforts, European countries across the continent have also benefitted since the early 1990s from the emergence of the **European Union (EU)**, which incorporated both cooperative and competitive ties between the 27 EU member states through a trans-national vision and policy framework combined with centralized direction and benchmarking initiatives to showcase digital leadership. The EU increased its economic strength through a common market and standardized system of laws and policies as well as the adoption of a single currency, the Euro, for 16 of its member states. With a population of almost 500 million, the EU generates nearly one-third of the world's wealth. Many EU countries, including those recently admitted to the union such as Bulgaria, Czech Republic and Hungary, have initiated additional e-government initiatives in response to standards set by the European Commission (Eastern European E-Government Days, 2008).

In a move towards greater administrative efficiency prompted by economic constraints, many EU countries have integrated ICT processes with public policies and strategies designed to transform citizen–government relationships and improve the quality of public services. One of the major advantages of a united Europe is the opportunity for citizens from very different backgrounds and cultures to share their thoughts,

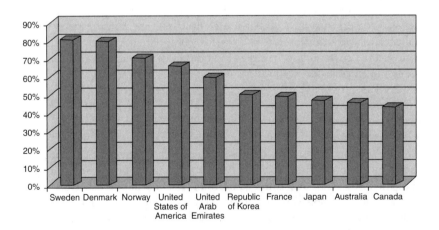

Figure 8.6 Transactional Services: Top 10 Countries

Source: UN Survey (2008: 75)

concerns and ideas on the future of the EU. Discussions on various forums such as **Debate Europe** allow European citizens to focus on the region's economic and social development, attitudes towards other member states, Europe's changing borders and its role in the world. Citizens can either participate in these debates or view the thoughts of other citizens on the website.[23] Debate Europe is available in the 24 languages of the European Union and citizens from various countries can participate in national debates concerning the political integration of their country as well as other nations.

The Dutch government employs common public sector e-government building blocks for providing seamless service to citizens, in the effort to improve efficiency and reduce administrative burdens.[24] Austria and France have established central bodies to coordinate information and data sharing policies within the public sector. In Austria, citizens could request birth certificates or marriage licenses in person or by mail; a national e-government registry automatically forwarded the information to the appropriate agency.[25] Austria ran into problems with online issuance of birth certifications and in 2009 reverted to the older method of positive identification in part as a result of unanticipated security concerns. Portugal has integrated its e-government and administrative simplification policies into the **SIMPLEX program**, a strategy designed to modernize public services by administrative simplification and better regulation.[26] To address the e-government and simplification strategy, the Office for Public Services Reform along with the Knowledge Society Agency and the Director General of Public Administration developed new ways to deliver public services, focusing on citizens' needs and based on a multichannel integrated structure. In Sweden, residents can review their letters and packages from the postal service online *by e-mail* and decide which to accept or reject *before* delivery, saving the **Swedish Postal Service** millions in distribution and fuel costs. Despite the apparent successes among many of the EU nations, there are vast differences in the ability and willingness of other governments to apply ICTs for improving civic responsibility and bureaucratic performance. Why are some countries and various agencies within them more willing to initiate changes?

One reason for such variations in motivation and performance is that the missions of individual agencies are complex and varied and digital governance systems cannot be "installed" and begin operating the next day. Given the immense number and variety of governmental agencies, branches, bureaus, departments and divisions in some 240 countries around the world, it is no small achievement to build the government-to-government (G2G) infrastructure and establish the basic government-to-citizen (G2C) trust needed to reach a level of technological sophistication and mutual confidence, the keys to successful implementation.

In Denmark, Europe's most digitized nation, Danish businesses have saved 50 million Euros and taxpayers 150 million Euros a year from online procurement processes. Denmark also has a national citizens' portal which includes all municipalities and several agencies and offers self-service solutions that can be accessed from this central site.[27] There is also a module supporting (non-binding) voting and discussion on the site. Currently, work is proceeding on **Denmark e2012** goals which state that integration shall continue (and improve) and that all communication between business, citizens and government will take place digitally by 2012. This will be a requirement for government agencies and an option for citizens. The Danish goal of the national government portal for businesses is to relieve Danish companies from administrative burdens and to provide a single linkage to the public sector.[28] Bedst På Nettet (Top of the Web) is an annual benchmarking competition where government websites at all levels (national, regional, local) are evaluated and awarded so-called Net Crowns. The concept has been developed from focusing on technical, navigational and functional aspects (i.e. requirements that can be tested automatically or semi-automatically) which have a more organizational and citizen-oriented focus. A citizen-centric self-assessment has been added where participants consider how much an individual website helps improve organizational processes and services. E-learning modules also support these projects as nationwide ICT education initiatives to digitally and democratically include those who do not use computers or have very low ICT skills.[29]

Conclusions and Future Directions

Few innovations have had a greater potential impact on politics and public administration than the global spread of the internet communication and New Media technologies. It may be too early to call this the next global revolution, but a practical working vision of the virtual state envisioned a decade ago may now be closer than ever before (Council for Excellence in Government, 2001; Fountain; 2001; Ronan, 2000). Even those who offer more modest predictions tout electronic and now digital governance as the fast-track to improve government efficiency, deliver services and respond to citizens. ICTs are being used to promote greater accountability and transparency, restore citizen trust in government and encourage political participation.

For nearly three decades, ICTs have revitalized public sector performance as well as advanced ideals of citizen participation and democratic values. Global internet use more than quadrupled in the decade from 2000 to 2010, with the largest percentage increases occurring in underdeveloped regions such as Africa, the Middle East and Latin America (Figure 8.1). Still, there is much unfinished as only 21% of citizens in emerging nations have access to the internet as compared to over 70% in developed nations.

One of the most promising aspects of digital governance is that all governments can make better use of available technology to address problems of access and democratic outreach (Chapter 2). With respect to infrastructure, mobilizing resources is only the beginning of the necessary transformation. While many countries await a digital future, some developed nations such as the United States are falling behind in broadband access, educational attainment, public sector innovation and the adoption of interactive tools and technologies. This weakens the most powerful democracy's ability to empower citizens and businesses. It also represents a dilemma where technology will either be framed or pursued as an inclusive project for the entire population or support the wealthiest and most educated segments of the population. Structuring online government in a broad and inclusive manner from the outset is critical to minimizing and reducing the potential for harmful digital divides that continue to persist in many developed as well as developing countries.

Digital technology has been embraced by many governments offering a wide range of options—from archived data, publications and databases to actual government services—online for citizen use. Some nations have succeeded in implementing full-scale digital governance by conducting political campaigns, holding elections and actually voting online. Most still lack the resources for full implementation. Such variation is not surprising in view of the extreme differences in electoral systems and forms of government which exist around the world. Some nations have begun to reconsider decisions to implement online e-voting systems and question the accuracy of online voting. Even the United States— one of the richest and most democratic and economically developed nations in the world—has major problems conducting elections, which may explain the reluctance of many Americans to institute online voting.

Despite promises of democratic enhancement and administrative advancement, public sector innovation has tended to be incremental and gradual, especially since the global fiscal collapse in 2007. Factors such as budget scarcity, group conflict, economic growth or decline, cultural norms and patterns of social and political behavior limit governmental actions. Moreover, governments are divided into factions reflecting competing interests, making it more challenging for policy makers to persuade bureaucrats to work collaboratively to promote technological innovation. The addition of an infinite number of open and transparent systems (polispheres) and the advance of cellular technology and social networking permits more groups to organize and make demands on the finite resources of political systems (Chapter 2). In democratic governments, politicians come and politicians go, but public officials tend to have longer careers. In addition, cultural norms, literacy rates and patterns of individual behavior affect how technology is used by citizens and policy makers. Developing countries which depend on global financial institutions (such as the OECD, IMF and World Bank) for assistance have even fewer incentives to change.

As mentioned in earlier chapters, lack of standardization severely limits the expansion of ICTs. For countries that can afford to improve connectivity by implementing broadband systems and enhanced websites, there are still inconsistencies in terms of models, execution and evaluation. Portals are only useful to citizens when they have integrated and standardized navigational features, lacking in many national and regional websites. Search engines such as Google, for example, are important tools that allow citizens to access information from a particular site. Currently, only about one-third of government websites are searchable, limiting ordinary citizens from finding information of interest to them. A smaller number of government websites are capable of making two-way online transactions over the internet; interactive portals are located primarily in economically advanced nations. Standardized navigational systems would help average citizens access the wealth of material that is available online. Yet, as we have seen even in wealthy countries such as the United States, local power brokers may view standards suspiciously as ways to usurp their political power.

No country is without challenges in developing more citizen-centric, interoperable and value-added technologies that balance central coordination (in some cases accompanied by centralized authority) with decentralized autonomy across a wide variety of organizational units that comprise the public sector. Integrating horizontal and vertical dimensions of ICTs is a major challenge in all countries: increasing numbers recognize the importance of upgrading and aligning front-line interface with the public as service recipients and back office capacities for processing information and conducting transactions. Another important and related lesson in terms of interoperability—applicable across both developed and developing countries—is the acceptance of a more collaborative and participative citizen-centric mindset on the part of public employees (Chapters 3 and 7). Working effectively with external partners such as international assistance organizations heightens a nation's ability to overcome fragmentation and internal jurisdictional boundaries and create integrated systems and positive outcomes. This remains the focus of sustained innovation to foster digital governance. Plainly, organizational collaboration is more difficult to achieve than the purchase and installation of information and communication technology. All too often, political considerations trump technological innovation.

The shift from traditional hierarchical management to networked digital governance is transforming the public sector in many countries; those which have made changes vary enormously in their overall performance. The global divide between the richest and poorest nations is narrowing as economies adopt ICTs to cope with the global financial crises. Wealthier nations appear to be ahead of poor and geographically isolated countries which have only a minimum web presence. However, during the last decade the most impressive percentage growth in the use of internet and PDA applications has occurred in the emerging regions of Africa, the Middle East and Latin America. All countries must continue to improve their national portals and websites to offer citizens more information and services, easier payment of fees and bills, and greater accountability and transparency, and promote citizen engagement and inclusion. Access must be provided on secure, seamless, integrated and confidential networks. Simply put, states that are not constantly providing more online applications, training and tools for citizen participation are more likely to fall further behind.

Key Terms

9   Globalization, Information Technology and Public Administration

Arguing against globalization is like arguing against gravity.

Kofi Annan

In this chapter, we return to the broader themes of how ICT-driven innovations are fueling the growth of the global economy, and how rapidly and permanently their use (and possible misuse) is changing organizational concepts, public policies and international trade relationships. As discussed in previous chapters, global struggles for control of ICT systems have become more than just efforts to install better communication and information technology or improve government efficiency. Just as British control of the seas once helped England dominate 19th century international trade and American dominance of the airways provided the same advantage for the United States in the 20th century, the nation or nations that hold a technological edge in the 21st century are more likely to prevail in an uncertain future.

What was once a controlled and gradual shift in the global economy has accelerated (and perhaps altered) the world's balance of economic power in the decade since the beginning of the 21st century. One indication of just how much the international political economy has changed is the decline in the world's wealth in 2009: the sum of goods and services produced by all nations (the world's **gross national product or GNP**) shrank for the first time in 60 years, forcing many nations to curtail liberal free trade policies and impose new **trade restrictions** to protect domestic industries.[1] The resultant decline in public and private sector revenues not only impacted corporations, but strained government budgets dependent on tax collection for resources. As overall trade volume declines, many of the 153 members of the World Trade Organization (WTO) are taking defensive actions to protect domestic industries and jobs. This, in turn, forces other nations to retaliate with actions to protect their own domestic industries, resulting in further mutually disadvantageous trade restrictions.

Retaliatory actions by nations to protect their own economies and counter global economic trends are often self-defeating. Among the many and often trivial examples of trade wars is action by the United States to enact **tariffs** on imported Italian water and French cheese to counter European Union (EU) restrictions on U.S. beef and chicken exports. Japan protects its domestic rice growers by restricting less expensive U.S. grown rice allegedly because of its "inferior" quality. According to the WTO, Russia has imposed import tariffs on dozens of products. Brazil and Argentina have asked *Mercosur*, the Latin American free-trade association, to increase tariffs on goods imported from the EU and in response the EU has placed anti-**dumping** duties and tariffs on Chinese building products. These restrictions exclude Chinese products from the 27-member European common market, inevitably resulting in job losses in China. In September 2009 the Obama administration imposed high tariffs on Chinese-made automobile tires for three years; the Chinese retaliated with threats to place punitive sanctions on U.S. exports of chickens and car parts. And so it goes … much to the detriment of economic development and global free trade.

All of these actions and counter-measures may temporarily protect domestic jobs, but they threaten the spread of wider trade sanctions which could accelerate declines in the value of goods and services and further shrink public sector tax revenues. Worse, economists and trade representatives express concern that the rush to enact protectionist legislation could threaten efforts to recover from the current economic slump. Forecasts by the WTO for an upsurge in the global economy in 2010 may have been dashed by the persistent European debt crisis and continuing U.S. real estate bust and foreclosure crisis. Global trade declined by 2.1% in 2010 after growing by 6.2% in 2006, according to the WTO.[2] The mega-trends described below reflect global economic changes as well as shifting international political relationships. There is little consensus on future trends. The same developments that are judged harshly by some are viewed favorably by others.

Policies which have encouraged free trade for centuries have been literally "flattened" by the horizontal extension of the global economy through **in-sourcing, outsourcing** and **off-shoring**—costing millions of American jobs (Friedman, 2005). In addition, such actions undermine the 200-year ideal of free trade among nations. One consequence is certain. Regardless how the process is defined or perceived, as more and more workers are displaced in some way from their home cultures by **corporate globalization**, governments and the public administrators assume greater responsibilities for enacting educational improvements and economic security measures to redress the inequities and job losses produced by this inexorable trend. Whether it is ignored, opposed or supported, globalization and its antecedents significantly impact roles and responsibilities of business, government and society worldwide.

In this chapter, we briefly trace how modern technology-driven free trade policies hastened the evolution of economic globalization, describe how free trade policies combined with ICTs contributed to recent swings in the global GNP, assess globalization's impact on the American economy and discuss how American corporatism and foreign policy are influencing other economies.

Differing Visions of Globalization, Technology and Trade

Globalization has increased the speed at which information, goods and services cross international borders. It has further concentrated wealth in developed nations and in the hands of a small number of oligarchs in developing countries. Trade relationships between nations have fundamentally changed—inevitably posing challenges, as well as opportunities, for many segments of the American economy.[3]

Globalization has spawned the rise of **multi-national** or **trans-national corporations** that are now so large that they wield nearly unchallenged independent economic power, especially against the weakest and most vulnerable emerging nations. The triumph of post-communist free market capitalism has led to the growth of corporations which are now among the largest free-standing entities in the world. For example, BP, Chevron, Exxon-Mobil and Wal-Mart's annual sales alone are larger than the *combined* economies of over 150 countries, giving them extraordinary power to exert pressure on suppliers to drive down labor costs in pursuit of lower prices and higher profits. Moreover, the environmental risks, lack of political accountability and social irresponsibility which often accompany corporate globalization have added to security threats in many traditional nation-states, especially in economically vulnerable less-developed nations. In many instances, even powerful developed nations are vulnerable.[4]

As multi-national corporations (MNCs) expand globally, they not only reshape regional cultures but may also breed hostility in countries where disaffected workers are taking violent anti-globalization and (sometimes) anti-democratic actions to preserve their economies, traditional cultures, values and traditions (Barber, 2001; Bello, 2005; Dobbs, 2004, 2006; Hertz, 2003; Veseth, 2005). Anti-globalization protests are aimed at MNCs as well as international organizations such as the G-8, IMF, OECD, World Bank and the WTO. Opposition groups focus on social justice issues, environmental protection, fair trade, labor standards and working conditions. Protesters claim that so-called "free trade" without governmental policies to protect the environment and the health and well being of workers only strengthens corporate power and reduces workers' wages. This includes the United States, where average hourly wages adjusted for inflation have not increased in 35 years.[5] Plainly, the technologies which spawned globalization are non-ideological: there is little correlation between forms of government (authoritarian, communist, democratic, socialist, etc.) and the pace of globalization or the success of ICT implementation. Nonetheless, there are significant disagreements about its definition and effects.

What is Globalization?

Globalization is touted by many as a promising means to spread peace, prosperity and democracy to more of the world's population—others believe that this mega-trend has damaged the global economy and will lead to further conflict, exploitation of labor, economic stagnation, environmental degradation, job losses and trade wars and bolster the power of a so-called global "superclass" of business elites (Barber, 2001; Dobbs, 2004; Hertz, 2003; Rothkopf, 2008; Veseth, 2005). Globalization is applauded as a vehicle for the advancing banking reforms, capitalism, democratic values, economic development, property rights and personal freedoms around the world (Bhagwati, 2004; DeSoto, 2000; Friedman, 2005; Prestowitz, 2006; Stiglitz, 2006). There is little agreement, however, about when globalization began, how much it has affected world markets or which groups or nations benefit long-term. Thomas Friedman (2005) credits the collapse of the **Soviet Union (USSR)** and **fall of the Berlin Wall in 1989** with the birth of modern economic globalization. Noreena Hertz (2003) believes that conservative policies beginning in the early 1980s with U.S. President Ronald Reagan and British Prime Minister Margaret Thatcher's support for global free markets, deregulation and government withdrawal from economic issues encouraged the rise of globalization. Hertz focused on problems facing the world with the rise of multi-national corporations following large multi-billion dollar mergers and acquisitions.

These conglomerates are now so huge, with ties all over the globe and direct access to private sources of capital, that they are accountable only to their boards of directors and shareholders. Multi-national corporations are stubbornly independent from host government regulation and exert control over around 20% of all global capital (Hertz, 2003: 22). In what turned out to be a prophetic warning, Noreena Hertz described the situation and its impact on the United States as follows:

> All over the world, concerns are being raised about governments' loyalties and corporations' objectives. Concerns that the pendulum of capitalism may have swung just a bit too far; that our love affair with the free market may have obscured harsh truths; that too many Americans are losing out. That the state cannot be trusted to look after our increased economic growth. They are worried that the sound of business is drowning out the voices of the people.
>
> (Hertz, 2003: 3)

Although one of the main roles of Western governments is to ensure that private business interests continue to prosper, many countries now enable businesses to do more than just survive. They are subsidized with incentives such as lower taxes, loans, public services, protective regulations, security and infrastructure at favorable rates to ensure competitive markets and profitable free trade. Government **fiscal** and **monetary** policies also help determine the relative export value of a country's goods or services in the global economy. Some nations are accused of unfair competition by deliberately manipulating currencies to favor exports over imports. Countries such as China and India which export more than they import enjoy **trade surpluses**. The United States and many other debt-ridden developing nations which import more than they export show **trade deficits**. Increasingly, a nation's **balance of trade** is a measure of its economic strength vis-à-vis other nations. Recent U.S. elections registered support for unregulated free trade, but public opinion tends to express greater support for protectionist legislation, especially in rust-belt states that have been heavily affected by outsourcing.

When U.S. companies outsource jobs to countries such as China, India and Mexico where wages and benefits are lower (and profits for American companies higher) some naïvely believe that local employees in these countries would identify with American products and buy American goods with the extra money they make. If the same work could be performed less expensively, while providing the same level of productivity and quality, U.S. industries could grow concurrently in other directions. This has obviously not happened. Outsourcing has instead led to an unanticipated form of **global income redistribution** (for some more than others), a lowering of wages coupled with rampant complaints about poor quality goods and customer service. As competitive labor costs fall, several multi-national corporations have been forced to reconsider outsourcing of services and instead in-source back to the United States. American companies such as Dell Computer, Delta Airlines and J.P Morgan/Chase experienced massive increases in customer complaints when they off-shored technical service, lost baggage recovery searches and online banking to India.[6] Wage differentials are now so extensive that they portend the further depression of income in the United States.

Without ICTs, it would have been impossible for less developed countries to compete for high-skilled jobs once concentrated only in nations with advanced economies. Common themes exist in all of the definitions of globalization, suggesting that the mega-trend is synonymous with the expansion of global markets including the growth of the technology, trans-national corporations, intergovernmental organizations and civil society. Without ICTs there would be no globalization; their contribution to democratic values is less certain.

Globalization and Free Trade

During the early 19th century (c. 1816), English political economist **David Ricardo** (1772–1823) formulated a **theory of comparative advantage** which stated that if each nation specializes in the production of particular goods which gives it a comparative cost advantage and trades those goods with other nations for the goods in which they specialize, there will be an overall net gain in trade—aggregate income levels will rise in each trading country. According to Ricardo's theory, even if a country could produce all types of goods or services on its own, specializing in exports of products it would benefit from most was the most efficient way to produce and sell to other nations.[7] Wages should be left to free market competition and there should be no restrictions on the importation of agricultural products.

Free trade theories generally reflect free market economics and are grounded in the belief that nations which trade with each other are less likely to engage in armed conflict or wars, an especially important assumption today with the destructive capacity of nuclear weapons. Beyond general agreement that nations should specialize in the production of goods and services that offer a competitive advantage and that trade partners are less likely to engage in armed conflict against each other, there is little consensus on the long-term economic effects of 21st century globalization.

Without strict trade restrictions promulgated by such organizations as the IMF and the WTO, countries are free to trade or not to trade goods or services with others, regardless of their political ideologies. This creates anomalies such as the United States doing business with China, but maintaining strict trade restrictions against Cuba—despite the fact that both are communist regimes. It also fosters the formation of large scale **trading blocs** such as the **North American Free Trade Agreement (NAFTA)** which theoretically places even the richest countries on par with the poorest. After 15 years, concerns still persist about the "fairness" of trade relationships between the United States and Mexico, resulting in punitive actions to restrict the importation of agricultural products and transportation of goods from Mexico to the United States.

When combined with corporate expansion, free trade agreements are among the major forces encouraging the proliferation of globalization. In the late 1990s, free trade increased emphasis on foreign investment and was followed by world financial chaos that lasted for nearly two years (Rubin, 2003: 212–298). Countries kept their respective currencies undervalued to encourage foreign capital investment and exports. This led to industrial overcapacity and the near collapse of some developing economies. The so-called Asian Contagion beginning in 1997 posed an enormous threat to the global economy and caused severe hardships in affected Asian economies, as well as other developing nations such as Brazil and Russia. During the economic expansion of the late 1990s and early 2000s, shortly after China was admitted to the WTO, free trade systems were again quickly implemented without the proper monitoring by regulatory mechanisms necessary to ensure growth, leading to expansion without proper financial controls (Bhagwati, 2004: 7, 12, 199–201).

In mid-2010, a similar pattern emerged with the Euro-contagion affecting the so-called debt-ridden P-I-G-S countries (Portugal, Ireland, Greece and Spain) with the possibility of spreading to other European economies.

Global markets have changed the way traditional economic theories, such as Ricardo's free trade concepts, apply—especially during international business downturns. If markets are left alone, **Adam Smith's** "invisible hand" may not necessarily steer business in the right direction; instead it may push some emerging countries with eager workers willing to work for less in the path of business expansion (Veseth, 2005: 47–57). Large multi-national corporations are at the forefront of globalization and among the staunchest advocates of unregulated free trade. Profits are used to fund many pro-free trade lobbying groups which exert tremendous influence over the governments of countries in which they operate (Dobbs, 2004: 52–55). At the same time, reliance on free markets alone cannot keep American middle-class consumers safe or industries secure, or protect employees from being downsized (Dobbs, 2006). National interests can be hijacked by special interests or small groups of powerful elites, and nowhere is this easier than at the global level.

Globalization also raises questions about **Keynesianism,** an established economic doctrine that calls for government intervention and spending in case of a recession or depression to boost the economy (Hertz, 2003: 19–22). With increasing globalization accompanied by the concentration of power in the hands of a few trans-national corporations, government spending may no longer be a viable solution for recession. The primary incentives for trans-national corporations to globalize have always been weaker labor laws and less stringent regulatory environments in emerging countries. This reality began in the 1970s and might again be taking place in the United States in the 2000s. Unrestrained global capitalism will continue at a cost to poor countries and lower income groups in all countries, whose jobs disappear as they wait in vain for the "trickle down" effects of supply-side economics, lower taxes and less regulation.

The current global financial crisis has prompted calls for more regulation by public and private organizations. This raises questions such as: In whose interest is the global economy being regulated? Under what conditions can global regulation serve broader interests? The new ICT-enabled global economy breeds institutions that are less transparent and held to a much lower standard of accountability by media and public officials than are most domestic institutions. Attempts at **global regulation** often fall prey to regulatory capture by powerful multi-national corporations. Still, positive regulatory changes have occurred in areas including environmental protection, human rights, shipping safety and global finance. Under new systems of networked governance, self-regulation and economic globalization, some argue that technocrats should be left to regulate with as little political oversight as possible (Mattli and Woods, 2009).

Globalization continues unabated as large trans-national corporations move more jobs overseas to cheaper labor markets and downsize millions of jobs in the United States and other higher labor cost economies. One estimate by economist Alan Blinder, published before the global economic meltdown, predicted that as many as 20 million U.S. jobs could be off-shored from 2007 to 2017 (Blinder, 2007). Those opposed to unregulated free-trade driven globalization seek government intervention to mediate, monitor and regulate the harmful effects of such massive job losses on American workers and their families. This, in turn, breeds domestic protectionism and limits participation in world markets. Radical shifts in recent U.S. elections (the Democratic sweep of the Senate and the House in the 2006 and the 2008 Congressional and Presidential elections, and Republican gains in 2010) confirm that more Americans are concerned about job losses but uneasy about additional regulation to prevent further losses. Many want Congress to enact laws to moderate the negative effects of free trade policies on the U.S. economy, especially those living in states in the upper Midwest which have suffered extensive and (perhaps) permanent job losses from outsourcing.

One painful example of this trend is the U.S. automobile industry which, despite billions of dollars in bailouts from the federal government, has suffered extensive job losses, plant closings and the bankruptcies of two of the Big Three auto makers, Chrysler and General Motors. Those wanting to subsidize **legacy industries**, rather than letting the global free market determine their fate, are at odds with others who promote policies to convert organizations to support a more sustainable, less fossil-fuel dependent future (Senge, 2008).

Impact of Globalization on the U.S. Economy

Globalization generally refers to increases in investment, technology and transportation caused by the easing of trade barriers among increasingly interdependent countries. Thomas L. Friedman (2005) describes how the modern process began about three decades ago with the global diffusion of computer software and information technology and has since accelerated due to 10 irretrievable flattening forces, some of which are political and many of which are technological. Among them: the break-up of the Soviet Union and fall of the Berlin Wall two decades ago and the dissemination of Windows software and the public offering of the Netscape browser in 1995. (Box 9.1 summarizes mega-trends which are discussed in detail below.)

Global Flattening Forces

While some disagree about the precise dates that these changes began, the cumulative impact of innovations such as **work flow software,**

Box 9.1: Ten Global Flattening Forces

1) Fall of Berlin Wall and creation of Windows
2) Netscape browser (1995)
3) Shared standards/workflow software
4) Open-sourcing such as Apache software
5) Outsourcing and the Y2K bug
6) Offshoring connected by fiber optic cables
7) Supply-chaining (Wal-Mart)
8) Insourcing and standardization
9) In-forming and Google issue networks
10) Digital mobility and smart phones

Source: Assembled by author from lecture notes to accompany *Improving Service in the Global Economy*. Adapted from and originally discussed by Thomas L. Freidman (2005)

open-sourcing, outsourcing, off-shoring, supply-chaining, in-sourcing, **informing** and wireless information transfer significantly accelerated globalization. In addition, contemporary flatteners include technological innovations such as the expanded use of computers in the workplace, fiber optic networks, ICTs, webcasting and proliferation of internet use. Although scholars noted in the bibliography—apologists, champions, malcontents, supporters and victims—still disagree about globalization's definition, effects and origins, there is less doubt that it continues to impact political, economic and social interactions on a broader scale than ever before. Use of ICTs and the spread of globalization have had both positive and negative impacts on the U.S. economy.

The first catalyst for globalization coincided with the standardization of Microsoft Windows software in the early 1990s. Workflow software helps individuals communicate with others across the office or collaborate and share information around the world (Friedman, 2005: 71–80). Following the capitulation of the Soviet Union and the collapse of the Berlin Wall, Eastern Europe opened up to the rest of the world. Within five years, the Netscape Web browser was launched, enabling anyone anywhere with a computer or smart phone to access the internet's vast reservoir of online knowledge (Friedman, 2005: 48–55). Open-sourcing is another form of ICT which facilitates revising and uploading programs to the internet and gives anyone the ability to use and improve them. The online phenomenon **Wikipedia** is an example of open-sourcing that has become so successful that it threatens the economic viability of traditional printed encyclopedias, now a classic and rapidly disappearing legacy industry. Likewise, the open-source **Mozilla Firefox** Web browser provides stiff competition for

Microsoft and the online mega-store **Amazon.com** has revolutionized retail sales. Not only can anyone use the free software, but companies can sell their own modified versions with their name on it as long as they credit those who first created the software.

Global flatteners heightened concerns about the decline of the American economy and the subsequent rise of developing societies, especially Brazil, China, India, Korea and Russia. Less developed countries have benefited from American companies outsourcing certain segments of their operations to lower cost labor markets, but it is difficult to assess the long-term impact of these changes. Honeywell, IBM, Dell and Hewlitt-Packard and other trans-nationals have all made substantial investments in India. The types of goods and services now being outsourced have expanded to include not only familiar manufactured products such as automobiles, books and computers, but technical support services, interpretation of x-rays and even online banking, copy editing, legal assistance, surgery and tax preparation.

One the reasons why outsourcing accelerated was the dot-com bubble burst in the late 1990s. Many Western companies suffered billions of dollars in losses from investing in miles of fiber optic cable that now span the globe. This was a boom to India, where call-center businesses purchased fiber optic cable networks at fire-sale prices and hired many skilled workers who showed their competence with complex service work by first fixing imaginary Y2K bugs, then receiving contracts for other higher skill level work.

Offshoring occurs when companies move entire factories to less developed countries where workers are paid less and receive fewer benefits than those working for companies producing similar goods in North America and Europe (Friedman, 2005: 114–127). For instance, automobile factories for "American" vehicles are now located in countries such as Mexico where labor costs are lower; paradoxically, "Japanese" cars are produced in the United States by American workers who are paid less than Japanese workers. When Congresspersons or President Obama call on Americans to buy American products, it is difficult to know whether they are referring to those produced and sold here or manufactured elsewhere and sold here. For most consumers, finding the best value for the least cost is more important that buying a particular national brand.

These and other flattening forces have contributed to the loss of many U.S. jobs, but have created opportunities for different types of foreign manufacturers of off-shore service processes, such as *supply chain management* (Chapter 3). This type of advanced just-in-time inventory control system enables companies to use bar codes to track products with such accuracy that they know when to resupply a specific product just before it is needed on the assembly line or to restock shelves (Friedman, 2005: 128–139). Pioneered by Xerox and Wal-Mart, this technology eliminates the need for warehousing component parts and traces every single item in stock to ensure constant supply. Wal-Mart, the largest employer in the United States and the world's largest retailer, uses supply-chaining to cut out the middlemen and purchase products directly from the companies in emerging nations to further reduce costs. United Parcel Service (UPS) implemented supply-chaining for its package delivery service and now offers additional features to companies through what is referred to as insourcing. Some companies have relocated warehouses near the UPS hub in Kentucky which facilitates faster packaging of products and shipping to customers (Friedman, 2005: 141–150). Pushing the world toward further globalization is informing, the rise in information technology search engines such as A9©, Yahoo!© and Google© enables anyone with computer access to get information, products or services or establish social contacts directly for themselves (Friedman, 2005: 150–159). The meteoric rise of social networks such as *Facebook*, *Twitter* and *YouTube* could not have occurred without expanded global connectivity.

According to Friedman, the final flatteners are high-tech ICTs which eliminate nearly all barriers to communication and access to global markets. He calls them "steroids" referring to new digital, mobile, personal and virtual technologies, such as wireless networks, which reduce overheads, pay and benefits, and enable companies to communicate with workers no matter where they are located. Traveling businesspersons can work from mobile offices that fit into a briefcase and allow them to work anywhere more efficiently. Mobile smart phones allow nearly everyone to be reachable almost anywhere at any time. (Thomas Friedman pointed out in 2005 there were already more cell phones in China than there were people in the United States.) That number continues to grow with advances in technology such as broadband and mobile access (Chapter 8). Mobile technology is already so developed that jet aircraft equipped with Rolls-Royce engines can self-diagnose and contact an engineer on the ground before the jet lands, eliminating costly delays and repairs (Friedman, 2005: 159–172). Other examples of such self-monitoring technologies are found in automobiles, computers, telecommunications and other manufacturing systems.

Friedman's 10 flatteners flowed together sometime in the early 2000s in what he called the **triple convergence**, eliminating vertical bureaucratic hierarchies, encouraging multiple forms of collaboration and transforming businesses. Organizational hierarchies are being "challenged from below or transforming themselves from the top into more horizontal and collaborative [structures]," across lines and within networks that no one had ever thought possible (Friedman, 2005: 45). This emerging form of top-down bottom-up organizational system is antithetical to traditional bureaucratic and corporate structure and resembles an hourglass rather than a pyramid.

Two decades ago, Friedman heralded the arrival of globalization in his seminal work *The Lexus and the Olive Tree* (1999) which predicted the emerging conflict between wireless warriors of the new global economy and holdovers from traditional legacy cultures. In *The World is Flat* (2005), he warned that borders, oceans and geographic distance no longer isolate anyone from the information revolution that is leveling the global economic playing field. In his most recent book, *Hot, Flat and Crowded: Why We Need a Green Revolution—And How It Can Renew America* (2008), he argues for less dependence on Middle Eastern sources of oil and updates and expands his prognosis of how population growth, pollution and the expansion of the world's middle class are producing an energy, climate and population disaster. The "hot" of the title obviously refers to global warming, or as he calls it **global weirding**, the bizarre climate changes we are encountering. "Flat" refers to globalization, enhanced with criticism of how unregulated trade growth fuels excessive energy use and hurts democracy and the environment. "Crowded" refers to humanity's relentless expansion and its perilous effects on biodiversity, energy poverty and the consumption of the planet's finite resources. If unchecked, these trends could produce dangerous political instability; the only solution to these ills is innovation in the form of a green revolution. Friedman remains guardedly optimistic that we can stave off the worst ecological nightmare, particularly if the United States changes its wasteful energy consuming habits by going green.

ICTs and the Green Revolution

Echoing many of the same concerns expressed by former Vice President Al Gore, media-commentator Fareed Zakaria and others, Friedman believes that Americans need to become "green hawks," turning conservation and cleaner energy into a national strategy in many different arenas, including household consumption, transportation and the military. Rather than references to the post-Cold-War era, he redefines our current epoch as an Energy-Climate Era marked by four major problems: 1) growing demand for scarcer supplies of petroleum; 2) massive transfer of wealth to **petro-dictatorships** in countries such as Nigeria, Saudi Arabia, Iran and Venezuela; 3) disruptive **climate change**, resulting in poor have-nots falling further behind; and 4) an accelerating and troubling loss of biodiversity. Friedman blames the American political system because the United States government has proven inept at developing a serious renewable energy strategy. Our approach, he says quoting one expert, is "the sum of all lobbies"; decisions continue to be driven by energy *politics* rather than energy policy. He cites the example of former president George W. Bush who, in the aftermath of 9/11, ignored calls for a $1 per gallon USA Patriot Tax on gasoline to curb consumption and instead offered tax cuts and urged Americans to "go shopping."

Rather than stimulating the economy to move forward with production of fuel-efficient vehicles and renewable sources of energy, the United States has become more dependent on China to finance our deficit and Saudi Arabia and other oil-rich Persian Gulf states to provide the 20 million barrels of oil *per day* to feed our fossil-fuel addiction. In exchange, we have committed scarce military resources and lives to protect those same oil-rich states. Americans were rewarded for these sacrifices by paying even more for gasoline, enabling oil producing countries (few of which are democracies) to reap windfall profits for multi-national corporations instead of using the revenues to alter fossil-fuel consumption. Friedman calls this a "No Mullah Left Behind" policy and quotes former CIA director James Woolsey as saying: "We are funding the rope for hanging ourselves." Friedman's opinion is shared by many others, who believe that a green strategy is not simply about generating cleaner sources of energy, but is an entirely new way of generating national power.

Neglect of serious energy policy, or more accurately its abdication to private corporate interests, obviously has national security implications. There's a simple, negative correlation, says Friedman, between the price of oil and democracy: as oil prices rise, dictators from oil-rich countries grow richer and democracies weaken. Conversely, as oil prices fall, petro-dictators grow weaker and democracies flourish. Think of the reforms in Russia and Iran in the 1990s, when oil prices were low, compared with these same countries' troublemaking in the present era of $100-per-barrel oil. In addition, petro-dictatorships threaten international security by undereducating their youth and creating unemployment and thus become breeding grounds for political instability and terrorism. How can this pattern be reversed? His answer: radically cut energy demand by investing in less energy-consuming substitutes, such as hybrid cars and solar-powered homes. This first proposal is being helped in a perverse way by the global recession and the second awaits research and development innovations. Despite the recession, which has lasted almost three years at this writing, the United States continues to rely on foreign sources of oil, even though prices have again reached record high levels.

To promote sustainable security, the United States and other rich oil-consuming countries may have to forge partnerships with China, India and other CO_2 emitting countries to develop a full range of creative ideas, technologies and policies to forestall the dangerous effects of climate change. This requires a rethinking of national security policy and a more inclusive and multi-lateral foreign policy. For the first time in September 2009, the United States proposed a **carbon emissions tax**, similar to policies that already exist in many European counties. A carbon emissions tax is similar to a **value-added tax**. For tax purposes, value is added whenever the value of a product increases as a result of the application of a company's factors of production, such as labor and equipment. The same principle could be applied to registration fees on automobiles, power generators and trucks that emit more CO_2 into the environment. The higher the emission levels, the higher the tax. Proposals based on this principle, known as **cap and trade**, await certain defeat in Republican-dominated 2011–2012 U.S. House of Representatives after deliberation and the full press of petro-lobbies. Under a cap and trade system, a government authority first sets a *cap*, deciding how much pollution in total will be allowed. Next, companies are issued credits, essentially licenses to pollute, based on how large they are, what industries they work in and so forth. If a company comes in below its cap, it has extra credits which it may *trade* with other companies.

Friedman and others are skeptical about the value of treaties, and argue that "a truly green America would be more valuable than fifty **Kyoto Protocols**. Emulation is always more effective than compulsion." He makes the case that outgreening other countries would contribute to America's soft global power as well as our hard military power. But the growing problem of strained U.S.–China relations could overshadow what we do to promote energy sustainability at home. In 2007, China surpassed the United States as the world's leading emitter of carbon dioxide. The Chinese argue that on a per capita basis each of their citizens is responsible for only one-fifth the emissions of an average American, and that developing countries should not have to cut back energy consumption until they reach parity with rich countries' CO_2 levels. This would be a formula for global disaster. As Friedman says, "Mother Nature isn't into fair. All she knows is hard science and raw math, (Friedman, 2008: 399)." Unfortunately, "Father Profit" often trumps efforts to reduce carbon emissions and outgreen other developed countries.

China uses coal, a particularly dirty CO_2-intensive fuel, for 70% of its commercial energy supply, while coal now accounts for only about one-third of America's total energy generation. China builds more than one new coal-fired power plant each week. Coal is cheaper and more widely available in China, which is important as the country tries to find energy resources to keep its many energy-intensive industries running. The thorny issue of cleaner coal in China is too controversial, and no amount of renewable energy in America will solve the problem. At the rate China is growing, a switch to renewable energy, if it comes at all, will probably come too late to have any perceptible effect on current pollution levels.

American industry must reconfigure itself with government help to remain competitive in global markets. This will require unprecedented cooperation among traditionally hostile stakeholders and a renewed focus on **alternative energy sources** to become energy self-sufficient. With backing from the **United Steel Workers**, the **Natural Resources Defense Council** and others, the **Center for American Progress** argues that a $100 billion green-stimulus package would generate job gains and larger energy savings than an equal expenditure on fossil-fuel subsidies or direct taxpayer refunds. Investment in more efficient fuel economy standards, incentives to purchase hybrid and battery-powered electric vehicles, development of natural-gas-fueled heavy duty vehicles and production of advanced biofuels would also help secure America's future by conducting research into alternative fuels, creating green economy jobs and reducing the effects of climate change caused by carbon emissions and environmental pollution.[8]

Catalysts for Change

The embargoes and weapons of traditional international security policy are increasingly irrelevant in today's interdependent global economy. A 2007 report from the International Energy Agency urged a cooperative approach to helping China and India become more energy efficient.[9] Chinese leaders unleashed two decades of environmental turmoil by replacing Communism with GDPism. But, increasingly, Chinese leaders recognize that environmental harm threatens not only the land, water and air resources but also their political futures (Friedman, 2008). If China had reacted by voluntarily setting a goal of decreasing carbon emissions, this would have resulted in five times more greenhouse gas savings than the targets set by Europe under the Kyoto Protocol. China already also has higher national targets for renewable energy than the United States (where there are none) and tougher mileage rules for its burgeoning fleet of vehicles. If China's leaders can see the necessity of this approach, says Friedman, why can't ours?

What can the United States do about this energy and security threat? The answer is as simple as it is hard to implement: shift to a renewable and sustainable energy (Senge *et al.*, 2008). Despite the massive scale of the challenge, many are optimistic that the political, technical and economic means are at hand to spark a U.S. economic revolution, assisted by ICTs. From wind-powered generators to advanced batteries, the results could mean new exports and more jobs. Friedman is certain the American public can tackle the challenge, even during recessionary times. Change will not be painless: it will require ugly political battles, the demise of dirty industries and the rise of new, clean ones. Friedman is convinced "that the public is ready; they're ahead of the politicians." For now, though, the petro-dictators are surely the only ones celebrating, as oil once again nears the $100 per barrel mark. Rational policy making offers a persuasive political, environmental and economic case for the greening of America. Leaders of trans-national corporations, members of Congress seeking reelection and newly emerging mega-states are less interested in environmental priorities than profit.

When multi-national corporations set up operations in other countries, they bring with them the ideals of their home countries and seek to influence host governments in a variety of ways that would benefit themselves and their shareholders. This was the essence of earlier forms of economic domination such as colonialism and continues unabated today. In many instances, free-market forces have encouraged wasteful practices, which are not likely to serve as catalysts for fundamental political change. For better or worse, capitalism is triumphant and has reinforced existing authoritarian regimes. The environmental damage caused by Chevron's drilling operations in Ecuador and Royal Dutch Shell Oil Company's nefarious affiliation with petro-dictatorial regimes in Nigeria are among the worst of several such examples.[10] Thomas Friedman and other green-hawks say we need to do better than "carbon neutral" because it is not ambitious enough: companies and institutions should seek a "carbon advantage" over competitors. This will require innovations in clean energy, greater energy efficiency (including the use of ICTs to create smart grids and smart buildings) and a new ethic of conservation. Although hard evidence for this is scant and political opposition is fierce, rather than costing too much, such initiatives can create investment opportunities, new jobs and global leadership for the U.S. economy. Competition from developing nations which have discovered the economic advantages of unregulated capitalism may become the most serious challenge to sustainable development.

Since the fall of the Berlin Wall two decades ago, globalization has added 3 billion ambitious new players from rapidly growing developing countries (primarily from China and India) many of whom are now able to work faster and cheaper than comparable workers in America and Europe (Prestowitz, 2006). Those who espouse globalization's positive effects claim that current trends put everyone on a "level playing field," promote economic equality and eliminate many of the past economic constraints such as colonial domination of developing countries. Citing data which suggests that poverty levels in China and India have decreased 19% and 25% respectively, Jagdish Bhagwati (2004) argues that economic globalization has neither widened income inequality nor increased poverty in poor nations. As China, Brazil, India and Russia benefit from economic globalization and (perhaps) shed their ideological legacies, they are producing highly skilled and tech-savvy workers that guarantee very different post-industrial economic futures (Kelly, Ramkishen and Goh, 2006). With the greening of globalization, millions of individual entrepreneurs and corporations in counties with fewer natural resources are becoming empowered with the ability to improve communications and transcend national barriers that once separated global trade partners. Others are less optimistic about the redistributive effects of globalization.

Economist Joseph Stiglitz challenges these positive assessments, arguing that without fundamental changes in financial institutions and greater sharing of wealth with emerging countries, globalization will continue to favor rich over poor countries (Stiglitz, 2006). Indeed, while there have been many positive results from economic globalization, there is another darker and more sinister side to the process described above which has increased since the international financial meltdown. Governments may be powerless to forestall its negative consequences.

What is the Role of Public Administration?

Globalization is encouraged by the promotion of free trade, economic deregulation and the elimination of trade barriers which limit growth in emerging economies. At the same time, free trade policies have flattened the global economy through in-sourcing, outsourcing and off-shoring, costing many American jobs. With the prospect of continued globalization looming over millions of American workers, trying to protect what remains is becoming increasingly difficult. Paradoxically, increase in ICT-driven globalization forces more people to rely on public services offering health care, public education, career retraining, retirement guarantees and unemployment compensation to protect them from the rigors of international economic competition. As it becomes cheaper and easier to move operations overseas, how will political leaders, educators and legislators respond to ensure that dislocated workers will have opportunities for productive employment?

As chief executive of the most powerful nation in the world, the president of the United States has nearly unlimited control over foreign policy, and sets the agenda for domestic and economic policy. Presidential efforts in the past have helped grow the economy, protect constitutional freedoms and maintain minimal social welfare policies. Presidents can be credited with encouraging free trade through free market policies, utilizing resources more efficiently and protecting American jobs. President Ronald Reagan (1981–1989) alongside British Prime Minister Margaret Thatcher received credit in the early 1980s for pressuring global markets through an increase in privatization. Reagan also provided tax cuts that were supposed to stimulate economic growth through excess capital that resulted from tax breaks. The reasoning was that a "trickle down effect" of tax cuts which benefitted the wealthy would encourage job growth and income redistribution. In theory, the extra money left over would be spent or reinvested and create more wealth at all income levels. This enabled the growth of corporations and removed most government intervention in the market (Hertz, 2003: 21–22). When Bill Clinton took office in 1993, his foreign policy became the expansion of free trade. He believed in the democratization of globalization—to ensure an adequate workforce, a social safety net was required to guarantee economic survival. President Clinton made some strides with passage of the North American Free Trade Agreement (NAFTA) and revisions to the WTO, eliminating many trade barriers that existed at the time. Clinton's plan for globalization, however, included a broad social safety net to ensure that growth would not be at a cost to jobs at home.

In contrast, former president George W. Bush's post-9/11 policies centered on encouraging the growth of corporations at a cost to global capitalism. He encouraged subsidies to ensure industry growth in some sectors nationally, but did not aggressively push for worldwide economic expansion

(Bhagwati, 2004: 128). At the same time, the Bush administration was obsessed with removing Iraq's Saddam Hussein and failed to recognize the importance of domestic educational and economic reforms as a means to hold jobs and compete globally. Policies of his administration demonstrate just how damaging neo-conservative unilateral foreign policy can be.

Bush's decisions to invade Iraq and authorize the use of torture to obtain information from so-called enemy combatants were especially harmful. His administration's case for **wars in Iraq** and later in **Afghanistan** suffered from three major flaws: 1) lack of reliable intelligence that Saddam had connections to *al Qaeda* (which were never verified); 2) questionable evidence presented to the United Nations that Iraq possessed weapons of mass destruction (WMDs); and 3) the fact that the United States had lost a potentially powerful ally in the war on terror: Saddam Hussein himself. He was a secular leader who believed in socialism rather than religious fundamentalism; he was not an Islamic extremist, but rather a military petro-dictator, not unlike others in the region and elsewhere. Despite Iraqi government attempts to convince Washington that it had no WMDs, the Bush administration had already decided to go to war with Iraq, WMDs or not. The lack of conclusive evidence of Iraqi ties with *al Qaeda* did not dissuade Bush from finishing the job that his father had started during the 1991 Gulf War. Prior to his invasion of Kuwait, Saddam was one of the most powerful U.S. allies in the region. His regime had a mutually supportive relationship with the United States, even receiving funds from the CIA.

The Bush administration failed to heed the accurate and factual intelligence findings presented to them by CIA officers and foreign diplomats who were later forced to resign under pressure from the White House. The administration's attention was selective and favorable only to intelligence that supported its plan to invade Iraq. They ignored evidence that Saddam had a WMD research facility modeled after the Manhattan project, although it had been shut down for almost 10 years. The CIA was aware of this because it had sent spies living in the United States to Iraq prior to the war to talk to research scientists employed by Saddam's regime. The scientists advised family members and tried to get the message across to the United States that there were no weapons of mass destruction, at least not anymore. There had been a research project but it was destroyed during a Desert Storm bombing raid in 1991. This information was apparently either ignored or never reached the White House. Bush steadfastly believed that Iraq possessed the capability to produce weapons of mass destruction.[11]

Another plausible reason for invading Iraq was to create a smokescreen for the U.S. media and citizenry to shift focus from *al Qaeda* and the *Taliban* in Afghanistan. Bush's extreme right-wing supporters believed that there must have been some linkage between the terrorist organization which had attacked New York and Washington and the Saddam regime, providing support needed to invade Iraq. The administration's primary objective may have been building support for the next presidential campaign and getting reelected in 2004. They succeeded and the same harmful policies continued for another four years. Why else would the United States invade Iraq telling the world that there were WMDs only to eventually admit they were wrong, and, in the process, lose a great deal of worldwide credibility and political capital? The real aims were domestic and the means to accomplish them entailed demonizing Saddam and invading Iraq (Milakovich and Gordon, 2009: 276–277).

In addition, the Bush administration authorized the capture and torture of both U.S. citizens and foreign nationals outside of the United States. To avoid conflict with U.S. civil liberties and criminal procedures, enemy combatants were transferred to Guantanamo prison in Cuba or to secret overseas U.S. administered detention facilities in at least 15 countries.[12] Leaked CIA documents reveal that combatants were denied due process rights, held incommunicado and even tortured for periods of months or years. CIA memos confirm that persons categorized as prisoners were abused, humiliated and tortured; their rights afforded under the Geneva Convention violated. One of President Obama's first actions upon assuming the presidency was to propose closing Guantanamo and many of the foreign detention facilities and authorize an investigation into the events surrounding the detention policy.

Another apparent consequence of U.S. neo-conservative post-9/11 foreign policy was the disappearance of the so-called intellectual advantage in research and development technology. The so-called "brain gain" that the United States once enjoyed turned into a "brain drain," as talented foreign students restricted from entering the United States because of their ethnicity decided to study elsewhere. Many went to Europe and found that they had the ability to achieve an equivalent standard of living in their home countries and chose to work in jobs created by outsourcing (Friedman, 2005: 260–275).

The Globalization of Education

Qualified persons from developing countries are generally more eager to work and compete directly with many American workers. The Indian Institutes of Technology, or ITTs, prepare students with educations comparable to that of preeminent U.S. institutions such as the Massachusetts Institute of Technology (MIT) for many high-skilled jobs. Furthermore, competition is challenging companies by forcing them to consider outsourcing operations to other countries that provide the same or higher quality work at a lower cost. The U.S. federal government hasn't seen this as enough of a threat to prevent the inevitable losses from happening. In particular, funding for science and engineering programs has been drastically cut, and every year fewer U.S. students study those fields in institutions of higher learning (Friedman, 2005: 256). To address the so-called "quiet crisis" of American higher education, former president George W. Bush called for a loosening of visa requirements so more high-skilled foreign workers could enter the United States to fill positions that Americans were unqualified for. At best, this was a short-term solution to a very challenging long-term problem.

The Obama administration realizes that to ensure the financial stability of future generations, education needs to be prioritized along with health care and job training. Citizens also need to be able to turn to the government for retraining and social insurance programs in the case of layoffs. Although the United States still has some of the world's best higher education institutions, the quality of its middle and high schools is dismal. Dropout rates have been increasing as math and science scores have declined. There are not enough educated scientists and engineers to replace those Baby Boomers who will soon retire, so the United States will have to outsource even more high-skill jobs. Although emphasis is placed on getting into college, there is no guarantee that students will graduate after four years. As a direct result of the recession, only 54% of entering students received a degree after six years. The percentage is even lower for Hispanic and black minorities. Some college students are worse off when they drop out because they still have to repay loans they assumed when they were in school. Concern has only focused on getting minorities into college—additional efforts need to be made to ensure that students graduate.

The only way to ensure economic survival and equalize opportunities for political participation is through improving the quality of education and other social programs preparing U.S. citizens for competition in rapidly changing global markets (Chapter 4). The best national strategy to avoid workers being outsourced is to make a commitment to higher education; it is not employment stability, but *employability* that is necessary for global competition (Friedman, 2005: 284–293). Everyone is going to have to be more adaptable and retrain to cope with new situations when old conditions change, as they have dramatically since 2007. Thomas Friedman refers to jobs that are less likely to be outsourced as "untouchable" and those who learn the skills needed for high-level value-added careers will be the least affected by globalization. Although the job market will necessarily shift, job growth in other sectors such as the green economy could be promoted, or new sectors stimulated through job training. This strategy does not rely on the government as in the case of unemployment compensation, but provides a means to continue working in the rapidly changing global economy. As factories close and industries move offshore, investment in education, job retraining and universal health insurance are the only ways to ensure employability and mitigate the negative impacts of globalization and recession on the U.S. economy.

Models of Corporate Globalization: McDonalds, Starbucks or Wal-Mart?

For many, the spread of American culture is symbolized by rap music, Hollywood films, fast food chains and giant conglomerates that are frequently accused of lowering wages and driving out family businesses— its rapid assimilation in the new world economy together with the aggressive foreign policy of the Bush administration has angered many in other countries. Bush administration policies reinforced a naïve view of the world and ignored shifting global economic realities. Ironically, the loss of high paying industrial jobs and the increase in lower paying service positions in the United States have generally benefited many of the same developing economies which disdain these symbols of American corporate globalization.

The genius of the much-maligned American "fast food" system was a division of labor which allowed for specialization along the assembly line to standardize menus and take and prepare orders more quickly. For over 50 years, McDonalds has been using standardized methods to increase efficiency and produce lower cost meals. When the Golden Arches make their way into other countries, they are not always met with open arms. McDonalds has expanded to 34,000 restaurants all over the world; some have even been identified with major moments in history, such as anti-American riots in Russia. McDonalds outlets symbolize American "cuisine" and have even been bombed as targets during anti-globalization demonstrations in several countries (Barber, 2001; Veseth, 2005: 215–218). Yet in China, half of all children under age 12 recognize McDonalds as an American brand. McDonalds, together with Kentucky Fried Chicken and Burger King (a British owned company) are among the most popular restaurants in China, where the concept of "drive-ins" has only recently been introduced. Japan's most popular fast food restaurant in 1992 was McDonalds which has been adapted to the Japanese culture and diet. McDonalds was also forced to scrap traditional menus and offer meat-free meals to its customers in India while Israel's McDonalds offer kosher meals (Veseth, 2005: 127). Despite customer preferences, compromises and efficiencies alone are not enough to satisfy many governments that the "fast food" model is the best alternative. In some countries, these concessions don't matter, as U.S. corporations are rejected outright.

Although some cultures are ready and willing to accept American corporations in their home country, others are not; foreign leaders have challenged the way companies do business internationally. England's Prince Charles accuses the fast food chains of social irresponsibility by contributing to obesity among British youth. Although France is McDonalds' third largest market, the French are adamantly opposed to the Americanization which they feel comes with the operation of American "fast food" companies in their country. On average, the French are less obese yet spend twice as long at meals than do Americans. In Germany as well as some regions in the United States, the construction of Wal-Mart outlets has been banned. The Chinese government limits the number of Western films that can be shown. In Italy and elsewhere in Europe, where McDonalds and other fast food outlets began to proliferate (including in the Eternal City of Rome) the **slow food movement** has gained momentum in consort with animal rights groups (PETA) and health-conscious vegetarians. The movement emphasizes less dependence on corporate agri-business and more organically grown food products from local farms. According to the slow food movement, the U.S. model is not only unsustainable from an ecological perspective but it is also devastating to the economic viability of small farmers.[13]

The slow food movement is not the direct antagonist of the fast food movement, although it promotes healthier lifestyles, ethical treatment of animals, vegetarian diets and the protection of cultural traditions that would otherwise be lost with the rise of the global corporate fast food industry. The movement criticizes the proliferation of fast food outlets and claims that society is becoming enslaved by this lifestyle. It is both an anti-obesity and anti-globalization movement that does not call itself that because, although it is based around the principles of food, it is not just food that concerns its supporters. This grassroots movement encourages the experience of local cuisine, rejects quick fixes, supports local chefs and opposes global menus and fast food franchises that exist today (Veseth, 2005: 191–203). As such, it has become a symbol for changing to healthier diets and an ally of opponents of trans-national corporate globalization.

Conclusions: Current Situation and the Future: How Far Have We Reached and Where Are We Going?

Governments are becoming increasingly aware of the importance of employing digital governance measures to improve the delivery of public services. Visions for online service delivery began several decades ago and, since then, many have had varying degrees of success in becoming reality. The benefits are clearer, faster, cheaper, more personalized and efficient service delivery that citizens and businesses can access literally whenever they need it. Realizing those benefits, however, has proven somewhat elusive as many states and local governments have reduced capital spending to meet budget crises. Challenges of moving government online are complex—administrative, budgetary, legal, regulatory, social and political forces combine to create a delicate mix of stakeholders that must be managed and led in the transition to digital governance.

The careers of many willing American workers have been disrupted or cut short by the expansionist strategies of multinational corporations in the new global economy: 15 million Americans are unemployed and it is estimated that another 15 million have given up or are underemployed. Jobs have been "outsourced" and health care and retirement benefits are being abandoned by companies seeking to avoid long-term responsibilities to employees. World politics has changed and multi-nationals now wield greater political power. Globalization stimulates economic growth for certain segments of the new global economy, while others are left behind. With the aid of powerful **free-trade lobbies**, private interests dominate American economic, energy and foreign policy. At the same time, overemphasis on efficiency and profits has its own inherent loss, eschewing America's most valuable asset, loyal employees. As a result, the way business is handled has dramatically changed. McDonalds and Wal-Mart pay less and cover fewer employees' medical benefits than many legacy companies. But at least they pay some portion as compared to millions of small businesses that pay nothing.

Prior to the passage of health care affordability legislation in 2010, small businesses with fewer than 50 employees accounted for most of the job growth in the United States and were exempt from most social legislation. Health care and retirement benefits, if available, were the employees' responsibility. This downsizing-benefits strategy became an issue in the 2006 Congressional and 2008 presidential elections, prompting the newly elected Democratic Congress and President Obama to propose enacting laws, similar to pension guarantee benefits, to protect the health care benefits of domestic workers. President Obama pledged and succeeded with the passage of near-universal health care coverage which many political conservatives still view as too expensive and too much under federal control. Republican candidates successfully campaigned on a platform to among other goals repeal health care coverage. The results of the 2010 Congressional elections suggest that Americans are in an impatient mood; politicians who fail to deliver on promises are likely to serve only one term.

Future challenges for elected officials and public administrators are to moderate the negative impacts of globalization through domestic policies that encourage economic competitiveness and job growth without sacrificing another generation of willing workers. Government intervention and the maintenance of minimum social safety nets that ensure basic access to health care and some degree of job security are the only ways to protect workers without enacting anti-competitive trade tariffs or import restrictions. One viable solution to this dilemma is to utilize existing ICTs to improve the delivery of government mega-services, such as education, health care and social security via the internet. Only educated workers have the ability to access online government support systems. The primary global developmental challenge for the advancement of digital governance is how to accomplish access without discriminating against those without knowledge.

Key Terms

gross national product (GNP), 216
trade restrictions, 216
tariffs, 217
dumping, 217
in-sourcing, 217
outsourcing, 217
off-shoring, 217
corporate globalization, 217
multi-national corporations
  (MNCs), 218
trans-national corporations, 218
Soviet Union (USSR), 219
fall of the Berlin Wall (1989), 219
fiscal policy, 220
monetary policy, 220
trade surpluses, 220
trade deficits, 220
balance of trade, 220
global income redistribution, 220
David Ricardo, 220
theory of comparative
  advantage, 220
trading blocs, 221
North American Free Trade
  Agreement (NAFTA), 221
Adam Smith, 222
Keynesianism, 222
global regulation, 222

legacy industries, 223
workflow software, 223
open-sourcing, 224
informing, 224
Wikipedia, 224
Mozilla Firefox, 224
Amazon.com, 225
triple convergence, 226
global weirding, 227
Green Revolution, 227
petro-dictatorships, 227
climate change, 227
carbon emissions tax, 228
value-added tax, 228
cap and trade, 229
Kyoto Protocols, 229
alternative energy sources, 229
United Steel Workers, 229
Natural Resources Defense
  Council, 229
Center for American
  Progress, 229
role of public administration, 232
Iraq and Afghanistan Wars, 233
Models of Corporate
  Globalization 236
slow food movement, 237
free trade lobbies, 238

10 Toward Digital Governance and Participatory Citizenship
Integrating Technology and Public Administration

This book has explored the conversion from traditional public administration enhanced by electronic government to expanded forms of digital governance, emphasizing the importance of citizen participation, interoperability and information technology to accomplish the change. Chapters concentrated on strategies for organizational transformation and their implications for improved and measurable government performance. This concluding chapter summarizes the main points of each section, highlights recurring themes, discusses paradoxes and outlines future challenges.

Chapter Summaries: Closing the Trust Deficit

Implementation of any ICT-enabled transformation is burdened by a multiplicity of challenges—attitudinal, financial, political, structural and technical. ICTs can be used to promote more participatory democracy, generally considered to be broader than representative democracy because of its implications for citizenship and the use of New Media to encourage citizens and government officials to communicate. Increased access to computers and smart phones allows more people to become active participants in economic, political and social development via the internet. In recent years, the information revolution has been slowed by the effects of a weak economy on many commercial enterprises, public agencies and other organizations. Following economic recovery, changes are likely to pick up at an even faster pace.

Why some government officials accept change and others resist is an elusive question with multiple answers. Conversion of public administration service delivery systems is more likely to result from the current dire financial conditions facing nearly all governments. Recession has limited but not curtailed the ability of many otherwise receptive governments to expand online access. Those who have begun the process have developed characteristics which are key to becoming high-performance governments: a citizen-centered perspective, meeting citizen expectations, working collaboratively across and within agencies, offering multiple channels of interaction, using innovative technologies to offer flexibility to citizens and reaching out proactively to make full use of the newly enhanced service offerings and deliver maximum public-sector value. Technical changes are less of an obstacle than lack of trust in political institutions.

Much of the anti-government wave which has swept the United States since the mid-1970s reflects a lack of faith in public institutions to deliver on promises of more accountable, cost-effective and responsive public services. Despite short-lived upward fluctuations during times of economic prosperity or national crisis, public trust in government has declined steadily over the past four decades (Figure 10.1). Trust in government spiked briefly after 9/11 but resumed its downward trend thereafter. This phenomenon represents a major challenge for both appointed and elected public officials because it reflects a more pervasive loss of confidence in political and administrative leadership, performance and capacity for service delivery. Factors that have contributed to the decline in citizen trust in government include anger over wasteful spending and deficits, jobs losses resulting from the economic recession, perceptions of governmental inefficiency and rising suspicions about sources of campaign financing, resulting from the U.S. Supreme Court decision in the **Citizens United v. Federal Election Commission** (discussed below).[1]

The long-term balance of trust and distrust in the United States and elsewhere presents major challenges for officials who have been supportive of innovative changes. The difference between the numbers of adults who distrust Washington compared with those who trust government is greater

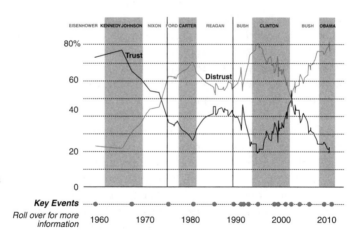

Figure 10.1 Trust and Distrust in Government Index, 1960–2010
   Source: Data from Pew Research Center, National Election Studies, Gallup, ABC/Washington Post, CBS/New York Times, and CNN Polls. Accessible at: http://people-press/trust/

now than at any time in the past 50 years (Figure 10.1). This **trust deficit** is another reason why confidence in government's ability to resolve basic economic and social problems has eroded. As discussed in this book, political and administrative changes are also being driven by the relentless forces of politics, administration and globalization.

Politics and Participation

Rapid breakthroughs in applications of digital technologies have empowered billions more citizens worldwide to influence commercial, political and administrative outcomes using ICTs in a variety of different ways. Political linkages between businesses, citizens and governments increase opportunities for commercial trade, public service and citizen participation. Blogs, social networks, multi-media and PDAs have become institutionalized as components of electoral processes. Moving from a traditional bureaucratic, hierarchical, paper-intensive and rule-driven environment (public administration as we know it) to a more citizen-centered, horizontal, integrated and networked governance system entails internal transformations as well as participation by informed citizens capable of making choices online. Citizen participation provides a source of special insight, information, knowledge and experience which contributes to the soundness of government solutions to public problems. This requires widespread adoption of digital ICTs capable of connecting governments with citizens who understand how to interact with newer forms of technology. For those unable or unwilling to learn how to access new technology-driven ICTs, massive re-education and training efforts must accompany the transition. Additional breakthroughs in political communication and virtual education are being made in newly emerging and rapidly expanding polispheres (Chapters 1, 2 and 4).

Major conflicts have erupted over the most effective methods to reform administrative and political systems. Health care reform or so-called "Obamacare" is just one of numerous policies buffeted by partisan divisions. Greater numbers of citizens are less tolerant of inefficiencies, mismanagement and lack of responsiveness in both the public and private sectors. Whether success can be achieved through more private sector involvement or greater governmental regulation remains a contentious political issue that divides the electorate, executives and legislators. Declining trust in federal employees is also linked to less political participation and lower voter turnouts. At a time when millions more people depend on public services, bureaucrats are often blamed, their salaries frozen and public agencies downsized (see Box 10.1). Citizens want choice, convenience and control over their interactions with public agencies. Better government decisions, by definition, benefit greater numbers of citizens. Yet, governments resist cost-benefit analysis to determine which among several alternative policies and strategies work best. Involvement in

Box 10.1: American Confidence in Federal Workers Eroded in 2010

The proportion of registered voters who have at least "some confidence" in civilian federal employees fell from 75% in July 2009 to 66% in October 2010, according to a Politico-George Washington University-Battleground Poll. Only about one in five randomly sampled respondents (19%) say they have a "great deal" or "a lot" of confidence in federal workers. While a large majority would still encourage "a young person who was considering going to work as a federal civilian employee" (72%), that proportion too has declined over the past year. In the 2009 survey, 79% said they would encourage such a career path. The partisan shift which emerged during the 2010 U.S. mid-term elections was driven by factors such as the intensified polarization of the parties about the role of government in health care and the economy, viewing federal workers as agents of a now less popular President, spillover from the anti-government rhetoric of the Tea Party movement, and blame toward perceived federal malfeasance both before and after the Gulf oil disaster. Decline in confidence regarding federal workers derives almost entirely from Republican disaffection, with almost four in ten Republicans now expressing "very little" confidence (38% in 2010 compared to 28% in 2009), and to a lesser extent from Independents. Only one in seven Democrats (14%) have so little confidence in the federal workers, virtually unchanged from 2009. Whether this trend develops into an even more dramatic split between Republicans and Democrats in their attitudes toward federal workers will determine policy success in the years to come. If Republican mistrust of federal workers continues to grow—and does not swing back markedly the next time a Republican captures the White House—that would signal that something deeper than temporary partisan politics is pushing this cleavage. President Obama's decision to freeze federal salaries for two years symbolizes the deep fractures in the U.S. polity over issues such as who should decide fundamental policy directions.

Source: Adapted from: William C. Adams and Donna Lind Infeld "Trust in Federal Workers Continues to Erode, Enthusiasm for Federal Careers Suffers as Well" *PA TIMES* print issue, October (2010)

public affairs also serves to check and balance political activities, thereby increasing accountability and reducing the likelihood of public officials making self-serving decisions. Unsupported leaders often become discouraged and drop activities that are potentially beneficial, but difficult to implement in divisive political environments.

Governments recognize citizen mandates and redesign programs with citizen-centric guiding principles in mind (Chapter 3). Mission statements increasingly identify the need for value-added digital exchanges with citizens, government employees and private sector organizations. Virtual learning is bolstered by recent evidence supporting the value of online education and training as alternatives to traditional learning and teaching methods (Chapter 4). Quality awards and national accreditation standards also provide a rich and varied resource for governments to define their main missions and purposes and reach out to all citizens. Rewards help improve the quality of public services, focus attention on new performance measures, rather than partisanship, and emphasize process improvements. The challenge and distinction that accompany the pursuit of an award or a prize can also motivate employees and enhance in-house customer service quality initiatives. Can the public sector emulate the private sector without a profit motive? Awards, benchmarks, citizen charters and audit standards will never entirely eliminate the differences between the missions of non-profit, public or private organizations, nor should they. They can, however, provide a rich database for assisting businesses and governments in implementing change strategies, developing successful performance measures and reaching out to all customers being served.

Administration and Performance

Past e-government efforts were supported by initiatives which applied new and emerging technologies to transform the operations and scope of government. ICTs were used to initiate top-down management reforms and achieve a wide variety of policy goals discussed in previous chapters, including customer service quality, online participation, privatization and results-driven management of federal, state and local programs. Making such profound organizational transitions in the operations of public agencies requires significant changes in administrative, legislative, technological and socio-cultural infrastructures as well as linkages to other civic institutions. In some instances, promises made by advocates for electronic government exceeded actual levels of performance and results, further dampening public trust. Still, online delivery of public services is emerging as a viable alternative to meet fiscal exigencies because of its lower costs, greater flexibility and potential to narrow the digital divide. Different incentives are being used to encourage public managers, especially those at the state and local level, to reorient management systems to become more customer-focused and results driven. ICTs are also used to promote other public policies, such as gender and racial equality, while reinforcing pre-existing commercial and governmental interests.

Improving public productivity via the expanded use of ICTs continues with a new sense of urgency resulting from the depth of the economic recession and fiscal stresses plaguing both business and government. Co-production is increasing as more citizens are making online choices involving health insurance, investments, mortgages, student loans, tax collection and retirement savings plans. Managing performance isn't a new challenge for the federal government; performance management has also been the goal of many states and local governments for decades. Digital governance is a primary area of interest and study for numerous public policy specialists as governments use ICTs to improve interoperability among agencies. Chapters 5, 6 and 7 in Part II also questioned the results of some past efforts to enhance availability, lower cost and improve the quality of co-produced public services. The ultimate effectiveness of many of these policies depends upon acceptance of New Media by citizens exercising democratic freedoms and responsibilities. Without enhanced citizen access to the internet and additional knowledge of how to utilize new technology, further efforts may be limited.

Globalization and Public Administration

In many developed and developing regions, public officials have overcome obstacles to the adoption of New Media technologies and implemented ICT-enabled breakthroughs in a wide range of public services. Governments in several countries now use ICTs as strategies to encourage participation, increase effectiveness and facilitate public sector reform; still others conduct elections online, collect more tax revenue and deliver public services more efficiently. Chapters 8 and 9 offered examples of successful applications; traced the history and advantages of free trade; discussed how rapidly the use (and possible misuse) of ICTs has changed the practice of public administration; showed how relationships between individuals, businesses and governments are being affected; and explained how U.S. foreign and military policy is influenced by dependence on foreign sources of energy. Progress in selected world regions was compared, highlighting benchmarks and best practices (lessons from leading countries), and examples of value-added public sector applications. Comparisons show how nations at different stages of economic development deploy ICTs to deal with financial and economic crises, overcome digital divides and respond to natural and made-made disasters. Even in the most advanced economies, obstacles to full implementation remain.

Innovations in communication, technology, transportation and trade will continue to drive global economic growth. The belief that government acts in the best interests of its citizens is being questioned with the rise of corporate power in world politics. Since the fall of the Berlin Wall two decades ago, globalization has added another 3 billion ambitious new players from rapidly developing countries (primarily from China and India) many of whom are now able to work faster and cheaper than higher-paid workers in North America and Europe. The **competitive challenges** confronting the United States and other developed nations should prompt concerted action rather than breed divisive rhetoric. Several recurring themes throughout the book demonstrated how ICTs are being used in several countries to mitigate the effects of global recession, reduce dependence on fossil fuels and convert Industrial Age legacy industries to less hierarchical future-oriented citizen-centric networked systems.

Recurring Themes

The transition from bureaucracy-centered to citizen-centered networked governance is proceeding, but at an uneven pace. Past Industrial Age political and social innovations required the application of advanced specialized technical skills inspired by the forward-looking leadership of politicians and administrators. These qualities appear to be in short supply since the advent of the Information Age. Leadership may be exercised in IT councils, boards, agencies or information systems departments. Agencies with positive working relationships between decision makers and those responsible for digital government implementation tend to be leaders in strategy and implementation. Strong and competent leadership by CIOs can influence success or failure, which is why these positions should be filled by professionals with relevant credentials, not political appointees. Unfortunately, many states experience frequent CIO position turnover, which deters consistent strategic management and implementation. The combination of changing political leadership and quixotic public support has made goals difficult to achieve under the best of circumstances: the first decade of the 21st century has not been the best of times for governments or public administration.

Civic reformers, government contractors, public administrators and other stakeholders need current knowledge of ICTs as well as practical administrative skills to take government to the next level of administrative efficiency and customer satisfaction. Using the power of the internet can make government more capable, competent and responsive in the eyes of all public sector stakeholders. Public trust is strengthened and relationships between government and its citizens are improved. This is not an easy task—if it had already been achieved, public confidence and trust in government would not be as low as it is today. Difficult issues remain.

At minimum, appointed and elected officials must be willing to guide citizens in the transition to digital governance. Although technology is becoming less expensive and more widely available worldwide, without political leadership its potential to convert governmental practices is problematic. Resources must be made available and devoted to acquiring the additional hardware, human assets and software necessary to link stakeholders together. Faster and more reliable internet connectivity, mobility and real-time contact, instant exchange of data, files and information offer powerful advantages for individuals, organizations and (eventually) governments. Although these investments must be carefully made, this book argues that the key impediments to applying such innovations are political, organizational and social—rather than technological.

The technology is available: what is lacking is the political will and administrative skill needed to adopt and apply ICTs to restructure existing political and administrative processes. The cynicism and skepticism mirrored in Figure 10.1 and Box 10.1 impact efforts to increase the use of ICTs. Several **recurring themes** have emerged as issues for public officials to address in the future.

Box 10.2: Recurring Themes

1) Cost-benefit analysis and productivity improvement
2) Establishing new value-added missions
3) Responding to demands to become citizen-centric rather than bureau-centric
4) Adjust to changing traditional sources of revenue
5) Acceptance of the entrepreneurial paradigm
6) Decreased vehicular traffic and the **greening of the net**
7) Closing digital divides and eliminating impersonal service
8) Responding to the exponential growth of social networking
9) Encouraging information sharing and greater public confidence in government
10) Beware of unsupervised contracting out

There are significant "up-front" costs involved in the construction and maintenance of digital service delivery channels. Initial costs of developing a website and putting services online (estimated at between $300,000 and $7 million) present a major obstacle to implementation, especially in developing nations (West, 2005: 32). In addition, many governments have undertaken changes in isolation from others. Public agencies often deny each other the opportunity to achieve economies of scale by not conducting *cost-benefit analysis*. Smaller and poorer countries or states could form regional alliances such as those created by European Union countries allowing them to pool resources and gain greater cost efficiency by building cooperative digital infrastructures. Such collective efforts would give citizens of a particular region more access to information that cuts across county, state or national borders. As detailed in Chapter 8, countries with limited resources can share knowledge and expertise as well as lower overall expenses. Many have a greater opportunity to become truly innovative because they are unencumbered by sunk costs of existing equipment or negative attitudes towards public sector spending. The extended use of regional networking is one reason why Europe is fast becoming the most competitive knowledge-based society in the world.

The costs of digital governance projects depend on initial conditions—whether an application replaces existing manual systems or obsolete computerized systems. Major cost elements include hardware and software at the front end, data cleaning and conversion, IT salaries, training, maintenance and communications infrastructure to link public access points at the back end. Costs vary dramatically according to scope and scale of a project. Projects involving website design may cost thousands of dollars, whereas full-service delivery portals for large agencies or an entire country might take millions of dollars to construct and maintain (Bhatnagar, 2004: 30). The capacity of existing systems vs. the costs of purchasing new hardware and software and hiring management personnel are key considerations. Mistakes made in hardware purchases can lead to unrecoverable costs, security problems and expensive error correction costs in the future. Finding the proper balance between software alternatives—open source or proprietary platforms and applications—can provide avenues for reducing costs. In addition to start-up costs of equipment and personnel, governments must assume continuous operating expenses after hardware has been installed, personnel hired and operating capabilities achieved. Because of its significant costs, virtual government must do more than duplicate channels for delivering the same services available elsewhere: it must confer higher-level tangible value-added benefits, operational efficiencies and cost-savings. Governments are gradually learning how to more accurately measure the costs and demonstrate the productivity gains of digital initiatives. Many studies cited in the proceeding chapters emphasize the value-added cost benefits of virtual government.[2]

Digital governance results in significant *benefits for consumers*, not just to the providers of expanded online public services. In the current era of budget austerity, downsizing and self-funding, many elected officials see only the start-up costs when asked to appropriate more money for new applications, without seeing the revenue potential or savings. Expected savings from ICTs strengthen the case for investments in online service: governments must not only calculate the direct service costs but also recognize savings that accrue to users. If governments make investment decisions based only on their own internal rate of return they may misallocate resources or underestimate return on investments. Online users save time by not waiting in lines and save money from not having to mail forms or commute to public offices for appointments. When fully operational, customer-focused digital governance makes interacting with public agencies much more convenient for all stakeholders. However, efficiency comes with a price: job losses for those unprepared for the new technology.

Throughout the book, a second recurring theme has been that government, in partnership with the private sector, must *find new value-added missions* for legacy industries such as U.S. postal service, General Motors, public schools and many health service providers to become greener and more competitive in the ICT-driven global economy. As service providers and regulators, governments are in a prime position to reap the benefits of all types of digital technology, not just the internet. For many agencies, change will require a transition period where multiple access points and duplicate systems must be maintained. Once websites are "embedded" within government infrastructures, staff can provide better service over the telephone or in person, without the need to focus on routine tasks being handled by computers. This permits more citizens to interact with government through cost-efficient self-selected online applications. Just as ICTs have positively impacted a wide range of services in the private sector, digital governance can provide significant savings to public agencies: for instance, filing forms online costs one-tenth that of filing paper forms.

The need to *become citizen-centric rather than bureau-centric* will help rebuild faith and trust in the competence of public servants to resolve intransigent problems. This requires an attitude change among public servants to ensure security and regain trust in government. Governments are slowly realizing their visions of improved service quality at lower costs. More importantly, there is a growing recognition that harnessing technology is just one of the many tools to transform the way governments operate. Governments are also learning that transformation comes not solely from moving services online, but from redesigning government organizations and processes to put the citizen at the center, integrating across agencies to simplify interaction, reduce cost and improve service. Transformation will only occur on a broad scale with the right configuration of governance structures, coupled with the political will to drive change.

To achieve the goal of user-friendly virtual services, governments must concentrate efforts to provide citizen-centric self-service and focus on the satisfaction of constituents. This is consistent with the **market-based approach** which considers citizens as clients or customers whose needs must be satisfied by providing higher levels of service quality. This approach contrasts with more traditional public administration which views citizens as having few participatory responsibilities beyond merely "consuming" various services provided by government. These two opposing theories are not necessarily incompatible and must be reconciled for self-directed digital governance to succeed.

The prolonged economic downturn has permanently *changed traditional sources of revenue* for governments. Voter opposition to new taxes has forced many governments to draw funds from proprietary services, designated trust funds or user fees collected *directly* from recipients. These funds are restricted to specific services such as highway operations, cable television, parking, non-emergency police services, responding to fire alarms, towing, utility franchises, water and sewer, or solid waste disposal. Proprietary fee-based shares of operating budgets of many large state and local governments now *exceed* the amount collected from general revenue sources (taxes). Economic pressures force governments to treat citizens as valued customers, especially when fines, license fees, service charges and tolls are paid directly by service recipients for specific purposes. Residual savings from greater use of e-mail, for example, caused a precipitous decline in paper mail usage, prompting the U.S. Postal Service (a highly "at-risk" legacy quasi-government corporation that is on the brink of bankruptcy) to enact steep cost cuts, close postal stations and local branches, raise postage rates and likely reduce mail delivery from six to five days per week.[3]

The widespread *acceptance of the entrepreneurial paradigm* encourages citizens to compare the quality of public services with those offered by private providers. Political debate will continue over such fundamental issues as who should receive how much of which valued public resources in society, and who should deliver services to whom at what costs. These questions cannot and *should not* be separated from multiple forms of delivering public services, whether online, by mail, telephone or in person. Many public employees and their professional associations continue to promote digital management practices and virtual government aimed at responding to citizens as valued customers. However, when compared to for-profit private businesses, it is nearly always more challenging for governments to balance conflicting interests, set performance standards and motivate employees to respond to citizens as valued customers. Still, citizen expectations about access to and quality of services provided by governments are likely to rise even higher in the future (Kettl, 2002b; U.S. General Services Administration, 2005). Predictably, offering customer-centric services may also conflict with partisan political agendas, bureaucratic processes and deeply rooted powerful vested interests.

Decreased vehicular traffic and the greening of the net are among the most highly anticipated environmental consequences of increased customer-driven digital governance. This change will result in less congestion, conversion to renewable energy sources, less use of paper and (hopefully) less pollution. The global energy crisis has also spurred a resurgence of interest in mass transit with the Obama administration encouraging funding of inner-city and intra-regional high-speed and light rail systems in the United States (Meinhold, 2009). In addition, existing outreach programs could be expanded to assist the disabled, poor and elderly who are otherwise likely to remain underserved. Expansion could come through developing partnerships with commercial, non-profit or public interest organizations or through traditional technologies such as scheduled service to rural American locations using 21st century "bookmobiles" with personal computers connected to the internet via mobile phone links.[4] This option is becoming more advantageous as more aspects of government service are accessible online. When the number of people using services online equals or exceeds those receiving traditional services, substantial energy savings can be expected.

Digital divides and impersonal service present other potential dilemmas with the transition from traditional to digital self-governance. Some citizens may be underserved because they lack the basic resources and skills necessary to access the internet; others already receive impersonal service vis-à-vis direct contact with public officials (Chapters 5 and 8). The digital divide has worsened since the beginning of the economic recession in 2007. While politicians articulate a vision of equality and digital government, bureaucrats are responsible for redefining the direct relationship between citizens and the public sector (Pavlichev and Garson, 2004). Instead of meeting with public officials face-to-face or conversing with them by telephone, digital governance requires interaction with computers or mobile phones, or sending an e-mail or text message to an official. With the passage of comprehensive health care reform in March 2010, millions of previously uninsured individuals will now have to make complex decisions about health insurance coverage online. One of the possible negative side effects of digital government is that certain individuals may be treated more equally than others. There are always those who would rather have more personal face-to-face communication with a service provider; public agencies must respect that preference.[5] Governments cannot neglect the needs of some people, especially the elderly and disabled, to receive personalized service. Therefore, citizens with special needs should be given a choice of how to communicate with government.

The recent *exponential growth of social networking* and use of smart phones demonstrates the potential to communicate in different ways with a much wider range of demographic groups. In addition to differences in culture, ideals and values, a generation gap undeniably exists when using online services and the internet, but especially with the use of social networking. Older generations, coached by their parents about the value of privacy, view ICTs differently. They do not always understand the attraction of such social networking tools as *Facebook*, *MySpace*, *Skype* or *YouTube*. On the other hand, younger generations see the tools as fun and necessary, a quick means of getting an answer to a question. **Networking** has always been an important element of developing leaders and managers. The difference today is that online *social* networking has created virtual communities without borders, age, race or class discrimination. Anyone can choose to use social networking to establish relationships that essentially augment what they know, which can benefit organizations when knowledge is translated into practice. While face-to-face networking will always be important, the exponential development of internet-based social networks greatly increases the ability of people to expand their contacts and knowledge. Social networking also serves the vital function of facilitating ICT literacy.

Decreased costs and increased productivity are illusory without computer literate citizens. Increased productivity, always a concern, now an obsession, is the engine of economic improvement in living standards for all societies without which governments could not exist.

Researchers generally agree that the use of ICTs by government is likely to raise levels of citizen satisfaction.[6] Social networking applications have not as yet been as widely used for the productivity improvement of public administrative services. When combined with social networking, digital governance has the potential to improve delivery of many types of public services, including dissemination of information about government operations and online transactions; access to information and services around the clock creates a one-stop-shopping "Amazon.gov" experience.

Encourage information sharing and greater public confidence in government. As governments continue to shift to virtual service delivery more diverse content becomes available. But it is not enough to merely upload information to a website: information, especially sensitive public documents, must be organized and secured. (The internet phenomenon, *Wikipedia*, an "open-source" online encyclopedia, has had problems controlling the accuracy of its content in the past.) Communication between citizens and government improves through e-mail and websites, enabling more direct participation in government decision making. Privacy and security needs of users must be taken into account; in some cases, too much disorganized information is available on websites, making them virtually unusable by citizens. Frustration with the lack of content, poor design and the passive nature of many websites further limits their usefulness for increasing public participation. Thus, editorial control and information management are vital to ensure citizens are getting accurate information while at the same time protecting individual privacy.

Various types of outsourcing have been discussed throughout the book and refer generally to the use of private sector companies to provide goods or services for governments. IT services can include: database maintenance, website maintenance, state portal site design and purchasing or help desk functions. Outsourcing is controversial because of the high costs of IT projects and contracting issues. Issues with contracting and purchasing processes can influence the public's perception of IT investment and take power away from responsible parties such as state CIOs and IT directors. Responsible officials should be careful not to initiate *unsupervised contracting out*. Costly, unsuccessful programs can influence a leader's ability to maintain funding because legislatures become more skeptical about supporting future projects.

Although more citizens are communicating directly with governments instantaneously using computers and wireless devices, the expansion of virtual government services has not kept pace with global exponential growth of the internet (Chapter 8). Citizens expect governments to overcome effects of globalization, such as job losses, market failures and restrictive tariffs. President Obama has emphasized exports, technology and manufacturing as critical components for competitive economic growth. Without economic recovery almost nothing else matters; governments are dependent on private sector growth to survive.

Paradoxes in Politics and Participation

Contradictory trends reflect general anxiety about the economy and pervasive negative attitudes towards government institutions in general. Lower productivity of the private economy and reduced housing values shrink tax bases which, combined with citizens' reluctance to pay higher taxes, place greater fiscal stresses on governments, especially states, counties and municipalities. This has muted somewhat the knowledge and technological explosion which gave rise to the use of ICTs in government, especially in advanced industrialized nations. Many citizens have developed a "where's my bailout?" attitude and want government to satisfy their individual demands; at the same time, they expect protection from economic perils, but lack confidence in the execution of service delivery and even regard government itself with hostility.

Several other paradoxes could also impact future citizen participation. Extensive ideological differences remain on policy issues between leaders of business and government, Republicans and Democrats, management and union members as well as questions about who should lead the transformation. Business and government often propose opposing solutions to the same problems. If business benefits, why can't government? There are differences, however, between the two sectors: the primary mission of government is *service* to citizens, most of whom do not pay directly for a public service. This contrasts sharply with the market-driven *for-profit* orientation of the private sector. Citizens use ICTs primarily to demand more accountability for their tax dollars and greater value for services they receive from public agencies. Current and potential users are frustrated: they are using commercial applications and asking why governments cannot or will not provide the same level of direct or virtual service. Competing political interests (sometimes referred to as iron triangles) conflict with persistent problems of defining citizen and customer needs. The political power of complex iron triangles provide effective representation for economic segments of society, but limit standardized public sector solutions to national policy issues.

As more organizations adopt new technologies to enhance quality of service delivery, productivity and performance, the adoption of ICTs at the individual level often does not proceed smoothly. Generational differences in today's workforce lead to conflict, frustration and poor morale for some workers, while at the same time those very differences have stimulated increased creativity and productivity. Today's workforce is comprised of different generations, each with different ideas, learning styles, needs and values that make managing such a diverse multi-generational workforce increasingly challenging. Different modalities have also created problems between the generations as their methods of communicating are very different. **Baby Boomers** highly value face-to-face and telephone communication, and have no problem getting up to walk to another office to ask a colleague a question; younger **Millennials** (also known as the Net Generation), however, are more comfortable and at ease sending quick e-mail or digital text message than having a face-to-face conversation or picking up the telephone. ICTs can be used to bridge generational conflict. Finding the right communication method for each generation is at the center of meeting these challenges. Change-oriented governments and organizations must create new methods of training and accommodating the needs of every generation in their workforce and encourage collaboration between them to enhance performance and productivity. Despite differences between generations, New Media technology can assist people in all age groups to learn from each other.

There is no easy resolution to the problems of educational reform and the closing of digital divides. Access to technology is easier for the information "haves" and less accessible for "have-nots." In many respects and on many comparable measures, the United States is becoming a developing country. Students' SAT scores have not increased and the United States continues to rank lower on comparable educational attainment measures. Even with its high level of economic development, accumulated wealth and historical advantage in technological research and development (R&D), the United States has fallen behind several less affluent industrialized democracies in the application of ICTs to public services (Chapter 8). Internet access is not guaranteed for all citizens. Difficulties arise for those living in remote areas, those who are homebound, people with low literacy levels and those in poverty. This paradox is inextricably connected to declining test scores and failure to reform educational systems. The inferior quality of some schools makes the employability of their graduates questionable. The extent of the divide is reflected in a nation's population and its political leadership. Citizens who are already inclined to use the internet and have better access are being rewarded with more interactivity and better websites. Citizens on the wrong end of the divide are less prepared to function as proactive 21st century citizens.

Centralized administrative structures needed to manage internet servers are often in conflict with decentralized political systems such as American federalism which promote local initiatives. Centralized systems allow IT requests to be filtered through one agency or private firm reducing duplication and variation; decentralized systems allow individual agencies more control over digital administration and content, rather than using one large portal to provide information. Agencies can choose which to use and many believe that decentralized information is more accurate because it is provided directly from the source. Decentralized systems can also provide agencies with a sense of ownership that encourages better site management and design. The decision to develop a centralized or decentralized delivery system depends on the economic and political circumstances. Information management plans demand a high level of central coordination across divisions as well as attention to new issues brought on by online access, such as electronic records management and data sharing. While these issues are not unique to government, they are closely associated with it in the public mind because of concerns about internet security, privacy and data aggregation. To meet high standards of public trust and to ensure compliance with standards, many governments have gone beyond simply improving administrative practices and policy measures by enacting laws and regulations in this area (Chapter 6). Standardization and uniformity are essential for implementing ICTs accessible on the same platforms. In general, centralized structures work to the fiscal benefit of governments by avoiding overlap, allowing for cooperation, data sharing and streamlining processes.

Although President Obama's 2008 political campaign was a breakthrough for internet fund raising (with the entire presidential campaign totaling $2 billion), the 2010 midterm elections were the most expensive yet in American history with twice as much money ($4 billion) spent, much of it financed by "unidentified" sources. As a consequence of the *Citizens United* decision, big money interests now have even greater impact on U.S. political campaigns. Conservative groups outspent liberals in the last election by more than a two-to-one margin. President Obama repeatedly criticized conservatives for their lack of accountability in the midterm elections and chastised the Supreme Court for its decision to allow unlimited corporate and union spending on election ads. Recent U.S. election results also registered support for unregulated free trade, despite public opinion expressing greater support for protectionist legislation. Ironically, although most Americans want government to protect jobs and to stimulate the domestic economy, Republicans elected to the 112th Congress in 2011–2012 are less committed to domestic economic development than to global free trade.

Citizen Perceptions, Attitudes and Internet Use

E-government was originally created by benchmarking private sector e-commerce applications, the best practices of leaders in various processes, including information and communication technologies. Organizations that received awards have themselves become models for benchmarking and self-promotion of newer, more innovative ideas (Chapter 3). The **International Benchmarking Clearinghouse** contains information about the best practices, networking opportunities, just-in-time practices and resources to discover, research, understand and implement emerging improvement methods.[7] Management improvements are being made and standards set on the basis of experience in other, similar jurisdictions. Public agencies are learning from each other, not just the private sector, how to respond to the needs of all those they serve. If effectively implemented, these changes increase the likelihood of producing better performance and results. For the past several decades, ICTs have been used extensively by private market-driven firms and to a lesser extent by governments to provide more efficient, higher level quality and lower cost service. The U.S. Patent and Trademark Office, Social Security Administration and Internal Revenue Service as well as many other federal agencies have demonstrated measurable results and cost savings (Noveck, 2010). Providing incentives, such as awards, charter marks and audit standards to achieve organizational goals encourages organizations to overcome barriers to innovation. Still, difficult issues remain.

Issues in Information Technology

When asked why they are reluctant to provide information to government agencies, the most frequently cited reasons given by citizens are concerns about privacy and security. How do citizens connect trust and the internet to government? One of the weaknesses of the internet is its anonymity; this is also one of its strengths. Before higher level relationships with government agencies can be established, the identities and other relevant data about citizens must be known. Without such information, it would be impossible to go past Stage 1 of posting data on a website. The Thompson/Lieberman Government Information Security Act established a comprehensive framework for federal agencies to make their information systems more secure while providing uninterrupted public service. Every federal agency is required to implement a computer security plan, undergo annual independent information security audits, report unauthorized intrusions and train its workers in security awareness (Chapter 6). Understanding and enforcing the provisions of other laws such as the Privacy Act of 1974 and the Electronic Government Act of 2002 are also inherently important for public managers. The need for a more secure internet access involves the expansion, creation and regulation of new trust mechanisms such as:

- utilizing the services of certified providers, which are essential institutions for the use of message encryption techniques;
- regulating e-commerce to establish the identity and specific responsibilities of organizations providing access to communications networks and the internet;
- creating legal and arbitration mechanisms and procedures to permit enforcement of regulations governing encryption and the responsibilities of encryption providers (Grönlund, 2002).

Technical problems with securing data content involve both public and private communications channels and raise critical questions. Are the messages sent from computer to computer secure? What if the integrity of a message or information was sent over a secure line but then forwarded to a non-secure line? Are mechanisms in place to keep hackers away from sensitive information?[8]

The field of **internet law** is expanding and legal principles are being applied to communication and privacy policies for privileged information and criminal investigations. Privacy and lack of security measures are more than technical issues. Privacy violations can also become criminal issues when information is used improperly. Technical solutions can at the very least give citizens a better feeling about the use of virtual government transactions. Public key encryptions, electronic signatures, certification and registration services can be deployed as technical measures to resolve perceived weaknesses of online communications. Each measure should be discussed and applied based on needs of individual agencies.

Towards Full-Scale Digital Participation

At the heart of digital governance is the attempt to increase citizen participation, lower administrative costs and make government more efficient and reliable. Several issues related to participation have been discussed: How is participation encouraged? What are the benefits of wider citizen participation? Why would any democratic government want to decrease citizen participation? What are the limitations to absolute freedom of information and participation through the World Wide Web? How do we define digital participation and what are the barriers to different levels of participation? These questions emerged as ICTs became more prevalent.

Public managers must promote digital governance as a non-partisan issue. Internet connectivity can make any public official portray his or her administration as modern, progressive, visionary and dynamic by making technology a priority initiative. Citizens who no longer have to stand in line to register cars, pay fines or register to vote are more likely to view government positively. In fact, most people expect to find services such as banking, investments and retail online and have grown accustomed to the Information Age and e-commerce/e-business applications. Web-enabled governments that require different departments to talk to each other with technologies such as certificates, digital signatures, electronic forms and smart cards demonstrate cutting edge technology. Government needs more specialized processes to provide a single data source to all queries in one contact with a call center, website or portal. As IT departments gain more experience, knowledge and direction, advanced processes and applications will be developed and implemented in the future.

Future Implementation, Issues and Challenges

It is difficult to forecast the expected progress of electronic and digital government in particular public agencies, especially those within the diverse U.S. federal system of government and in other regions in the world. Several agencies have been profiled in this book. The types of applications and stages of development among over 88,000 U.S. general and special purpose governments vary significantly, as do those in other countries. Further development and success depends on a careful study of the economic, social and technical implications.

The challenge for citizens and public officials is to acquire the best available knowledge and learn how to apply democratic tools responsibly in the best interest of their local communities, states or nation. Future political support for effective information management systems linking citizen to government cannot be assumed. Government must improve the security of inter- and intra-governmental communication channels and provide clear information strategies on issues such as goals, means/modes, time-space and evaluation for effective development of citizen partnerships. The incorporation and synthesis of large volumes of comments, e-mail messages and opinions received and stored online will become increasingly difficult as the use of the internet for two-way communication and participation increases. The challenge for public managers and policy analysts is to interpret the significance of these data and present decision options to citizens and political decision makers in a comprehensible and understandable format.

Each local community in every country is challenged to adopt more citizen-centric, interoperable and value-added technologies that balance central coordination (in some cases accompanied by centralized authority) with decentralized autonomy across a wide variety of public sector organizational units. Many countries are adapting digital governance systems in accordance with changing global environments. Integrating horizontal and vertical dimensions of ICTs is a major challenge for both developed and developing countries: increasing numbers of public agencies recognize the importance of upgrading and aligning front-line interface with citizens as service recipients and back office capacities for processing information and conducting transactions. Another important and related lesson in terms of interoperability—applicable across both developed and developing countries—is the acceptance of a more collaborative and participative citizen-centric mindset on the part of public employees.

ICTs have great potential to increase productivity, decrease costs, save time, improve citizen service, enhance citizen engagements, share information and open government. But there have been many failures in implementing e-government in the past years. It is not enough to add "d" to traditional government service and expect successful implementation. It takes a great deal of behind-the-scenes work that is customer-focused and comprehensive, but invisible to most citizens. Furthermore, there are also many obstacles that governments need to overcome when implementing technological solutions to public problems. Citizens have to be able to trust government agencies to secure data and files. Otherwise both sides will be reluctant to use the online applications and services. From a public policy perspective, the most important of these are privacy concerns and closing the digital divide. All governments in countries which have initiated ICT-enabled initiatives have to find ways to resolve these two important limits on implementation. Many governments have succeeded in doing so, but there is a great deal more to be achieved. When effectively implemented, ICTs can do extraordinary things to change how government works and improve public services for the benefit of all citizens. In closing, here is a summary of guidelines managers can use to lead the transition:

- Plan carefully in advance: government should analyze and evaluate the feasibility of projects by defining the mission and vision of their website. A strategic plan that includes citizen inputs should be developed before websites are created.
- Seek partnerships and support from top leadership: government should adopt cross-government services by pooling resources to reach more constituents, thereby providing more efficient standardized services. Leadership support is necessary to ensure implementation.
- Establish incentives for adopting digital governance: innovation can be encouraged by recognizing agencies' or governments' initiatives in e-government, promoting excellence and institutionalizing awards for digital service quality.
- Provide user-friendly service: the needs of end-users must be considered when developing websites. An easy and friendly interface increases effective usage of sites.
- Educate and train all citizens about the availability and expanded use of virtual government services. This can be accomplished with the extended use of social networking.

Strategies for improving online customer service quality are well known, if not widely practiced; many local and state governments emphasize customer service training as one of their highest priorities. Several governments have increased market exposure and now have specific guidelines for implementing customer service programs, many of which focus on the expanded use of information technology. Information and communication technology applications, especially innovative programs, are increasingly becoming cornerstones of progressive government operations. The potential for digital governance as a developmental tool hinges upon three prerequisites: 1) a minimum threshold level of technological infrastructure; 2) inspired leadership and motivated human resources; and 3) digital connectivity—for all. Digital governance readiness strategies will be effective and inclusive only if all citizens have equal access and functional ICT literacy and are willing to use computers, PDAs or smart phones for two-way communication with governments.

Key Terms

Appendix A: Why Participants Contacted Government

Births, Deaths and Marriages

Apply for marriage license
Checking family history
Copy of birth certificate
Copy of marriage certificate
Historic data and status of online research facilities
New birth certificate
Procedure for obtaining birth certificate

Benefits

Application for student allowance
Application for student allowance/loan while overseas
Applications, problems with payment
Availability of student allowance for myself, support for
    my partner
Confirming date of superannuation
Disability allowance
Eligibility for grants and financial support while studying
Find out benefit eligibility
Inquiry about niece's requirements
Proving level of income
Requirements for disability allowance and sickness benefits
Unemployment benefit

Broadcasting

Radio
News
Seeking program information

Business-Related Issues

Environment grants for fencing waterways
Grants
New Business funding
Rules for incorporated societies

City Council Matters

Building and zoning permits (extension of house)
Bylaw information
Drainage from house going down neighbor's land
Information on history of area
Liaising with council on issues affecting disabled students
Meeting (minutes and policy)
Paying rates
Policy plans and statements of local council
Safety and environmental regulations, building codes
Street matters
Summer events in region
Water supply and concern over trees in a local park

Consumer Affairs

Issues related to vehicle ownership and use
Ongoing work relationship
Product recalls
Things for sale

Customs

Travel Restrictions
Visas
What to declare

Driver's License

Checking what is needed to change license
Regulations for replacing lost items
Reissue/renewal of driver's license

Education

Consultation appointments
Cost of university for foreigners
Find out about learning sign language

Find out entitlements as a returning student
Funding for students
Information about grants and loans

Information on student support

List of university courses
Looking at new schools
Looking into private schooling
Research grant applications
Status of peer support programs
Status of tertiary project
Teacher registration

Elections

Accurate electoral roll information
Application for absentee ballot
Polling booth
Registration (available in some states)
Time frame for next election, employment possibilities

Employment

Employment opportunities
Government jobs listings
Seeking research work
Staff recruitment
Where we stand with time off and wages for our workers

Environment

Issues related to technology, science in society, etc.
Lease conditions, buildings, etc.
Policy wording for a contract project
Politics being introduced on environmental issues
Resource management
Weather information

Fisheries

Update law books fisheries

Funding Agencies

Information about federal research funding

Links to social benefits
See what is going on

Health

Issues related to technology, science in society, etc.
A matter regarding compensation
Mental health issues and publications
Seeking a copy of a discussion document

Housing and Tenancy

Had bad tenant and wanted to know rights as landlords
Information on costs as a result of a dispute
Tenancy rights/agreement

Immigration, Passport and Citizenship

Apply for, reissue, or renew passport
Changes in immigration policies that affected new immigrants
Details required about getting into country
Family overseas trip
Family passport problems
Immigration requirements for my partner
Information on costs as a result of a dispute
Migration information for parents
Residency status
Rights of refugees
Rules for citizenship
Visa information (e.g., requirements for travel)

Legislation (Laws and Regulations)

Bills in the House and Senate
Copyright law
Employment law
Information for study
Issues related to technology, science in society, etc.
Legalities of paternity tests
Staff information
Statutes (contents of various acts)

Maps and Land Information

Boundaries of property

Finding streets
Finding the quickest routes
Information on a site for a geography project
Land information
Land title
LINZ data
Maps for holidays
Maps of major cities
Mapquest

Occupational Safety and Health

Paying OSH

Personal/Family Issues

Accident Compensation (SSI)
Reporting on an incident
Pregnant and working with child, youth and family

Police/Justice

Handing in a law related to a burglary
Homeland Security
Information on sexual abuse
Issues related to technology, science in society, etc.
Prowler and car theft in neighborhood
Reporting on an incident
Respond to a submission to law commission
Seeking clarification on facts or official interpretation of what I have
    read or heard
Statements by elected representatives

Policy and Politics

Concerns about a child
Latest policy and statements that the government has issued
Politics
Release from restricted security rating for thesis written while
    in the defense force
Reserve Bank exchange rates
Seeking general information and policies
Research work
Various government policies

Recreation and Sport

Book a play trailer for kindergarten
Grants for sports club
Results of sports events
What is occurring around town?

Regional Council Matters

Building permit for local community meeting centers
Installation of water meters
Permits and consents
Regional district plan information
Regional growth plan
Timetables
Treaty issues
Update law books regional council
Water supply information

Statistics

Copies of forms
Seeking data (e.g., on research work on sales tax)
Seeking population and other online statistics

Tax and Finance

How to get a social security number
Paying taxes
Personal income tax regulations
Refund of taxes for charitable donations
Signed up online
Tax codes—state and federal
Tax forms
Tax refund
Tax return

Tourism

Information about immigration
Tourism (general information)

Transportation

Information on policy for disabled access to public
transportation

New RV regulations
Policies being introduced on transport issues
Public transport (fares and timetables)
Warrant of fitness regulations

Treaty Issues

Information for study
Information on specific issues or fact

Other

Copies of submissions and commission pages
Disability issues, strategies and pertinent building codes
Events: date of birth of a friend's child that had been advertised
Seeking career information
Seeking information on a government department
Updating status on *Facebook* or other social media: finding out what is
   going on (especially in relation to key personal interests)

Appendix B: Use of Government Websites for Transactions and Information, by Gender, Race, Age, Education and Income

Use of government websites for transactions and information

The proportion of internet users within each group that has used a government website in the last 12 months to conduct a specific transaction or get information

	% online government users
Total internet users (n=1676)	82%
Gender	
Male (n=748)	83
Female (n=928)	81
Race/Ethnicity	
White, non-Hispanic (n=1273)	83
Black, non-Hispanic (n=158)	72
Hispanic (n=135)	78
Age	
18–29 (n=318)	83
30–49 (n=560)	83
50–64 (n=505)	80
65+ (n=259)	74
Educational Attainment	
Less than high school (n=80)	68
High school graduate (n=435)	71
Some college (n=438)	83
College+ (n=711)	93
Annual Household Income	
Less than $30,000 (n=338)	70
$30,000–$49,999 (n=313)	85
$50,000–$74,999 (n=261)	90
$75,000 or more (n=510)	91

Source: Pew Research Center's Internet & American Life Project, November 30–December 27, 2009 Tracking Survey. N = 2.258 adults 18 and older, including 1.676 internet users. Please see the Methodology section for margin of error calculations.

Pew Internet
Pew Internet & American Life Project

Appendix C: 2010 UN DATA survey

Rank	Country	Index value	Of which		
			Online service component	Telecom-munication Infrastructure component	Human capital component
1	Republic of Korea	0.8785	0.3400	0.2109	0.3277
2	United States	0.8510	0.3184	0.2128	0.3198
3	Canada	0.8448	0.3001	0.2244	0.3204
4	United Kingdom	0.8147	0.2634	0.2364	0.3149
5	Netherlands	0.8097	0.2310	0.2530	0.3257
6	Norway	0.8020	0.2504	0.2254	0.3262
7	Denmark	0.7872	0.2288	0.2306	0.3278
8	Australia	0.7863	0.2601	0.1983	0.3278
9	Spain	0.7516	0.2601	0.1683	0.3231
10	France	0.7510	0.2321	0.1965	0.3225
11	Singapore	0.7476	0.2331	0.2107	0.3037
12	Sweden	0.7474	0.1792	0.2482	0.3200
13	Bahrain	0.7363	0.2483	0.1932	0.2948
14	New Zealand	0.7311	0.2170	0.1864	0.3278
15	Germany	0.7309	0.1867	0.2295	0.3146
16	Belgium	0.7225	0.2126	0.1880	0.3218
17	Japan	0.7152	0.2288	0.1730	0.3134
18	Switzerland	0.7136	0.1511	0.2537	0.3088
19	Finland	0.6967	0.1630	0.2059	0.3278
20	Estonia	0.6965	0.1705	0.2070	0.3190
21	Ireland	0.6866	0.1695	0.1894	0.3277
22	Iceland	0.6697	0.1349	0.2110	0.3238
23	Liechtenstein	0.6694	0.1781	0.1786	0.3127
24	Austria	0.6679	0.1619	0.1893	0.3167
25	Luxembourg	0.6672	0.1295	0.2355	0.3021
26	Israel	0.6552	0.1986	0.1430	0.3136
27	Hungary	0.6315	0.1716	0.1432	0.3167
28	Lithuania	0.6295	0.1641	0.1456	0.3198
29	Slovenia	0.6243	0.1360	0.1659	0.3224
30	Malta	0.6129	0.1597	0.1605	0.2927
31	Colombia	0.6125	0.2418	0.0799	0.2908
32	Malaysia	0.6101	0.2148	0.1134	0.2819
33	Czech Republic	0.6060	0.1543	0.1405	0.3112
34	Chile	0.6014	0.2072	0.0895	0.3047
35	Croatia	0.5858	0.1436	0.1393	0.3030
36	Uruguay	0.5848	0.1630	0.1050	0.3168
37	Latvia	0.5826	0.1414	0.1241	0.3171
38	Italy	0.5800	0.0982	0.1622	0.3196
39	Portugal	0.5787	0.1317	0.1382	0.3088
40	Barbados	0.5714	0.0680	0.1819	0.3215
41	Greece	0.5708	0.1209	0.1263	0.3235
42	Cyprus	0.5705	0.1263	0.1428	0.3015

			Of which		
Rank	Country	Index value	Online service component	Telecom-munication infrastructure component	Human capital component
43	Slovakia	0.5639	0.1177	0.1390	0.3072
44	Bulgaria	0.5590	0.1392	0.1112	0.3086
45	Poland	0.5582	0.1317	0.1113	0.3152
46	Kazakhstan	0.5578	0.1792	0.0593	0.3194
47	Romania	0.5479	0.1414	0.1021	0.3045
48	Argentina	0.5467	0.1403	0.0928	0.3136
49	United Arab Emirates	0.5349	0.0853	0.1793	0.2703
50	Kuwait	0.5290	0.1565	0.0833	0.2892
51	Jordan	0.5278	0.1813	0.0596	0.2869
52	TFYR Macedonia	0.5261	0.1090	0.1255	0.2916
53	Mongolia	0.5243	0.1889	0.0342	0.3012
54	Ukraine	0.5181	0.1177	0.0821	0.3184
55	Antigua and Barbuda	0.5154	0.0410	0.1730	0.3014
56	Mexico	0.5150	0.1500	0.0713	0.2936
57	Andorra	0.5148	0.0788	0.1457	0.2903
58	Saudi Arabia	0.5142	0.1058	0.1330	0.2754
59	Russian Federation	0.5136	0.1123	0.0913	0.3101
60	Montenegro	0.5101	0.1069	0.1093	0.2940
61	Brazil	0.5006	0.1252	0.0838	0.2916
62	Qatar	0.4928	0.0950	0.1046	0.2932
63	Peru	0.4923	0.1392	0.0590	0.2941
64	Belarus	0.4900	0.1025	0.0687	0.3188
65	Bahamas	0.4871	0.0788	0.1156	0.2927
66	Tunisia	0.4826	0.1641	0.0641	0.2544
67	Trinidad and Tobago	0.4806	0.1155	0.0760	0.2891
68	Brunei Darussalam	0.4796	0.0961	0.0892	0.2943
69	Turkey	0.4780	0.1177	0.0852	0.2752
70	Venezuela	0.4774	0.1036	0.0766	0.2971
71	Costa	0.4749	0.1036	0.0800	0.2913
72	China Rica	0.4700	0.1252	0.0631	0.2817
73	El Salvador	0.4700	0.1446	0.0635	0.2619
74	Bosnia and Herzegovina	0.4698	0.0939	0.0827	0.2932
75	Saint Kitts and Nevis	0.4691	0.0345	0.1417	0.2929
76	Thailand	0.4653	0.1133	0.0576	0.2943
77	Mauritius	0.4645	0.1004	0.0874	0.2768
78	Philippines	0.4637	0.1338	0.0368	0.2931
79	Panama	0.4619	0.0961	0.0727	0.2932
80	Republic of Moldova	0.4611	0.1004	0.0638	0.2970
81	Serbia	0.4585	0.0756	0.0889	0.2940
82	Oman	0.4576	0.1252	0.0690	0.2633
83	Azerbaijan	0.4571	0.1101	0.0439	0.3031
84	Dominican Republic	0.4557	0.1241	0.0547	0.2769
85	Albania	0.4519	0.1058	0.0538	0.2924
86	Egypt	0.4518	0.1803	0.0414	0.2301
87	Uzbekistan	0.4498	0.1284	0.0282	0.2931
88	Saint Lucia	0.4471	0.0378	0.1158	0.2934
89	Jamaica	0.4467	0.0777	0.0930	0.2759
90	Viet Nam	0.4454	0.1036	0.0746	0.2672
91	Kyrgyzstan	0.4417	0.1079	0.0303	0.3035
92	Maldives	0.4392	0.0550	0.0952	0.2889
93	Lebanon	0.4388	0.0907	0.0648	0.2833
94	Saint Vincent and the Grenadines	0.4355	0.0443	0.1216	0.2697

Rank	Country	Index value	Online service component	Of which Telecom-munication Infrastructure component	Human capital component
95	Ecuador	0.4322	0.1079	0.0526	0.2716
96	Cuba	0.4321	0.0820	0.0206	0.3296
97	South Africa	0.4306	0.1047	0.0476	0.2783
98	Bolivia	0.4280	0.1036	0.0302	0.2942
99	Grenada	0.4277	0.0637	0.0795	0.2845
100	Georgia	0.4248	0.0842	0.0384	0.3022
101	Paraguay	0.4243	0.0896	0.0473	0.2875
102	Iran (Islamic Republic of)	0.4234	0.0907	0.0712	0.2616
103	Palau	0.4189	0.0183	0.0840	0.3165
104	Seychelles	0.4179	0.0194	0.1002	0.2983
105	Dominica	0.4149	0.0173	0.1177	0.2800
106	Guyana	0.4140	0.0615	0.0424	0.3101
107	Honduras	0.4065	0.1004	0.0419	0.2642
108	Cape Verde	0.4054	0.0917	0.0543	0.2593
109	Indonesia	0.4026	0.0831	0.0377	0.2818
110	Armenia	0.4025	0.0594	0.0422	0.3009
111	SriLanka	0.3995	0.0885	0.0357	0.2753
112	Guatemala	0.3937	0.1047	0.0504	0.2386
113	Fiji	0.3925	0.0626	0.0461	0.2839
114	Libya	0.3799	0.0464	0.0371	0.2963
115	Samoa	0.3742	0.0486	0.0270	0.2986
116	Tonga	0.3697	0.0237	0.0419	0.3040
117	Botswana	0.3637	0.0680	0.0357	0.2601
118	Nicaragua	0.3630	0.0863	0.0250	0.2516
119	India	0.3567	0.1252	0.0192	0.2123
120	Belize	0.3513	0.0540	0.0462	0.2511
121	Lesotho	0.3512	0.0896	0.0132	0.2484
122	Tajikistan	0.3477	0.0302	0.0203	0.2972
123	Gabon	0.3420	0.0270	0.0366	0.2784
124	Kenya	0.3338	0.0810	0.0210	0.2319
125	Namibia	0.3314	0.0227	0.0402	0.2685
126	Morocco	0.3287	0.0810	0.0584	0.1894
127	Suriname	0.3283	0.0076	0.0400	0.2807
128	SãoTomé and Príncipe	0.3258	0.0302	0.0273	0.2683
129	Zimbabwe	0.3230	0.0432	0.0193	0.2605
130	Turkmenistan	0.3226	0.0097	0.0137	0.2992
131	Algeria	0.3181	0.0335	0.0412	0.2435
132	Angola	0.3110	0.1155	0.0149	0.1806
133	Syrian Arab Republic	0.3103	0.0140	0.0399	0.2564
134	Bangladesh	0.3028	0.1209	0.0109	0.1710
135	Congo	0.3019	0.0270	0.0195	0.2555
136	Iraq	0.2996	0.0518	0.0182	0.2295
137	United Republic of Tanzania	0.2926	0.0594	0.0111	0.2221
138	Equatorial Guinea	0.2902	0.0108	0.0198	0.2596
139	Madagascar	0.2890	0.0561	0.0099	0.2230
140	Cambodia	0.2878	0.0464	0.0098	0.2316
141	Myanmar	0.2818	0.0281	0.0015	0.2522
142	Uganda	0.2812	0.0345	0.0158	0.2309
143	Zambia	0.2810	0.0356	0.0141	0.2313
144	Côted'Ivoire	0.2805	0.1101	0.0205	0.1498
145	Swaziland	0.2757	......	0.0202	0.2555
146	Pakistan	0.2755	0.0842	0.0254	0.1658
147	Ghana	0.2754	0.0507	0.0195	0.2051
148	Rwanda	0.2749	0.0594	0.0067	0.2089

Rank	Country	Index value	Online service component	Of which Telecommunication Infrastructure component	Human capital component
149	Cameroon	0.2722	0.0518	0.0136	0.2069
150	Nigeria	0.2687	0.0324	0.0196	0.2167
151	Lao People's Democratic Republic	0.2637	0.0270	0.0109	0.2259
152	Bhutan	0.2598	0.0637	0.0204	0.1757
153	Nepal	0.2568	0.0572	0.0075	0.1921
154	Sudan	0.2542	0.0529	0.0235	0.1778
155	Vanuatu	0.2521	0.0043	0.0124	0.2354
156	Solomon Islands	0.2445	0.0151	0.0063	0.2232
157	Mauritania	0.2359	0.0302	0.0263	0.1793
158	Democratic Republic of the Congo	0.2357	0.0302	0.0046	0.2009
159	Malawi	0.2357	0.0054	0.0060	0.2243
160	Comoros	0.2327	0.0097	0.0067	0.2162
161	Mozambique	0.2288	0.0583	0.0083	0.1623
162	Timor-Leste	0.2273	0.0453	0.0022	0.1797
163	Senegal	0.2241	0.0604	0.0235	0.1403
164	Yemen	0.2154	0.0162	0.0098	0.1894
165	Togo	0.2150	0.0237	0.0150	0.1763
166	Liberia	0.2133	0.0216	0.0062	0.1855
167	Gambia	0.2117	0.0281	0.0315	0.1521
168	Afghanistan	0.2098	0.0788	0.0108	0.1202
169	Haiti	0.2074	0.0065	0.0221	0.1789
170	Djibouti	0.2059	0.0162	0.0049	0.1848
171	Papua New Guinea	0.2043	0.0248	0.0075	0.1719
172	Ethiopia	0.2033	0.0680	0.0024	0.1329
173	Benin	0.2017	0.0399	0.0150	0.1468
174	Burundi	0.2014	0.0140	0.0030	0.1844
175	Eritrea	0.1859	0.0076	0.0037	0.1746
176	Mali	0.1815	0.0626	0.0096	0.1093
177	Sierra Leone	0.1697	0.0011	0.0059	0.1627
178	Burkina Faso	0.1587	0.0529	0.0066	0.0992
179	Guinea-Bissau	0.1561	0.0054	0.0118	0.1388
180	Guinea	0.1426	0.0119	0.0094	0.1213
181	Central African Republic	0.1399	0.0000	0.0015	0.1384
182	Chad	0.1235	0.0065	0.0060	0.1110
183	Niger	0.1098	0.0130	0.0038	0.0930

Other UN Member States

Rank	Country	Index value	Online service component	Telecommunication Infrastructure component	Human capital component
184	Democratic People's Republic of Korea	......	0.0065	......	......
184	Kiribati	......	0.0097	0.0049	......
184	Marshall Islands	......	0.0086	0.0138	......
184	Micronesia (Federated States of)	......	0.0432	0.0268	......
184	Monaco	......	0.0464	0.2297	......
184	Nauru	......	0.0043	......	......
184	San Marino	......	0.0626	0.1759	......
184	Somalia	......	0.0000	0.0040	......
184	Tuvalu	......	0.0043	0.0567	......

Regional and economic groupings

	Africa	0.2733	0.0489	0.0221	0.2039
	Americas	0.4790	0.1069	0.0857	0.2864
	Asia	0.4424	0.1085	0.0657	0.2659
	Europe	0.6227	0.1480	0.1598	0.3123
	Oceania	0.4193	0.0532	0.0548	0.2766
	Developed countries	0.6542	0.1369	0.1719	0.3136
	Developing countries other than LDCs	0.4443	0.0960	0.0675	0.2774
	Least developed countries	0.2424	0.0381	0.0147	0.1895
	Small island developing States	0.3924	0.0479	0.0657	0.2685

Glossary

accountability holding politicians and bureaucrats responsible for their actions by externally defined review standards.

accountability for performance evaluations and objective measures of how well governments meet externally defined demands for services and at what level of quality.

Adam Smith (1723–1790) Scottish moral philosopher and author of *The Theory of Moral Sentiments* and *An Inquiry into the Nature and Causes of the Wealth of Nations* (*The Wealth of Nations*); pioneer in field of political economics.

administrative effectiveness refers to how well a program is administered, including clear and rational ways to implement a decision, project or program. Characteristics include well-defined goals or objectives, well-trained staff, decision-making guidelines, established lines of authority and a clear definition of roles and responsibilities.

Administrative Procedure Act (APA) of 1946 spells out how federal administrative agencies are required to issue regulations; also established a process for courts to review agency decisions.

administrative values rational model applied to public policies including but not limited to promoting efficiency, effectiveness and discretionary authority aimed at better **performance management**.

Advanced Research Projects Administration (ARPA) the agency responsible for the development of new internet communication technology for the military during the 1970s.

alternative energy sources are different from those in widespread use presently (referred to as conventional). Alternative energy usually includes solar, wind, wave, tidal, hydroelectric and geothermal.

Amazon.com online retail store that revolutionized internet commerce.

American Recovery and Reinvestment Act (ARRA) of 2009 an economic stimulus package proposed by President Obama and enacted by the 111th United States Congress in February 2009. The stimulus bill was intended to create jobs and promote investment and consumer spending to help recover from recession.

ARPANET the first operational packet switching system and one of the networks that would eventually form the internet.

Athenian Democracy direct democracy in early Athens, Greece, where citizens could (and all public-spirited citizens were expected to) attend a sovereign assembly. Also an "elitist" form of citizenship with representatives.

Baby Boomers large post-World War II age group born between 1946 and 1964, best recognized as the generation that enjoyed post-war prosperity.

balance of trade the difference between the value of a nation's exports vs. imports over time adjusted for currency valuations.

balanced performance standards reflect attempts to accommodate diverse preferences of individuals and groups. Public agencies must constantly stretch resources to meet standards for citizens, businesses, interests, as well as elected officials. Public managers are continuously challenged to fill gaps between citizen expectations and the level of service provided by bureaucracies.

barriers to acceptance obstacles to applying quality improvement methods, standards and services. They persist because of public agencies' inability to abandon existing **Industrial Age** management systems which emphasize routine protocols for all demands, processes and systems.

benchmarking compares existing business processes, practices and performance metrics to industry bests and/or best practices from other industries.

benefits.gov (formerly known as Govbenefits.gov) website that provides citizens with easy, online access to government benefits and assistance programs, accessible at: www.benefits.gov.

Berlin Wall concrete and barbed-wire barrier which separated East and West Germany during the Cold War period from 1961 to 1989. Its fall symbolized German reunification and end of Communism in Eastern Europe.

Bernard Madoff (b. 1938) infamous investment adviser who admitted his transformation of Madoff Investment Securities LLC into the largest **Ponzi scheme** in history. Plead guilty to 11 federal crimes and serving prison sentence.

Blackboard an electronic course management system that enables faculty and students to communicate and collaborate online through course content, discussion boards, e-mail, tests and online file exchanges.

blended learning combining two or more teaching methods or learning environments designed to affect more students positively. Also referred to as hybrid approach to learning.

"blogs" short for **weblogs** a type of website, usually maintained by an individual with regular entries, commentary, descriptions of events or other material such as graphics or video. Facilitates and promotes online communication and amateur journalism.

blogosphere that portion of the internet consisting of weblogs or **blogs** and their interconnections. Community of amateur journalists commenting on a variety of subjects on the World Wide Web.

bottom-up management innovative customer-oriented management system in which employees are encouraged to become involved with planning and decision making as well as provide feedback. Employees are **empowered** to become more motivated and accept accountability for program results.

broadband internet connectivity faster internet access at a high data transfer rate. Internet access that supplies more than double the rate of 56kbit/s (kilobits per second) generally without disrupting telephone service.

Brookings Institution a non-profit "think tank" based in Washington D.C. which provides educational services and conducts research on public policy issues (www.brookings.edu).

budgetary constraints accounting limits that prescribe consumption options available to allocate among various goods or services.

Business Process Reengineering (BPR) systematic, disciplined strategy that critically examines, rethinks and redesigns mission-delivery processes to achieve dramatic performance improvements in areas important to customers and stakeholders.

business vs. government strategies contrasting approaches to managing public agencies derived from theories such as **NPM**, **NPR** and **PMA**. As public services depend more on user fees, there is greater agreement that they should provide the best-quality service at the lowest costs.

Business.gov single one-stop website for businesses seeking access to government services and information on how to improve the quality of their own business operations. Managed by the U.S. Small Business Administration.

cap and trade is a method for managing carbon emissions, with the end goal of reducing the overall pollution in a nation, region or industry.

carbon emissions tax levies a fee on the production, distribution or use of fossil fuels based on how much carbon emitted. Government may set a price per ton on carbon and then translate it as a tax on electricity, natural gas or oil. Encourages utilities, businesses and individuals to reduce consumption and increase energy efficiency.

Center for American Progress public policy research and advocacy organization dedicated to improving the lives of Americans through progressive ideas and action.

Central Personnel Data File (CPDF) and **Enterprise Human Resources Integration (EHRI)** are human resources reporting systems used by the federal executive branch, archive at http://listserv.opm.gov/archives/cpdf.html.

charter marks informal awards recognizing agencies and organizations that are particularly effective at following a charter and delivering services consistently at a superior level of quality.

charter schools publicly funded privately operated K-12 schools; public schools staffed without teachers' unions.

Chief Information Officers (CIOs) high level corporate or governmental officials responsible for maintenance of communications and information technology systems in public or private organizations.

Chief Information Officer (CIO) Council established by Title I of the Clinger-Cohen Act, group focuses on enhancing e-government, establishing performance measures and further confirms **U.S. Office of Management and Budget (OMB)** as the federal e-government services leader.

Chief Performance Officer (CPO) a position in the Office of Management and Budget (within the Executive Office of the President of the United States), first announced on January 7, 2009 by President-elect Barack Obama. The new post concentrates on the federal budget and government reform.

Chief Technology Officer (CTO) focuses on overall technology policy and innovation strategies across federal agencies and departments. President Obama appointed the first CTO in April 2009.

CitiStat database designed for managers to better track the performance of city services such as crime control, trash pick-up, street repairs or snow removal. The program also records data from residents' service calls so public officials can identify trends, allocate resources and respond appropriately.

citizen-centric multi-channel integrated approach to public services oriented toward meeting citizens' needs. Technology is prerequisite but attitudinal changes and **performance management** strategies are equally important to encourage public officials to become citizen-centered.

citizen charters are similar to a "bill of rights" designed to encourage and reinforce high standards for service delivery and participation on the part of the citizens. Charters have been enacted by governments in countries ranging from India to the UK, among others.

citizen participation the involvement of individuals in federal, state and local governmental decision-making processes.

Citizen Relationship Management (CzRM) business strategy designed to deliver a broad range of government services to citizens and facilitate dialogue among all stakeholders. Objectives are to optimize service quality, timeliness and citizen satisfaction and to increase the level of engagement with citizens in all aspects of public administrative processes.

citizen responsiveness acceptance of new innovations, suggestions, ideas, influences or opinions from members of a state or nation. The quality of being responsive, reacting quickly and responding to emotional needs of people receiving public services.

citizenship the state of being a citizen of a particular social, political or national community.

Citizens United v. Federal Election Commission, 130 S. Ct. 876 (2010), was a controversial Supreme Court decision that corporate funding of independent political broadcasts in candidate elections cannot be limited under the U.S. Constitution. The 5–4 decision resulted from a dispute over whether the lobbying group could air a film critical of Hillary Clinton, and whether they could advertise the film in broadcast ads featuring Clinton's image, in apparent violation of the 2002 Bipartisan Campaign Reform Act, commonly known as the McCain–Feingold Act.

civic obligation the responsibilities of democratic citizenship such as voting.

Clark County Nevada Urban Area Working Group (UAWG) application of **SAFECOM** in Las Vegas; sought to improve the quality of communications **interoperability** between urban areas within the state of Nevada.

climate change a change in global temperatures and precipitation over time due to natural variability or to human activity. Global climate change is caused by the accumulation of greenhouse gases in the lower atmosphere. The global concentration of these gases is increasing, mainly due to human activities, such as the combustion of fossil fuels (which release carbon dioxide) and deforestation.

Clinger-Cohen Act of 1996 federal law designed to improve the way government acquires, uses and disposes of information technology (IT). Establishes comprehensive standards for executive agencies to improve the acquisition and management of information resources. Mandates the development and maintenance of Information Technology Architectures (ITAs) by federal agencies to maximize the benefits of information technology (IT) within government agencies.

collaboration cooperative process where two or more people or organizations work together to achieve common goals.

collective bargaining formal process by which unions negotiate with management over wages, working conditions and benefits.

command-and-control bureaucratic management structure commonly found in rules-driven, rather than customer-driven, public bureaucracies. Refers more generally to the maintenance of organizational structures which limit the discretionary decision-making authority of workers. Also referred to as Theory X management style.

community organization a civic non-profit group operating in a local community or neighborhood.

competitive challenges faced by the United States and other developed countries as a result of globalization and the industrialization of 3 billion new workers in countries such as Brazil, China, India and Korea.

competitive sourcing the policy of opening government activities to competition with the private sector. See **President's Management Agenda (PMA)**, **outsourcing** and **privatization**.

Computer Security Act of 1987 federal law passed to improve the security and privacy of sensitive information in federal computer systems and to establish minimum acceptable security practices for such systems. Requires the creation of computer security plans and appropriate training of system users or owners of systems which house sensitive information.

Consumer Product Safety Commission (CPSC) product safety agency that was heavily scrutinized after toys manufactured in China were found to contain toxic chemical melamine which, after evaluation, was replaced in 2010 by a new agency, the **Consumer Financial Protection Bureau**.

Consumer.gov website for consumer protection super-agency to better protect American consumers from mortgage fraud and predatory lending practices.

content providers individuals or organizations providing online content. Each internet user is a potential supplier of content, but providers are usually limited to academics, bloggers and subject matter producers, comprising about 3% of all those using the internet.

contracting out engaging persons or groups outside an organization to undertake or produce goods or services. Widely used in procurement and purchasing. See also **outsourcing** and **privatization**.

cooperative agreements contracts between business and governments specifying mutual accountability and responsibilities for program or project completion.

corporate globalization refers to corporations that manage production or deliver services in more than one country.

cost-benefit analysis an economic analysis of the total expected costs of different alternatives weighed against the estimated total returns or benefits of one or more actions to determine if benefits outweigh costs.

crisis management processes by which organizations deal with major unpredictable events that threaten harm to their stakeholders or the general public. Requires skills and techniques to identify, assess, understand and cope with non-routine situations, especially from the moment they first occur to the point that emergency assistance and recovery procedures begin.

critical analysts those assessing or critiquing online information, thus further supplying potential information in the form of opinion and evaluation, comprising about 12% of users.

cross-agency cooperation mutually beneficial and well-defined relationships involving personnel from different agencies or sectors of the community joining together to achieve a common goal. See also, **interoperability.**

curriculum set of courses and content offered by a school, college or university. A curriculum is prescriptive, and based on a more general syllabus which specifies what topics must be understood and at what level to achieve a particular grade or standard.

Customer Relationship Management (CRM) business strategy designed to optimize profitability, revenue and customer satisfaction. To realize CRM, organizations must implement processes and technologies that support coordinated customer interactions throughout multiple channels.

customer service quality ratings assessment of the quality of a service obtained by surveying customers for their opinions about satisfaction with the service.

customer service standards measures used to gauge agency performance through explicit standards to identify customers and meet their needs. First published by federal agencies in September 1995, performance indicators have been integrated to a limited extent with budgetary requests. See also, **Government Performance and Results Act (GPRA) of 1993.**

"cyberellas" women with industry recognized IT skills and qualifications who are able to benefit from the lifelong potential that IT careers offer.

data cleaning technical evaluation of available data from multiple sources, requiring an integrated, comprehensive system with well-defined structures and high quality data processing capability. See also, **data points.**

data points type of measurement used to specify results in a yes or no format, integer or real number, or some vector or array. Data may be plotted in a graphic display, but in many cases points are processed numerically before they can be displayed graphically.

Data.gov open-source portal that publishes government data and employs new technologies for publicly disseminating such data; provides online network for citizens to converse with one another on related issues.

David Ricardo (1772–1823) English political economist who formulated the **Theory of Comparative Advantage**, a fundamental argument in favor of free trade among countries. He argued that there is mutual benefit from trade (or exchange) even if one party (e.g. resource-rich country, highly skilled artisan) is more productive in one area than its trading counterpart (e.g. resource-poor country, unskilled laborer), as long as each concentrates on the activities where it has a relative productivity advantage.

Debate Europe online forum using a variety of communication strategies to amplify and integrate citizen voices into policy making on a number of EU-related subjects.

deliberative democracy system of political decision making that relies on popular consultation before making policy.

Deming Prize the oldest international award for quality recognition. Established by quality guru W. Edwards Deming in Japan in 1950, the prize is highly prestigious and influences the development of total quality control practices throughout Asia. The prize is overseen by the **Japanese Union of Scientists and Engineers** and awarded to both Japanese and non-Japanese companies who have made improvements in the advancement of total quality control.

Denmark e2012 goals which state that integration shall continue (and improve) and that all communication between citizens, business and government in Denmark will take place digitally by 2012.

digital cities municipalities premised on the idea that local people, ideas and information are valuable; ambitious attempt to present "virtually" all aspects of city life; connected communities that combine ICT infrastructures and provide internet-based communication and government services.

digital divide the gap between those *with* access to ICTs and those *without* or with little access. Also refers to the disparity in access to technology between wealthy, highly developed countries and the majority of technologically underdeveloped, poorer developing nations. This gap pertains to items such as electrical power and personal computers, but also includes simpler technologies such as telephones. For a list of nations in order of wealth, see Appendix C.

digital governance the networked extension of ICT relationships to include faster access to the Web, mobile service delivery, teleconferencing and multi-channel information technology to achieve higher level two-way communications. Used to enhance access to and delivery of governmental services to benefit citizens, business partners and employees.

digital government use of ICTs to enhance access to and delivery of government services to benefit stakeholders as well as strategy to achieve better performance. Provides citizens with information and delivers services online. Differs from traditional "in office" public service delivery in that it is: 1) digital and becoming mobile and wireless, rather than paper-based; 2) available to citizen/customers 24 hours a day, seven days a week; and 3) provides information and service delivery of various types and levels of detail not found in existing government systems.

direct democracy form of democratic governance in which citizens participate directly in public decision making. Includes direct electoral processes for amendments, initiatives, recalls and referenda.

Disaster Assistance Improvement Plan (DAIP) online application to enhance the quality of G2C services by establishing an all-in-one disaster assistance portal; offers numerous advantages such as reduced paperwork, increased speed and efficiency and the overall simplification of assistance application processes.

Disaster Management Interoperability Service (DMIS) applies ICTs to enhance the ability of public, private and non-profit agencies to respond to emergencies. DMIS offers emergency managers open online access to disaster-management information and planning and response tools. DMIS provides participating agencies with the resources and capability for enhanced cost-effective situational awareness, disaster response, resource requests and access to collaborative environments for training and preparedness exercises.

distance learning education obtained remotely; process by which technology is used for online education in ways that the student does not have to be physically present in the location where the teaching is taking place.

distributive and redistributive services distinction between individual and group benefits based on policy impact; permits managers to maintain **point-of-contact accountability** by defining parameters for responding to citizen demands in conflict with government procedures.

domain space used in various networks for application-specific naming and addressing purposes. Domains are used by individual internet host computers as unique identifiers. They provide easily recognizable names associated with numerically addressed internet resources.

downsizing organizational restructuring involving **outsourced** activities, replacing permanent staff with contract employees and reducing the size of the workforce to be more competitive, efficient and cost-effective.

dumping a trade practice by which nations flood markets with below cost goods in order to increase market share and eliminate competition.

economic stimulus an investment designed to jumpstart economic growth, provide more jobs, increase consumer confidence and generate more private investment. See **American Recovery and Reinvestment Act of 2009**.

e-government maturity extent to which a government has developed an online presence.

e-learning any form of education, learning or training in which technology is utilized to facilitate the learning process. Examples include internet, intranet, audio/visual and virtual classrooms, among others. E-learning environments can be either *synchronous* (students and teacher participate together in real-time), or *asynchronous* (students and teacher interact with the aid of e-mail, social networks and class discussion boards, though not at the same time).

electoral activist the role of elected representatives who carry out responsibilities for resolving disputes between government officials and individuals who feel they have been treated unfairly. Federal, state and elected officials are responsible for carrying out this role.

Electoral College established under the U.S. Constitution to choose the president and the vice president of the United States. Each state has as many electoral votes as members in Congress and its delegates, called *electors*, can be selected by any method. Candidates who win the popular vote in each state receive all of that state's electoral votes (except in Maine and Nebraska where votes are split according to the proportion received by each candidate). Under this system, a presidential candidate can lead in the nationwide popular vote and can still fail to win the required majority in the Electoral College. For example, Bush vs. Gore in 2000.

electorate the registered voting public, comprising about two-thirds of all those over 18 who are eligible to vote.

Electronic Business Resource Centers (EBRCs) online government resources available to businesses.

electronic community networks offer a way to close the **global digital divide** through multiple ICT access points, including libraries, post offices, schools and other public places.

electronic government integration of multiple data sources into one-stop websites or portals to improve access and communication between governments, businesses and related interests.

Electronic Government Act of 2002 important federal statute to improve the management and promotion of electronic government services and processes by establishing a **Chief Information Officer (CIO)** within the Office of Management and Budget and a framework of measures that require using ICTs to improve citizen access to government information and services.

electronic procurement processes for purchasing goods and services over the internet.

elitism the belief or attitude that some individuals, who supposedly form an elite—a select group of people with intellect, wealth, specialized training or experience, or other distinctive attributes—are inherently fit to govern.

empowerment approach to organization, political participation or public management which stresses extended customer satisfaction, examines relationships among existing management processes, seeks to improve internal agency communications and responds to valid customer demands; in exchange for the authority to make decisions at the point of customer contact, all empowered employees must be thoroughly trained, and the results of their work must be carefully monitored. See also, **point-of-contact accountability**.

Enterprise Human Resources Integration (EHRI) a second generation human resources reporting system used by the federal government with three sophisticated enhancements: 1) a central data repository for all executive branch employee records; 2) an electronic Official Employee Record; and 3) a set of analytical tools for human capital forecasting and trend analysis.

entitlements transfer payments made to individuals with certain designated characteristics and circumstances, such as age or need.

entrepreneurial paradigm market-based approach encompassing various concepts such as **Business Process Reengineering (BPR)**, **Customer Relationship Management (CRM)**, continuous quality improvement (CQI), **Total Quality Management (TQM)** or **Six Sigma** applied to the public sector.

environmental protection enforcement of environment protection laws and regulations on individuals, organizations or governments for the benefit of the natural environment.

e-participation index comparative measure used by the United Nations to evaluate the extent of a country's political participation.

E-rulemaking use of digital technology by government to enable agencies to manage the rulemaking processes more productively.

European Quality Awards given to different types of organizations based on their leadership, strategic planning, human resource management, information analysis, quality systems, focus, satisfaction, corporate governance and social responsibility, relationships and results. Awarded to organizations that follow the framework for organizational management designed by the European Foundation for Quality Management.

European Union (EU) economic and political union of 27 member states with approximately 500 million people in Europe. Common currency (the Euro) is used by 16 states.

E-Verify controversial voluntary web-based system operated by Department of Homeland Security (**DHS**) and the Social Security Administration (**SSA**) which enables employers to verify citizenship and employment eligibility of job applicants by validating their social security numbers.

Evolution of Governance Models describes the process of changing from old public management to new public management and networked governance. See Table 5.1, p. 114.

Expanded Electronic Tax Products for Businesses (EETPB) online system that reduces the tax-reporting burden on businesses while improving the efficiency and effectiveness of government operations. Provides for timely and accurate tax information from businesses and simplifies federal and state reporting processes.

Fair Credit Billing Act federal law designed to facilitate the handling of credit complaints and eliminate abusive credit billing practices.

Fair Credit Reporting Act a law enforced by the Federal Trade Commission (FTC) that promotes accuracy and ensures the privacy of information contained in consumer reports.

Fair Deal domestic legislative program from 1948 to 1949 which expanded the federal government's role in promoting economic development and social welfare. The program is credited with raising living standards during the 1950s.

Fall of the Berlin Wall (1989) symbolized the end of Communist rule in Eastern Europe.

Family Educational Rights and Privacy Act federal law that protects the privacy of student educational records.

federal contractor rule requires all firms that accept federal stimulus funds to clear all employees with **E-Verify** system.

Federal Financial Assistance Management Act (Public Law 106-107) goal was to improve the effectiveness and performance of federal grant programs, simplify application and reporting requirements, improve the delivery of services to the public and facilitate greater coordination among those responsible for delivering such services.

Federal Housing Administration (FHA) mortgage assistance financing agency of the U.S. Department of Housing and Urban Development (HUD) working to strengthen the housing market, meet the need for quality affordable rental homes and use housing as a platform for improving quality of life.

Federal Information Security Management Act (FISMA) of 2002 amended the Clinger-Cohen Act and restructured security standards for federal information systems; replaced the existing Computer System Security and Privacy Advisory Board with the Information Security and Privacy Advisory Board, as well as established limits on the disclosure of data and confidentiality policies.

Federal Register official daily journal of the United States federal government that contains most routine publications and public notices of government agencies.

federalism political concept describing a constitutional division of governmental power between central or national government and regional units (such as states), each having independent authority over its citizens. Used in the United States and a few other countries. See also, **fragmented federalism**.

fiscal control policy that avoids deficit spending and debt. Considerations include reduction of overall government spending and lowering debt by balancing budgets. In theory, prevents governments from spending more revenues than collected in taxes and user fees.

fiscal policy revenue and expenditure policies adopted by government.

fragmentation the absence of cooperation/information sharing across agencies, jurisdictions or political districts. See also **fragmented federalism**.

fragmented federalism negative description of U.S. intergovernmental relations under constitutional division of powers between federal, state and local government. See also, **federalism**.

Freedom of Information Act of 1966 provides for full or partial disclosure of requested government documents. Places the responsibility on the government agency to prove why it should not disclose such information, rather than on the individual requesting information to prove why he or she should have it.

free trade lobbies corporations and interest groups advocating less government intervention in international business.

G-20 countries a group of finance ministers and central bank governors from 20 economies committed to democracy and free trade: includes 19 countries and the EU.

G-8 countries forum for the leaders of seven countries with strongest economies and Russia to discuss economic and trade matters. European Union is represented and recent summits have considered assistance to the developing world, global security, Middle East peace and reconstruction in Iraq.

gender and racial mainstreaming public policy of assessing different implications for gender and race of any planned policy action, including legislation and programs, in all areas and at all levels.

geographic districts distinct legal territorial subdivisions of governments which exist within specific boundaries or sub-divisions, such as cities, counties, districts, townships or states.

Germany.info web portal which provides information about modern Germany. Provides basic facts of Germany's geography and demographics, free electronic newsletters and outreach through special events and partnerships with non-profit organizations.

global digital divide disparities in opportunity to access the internet and the information and educational/business opportunities tied to access between developed and developing countries.

global income redistribution increasing wages in developing countries and lowering of wages in developed countries caused by outsourcing from richer to poorer nations.

global north refers to about 60 countries generally in the northern hemisphere which have more internet access and users than the less economically developed countries in the **rural south**.

Global Positioning Systems (GPS) navigational systems involving satellites and computers that can determine the latitude and longitude of a receiver anywhere by computing the time difference for signals from different satellites to reach the receiver.

global regulation networked governance among nations calling for regulation in various areas, including the economy and the environment.

global "weirding" term used by author Thomas Friedman to describe changes occurring as a result of the Energy-Climate-Era.

globalization a continuing process by which cultures, economies and societies become more integrated through a global ICT network linking telecommunications, transportation and trade.

Government Performance and Results Act (GPRA) of 1993 one of a series of laws designed to improve government program management. Requires agencies to set goals, measure results and report their progress. Results used in program evaluation and budgetary decisions.

Government-to-Business (G2B) interactions involve providing information to the business community on topics such as applications, electronic procurement, permits, regulatory compliance and zoning.

Government-to-Citizen (G2C) online contacts between government agencies and citizens.

Government-to-Employee (G2E) relationships cover virtual relationships between government agencies and their employees as well as how government workers serve citizens.

Government-to-Government (G2G) Services intra- and inter-agency networks as well as interoperable linkages between federal, state and local agencies; all forms of communications, exchanges and other transactions taking place among government agencies, branches and departments at different levels within public administrative systems. G2G targets the elimination of barriers preventing the exchange of information, thus reducing bureaucratic overhead structures and allowing more access to information regarding a wider range of public issues.

Grants.gov U.S. government's primary online service portal to assist potential recipients to find and apply for government-wide competitive grants-in-aid.

Green Revolution refers specifically to the introduction of pesticides and high-yield grains and better management during the 1960s and 1970s which greatly increased agricultural productivity; more generally describes actions taken to prevent harm caused by CO_2 emissions and climate change.

Greening of the net is the expected energy saving consequences of full-scale digital governance which will lessen demand for paper, reduce commuting time, save energy and encourage telenetworking.

gross domestic product (GDP) aggregate measure of a country's overall economic output; the market value of all goods and services produced within the borders of a country in a year.

gross national product (GNP) the market value of all goods and services produced by all citizens of a nation during a calendar year.

Health Care and Education Reconciliation Act of 2010 (P.L. 111-152, 124 Stat. 1029) compromise legislation addressing comprehensive health care and student loan reform.

Health Maintenance Organizations (HMOs) type of managed care organization that provides health care coverage in the United States through hospitals, doctors and other providers with which the HMO has a contract. Application of business model to health care services.

high-performance governments take a citizen-centered perspective, delivering services in terms of needs, expectations and perceptions of citizens. Work collaboratively within and across agencies, offer multiple channels of interaction and use innovative technologies to provide accountability and flexibility to citizens. Governments that reach out to citizens proactively while delivering maximum public sector values. See also, **CzRM** and **cross-agency cooperation**.

high-tech countries wealthy countries such as Canada, Denmark, Japan, Korea, Norway, Sweden and Switzerland which use ICTs to overcome financial and political obstacles to development.

Housing Act of 1949 passed as part of Truman's **Fair Deal** program, law expanded the federal government's role in public housing and mortgage insurance.

identity theft stealing another person's personal information (e.g., name, Social Security number, credit card number, passport) without that person's knowledge and the fraudulent use of such information.

Immigration and Customs Enforcement (ICE) federal law enforcement agency under the Department of Homeland Security (**DHS**) responsible for identifying, investigating and dismantling vulnerabilities regarding the nation's border, economic, transportation and infrastructure security.

incremental continuation of previous government activity, with minimal changes. Also refers to gradual change, or slow improvement.

Industrial Age also known as **Industrial Revolution** a period from the 18th to 19th century marked by rapid development of manufacturing through the introduction of machines, concentrating work in factories, where industrial towns grew around them. This period saw great advances in agriculture, manufacturing, mining, transportation and technology affecting organizational and socioeconomic conditions. See Table 5.1, p. 114.

Information Age shift from traditional **Industrial Age** economy to one based on the manipulation of information. Period marked by the increased production, transmission, consumption of and reliance on technology. Many consider the new role of information to be changing economic and social behavior as dramatically as did the Industrial Revolution. See also, **knowledge revolution** and Table 5.1, p. 114.

information and communication technologies (ICTs) are various forms of New Media technology connecting internet users with service providers and websites. ICT methods include communication protocols, transmission techniques, communications equipment as well as systems for computer storage and information retrieval.

information continuum describes the information or **infrastructure** of a people, a species, a scientific subject or an institution. Includes three important steps: the means by which information is delivered; the "decoding" of information matched against institutional and personal needs (information processing); and information feedback (how citizens respond to information).

information overload occurs when there is so much information that it is difficult for individuals to focus on a particular subject because of the "noise" (high levels of redundancy or inaccurate, irrelevant information). Characteristic of modern American political campaigns and a deliberate tactic by candidates and interest groups to obscure political issues.

information quality management an information technology management discipline which encompasses the COBIT (Control Objectives for Information and Technology) information criteria of efficiency, effectiveness, confidentiality, integrity, availability, compliance and reliability.

information resources management (IRM) techniques for managing information as a shared organizational resource. IRM includes: 1) identification of information sources; 2) type and value of information; and 3) ways of classification, valuation, processing and storage of that information.

information technology (IT) established academic and practical discipline to study, design, develop, implement, support and manage computer-assisted information systems, particularly computer hardware, networks and software.

Information Technology Management Reform Act (ITMRA), see **Clinger-Cohen Act of 1996.**

informing the rise in information technology search engines such as A9©, Yahoo!© and Google© enabling anyone with access to a computer or smart phone to search for information, knowledge, products and services.

infrastructure physical and organizational structures necessary for the operation of a society or facilities and services needed for an economy to function. Typically refers to the technical structures that support a society, such as power grids, roads, sewers, water supply and telecommunications systems.

innovation introduction of something new into an existing system that *adds value* to processes; change in processes for doing something, or the useful application of new inventions or discoveries; emergent, radical and revolutionary changes in thinking about products, processes or organizations. See also, **value added.**

in-sourcing one of Thomas Friedman's 10 noted accelerants to globalization, generally defined as the opposite of **outsourcing**; delegation of operations or jobs from production within a business to an internal (stand-alone) entity that specializes in that operation.

Intelligent Community Forum studies the economic and social development of 21st century communities. Mission is to research and share best practices by communities in adapting to the changing economic environment and positioning their citizens and businesses to prosper. (www.intelligentcommunity.org).

internal and external operations internal operations refer to the use of information technology (IT) for automation, cooperation, infrastructure development and integration *among* agencies and as a decision-making tool. External operations occur when government agencies use ICTs and the internet to conduct transactions, provide and receive information and deliver services to citizens, clients or customers.

International Baccalaureate (IB) rigorous academic curriculum offered in public and private schools as a more challenging alternative to a more traditional high school curriculum. Students are required to learn a second language and write an extended essay, as well as achieve a minimum cumulative score on standardized assessment tests given at the conclusion of the course in order to graduate with an IB Diploma.

International Benchmarking Clearinghouse non-profit consulting organization specializing in benchmarking, knowledge management, measurement and process improvement through the application of benchmarks and best practices.

International Monetary Fund (IMF) international organization created in 1944 that oversees the global financial system by following the macroeconomic policies of its member countries, in particular those with an impact on exchange rates and balance of payments.

International Organization for Standards (ISO) 9000–14000 certification criteria and standards for multi-national quality management systems. Fastest growing quality assurance system in the world and applicable to most types of organizations. ISO 9000 series addresses quality management while ISO 14000 deals with standards for environmental management.

internet browser software application for retrieving and presenting information on the World Wide Web; also used to access information provided by web servers in private networks or files in file sharing systems.

internet law growing subfield within the legal profession specializing in cyber-law, intellectual property laws, and international legal and regulatory issues.

internet participation (or e-participation) ICT-supported participation in processes involved in administration and governance. Processes may include decision making, service delivery and policy making.

internet readiness having the capacity, expertise, infrastructure and human resources necessary to fully implement online government.

internet subscribers per household measure of ICT development derived from dividing the number subscribers to internet services by the number of households in a country.

internet use accessing information on the internet privately, securely and efficiently.

interoperability refers to the ability of two or more systems (as well as the people and processes within them) to share data protocols and tools effectively and seamlessly, independent of location, data models, technology platforms or specialized agency terminologies. Example is U.S. federal government **SAFECOM** emergency communication system.

Iraq and Afghanistan Wars invasions in the Middle East by a multinational force led by troops from the United States under the administration of President George W. Bush. Justified by possible connections to *al Qaeda* and *Taliban* supporters and the existence of weapons of mass destruction.

iron triangles political alliances uniting members of an administrative agency, a legislative committee or subcommittee and an interest group according to shared values and preferences in the same substantive area of policy making.

Issy-les-Moulineaux, France industrial suburb of Paris with 65,000 inhabitants which recognized in 1997 that e-government and e-democracy would be 21st century trends. Conducts **town meetings** via cable television or internet; citizens pose questions to lawmakers via e-mail or a toll-free number and potentially watch live as questions are answered; has become a recognized cyber-city.

just-in-time learning acquisition of knowledge or skills as they are needed; used to describe ways in which information is made available to persons when they need it and at a level equal to their ability to understand it.

Keynesianism economic theory that argues that private sector decisions sometimes lead to inefficient macroeconomic outcomes and therefore advocates active policy responses by the public sector.

knowledge management strategies and practices used by high-tech organizations to identify, create, represent, distribute and enable adoption of insights and experiences. Shift in emphasis from physical management of data to the management of electronic information content. Process of capturing, organizing and storing information and experiences and making them available to others through sharing and collaboration. Supported by advanced IT tools and methods to enhance an organization's efficiency, productivity and profitability. See also, **information technology (IT)**.

knowledge revolution global mega-trend evolving in the past 40 years creating and applying new research to vast areas of biogenetic engineering, computers, education, government, space exploration, communications, nuclear technology and energy; creating a global paradigm shift comparable to the previous agricultural and industrial revolutions. Fundamental socioeconomic change by *adding value,* creating and using knowledge to improve the lives of individuals and the efficiency of organizations. See also, **value added**.

Kyoto Protocol international agreement that aims to reduce carbon dioxide emissions and the presence of greenhouse gases.

legacy industries term used to describe industries that have been phased out or are destined to be eliminated due to failure to change and pressure from emerging global technological advances.

lifelong learning idea that learning is an ongoing process that occurs throughout one's life and is not confined to a particular environment or time period. Technology, e-learning and virtual learning communities can enhance lifelong learning.

Linked Area Networks (LANs) also referred to as Local Area Networks, consist of groups of computers or associated devices that share a common communications line or wireless link. They usually share a single processor or server within a small area (house, office setting). In addition, the server has applications and data storage capacity that are shared in common by multiple users. LANs may serve a few people in a home setting or as many as thousands of individuals in an office environment.

Malcolm Baldrige National Quality Award (BNQA) originally created by federal legislation in 1987 to improve the quality of American manufactured goods, awarded to organizations which demonstrate productivity, results and the highest levels of customer service in the United States. Business, health care, education and non-profit organizations are eligible to apply for and receive the award. Winners then share their strategy with the public in order to improve the quality of other organizations: further information accessible at: www.NIST.gov.

market-based approach the use of private market mechanisms to determine cost, price and other factors relating to supply and demand for goods and services. Generally considered the opposite of government regulation.

mass media means of communication such as radio, television or the internet available for connecting large numbers of people.

Millennials born after 1982, they are the first entirely technologically savvy generation to enter the workplace with a "why not me?" attitude and a self-accommodating approach to work. See also, **Net Generation**.

Millennium Development Goals (MDGs) United Nations initiative focusing on life issues facing women and minorities in developing nations (www.un.org/millenniumgoals/).

mini-Baldrige Awards non-profit or state-sponsored programs in the United States and elsewhere that recognize quality at the sub-national state and local levels. Used in 45 of the 50 U.S. states and many other countries to reward local organizations for quality and productivity improvements.

Models of Corporate Globalization involve the consolidation, partially through so-called "free trade" treaties, of economic and political power into the hands of trans-national corporations, with minimal regard for labor rights, the environment or national sovereignty.

Moncton, New Brunswick city in Atlantic Canadian province which formed creative partnerships with public and private providers to enhance public sector enterprises.

monetary policy policies by the Federal Reserve Board that influence supply of money, circulation of money and availability and cost of credit.

Moodle (abbreviation for Module Object-Oriented Dynamic Learning Environment) is an open-source distance learning course management system that is used for discussion forums, assignment submissions, grade/feedback tracking and teams/people pages.

Mozilla Firefox open-source web browser that competes with Microsoft.

multi-national corporations (MNCs), see **trans-national corporations**.

National Digital Governance Awards recognize excellence in applications of and projects involving ICTs by state and local governments. Awarded by the Center for Digital Government, which advocates using the best technology practices at all levels of government.

National Educational Association (NEA) organization of educators concerned with the overall improvement of education and the conditions of the teaching profession.

National Institute of Standards and Technology (NIST) federal government agency within the U.S. Department of Commerce with the mission of working with industry to develop and apply technology, measurements and standards in the national interest. Also administers **Malcolm Baldrige National Quality Awards**.

National Performance Review (NPR) an interagency task force which recommended reforms in the U.S. federal government during the Clinton Administration.

National Science Foundation (NSF) a government agency supporting research in all non-medical fields of science and engineering, accessible at: www.nsf.gov.

natural monopolies groups that provide services in confined geographic locations or defined industries without competition, often provided by public agencies.

Natural Resources Defense Council a New York City-based, non-profit, non-partisan, international environmental advocacy group.

need-to-know basis principle set by the APA requiring agencies to provide information to inquiring citizens; those who request information must demonstrate why they need to know it.

Net Generation demographic group born after 1982 following Generation X, often referred to as **Millennials**. Characteristics of the "NetGens" vary by region, depending on social and economic conditions.

Generally recognized by increased use of and familiarity with **New Media** and all forms of ICTs.

Netscape internet browser developed in 1994 using *Secure Sockets Layer Protocol* (SSL) for online communication and *Javascript*, still the most widely used language for scripting of web pages. The usage share of Netscape dropped from over 90% in the mid-1990s to less than 1% in 2006, largely due to competition from Microsoft's Internet Explorer. Netscape was purchased by AOL in 1998.

networked government public services connected electronically through the use of ICTs to improve interaction between government and citizens.

networking broad term describing interconnections between individuals using **New Media** technology and personal data assistants.

New Media the amalgamation of traditional media such as film, images, music, spoken and written word, combined with the interactive power of ICTs, computer-enabled consumer devices and the internet.

New Public Management (NPM) philosophy used by governments since the 1980s to modernize the public sector by applying private sector business strategies to delivery of public services.

New Public Service (NPS) asserts that the public interest should be the result of democratic dialogue and deliberation about shared values.

NIMBY "Not in My Back Yard" colloquial term for local opposition to many controversial government projects, including highways, sewage treatment plants and prisons located in residential neighborhoods.

"311" non-emergency telephone numbers are used to contact public officials for routine services, making it easier for citizens to access government agencies and freeing up "911" channels for true emergencies.

non-governmental organizations (NGOs) legal organizations without local, state or federal government affiliation. Examples include the Red Cross and United Way.

North American Free Trade Agreement (NAFTA) is a trading bloc composed of Canada, Mexico and the United States.

O3b (Other 3 billion) ambitious network of interlinked satellites to bring the "other 3 billion" global inhabitants consistent access to the internet and modern technology. Founded in 2007 by pioneering high-technology entrepreneur Greg Wyler, who also helped to create Africa's first commercial 3G mobile and fiber-to-the-home networks in 2008 (www.O3bnetworks.com).

Office of Electronic Government headed by the Chief Information Officer (CIO), develops and provides direction for use of ICTs to make it easier for citizens and businesses to interact with federal agencies, save taxpayer dollars and facilitate citizen participation.

Office of Information and Regulatory Affairs (OIRA) located within the OMB to carry out several important functions, including reviewing federal regulations, reducing paperwork burdens and over-seeing policies relating to privacy, information quality and statistical programs.

Office of the Director of National Intelligence (DNI) federal executive-level agency created by Congress in 2005 by merging 15 disparate agencies located in other bureaus and departments—including the CIA and various defense intelligence agencies—to establish greater **interoperability** among federal, state and local agencies and functions.

off-shoring describes the relocation by a company of a business process from one country to another, typically an operational process, such as manufacturing, or supporting processes, such as accounting. A type of **outsourcing**.

oligarchy form of government in which power effectively rests with a small segment of society distinguished by royalty, wealth, family ties or military control.

online citizen participation model describes how public information is shared via the internet with citizens and how information is received, processed and used to modify values, behaviors and norms; requires knowledge of how various sources connect to the internet to obtain necessary information to participate in the public sphere.

Open Educational Resources (OERs) educational content or material that is free to be used, distributed or redistributed. This includes soft-ware tools for **open source** content creation, management, organiza-tion and accessibility. Content can include online journals and publications, virtual textbooks and full-featured courses utilizing open source content.

open source refers to software that is publicly shared intellectual prop-erty. One of the best-known open source software applications is the Linux operating system. All of the source code is open and available for any and all developers to add to and improve, on the condition that it remains open and free; the software cannot be sold. Used by federal government website **Data.gov**.

open-sourcing form of communication and information technology which permits anyone to use and improve existing open source software.

Organization of Economic Cooperation and Development (OECD) an international economic organization established in 1961 and comprised of 34 countries established to stimulate economic progress and world trade.

Organizing for America President Obama's political website operated by the Democratic National Committee at: www.my.barackobama.com/page/content/ofasplashflag/.

outsourcing refers to a company that contracts with another company as sub-contractor to provide services that might otherwise be performed by in-house employees. See also, **contracting out**.

ownership of educational processes sense of commitment and connection felt by stakeholders when they feel involved with a common goal of quality education and are committed to accomplishing its mission.

Paperwork Reduction Act (PRA) of 1980 law established in order to reduce the amount of paperwork which is handled by federal agencies, businesses and private citizens, reducing the burden on people who routinely file government forms and regulatory documents.

partnerships cooperation between customers and suppliers who could be recipients of government services as well as co-producers of the services.

Patient Protection and Affordable Care Act (PPACA) of 2010 was signed into law by President Obama on March 23, 2010 along with the **Health Care and Education Reconciliation Act of 2010**.

patronage rewarding supporters of winning politicians and political parties with positions in government based on loyalty and aid during political campaigns. Opposite of meritocracy.

per capita gross domestic product total sum of goods and services produced by a country divided by its population. See also **gross domestic product (GDP)**.

Performance Assessment Rating Tool (PART) "scorecard" system passed in 2003 by the Bush administration and effectively discontinued by Obama administration.

performance management methods and strategies that can and should be used to reinforce organizational values and help measure results.

petro-dictatorships leaders of countries whose economies are primarily dependent upon the export of petroleum. As these oil prices rise, dictators from oil-rich countries grow richer and democracies weaken. As oil prices fall, petro-dictators grow weaker and democracies flourish.

pluralism political theory in which the diversity of racial, religious, ethnic or cultural groups is accepted by guiding principles which permit the peaceful coexistence of different interests, convictions and lifestyles. Opposite of **elitism** in that the theory holds that any member of society (regardless of wealth, intellect, education or experience) can be fit to govern.

point-of-contact accountability guidelines for **empowering** employees to apply certain techniques at critical points in service transactions to improve both customer responsiveness and utilization of resources. These include: 1) empowering public employees; 2) conducting online surveys and assembling focus groups; 3) prioritizing routine customer expectations and establishing performance standards for both routine and non-routine situations; 4) analyzing gaps between expectations and perceptions of service; 5) recognizing that non-routine and regulatory services present unique measurement and enforcement problems;

6) separating regulatory from distributive and redistributive services; 7) applying customer service measures in agencies on the basis of function/impact; and 8) defining specific guidelines for responding to citizens in both extreme and routine situations.

polisphere describes political and policy information available on the internet.

political accountability the accountability of government officials, civil servants and politicians to the public and to legislative bodies such as Congress. Requirement that representatives answer to the represented on the execution of their powers and duties, act upon criticisms or requirements made of them and accept accountability for corruption, incompetence, failure or deceit.

Political Action Committees (PACs) type of interest group legally organized to receive campaign contributions and contribute to political campaigns for the purpose of influencing the outcome of an election.

political participation citizen involvement in local, state and federal politics.

political responsiveness how public officials react to major issues by prioritizing political issues, responding to majority preferences by enacting legislation, and implementing policies consistent with majority public opinion measured by citizen evaluations.

political values ideas expressed by interest groups towards the needs of others and of society as a whole, including accountability, democracy, majority rule and **political responsiveness**.

Ponzi scheme form of investment fraud in which returns are paid to early investors with money from later investors, instead of actual profit earned on the investment. See also, **Bernie Madoff**.

portals internet gateways or comprehensive websites that provide access to multiple sources of information and applications.

President's Management Agenda (PMA) an initiative by U.S. President George W. Bush in 2001 to make the U.S. federal government more efficient and effective by emphasizing results. The strategy incorporated five government-wide initiatives: 1) strategic management of human capital; 2) **competitive sourcing**; 3) improved financial performance; 4) budget and performance integration; and 5) expanded e-government.

President's Management Council (PMC) high ranking administrative officials assigned the task of improving management within the Executive Office of the president, resolving interagency management issues and establishing mechanisms for the efficient exchange of information throughout the executive branch. Council includes the Chief Operating Officers from all federal executive departments (minus the Department of Homeland Security), the Deputy Director for Management of OMB, Director of the Office of Personnel Management,

Administrator of General Services, the Chief Operating Officers of three other Executive branch agencies designated by the Chairperson, Secretary of the Cabinet, as well as officials of executive departments and agencies as designated by the president.

Privacy Act of 1974 protects certain federal government records pertaining to individuals. In particular, the Act covers systems of records that an agency maintains and retrieves by an individual's name or other personal identifier.

Privacy Protection Study Commission established by Section 5 of the original **Privacy Act of 1974** to evaluate implementation of the statute and issue reports containing recommendations for its improvement.

privatization see **contracting out** and **outsourcing**.

proxy servers linkage to computer systems that act as intermediaries for requests from clients seeking resources from other servers.

public administration study of public sector governmental decision making, analysis of policies and various inputs that have produced them, and the changes necessary to produce alternative results.

Public Sector Value Model analytical tool designed to help government agencies deliver increased value at a time when budgets are shrinking. Based on **value added** principles that can be applied to help governments better manage online programs.

quality assurance program of systematic monitoring of a good or service to ensure that a certain standard of quality is being met.

quality awards given to agencies, businesses and organizations recognizing excellence in categories such as performance-based changes, customer-oriented services and quality management. See **Deming Prize, European Quality Awards, Malcolm Baldrige National Quality Awards** and **National Digital Governance Awards,** among others.

quality management guidelines strategies for enhancing government services at all levels, emphasizing organizational goals, responsiveness to both internal and external customers, and continuous improvement of internal processes. Overlaps with e-commerce and digital technology and guided by the following principles: customer orientation; top management commitment; education and self-improvement; process orientation; continuous process improvement; freedom from fear; teamwork; communication rather than inspection; statistical and systemic thinking; and personal commitment. See also, **Deming Prize**.

Race to the Top is a $4.35 billion U.S. Department of Education program designed to encourage reforms in state and local district K-12 education. Funded as part of the **American Recovery and Reinvestment Act of 2009**.

racial and gender equality concept which promotes gender and racial gains, or at least equal opportunities, often through the use of ICTs.

Various policies, at the local, regional, national and international levels, support this initiative.

Real ID controversial U.S. federal law that imposes certain authentication, issuance, security and procedures standards for receiving state driver's licenses and state ID cards in order to be accepted by the federal government for official purposes, as defined by the Secretary of Homeland Security.

Recovery.gov online portal that gives citizens the ability to follow the government contracting processes for the allocation of federal stimulus resources, offering an unprecedented level of transparency for the distribution of federal stimulus funds.

regional differences variations in culture, economy, geography and language between different regions.

regulatory compliance enforcement of regulations which often reflect hostile relationships between citizen, businesses and government; should be differentiated from routine service delivery issues.

resource management efficient and effective deployment of an organization's resources when they are needed.

role of public administration to provide information and advance management and policies so that government can function.

rural south refers to developing countries in the southern hemisphere which have more people, less internet access and fewer users.

SAFECOM a digital communications system developed in 2002 and supported by the **DHS** which provides templates for **interoperable** communications-related issues to local, state, tribal and federal emergency responders.

Sakai is an open source collaborative community-based learning system available in 12 languages released in March 2005.

secondary recovery techniques procedures to correct errors after they have occurred; must be taught to all employees, not just managers.

SIMPLEX program strategy designed to modernize public services by administrative simplification and better regulation.

Six Sigma statistical quality control method originally developed by Motorola USA in 1981. Improves quality of processes by identifying and removing the causes of defects (errors) and minimizing variability in manufacturing and business processes. Describes the yield of a manufacturing process, or the percentage of defect-free products it produces. A six-sigma process is one in which 99.99966% of the products manufactured are statistically free of defects (3.4 defects per million). Motorola set Six Sigma as a goal for all of its manufacturing operations and engineering practices used to achieve it.

Skype.com software originally developed in Estonia using two-way cameras now built into most personal computers to link citizens directly to public officials; increases capability to overcome impersonality of online citizen-service contacts.

slow food movement emphasizes less dependence on corporate agribusiness and promotes organically grown food products from local farms. Has gained momentum in consort with animal rights groups (PETA) and health-conscious vegetarians.

social networks are made up of individuals (or organizations) connected by one or more specific types of interdependency, such as common interest, friendship, kinship, financial exchange, likes and dislikes, sexual relationships, or relationships of beliefs, knowledge or prestige. *Facebook*, *MySpace*, *Twitter* and *YouTube* are among the leading examples.

Soviet Union former Union of Soviet Socialist Republics (USSR) a socialist state that existed on the territory of most of the former Russian Empire between 1922 and 1991.

standard operating procedures (SOPs) guidelines for handling routine activities in bureaucratic organizations.

standardization concept which encompasses a broad range of issues from the actual development of a standard to its promulgation, acceptance, implementation and demonstration of compliance. Standards arise from an open process of data gathering and a vigorous discussion of all viewpoints, talents and efforts at standard-setting activities.

Substance Abuse and Mental Health Services Administration (SAMHSA) federal agency under the U.S. Department of Health and Human Services.

sunk costs are expenses that have already been incurred and cannot be recovered. Once a decision has been made to proceed in a particular policy direction, additional costs would be incurred if that direction were later reversed.

sunset (closure) laws statutes that deal with the tendency of government agencies and programs to be self-perpetuating by providing for their periodic review. Purpose is to limit growth of bureaucracy, government spending and power of special interests through predetermined expiration dates for legislation.

sunshine (open government) laws U.S. federal and state laws requiring regulatory authorities' meetings, decisions and records to be made available to the public through the mass media.

supply-chain management integration of key business components and distribution processes to create value for customers and stakeholders by optimizing the flow of products, services and related information from provider to customer.

Swedish postal service national postal service which allows residents to review their letters and packages online before deciding which to accept or reject before delivery, saving Swedish postal services millions in distribution and fuel costs. Benchmark for other postal services to follow.

Tallinn, Estonia recognized as one of the top seven technologically advanced cities. The Estonian capital has provided computerized schools, a large-scale digital skills training program and a smart ID card and has made WiFi connections available throughout the city via over 700 public access kiosks. See **Intelligent Community Forum**.

tariffs taxes imposed on exported or imported goods for political reasons to protect domestic industries from global competition from other countries which offer agricultural products, goods or services at lower prices. Associated with protectionism, the economic policy of restraining trade between nations.

teacher certification earned through completing a bachelor's or master's degree in education, as well as other state requirements. Results in award of teaching license.

technological change process of invention, innovation and diffusion of **value added** technology.

telenetworking at-home work options for employees wanting to save commuting time, fuel and parking expenses. Systems are modeled after "virtual teller" options offered by many commercial banks which provide secure face-to-face banking services and also promote reductions in energy consumption and environmental conservation.

testing one of a number of educational processes controlled and operated by independently elected state and local boards of education, district superintendents and administrators, as well as individual faculty members.

textbook selection process of purchasing textbooks that individual districts and schools are permitted to use; can create controversies in school curricula due to rising costs, influence from publishers and disagreement among local community values.

Theory of Comparative Advantage theory proposing the advantage to a provider of producing and exporting a particular good or service at a lower cost than another.

third party intermediary model enables citizens to select an organization or person through whom they would like to submit their vote. This trusted party could be anyone: an individual person with a public opinion about the topic, a government, an interest group—or even a political party.

Total Quality Management (TQM) comprehensive organizational management and customer service strategy that seeks to improve the quality of products and services through ongoing refinements, responsiveness and continuous feedback. See also, **quality management guidelines**.

town meetings forums at which voters can ask public officials direct questions about their government and community.

trade deficits an excess of imports over exports.

trade liberalization removal of or reduction in the trade practices that thwart free flow of goods and services from one nation to another. Opposite of **trade restrictions**.

trade restrictions tariffs and quotas placed by one nation on imported of goods from another to protect domestic industries.

trade surplus the value of goods and services that a country exports that is in excess of the amount of goods and services it imports.

trading blocs groups of countries agreeing to minimize or eliminate tariffs and other barriers against trade with each other, and possibly to impose protective tariffs on imports from outside the bloc. Also inter-governmental agreement where regional barriers to trade are reduced or eliminated among the participating states.

training and performance improvement consulting with all levels of management to identify the technical, non-technical and management development training needs of an organization to improve overall productivity and quality.

transactional services opportunity for online financial transactions and citizen e-consultation and e-decision making.

transformational outsourcing broadly describes reconfiguration of business and governmental processes designed to create value, provide flexibility and reduce costs.

trans-national corporation businesses that manage operations in more than one country. See also, **multi-national corporations**.

trust deficit statistical measure of the difference between those that trust the federal government to do what is right and those that do not.

triple convergence Thomas Friedman's description of the confluence of three global flattening trends including the creation of collaborative work platforms such as Windows, the change from vertical to horizontal networked production and the connection through ICTs of 3 billion new willing capitalist workers from developing countries.

Troubled Asset Relief Program (TARP) federal program signed into law by U.S. President George W. Bush on October 3, 2008 designed to address the subprime mortgage crisis by purchasing assets and equity from private corporations. Loans are expected to be paid back when businesses again become profitable.

two-way video imaging refers to the ability of computers to connect people or groups via live video stream. Example is **Skype.com**.

U.S. Department of Education (DoE) cabinet-level department of the U.S. federal government that deals with topics relating to education; administers several federal student financial aid programs, including the Federal Pell Grant, the Work-Study Program, Perkins Loans, Stafford Loans and the Federal PLUS Loans. Administers President Obama's **Race to the Top** program.

U.S. Congressional Budget Office (CBO) independent government agency that provides economic data to Congress; analyses economic and budgetary decisions on the wide array of programs in the U.S. federal budget.

U.S. Department of Commerce cabinet-level executive department of the federal government concerned with promoting economic growth.

U.S. Department of Homeland Security (DHS) U.S. executive-level agency formed in 2002 to better coordinate such diverse functions as customs, immigration, transportation security and emergency management (formerly located in other federal agencies) into one central federal department for more concerted responses to border security and prevention of terrorist attacks.

U.S. Government Accountability Office (GAO) is known as "the investigative arm of Congress" and "Congressional watchdog." Supports Congress in meeting its constitutional responsibilities and helps improve the performance and accountability of federal agencies.

U.S. Internal Revenue Service (IRS) division of the U.S. Department of Treasury responsible for tax collection and income tax code regulatory enforcement. Distributes tax forms and provides other services online.

U.S. Office of Management and Budget (OMB) assists the President in overseeing the preparation of the federal budget and supervises its administration in Executive Branch agencies. Helps formulate budgets and spending plans, evaluates effectiveness of agency programs, assesses competing funding demands among agencies and sets funding priorities.

U.S. v. Landano (508 U.S. 165) Supreme Court decision based on Vincent Landano's 1976 conviction in a New Jersey state court for the murder of a police officer. Landano sought complete FOIA access to all related FBI records which had been edited or redacted to protect personal privacy and confidentiality. Court ruled that agencies must disclose information withheld when someone is seeking to prove their innocence.

U.S. Securities and Exchange Commission (SEC) federal regulatory agency for the U.S. securities industry, stock markets and options exchanges.

Uniform Resource Locators (URLs) internet addresses specifying where an identified resource is available. The first part of a URL indicates what protocol to use (usually http). The second part consists of the IP address and domain name, denoting where the resource is located.

Union of Japanese Scientists and Engineers professional organization that awards the **Deming Prize**, given to individuals and firms that make notable advances in total quality control.

United Nations international organization whose stated aims are facilitating cooperation in international law, security, economic development, social progress, human rights and achievement of world peace.

United Nations Education, Scientific and Cultural Organization (UNESCO) specialized agency created to contribute to peace and security by promoting international collaboration through education, science and culture to further universal respect for justice, rule of law and human rights along with fundamental freedoms proclaimed in the UN Charter, accessible at: www.unesco.org.

United Steel Workers the largest industrial labor union in North America, representing workers in a diverse range of industries, including primary and fabricated metals, chemicals, glass, rubber, heavy-duty conveyor belting, tires, transportation, utilities, container industries, pharmaceuticals, call centers and health care.

USA.gov comprehensive portal to access federal, state and local government websites in the United States, accessible at: www.USA.gov.

value added the amount by which the value of a good, process or service is increased at each stage of its production, exclusive of the cost of materials, parts and labor.

value-added tax levies imposed on businesses at all levels of the manufacture and production of a good or service and based on the increase in price, or value, provided at each level.

virtual learning education and training presented over the internet. Provides a collection of tools for assessment, communication, uploading content, returning students' work, peer assessment, administration of student groups, collecting and organizing student grades, questionnaires and tracking progress. Alternative to traditional classroom lecture-discussion method of learning.

Virtual Learning Communities (VLCs) alternative educational environment to more conventional classroom atmosphere of instruction. Used for a variety of purposes from technical training to fully integrated online degree programs.

virtual services connecting citizens, patients, recipients or any other stakeholders with relevant services via the internet, government websites, smart phones or other ICTs.

Vision 2010 strategic future vision for **Moncton, New Brunswick**, focusing on collaboration with regional universities to promote tech-based entrepreneurship and a diversified ICT-enabled economy.

vouchers government issued certificates that parents can use to pay costs of education at schools of their choosing. Used to implement controversial policy to privatize public schools.

Web 2.0 World Wide Web applications that facilitate information sharing, **interoperability**, user-centered design and collaboration.

WikiLeaks controversial international organization based in Sweden that publishes anonymous submissions and leaks of otherwise secret documents while preserving the anonymity of sources; publishes and comments on leaked documents alleging government and corporate misconduct.

Wikipedia open-source online encyclopedia that is so successful that it threatens the economic viability of traditional printed encyclopedias.

wikis website that allows the creation and editing of any number of inter-linked web pages via a web browser using a simplified markup language.

workflow software application which automates, at least to some degree, a process or processes; processes are usually business-related, but could include any series of steps that can be automated via software.

World Bank financial assistance institution initially created in 1944 to aid recovery in war-torn Europe, now focused on providing loans to developing countries. Criticized for setting debt restrictions which enforce dominance of affluent industrialized countries and trans-national corporations over less developed nations.

World Trade Organization (WTO) international organization based in Geneva, Switzerland, that supervises world trade, encourages lower trade barriers and encourages multilateral trade. Created in 1995 to replace the General Agreement on Tariffs and Trade (GATT).

www.ExpectMore.gov archived website developed by the U.S. Office of Management and Budget to assess the performance of federal programs and hold agency heads accountable for results.

Notes

1 The Transition from Electronic Government to Digital Governance

1 Max Weber (1864–1920) was a noted German sociologist who formulated the most prominent model of bureaucracy as an explicit form of social organization in the late 19th century. Although widely applied in Europe during the early 20th century, Weber's work was not translated into English until after World War II in the late 1940s.

2 Internet portals are multi-access websites with links to the wide variety of information from multiple sources. For a comprehensive and useful public sector example, see USA.gov, the official United States government portal. On its home page, the three layer column design specifically states which column is for citizens, businesses and governments. USA.gov first went online on September 22, 2000 (as Firstgov.gov) and now connects more than 51 million web links from local, state and federal governments; during 2008, it had almost 100 million "hits" and continues to grow at an exponential rate.

3 The polisphere is that portion of internet space devoted to candidates, campaigns, politics, political issues or public affairs and administration.

4 During the 2008 Summer Olympics, China lifted media restrictions (at least temporarily) to avoid international media scrutiny and possible sanctions. The repressive Castro regime in Cuba has changed information and visitation policies, allowing limited internet satellite usage. Since 2008, Cuba has permitted residents to obtain cell phone service (with the Cuban government taking a hefty percentage of the fees) to communicate with friends and relatives in the United States and elsewhere. The U.S. government licensed TeleCuba Communications, Inc. to lay the first fiber-optic cable between Florida and Cuba. The massive protests and brutal repression following the purloined results of the June 2009 Iranian election further demonstrated the potential power of ICTs to generate what has been called the first, albeit unsuccessful, "internet insurrection." In many parts of the American and international press, opposition groups were viewed as oppressed people fighting a just cause, as patriots. In Iran, they were viewed as traitors subject to the death penalty. For decades, the indigenous people of Mexico have used the internet in their struggle against the Mexican government. The Chiapas Indians of Southern Mexico show remarkable strength in moving between the global and the local, creating their own international information flows. In Venezuela, imprisoned dissident groups communicate with each other via *Twitter*. These and other examples of internet

insurrections in Egypt and Tunisia are forceful reminders of the empowering capacity of New Media technology and its ability to reflect the plurality of the world.

5   Governments increasingly depend on intermediaries and principal agents for policy implementation. Intermediaries serve as power brokers between government agencies and private contractors. Principal agents are individuals or corporate entities working on behalf of another (the principal). When the agent is an expert at making necessary decisions this arrangement works well. It doesn't work as well when the interests of the agent or principal differ substantially from public interests. When used to implement public policies, there is danger of conflicts of interest. Contracts are often used to specify the terms of a principal agent–government relationship.

6   *Co-optation* is a process by which one group acquires the power to influence the actions of another. *Incrementalism* is an established public sector decision-making model that stresses making decisions through limited successive comparisons; it contrasts with the *rational model* often used in economics and focuses on simplifying choices rather than aspiring to complete problem analyses. Maintaining the status quo rather than attempting to achieve abstract goals is a key point of reference; emphasis is placed on "satisfying" rather than "maximizing" goals and on remedying ills rather than seeking positive goals. Stability is preferred over radical change.

7   Innovation, the introduction of something new into an existing system which *adds value* to a process or product, plays a vital capacity-building role as well as restoring public confidence that government can successfully initiate changes designed to compete in technology-driven global markets.

8   The full report is available at www.pewcenteronthestates.org.

9   Among many contemporary examples of this dilemma was the protracted 13-month debate over President Obama's health insurance reforms and the lack of a coordinated national government response to the massive Gulf of Mexico oil disaster in 2010.

10   The USA.gov portal and its British counterpart Direct.gov.uk are examples of online gateways for accessing information about federal, state or local governments in these countries.

11   Value is added to administrative processes by reducing internal costs and system variation leading to more efficient systems without additional costs to producers or consumers. Many European countries use a Value Added Tax (VAT) on the consumption of goods and services as a means to generate government revenues.

12   California's Life Event and Affinity Design (L.E.A.D.) effort was spearheaded by the Office of Innovation in Government and asked citizens and businesses to attend focus group activities. Three regional conferences were held with 120 people gathered to discuss and document the government services needed at specific stages in life. People were grouped into seven age categories and three miscellaneous categories (starting business, non-age-related events and professional licensing). Each group was then asked to think about information needed or business that would be transacted with a government agency during their particular stage of life or perspective. The results from the three conferences were analyzed and incorporated into California's Web portal and e-gov services. For details, see: California: Life Events and Affinity Design (L.E.A.D.) Program. Available at: www.egovernment.homestead.com/lead.htm.

13 Details available at www.burgerlink.nl. The author wishes to thank Matt Poelmans, Director, *Citizenlink*, The Hague, Netherlands, for providing this information.

14 Citizen satisfaction with electronic government and websites has risen steadily to its highest levels since surveying began (see also: Bailor, 2007; Anonymous, 2008, accessed January 15, 2009 at http://www.foreseeresult. com; and "Report: Citizen Satisfaction with e-Government Hits All-Time High," *Social Security Online*, February 3, 2009, accessed March 2, 2009 at http://www.govtech.com). The Social Security Administration has set a goal to increase online filing of new applicants by 50% by 2012. The conversion to direct deposit of benefits is projected to save $1 billion over the next 10 years.

2 From Representative to Digital Democracy: Using the Internet to Increase Citizen Participation in Governance

1 Earlier versions of this chapter were presented in a paper delivered by the author at an Electronic Democracy Conference in Vienna, Austria, in September 2009 and an article in *JeDEM—eJournal of eDemocracy and Open Government*, 2010. (Reprinted with permission and referenced in Bibliography.)

2 *eJournalUSA* is available at: www.america.gov/publications/ejournalusa.html. Source: www.nua.ie/surveys/how_many_online/index.html.

3 Available at: www.virginiadot.org/travel/citizen.asp.

4 Available at: www.thedailybeast.com/, www.dailykos.com/, www.huffingtonpost. com/, www.powerlineblog.com/ and http://techpresident.com/blog.

5 This often quoted statistic is available from numerous sources, including: Grant Eskelsen, Adam Marcus, W. Kenneth Ferree with Kate Schumacher and Alex Liopiros, *The Digital Economy Fact Book: 10th Edition 2008–2009*. Available at: www.pff.org/issues-pubs/books/factbook_10th_Ed.pdf.

6 In 2001, the now defunct Council on Excellence in Government published a study showing that 77% of respondents favored "investing government funds in e-government." Opinion surveys continue to indicate support for technologies which improve government-to-citizen communication and information (Chapter 1).

7 For a description of how top global "intelligent communities" integrate these and other resources, see www.intelligentcommunity.org/index.

8 See for details: http://worldwatch.org; and http://oxfam.org.

9 Available at: www.gatesfoundation.org/Pages/home.aspx.

10 For an article on the demographics of the site, see: www.insidefacebook. com/2008/09/18/latest-data-on-us-facebook-age-and-gender-demographics/.

11 Thanks to Nicole M. Milakovich for researching this discussion. Source: "Propelled by Internet, Barack Obama Wins Presidency" by Sarah Lai Stirland, November 4, 2008. Available at: www.wired.com/threatlevel/2008/11/ propelled-by-in/.

12 "Obama Announces Organizing for America," by Chris Cillizza, *Washington Post,* January 17, 2009. To view the blog, go to: www.barackobama.com/

13 This group was broken into four teams: Innovation and Government, Innovation and National Priorities, Innovation and Sciences, and Innovation and Civil Society. The focus of the Policy Working Groups was to develop the

priority policy proposals and plans from the Obama Campaign for action during the Obama-Biden Administration. The Policy Working Groups focused on: Economy, Education, Energy and Environment, Health Care, Immigration, National Security, and Technology Innovation and Reform.

3 Managing Citizen-Centric Digital Governance

1 Internal customers are employees and external customers are those being served by public agencies (Grönlund, 2002: 2).
2 See Singapore, E-Citizen: Your Gateway to All Government Services. Accessed June 30, 2009 at: www.ecitizen.gov.sg/.
3 The full report is available at: www.cbc.ca/news/background/auditorgeneral/ ag_report2004/20031101ce.pdf.
4 For further information, see: www.accenture.com/.
5 Available at: www.nstore.accenture.com/acn_com/PDF/2007LCSDeliv PromiseFinal.pdf and www.egov.vic.gov.au/index.php?env=-innews/detail: m2360-1-1-8-s-0:n-1328-1-0. Accenture (2002). *eGovernment Leadership— Realizing the Vision.* Accenture, The Government Executive Series. Available online at: www.accenture.com/Global/Research_and_Insights/By_Industry/ Government/EGovernmentVision.htm
6 The countries were Australia, Belgium, Brazil, Canada, Denmark, Finland, France, Germany, Ireland, Italy, Japan, Malaysia, Mexico, the Netherlands, Norway, Portugal, Singapore, South Africa, Spain, Sweden, the United Kingdom and the United States. Cited in V. Jupp, 2003: 129–145.
7 For details, see: www.e-tenders.gov.ie/.
8 Source: www.intelligentcommunity.org.
9 Portions of the following sections are abstracted with permission from Larsen and Milakovich, 2005: 57–68.
10 During the 1990s, the Clinton administration failed in its attempt to install computers in every classroom to "wire all schools together" largely because of the decentralized and locally controlled and funded structure of U.S. public education.
11 According to a 2004 report by the Kaiser Family Foundation, 75% of children from families with median incomes above $75,000 reported having access to the internet, compared to only 37% of children whose family incomes were under $20,000. This disparity is amplified by school failures in geographically definable districts with significantly higher school drop-out rates among low income and minority students in rural and urban school districts. Accessed at: www.kff.org/.

4 Virtual Learning: Using the Internet for Education, Training and Quality Improvements

1 Thirty-one states have recognized the extent of the problem and formed partnerships to develop a common proficiency examination. Even if this effort is successful, however, 19 states will still have their own separate examinations.
2 Examples of the potential for direct faculty to student interaction are websites such as www.AcademicEarth.com and www.flatworldknowledge.com.
3 The results of the 2006 U.S. Congressional and 2008 Presidential elections strongly suggest that the **electorate** (the voting public) is more willing to

entrust public agencies with critical policy decisions. This may be only a temporary condition resulting from the economic recession and frustration with the radical deregulatory policies of the George W. Bush administration; it may be changing as a result of the 2010 midterm elections.

4 Other U.S. federal agencies, including the Securities and Exchange Commission (SEC), the U.S. Immigration and Customs Service (ICE) (formerly the Immigration and Naturalization Service (INS)), the Federal Aviation Administration (FAA), Health and Human Services (HHS), particularly the Medicare program, and the Transportation Security Administration (TSA) have also been scrutinized for lax oversight procedures, poor record-keeping and "loose" interpretations that grant individual officials either too much discretion in applying administrative rules or too much power too make decisions without due process or judicial review. The Central Intelligence Agency (CIA), National Security Agency (NSA) and the Federal Bureau of Investigation (FBI) were under scrutiny by Congress for their handling of sensitive information regarding known terrorist threats prior to the September 11th attacks on the World Trade Center in New York.

5 Source: "California scraps IT department after Oracle debacle." July 5, 2002. Retrieved at: www.computerweekly.com/Articles/2002/07/05/188238/california-scraps-it-department-after-oracle-debacle.htm.

6 When appropriately researched, documented and summarized, comparative methodologies offer administrators detailed "benchmarks" for understanding customers' needs and training employees to meet them. Customers and managers benefit from empirically based knowledge and theory gained from customer surveys that evaluate the level of service expected and delivered, especially by intelligence, law enforcement and regulatory compliance agencies.

7 The prize was originally funded by international quality guru W. Edwards Deming (1900–1993) who pioneered the quality management movement first in Japan and then in the United States. His cumulative works still represent the definitive reference for statistical process control and quality improvement in manufacturing. For example, see: W. Edwards Deming, *Out of the Crisis.* Cambridge, MA: MIT Center for Advance Engineering Study, 1993 and the *New Economics of Industry, Government, and Education.* Cambridge, MA: MIT Center for Advance Engineering Study, 2004.

8 For details, see: www.juse.or.jp/e/deming/.

9 For details, see: www.efqm.org/en/.

10 Winners of the 2009 Digital Governance Awards were, in their respective categories: Tennessee General Assembly; Town of Blacksburg, VA: Leadership in Digital Access; County of Arlington, VA, Honorable Mention; City of Calabasas, CA: Excellence in Disseminating Government Information; City of Port of St. Lucie, FL, Honorable Mention; City of Sarasota, FL; Excellence in Government Efficiency Winner: Village of Rye Brook, NY; Honorable Mention, Superior Court of California, Ventura County: Excellence in Constituent Engagement Winner.

11 Accessed at: www.centerdigitalgov.com/survey/88.

12 Granicus provides integrated streaming media, legislative management and online training solutions built to help government agencies enhance Web-based transparency, citizen participation and communication. Over the past

decade, over 550 public agencies in 47 states and Canada have deployed Granicus technologies for streaming public meetings and managing legislative data, resulting in the development of one of the largest networks of government data online. This data includes audio/video public meeting recordings and digital public records all archived, cross-linked, keyword searchable and RSS-enabled. The collection of data has enabled Granicus to form a national ranking of webcast government content. The statistics are now publicly available at: www.granicus.com/Clients/Client-Stats.aspx? stats=PR.

13 In 2007, the city of Coral Springs, Florida, and the U.S. Army Armament, Research and Development Center were award recipients in the non-profit category. In 2008, only three awards were given: Cargill Corn Milling North America, Wayzata, Minn. (manufacturing); Poudre Valley Health System, Fort Collins, Colo. (health care); and the Iredell-Statesville Schools, Statesville, N.C. (education). In 2009, six awards were presented including a division of Veterans' Administration in the non-profit agency category. In 2009, the five winners were: Honeywell Federal Manufacturing & Technologies, Kansas City, Mo. (manufacturing); MidwayUSA, Columbia, Mo. (small business); AtlantiCare, Egg Harbor Township, N.J. (health care); Heartland Health, St. Joseph, Mo. (health care); and VA Cooperative Studies Program Clinical Research Pharmacy Coordinating Center, Albuquerque, N.M. (non-profit). For further details and current recipients, see: www.nist.gov/public_ affairs/releases/2009baldrigerecipients.htm.

14 The U.K. national charter program began in 1991 and was renamed *Service First—The New Charter Programme* by the Labour Administration in 1998. Nine principles underlie the New Charter Programme for every public service: 1) set published standards of service; 2) be open and provide full information about costs and performance; 3) consult and involve present and potential users; 4) encourage access and promotion of choice; 5) treat everyone fairly, respect their privacy and dignity, be helpful and friendly, pay particular attention to those with special needs; 6) put things right when they go wrong; 7) use resources effectively to provide the best value for taxpayers and users; 8) innovate and improve service and facilities; and 9) work with other providers. For a detailed and indexed guide to the use of charters, citizen participation, performance standards, charter mark awards, networks, best practices and how to complain in the United Kingdom, see the excellent Modernizing Public Services Group website at: www.servicefirst.gov.uk/.

15 Retrieved at: www.whitehouse.gov/administration/eop/nec/ StrategyforAmericanInnovation/.

5 Accountability and Equality of Access: Balancing Political Responsiveness with Administrative Effectiveness

1 Portions of this chapter were drawn with permission from an earlier version of an article published by the author: "Balancing Customer Service, Empowerment, and Performance with Citizenship, Responsiveness, and Political Accountability," *International Public Management Review*, 4 (1) 2003: 61–83.

2 For example, the Defense Department projects cost savings of over $1 billion in travel expenses; Social Security Administration answers 95% of its 800-number calls within five minutes; the U.S. Postal Service delivers 92% of its

first-class mail within three days; the Occupational Health and Safety Administration responds to worker complaints in less than one day; and the Federal Communications Commission is raising millions of dollars by auctioning new radio frequencies.

3 For details, see: www.intelligentcommunity.org/index.

4 The Brownlow Commission, named after its Chairman, Lewis Brownlow, was officially known as the President's Committee on Administrative Management that was appointed by President Roosevelt in 1937 and recommended major changes in the administration and management of the federal government.

5 The Grace Commission, named after its Chairman R. Peter Grace and officially known as the Private Sector Survey on Cost Control, was appointed by President Reagan in 1982. It made over 400 specific (and sometimes controversial) recommendations of streamlining the operations of the federal governments and reducing federal spending. One recommendation to close several obsolete military bases took over 10 years to complete.

6 For information on the history of the NPR, see its archived website at: www. govinfo.library.unt.edu/npr/index.htm. Two other comprehensive websites for information on recent reforms are: www.USA.gov and www.planetgov.com. To establish stronger ties with other governmental reforms such as the Government Performance and Results Act (GPRA), high impact agencies must publish their customer service standards, performance goals, specific measures and results on the GPRA website at www.opm.gov.gpra/index.htm.

7 This cliché was inspired by the best-selling 1992 book *Reinventing Government: How the Entrepreneurial Spirit is Transforming the Public Sector* by David Osborne and Ted Gaebler, which provided its theoretical foundations, a controversial mix of theory and ideology that focused on "market-driven" solutions to correct the perceived inefficiencies in the delivery of federal government services.

8 By late 1998, Congress had enacted and the president had signed 83 laws incorporating NPR recommendations. The "reinventors" claim to have implemented two-thirds of the original 1993 recommendations by eliminating 250 outdated government programs and 16,000 pages of regulation; cutting more than 640,000 pages of internal rules; reducing the federal budget by more than $137 billion; establishing nearly 4,000 customer service standards in 570 federal organizations or programs; giving out more than 1200 "Hammer Awards" to teams of federal employees responsible for $37 billion in cost savings; creating more than 350 "reinvention laboratories" to stimulate innovation, improve performance and eliminate unnecessary regulations (Thompson, 2000); and downsizing the federal civilian workforce by 13%—more than 317,000 employees. These reforms resulted in the smallest federal government, on a percentage basis, since the 1950s.

9 Reform efforts focused on partnerships with 29 "high-impact" federal agencies that employ 1.1 million of 1.8 million civilian employees and have the most contact with the public and businesses, including the Internal Revenue Service (IRS), Environmental Protection Agency (EPA), Federal Aviation Administration (FAA), Food and Drug Administration (FDA), Federal Emergency Management Agency (FEMA), Occupational Safety and Health Administration (OSHA) and the Social Security Administration (SSA). The U.S. Customs Service, now Immigration and Customs Enforcement (ICE), was identified as a model federal reinvention effort for reducing the time required to process inbound

airline passengers. The Social Security Administration (SSA) has been recognized for improving the responsiveness of its e-application processes and 800-number information systems. In 1997, the name of the NPR was changed to the National Partnership for Reinventing Government and the effort was given a new slogan—"America@Its Best"—which read like a website address to emphasize the commitment to greater public access through the expanded use of information and communication technology (ICT) and the internet.

10 For further details, see: www.eeoc.gov.

11 For details, see: www.un.org/millenniumgoals/.

12 For further details, see: www.schoolnetafrica.org/.

13 Thanks to Amber Stephens for researching this topic.

14 See for example, the 1999 report on "A Government to Trust and Respect: Rebuilding Citizen—Government Relations in the 21st Century" released by the National Academy of Public Administration at www.napawash.org/napa/index.html. See also, the 1989 Volcker Commission on the public service, National Commission on the Public Service, *Leadership for America: Rebuilding the Public Service.* New York: Lexington Book.

15 Technology may also provide a bridge to help guide improved customer service and enhance the development of theory to guide managers in their choice of strategies. For example, the American Customer Satisfaction Index (ACSI) rankings of customer satisfaction show that 93 million taxpayers filing tax returns electronically with the Internal Revenue Service (IRS) were much more satisfied (74%) than those filing paper returns in the traditional manner (48%). For full results, see: www.bus.umich.edu/researchh/nqrc/government.html.

16 For a discussion of the potential for two-way technology, see: www.pewinternet.org/Media-Mentions/2010/Video-calls-gaining-traction.aspx.

6 Advancing Digital Governance and Performance Management

1 For details, see: www.archives.gov/federal-register/laws/administrative-procedure/.

2 For details of implementation problems with these and similar federal programs, see: Bardach, 1977; Kettl, 1987; Maier, 1993; and Pressman and Wildavsky, 1984.

3 For details, see: www.usdoj.gov/oip/foia_updates/Vol_XVII_4/page2.htm.

4 In subsequent disclosures of tactical decisions in the wars in Iraq and Afghanistan, WikiLeaks redacted much of the top secret information. For details, see: http://wikileaks.org/.

5 For implementation details, see: www.csrc.nist.gov/groups/SMA/ispab/index.html.

6 For details, see: www.usdoj.gov/opcl/1974prostudy.htm.

7 For a study of the problem, see: www.consumerwebwatch.org/dynamic/press-release-princeton.cfm.

8 "Open Government Directive," Memorandum for the Heads of Executive Departments and Agencies from Peter Orszag, OMB Director. December 8, 2009. Accessed March 15, 2010 at: www.whitehouse.gov/sites/default/files/omb/assets/memoranda_2010/m10-06.pdf.

9 For details, see: www.ed.gov/policy/gen/leg/cca.html.

10   Available at: www.whitehouse.gov/omb/egov/.

11   United States House of Representatives, "The Electronic Government Act of 2002," p. 4. Available at http://csrc.nist.gov/policies/HR2458-final.pdf

12   Retrieved at: www.whitehouse.gov/omb/part/.

13   The awards recognize outstanding examples of creative problem solving in the public sector. Privately sponsored by the Roy and Lila Ash Center for Democratic Governance and Innovation formerly funded by the Ford Foundation, all units of government are eligible. Twenty finalists are chosen annually. Ten winners receive $100,000 in grants; others receive $20,000 in prizes. Since 1986, over 300 programs have been recognized and nearly $20 million in grants has been awarded. For details, see www.innovations.harvard.edu.

14   Source: www.cisco.com/web/about/ac79/docs/011001_TPM_winter_ articlereprint.pdf.

15   Hart-Teeter, Council for Excellence in Government E-Government: The Next American Revolution, available at: www.excelgov.org/egovpoll/index.htm.

16   For example, see www.miamidade.gov.

17   Information Technology Association of America, *US Public Concerned Over Government Held Data*, October 17, 2000. Accessed at: www.nua.ie/surveys. index/.

18   Momentum Research Group, Benchmarking the eGovernment Revolution: Year 2000 Report on Citizen and Business Demand, July 26, 2000. Accessed at: www.egovernmentreport.com.

7 Applying Digital Technologies to Improve Public Services

1   "Mayors of Hoboken, Secaucus, Five Rabbis Arrested," *Bloomberg News*, accessed at: www.bloomberg.com/apps/news?pid=email_en&sid=aGWQjW0qO6qg; "Governor Suspends Eggelletion, Gallagher, in Wake of Corruption Arrest," *Ft. Lauderdale Sun-Sentinel*, September 23, 2009; and "Corruption Probe Expanded to Broward Transit," by Amy Sherman, *Miami Herald*, September 25, 2009.

2   Source: 2009 National Survey of Local Governments report based on responses from more than 1,500 randomly polled city, county, township and special district governments across the county. Reported in *PATimes*, October, 2009.

3   Accessible at: www.disasterhelp.gov/disastermanagement/.

4   The website provides members of the community and other constituents with information and resources to help meet communications and interoperability needs. For additional details, see: www.safecomprogram.gov/SAFECOM/.

5   According to a report published in February 2003 by the National Task Force on Interoperability, the emergency response community views the following as key issues which limit responsiveness: hampering emergency response wireless communications; incompatible and aging communications equipment; limited and fragmented budget cycles and funding; limited and fragmented planning and coordination; limited and fragmented radio spectrum; and limited equipment standards. Accessed at: U.S. Department of Homeland Security: www.safecomprogram.gov/SAFECOM/interoperability/default.htm.

6   U.S.   Department   of   Homeland   Security.   Accessed   at: www.safecomprogram.gov/SAFECOM/library/interoperabilitycasestudies/ 1223_statewidecommunications.htm.

7 U.S. Department of Homeland Security. Accessed at: www.safecomprogram. gov/SAFECOM/currentprojects/project25/.

8 SAFECOM-Clark County Urban Area Project Action Planning Session Report held on February 23, 2006. Accessed at: www.safecomprogram. gov/NR/rdonlyres/54906E2B-47B0-4270-90F8-A12F01A160D7/0/NV UrbanActionPlanningMeeting_031306_v422.doc.

9 www.epa.gov—Grants and Debarment; Government/Federal Agency Benefits. Accessed at www.epa.gov/ogdunix1/guide/benefits.htm.

10 Grants.gov—Finding Grants: Washington, DC's Success Story. Accessed at: www.grants.gov/applicants/DCSuccessStory.pdf.

11 Agency officials responsible for preparing and correcting CPDF and EHRI data will find submission instructions for both systems at: www.opm.gov/ feddata/guidance.asp.

12 Quoted in "Pay stubs for some federal workers going electronic" by Ed O'Keefe, *Washington Post* Staff Writer, Tuesday, March 30, 2010, B03.

13 Quoted in "To save $1 trillion, Uncle Sam should take cues from CEOs, group says" by Jia Lynn Yang, *Washington Post*, October 12, 2010.

14 Available at: http://dms.myflorida.com/business_operations/state_purchasing/ myflorida_marketplace.

15 For a critical review, see Coursey and Killingsworth, 2010.

16 E-Gov; the president's goal of utilizing technology to improve how the Federal Government serves citizens, businesses and agencies: Available at: www.whitehouse.gov/omb/egov/.

17 For example, according to unaudited internal estimates, in fiscal year 2003, the business community spent 8.2 billion hours and over $320 billion on paperwork related to government regulatory compliance requirements. This includes negotiating with complex government hierarchies, devoting time to meeting government laws and regulations and filling out mountains of forms.

18 This is the second time Business.gov has been recognized for excellence in quality of service. In March 2008, Business.gov won the Government Information Technology Executive Council (GITEC) Project Management Excellence Award for project management excellence in the category of Delivering Mission Critical Services/Practical Innovations. Business.gov: "SBA's Business Gateway Initiative Wins 'Excellence.Gov' Award." Retrieved at: www.business.gov/press/.

19 Cindy Skrzycki, "Project Aims for One-Stop Online Shopping for Federal Rules," *Washington Post*, March 30, 2004, E1; and Cindy Skrzycki, "U.S. Opens Online Portal to Rulemaking," *Washington Post*, January 23, 2003, E6.

20 For details, see: www.georgewbush-whitehouse.archives.gov/omb/egov/c-3-2-eetpb.html.

21 For a detailed study of this application, see: www.epic.org/privacy/id-cards/ epic_realid_0508.pdf.

22 Available at: www.regulations.gov.

23 "E-Verify contractor rule delayed again," Gautham Nagesh, January 30, 2009: National Journal Group. Retrieved at: www.numbersusa.com/content/ news/september-8-2009/e-verify-executive-order-goes-effect-today.html. Find nextgov.com at: www.nextgov.com/nextgov/ng_20090130_5459.php.

24 "E-Verify fails to catch half of unauthorized workers, study reveals," Alice Lopowitz, *Federal Computer Week*, March 3, 2010. Available at: http://fcw.com/ articles/2010/03/03/everify-error-rate-illegal-workers.aspx.

25 Access benefits.gov at: www.benefits.gov.

26 Benefits.gov has received numerous quality awards over the last five years. The impressive list of awards includes: 2007 Top 50 Program—*Harvard Ash Institute for Democratic Governance and Innovation*; 2006 Laureate—*The Computer World Honors Program*; 2004, 2005, 2006 Intergovernmental Solutions Award Finalist—*American Council for Technology*; 2004, 2005, 2007 Excellence.gov Award Finalist—*Industry Advisory Council*; and 2003 E-Gov Pioneer Award—*Government Solutions Center*.

27 Available at: www.samhsa.gov/About/background.aspx. See also: www. whitehouse.gov/omb/inforeg/egovstrategy.pdf.

28 Source: www.samhsa.gov/About/background.aspx.

29 Available at: www.consumer.gov/about.htm.

30 FEMA: www.fema.gov/about/programs/daip/plan.shtm.

31 FEMA: www.fema.gov/about/programs/daip/benefits.shtm.

32 The White House issued a detailed report in 2002 stressing the need to foster leadership support and strengthen connections/communication between lead agencies, partner agencies and other governmental departments. For full text and specifics, see: www.whitehouse.gov/omb/inforeg/egovstrategy.pdf.

33 For a more detailed account of the struggle to decode the human genome, see: J. Craig Venter, *A Life Decoded: My Genome: My Life.* New York: Viking, 2007.

34 Stephanie Condon, "Obama's CIO wants more citizen activity on Web" March 5, 2009. Accessed April 4, 2009 at: http://news.cnet.com/8301-13578_3-10190069-38.htmlYe; and Kim Hart, "Local Tech-Savvy Duo Steps On to Federal Stage to Lead Work on Obama's Bold Digital Ambitions," *Washington Post*, April 27, 2009. Unfortunately, Vivek Kundra resigned in August, 2011.

8 Global Inventory of Digital Governance Practices

1 In 2008, Barbados ranked in the top 25% on the United Nations e-government readiness index and, in 2009, became the first Caribbean country to implement online tax administration. In Mauritius, the joint public and private sector Contributions Network Project (CNP) connects all large firms, and the majority of small ones, to the relevant government tax departments via a single channel for electronic submission of payments such as contributions, tax returns, etc. that Mauritian firms make to various government departments. For more information on the project see: www.siteresources.worldbank.org/INTEGOVERNMENT/Resources/702478-1129947675846/mauritiusCNPcs.htm.

2 Half of the total available points for online services are assigned to these stages. Specifically, the survey instrument allocates 68 points to characteristics of an emerging online presence (16.9%), 116 points to an enhanced online presence (28.8%), 169 points to a transactional presence (41.9%) and 50 points to a connected presence (12.4%) for a maximum possible score of 403.

3 G-20 countries will encourage national regulators to prevent excessive executive bonuses and urge banks not to permit excessive compensation and to cut into the reserve capital they need to deal with potential losses. Excerpted from original story in *The Wall Street Journal*, Friday, September 25, 2009.

4 David K. Correa, "Assessing Broadband in America: OECD and ITIF Broadband Rankings," April, 2007. Available at www.itif.org/files/BroadbandRankings.pdf.

5 Leonard Waverman, Kalyan Dasgupta, with assistance of Nicolas Brooks, "Connectivity Scorecard 2009." Available at: www.connectivityscorecard.org/images/uploads/media/TheConnectivityReport2009.pdf.

6 For utility bills, see: www.egovernmentaccess.com/Utility.htm. For parking tickets: www.egovernmentaccess.com/Parking.htm; building permits: www.gocolumbiamo.com/PublicWorks/Inspection/bptracking.php.

7 Source: www.germany.info/Vertretung/usa/en/Startseite.html.

8 Rajesh Makwana discusses how the three organizations help developing countries, why they do so and the restrictions they create. "IMF, World Bank, and Trade." Accessed May 19, 2009 at: www.stwr.org/imf-world-bank-trade/decommissioning-the-imf-world-bank-and-wto.html.

9 See: www.futuregov.net/articles/2009/mar/23/it-chief-e-gov-south-africa-has-long-way-go/.

10 O3b is company planning to launch 16 satellites to connect the "Other 3 billion" people in the world who do not have reliable internet connections or power sources.

11 Source: www.yoursdp.org/index.php/news/singapore/81-Asian-countries-are-below-average-in-e-government-readiness-UN-Survey.

12 The violent aftermath of 2009 Iranian elections, the overthrow of the Tunisian government and the internet uprising in Egypt are dramatic examples of the effect that cellular technology can have on government transparency and openness. When the governments in power in each of these countries cut off internet connections, cell phone users connected to other computers and networks with **proxy servers** and were still able to transmit photos and videos of anti-government protests.

13 Sweden had a newly revamped e-services portal at: www.sverige.se. Norway displayed its redesigned primary site at www.regjeringen.no. Denmark still led the way among Scandinavian countries and globally with integrated services at www.borger.dk.

14 For details, see: www.madridparticipa.es/.

15 Accessible at: www.premier-ministre.gouv.fr.

16 Accessed July 18, 2010 at: http://www.gomonews.com/digital-dividend-france-is-paving-the-way-for-harmonised-decisions-across-europe-says-analysys-mason/.

17 OECD. "E-Government as a Tool for Transformation. 2007," p. 16. Retrieved at: www.olis.oecd.org/olis/2007doc.nsf/8d00615172fd2a63c125685d005300b5/c5bfb886ebcafe06c12572ac0057513c/$FILE/JT03224646.pdf.

18 John Gerlach and Urs Gasser, "Three Case Studies from Switzerland: E-Voting," March, 2009, accessed June 18, 2009 at www.cyber.law.harvard.edu/sites/cyber.law.harvard.edu/files/Gerlach-Gasser_SwissCases_Evoting.pdf.

19 According to Ernsdorff and Berbec, (2007: 177), "the progress of ICT in a small country with less than 1.4 million inhabitants proved successful and that is why the Harvard University Global Information Report ranked the development of ICT in Estonia in 22nd place in the world among the 75 countries surveyed, surpassing countries such as France, Italy and Spain." In addition, over 91% of tax declarations were filed online in 2009. For details, see: www.vm.ee/estonia/kat_175/pea_175/1163.html.

20 See the section "Percentage of Customs Declarations Filed Online in Estonia Doubled within Year" at: www.estemb.se/estonian_review/aid-605.

21 Alexander H. Treshsel, in collaboration with Guido Schwerdt, Fabian Breuer, Michael Alvarez and Thad Hall, *Internet Voting in the March 2007: Parliamentary Elections in Estonia*, Report to the Council of Europe: Florence, Italy: European University Institute, July 31, 2007. Retrieved at: www.vvk.ee/public/dok/CoE_and_NEC_Report_E-Voting_2007.pdf.

22 Retrieved at: www.skype.com/.

23 For details, see: www.europa.eu/debateeurope/index_en.htm.

24 OECD E-Government Studies: Netherlands. Accessed June 10, 2009 at: www.oecd.org/document/15/0,3343,en_33873108_33873309_38988943_1_1_1_1,00.html.

25 Cap Gemini, *The User Challenge Benchmarking the Supply of Online Public Services:* 7th Measurement, September, 2007 prepared for the European Commission Directorate General for Information Society and Media (Belgium: Cap Gemini, 2007). Accessed January 8, 2009 at: www.ec.europa.eu/information_society/eeurope/i2010/docs/benchmarking/egov_benchmark_2007.pdf, p. 30.

26 For details, see: www.simplex.pt/downloads/SimplexAutarquicoEng.pdf.

27 Available at: www.borger.dk.

28 Available at: www.virk.dk.

29 The author wishes to thank Thomas Holstrom Frandzen, Coordinator, Division of ICT Skills and eAccessibiliy, Ministry of Science, Technology and Innovation, Copenhagen, Denmark, for the detailed and useful examples. See also, "E-gov would save countries billions of Euros, EU says," ZDNet, April 27, 2006, available at www.government.zdnet.com/?p=2241.

9 Globalization, Information Technology and Public Administration

1 The U.S. International Trade Commission determines which goods are subject to protective tariffs and quotas. For more information, go to: www.usitc.gov/tata/hts/.

2 John W. Miller "Nations Rush to Establish New Barriers to Trade," *Wall Street Journal,* February 6, 2009.

3 Portions of earlier versions of this chapter were presented in a paper delivered at the 27th International Congress of Administrative Sciences, Abu Dhabi, UAE, July 11–14, 2007.

4 The massive eco-disaster in the Gulf of Mexico during the summer 2010 was caused by the negligent and reckless actions of BP and its sub-contractors in their deep-water offshore drilling operations.

5 For chart on real hourly wages over time, see: www.creditwritedowns.com/2008/06/chart-of-day-real-hourly-earnings.html.

6 Each of these corporations dealt with customer complaints by in-sourcing these services back to the United States.

7 China specializes in producing low-cost consumer goods for large retail corporations, who then buy and sell them in bulk at prices considerably below what it would cost to mass produce the same products in more developed consumer nations.

8 Christopher Beddor, Winny Chen, Rudy deLeon, Shiyong Park, Daniel J. Weiss, "Securing America's Future: Enhancing Our National Security by Reducing Oil Dependence and Environmental Damage." Center for American Progress, 2009.

9 The Action Plan is accessible at: www.unfccc.int/resource/docs/2007/cop13/eng/06a01.pdf.

10 Using its own predictive models, Royal Dutch Shell claims that it takes 25 years for a new form of energy such as solar power to capture 1% of the world market. Shell predicts that if we do things according to their own self-serving forecasts, renewable energy will provide 30% of global needs by 2050, but fossil fuels will still account for 55%.

11 George W. Bush, *Decision Points.* New York: Crown Books, 2010; for a contrary view, see: Nicholas S. J. Davies, *Blood on Our Hands: the American Invasion and Destruction of Iraq.* New York: Nimble Books, 2010.

12 Thailand, the Philippines, Pakistan, Afghanistan, Uzbekistan, Azerbaijan, Jordan, Egypt, Iraq, Kuwait, UAE, Saudi Arabia, Morocco, Cyprus, Cuba, Diego Garcia and unspecified South Pacific island nations. In addition, individuals have been held in temporary or permanent U.S. controlled facilities in Indonesia, El Salvador, Nigeria, Equatorial Guinea, Libya, Israel, Denmark, Poland, Romania, Bulgaria, Albania, Hungary, Germany and Scotland.

13 Many small farmers in Europe are experiencing their most serious crisis since the end of World War II, accompanied by complete silence and lack of interest on the part of the European media. Prices of all types of raw materials have plummeted to historic minimums and farmers—irrespective of what crops they grow or animals they raise—are producing at a loss. Farmers have lost much of their independence and the ability to set a price according to the quality of their produce. They are being suppressed by the agro-industrial, monocultural approach to farming, which serves the interests of the large-scale retail trade.

10 Toward Digital Governance and Participatory Citizenship: Integrating Technology and Public Administration

1 The Supreme Court's highly controversial and partisan 5–4 decision in January 2010 effectively ended public accountability by removing restrictions on private campaign contributions. This decision influenced outcomes of the 2010 American midterm elections and, unless overturned, will doubtless affect campaign financing in the future.

2 "State Elections Websites Have Significant Room for Improvement," *PATimes:* 31(12), December, 2008. For examples, see: www.bschool.nus.edu.sg/staff/bizteosh/TeoSrivastavaJiangJMIS2008TrustEGovSuccess.pdf. See also, Sorin Kertesz, "Cost-Benefit Analysis of E-Government Investments," John F. Kennedy School of Government, Harvard University, May 2003. Available at: www.egov.sonasi.com/repository/cost-benefit-analysis-of-e-government-investments/download.

3 Many established newspapers and television networks are also converting to online delivery due to lower labor and material costs, reduced advertising revenue and declines in readers and viewers.

4 The U.S. Postal Service (desperately in need of a new mission) has the technical and logistical capability to provide and maintain such a vehicle-based delivery system through its 32,000 branch offices. The development of a prototype vehicle, which could then be field-tested and assessed by customers, should be undertaken as soon as possible. Kiosks and terminals could be placed in public places such as malls, libraries, schools, senior centers, government offices and office buildings where it is possible to insure easy access to underserved populations.

5 The same resistance to technological innovation took place with the introduction of "911" emergency telephone numbers in the 1960s and with automated bank teller machines in the 1970s.

6 See among others: Welch, Hinnant and Moon, 2004: 372 and Tolbert and Mossberger, 2006: 355.

7 Available at: www.apqc.org.

8 Government websites are under continuous attacks from computer hackers. Governments have been forced to devote more attention to security of their websites and descriptions of their privacy policies, especially since September 11, 2001. The WikiLeaks debacle has generated complex legal and ethical issues which have far-reaching consequences for U.S. foreign and technology policy.

Bibliography

Accenture. (2002) *eGovernment Leadership—Realizing the Vision*. Accenture, The Government Executive Series. Available at: www.accenture.com/Global/Research_and_Insights/By_Industry/Government/EGovernmentVision.htm.

Accenture. (2004) "eGovernment Leadership: High Performance, Maximum Value." Accessed April 15, 2009 at: www.accenture.com/Global/Research_and_Insights/By_Industry/Government_and_Public_Service/HighValue.htm.

Accenture. (2005) *Leadership in Customer Service: New Expectations, New Experiences*. Accenture, The Government Executive Series. Available at: www.accenture.com/Global/Research_and_Insights/By_Industry/Government/LeadershipExperiences.htm.

Accenture. (2009) "E-Government Leadership: Engaging the customer." Accessed March 18, 2009 at: www.accenture.com/xdoc/en/newsroom/epresskit/egovernment/egov_epress.pdf.

Agor, W.H. (1997) "The Measurement, Use, and Development of Intellectual Capital to Increase Public Sector Productivity," *Public Personnel Management*, 26 (2): 175–187.

Alford, J. (2002) "Why do Public-Sector Clients Coproduce? Toward a Contingency Theory," *Administration and Society*, 34 (1): 32–56.

Al-Hakim, L. (Ed.) (2007) *Global E-Government: Theory, Applications and Benchmarking*. Hershey, PA: Idea Publishing Group.

Alvarez, M. and Nadler, J. (2001) "The Likely Consequences of Internet Voting for Political Representation," *Loyola of Los Angeles Law Review*, 34: 1115–1152.

Arnold, P.E. (1995) "Reform's Changing Role," *Public Administration Review*, 55 (5): 407–417.

Atkinson, R.D. and Leigh, A. (2003) "Customer-Oriented E-Government: Can We Ever Get There?," in Curtin, G.G., Sommer, M.H., Vis-Sommer, V. (Eds.) *The World of E-Government*. New York: The Haworth Political Press, pp. 159–181.

Bailor, C. (2007) "E-Government: Satisfaction on the Rise," *CRM*.com, June 20. Available at www.destinationcrm.com/Articles/ReadArticle.aspx?ArticleID=42102.

Barber, B.R. (2001) *Jihad vs. McWorld: Terrorism's Challenge to Democracy*. New York: Ballantine Books.

Bardach, E. (1977) *The Implementation Game: What Happens after a Bill Becomes a Law.* Cambridge, MA: MIT Press.

Barlow, A. (2007a) *Blogging America: The New Public Sphere.* New York: Praeger.

Barlow, A. (2007b) *The Rise of the Blogosphere.* New York: Praeger.

Barquin, R. (2004) "Citizen Relationship Management (CZRM)—The Challenge and the Promise," U.S. General Services Administration Newsletter issue 14, January.

Barquin, R., Bennet, A. and Remez, S. (2001) *Knowledge Management: The Catalyst for Electronic Government.* Vienna, VA: Management Concepts.

Beam, G. (2001) *Quality Public Management: What It Is and How It Can be Improved and Advanced.* Chicago: Roman and Littlefield.

Beamish, A. (1995) *Communities Online: Community-Based Computer Networks,* unpublished Master's thesis, Massachusetts Institute of Technology, February 1995. Available at http://alberti.mit.edu/arch/4.207/anneb/thesis/toc.html

Beckett, J. (2000) "The 'Government Should be Run Like a Business' Mantra," *American Review of Public Administration,* 30 (2): 185–204.

Behn, R. (1995) "The Big Questions of Public Administration," *Public Administration Review,* 55 (4): 10–17.

Behn, R. (1999) "The New Public Management Paradigm and the Search for Democratic Accountability," *International Public Management Review,* 1 (2): 131–165.

Bekkers, V.J.J.M., Dijkstra, G., Edwards, A. and Fenger, M. (2007) *Governance and the Democratic Deficit: Assessing the Democratic Legitimacy of Democratic Practices.* Hampshire, UK: Ashgate Publishing.

Bello, W. (2005) *Dilemmas of Domination: The Unmaking of the American Empire.* New York: Metropolitan Books.

Berman, E. (1997) "Dealing with Cynical Citizens," *Public Administration Review,* 57 (1): 57–66.

Berman, E., West, J. and Milakovich, M.E. (1994) "Implementing TQM in the States," *Spectrum: The Journal of State Government,* 67 (2): 6–13.

Berry, L. and Parasuraman, A. (1991) *Marketing Services: Competing Through Quality.* New York: The Free Press.

Bhagwati, J. (2004) *In Defense of Globalization.* New York: Oxford University Press.

Bhatnagar, S. (2004) *E-government: From Vision to Implementation, a Practical Guide with Case Studies.* Thousand Oaks, CA: Sage Publications.

Blackstone, E.A., Bognanno, M.L. and Hakim, S. (2005) *Innovations in E-Government: The Thoughts of Governors and Mayors.* Lanham, MD: Rowman & Littlefield Publishers.

Blinder, Alan. (2007) "How Many U.S. Jobs Might be Offshorable," CEPS Working Paper No. 142, March 2007. Accessed at www.princeton.edu/~blinder/articles.htm.

Block, P. (1991) *The Empowered Manager.* San Francisco: Jossey-Bass Publishers.

Box, R.C. (1999) "Running Government Like a Business: Implications for Public Administration Theory and Practice," *The American Review of Public Administration*, 29 (1): 19–43.

Box, R.C., Marshall, R.S., Reed, B.J. and Reed, C.M. (2001) "New Public Management and Substantive Democracy," *Public Administration Review*, 61 (5): 608–619.

Bygrave, L. and Bing, J. (Eds.) (2009) *Internet Governance: Infrastructure and Institutions*. London: Oxford University Press.

Camp, R. (1989) *Benchmarking: The Search for Industry Best Practices that Lead to Superior Performance*. Milwaukee: ASQC Press.

Cap Gemini. (2007) *The User Challenge Benchmarking the Supply of Online Public Services*. 7th Measurement, prepared for the European Commission Directorate General for Information Society and Media (Belgium: Cap Gemini Group).

Carlstrom, G. (2008) "Obama's Bold Vision for E-Gov," *Federal Times*, November 18.

Carr, D., Kehoe, J., Barker, I. and Littman, D. (1999) *Transforming Government Services: A Global Perspective*. Washington, D.C.: PriceWaterhouseCoopers.

Carter, L. and Belanger, F. (2005) "The Utilization of E-Government Services: Citizen Trust, Innovation and Acceptance Factors," *Information Systems Journal*, 15 (1): 5–25.

Cassidy, J. (2008) *Enterprise GIS Strategies Strengthen Government Operations*, Government Technology Online. Available at: www.govtech.com/pcio/articles/265061.

Chadwick, A. (2006) *Internet Politics: States, Citizens, and New Communication Technologies*. New York: Oxford University Press.

Chadwick, A. and Howard, P. (2009) *The Routledge Handbook for Internet Politics*. London: Routledge.

Chen, H., Brandt, L., Gregg,V., Traunmüller, R., Dawes, S., Hovy, E., Macintosh, A. and Larson, C. (2008) *Digital Government: E-Government Research, Case Studies, and Implementation*. New York: Springer Science and Business Media.

Chen, I., Chen, N. and Kinshuk. (2009) "Examining the Factors Influencing Participants' Knowledge Sharing Behavior in Virtual Learning Communities," *Educational Technology & Society*, 12 (1): 134–148.

Chen, Y. and Thurmaier, K. (2008) "Advancing E-Government: Financing Challenges and Opportunities: New Perspectives on E-Government," *Public Administration Review*, 68 (3): 537–548.

Chu, P-Y. and Wang, H-S. (2001) "Benefits, Critical Process Factors, and Optimum Strategies of Successful ISO 9000 Implementation in the Public Sector," *Public Performance and Management Review*, 25 (1): 105–121.

Chuan, T.K. and Soon, L.C. (2000) "A Detailed Trends Analysis of National Quality Awards World-Wide," *Total Quality Management*, 11 (8): 1065–1080.

Clift, S. (2004) "E-Government and Democracy: Representation and Citizen Engagement in the Information Age." Report Prepared for United Nations–UNPAN/DESA, 2003, World Public Sector Report.

Coffman, L. (1986) *Public-Sector Marketing*. New York: John Wiley and Sons.

Coglianese, C. (2004) *E-Rulemaking: Information Technology and Regulatory Policy: New Directions in Digital Government Research*. Regulatory Policy Program, John F. Kennedy School of Government, Harvard University.

Coleman, C. (2004) "Citizen Relationship Management," U. S. General Services Administration, Newsletter issue 14, January.

Connelly, C. (2008) "Obama Policymakers Turn to Campaign Tools: Network of Supporters Tapped on Health-Care Issues," *Washington Post*, November 4, p. 1.

Coplin, W. and Dwyer, C. (2000) *Does Your Government Measure Up?: Better Tools for Local Officials and Citizens*. Syracuse, NY: Syracuse University Community Benchmarks Program.

Coulthard, D., Castleman, T. and Batten, L. (2001) "eCommerce Strategy in a Multi-Sector Trading Council for Excellence in Government," *E-Government: The Next American Revolution*. Accessed June 10, 2009 at: www.netcaucus.org/books/egov2001/pdf/Bluecove.pdf.

Coursey, D.H. and Killingsworth, J. (2010) "Managing IT in Florida: Consequences and Aftermath of the Bush Era," in Shea, C.M. and Garson, D. (Eds.) *Handbook of Public Information Systems*. Boca Raton, FL: CRC Press: 149–168.

Coursey, D. and Norris, D.F. (2008) "Models of E-Government: Are they Correct? An Empirical Assessment," *Public Administration Review* 68 (3): 523–536.

Culbertson, S. (2004) "Building E-government: Organizational and Cultural Change in Public Administration," in Oliver, E.L. and Sanders, L. (Eds.) *E-Government Reconsidered: Renewal of Governance for the Knowledge Age*. Canadian Plains Research Center and the Saskatchewan Institute of Public Policy, Regina, Canada, pp. 59–75.

Curtin, G.G., Sommer, M.H. and Vis-Sommer, V. (2003) *The World of E-Government*. New York: The Haworth Press.

Davison, J. and Grieves, J. (1996) "Why Should Local Government Show An Interest in Service Quality?," *The TQM Magazine*, 8 (5): 32–38.

de Tocqueville, A. (1948) *Democracy in America*. New York: Vintage Books (translation).

Dearstyne, B. (2001) "E-Business, E-Government & Information Proficiency," *Information Management Journal*, 34 (4): 16–24.

DeLancer Julnes, P. and Holzer, M. (2001) "Promoting the Utilization of Performance Measures in Public Organizations: An Empirical Study of Factors Affecting Adoption and Implementation," *Public Administration Review*, 61 (6): 693–708.

DeLeon, L. and Deleon, P. (2002) "The Democratic Ethos and Public Management," *Administration and Society*, 34 (2): 229–251.

DeLeon, L. and Denhardt, R. (2000) "The Political Theory of Reinvention," *Public Administration Review*, 60 (2): 89–98.

Denhardt J.V. and Denhardt, R.B. (2007) *The New Public Service: Serving, Not Steering*. Armonk, NY: M. E. Sharpe.

DeSoto, H. (2000) *The Mystery of Capital: Why Capitalism Triumphs in the West and Fails Everywhere Else.* New York: Basic Books.

Dobbs, L. (2004) *Exporting America: Why Corporate Greed is Shipping American Jobs Overseas.* New York: Warner Books.

Dobbs, L. (2006) *War on the Middle Class: How the Government, Big Business, and Special Interest Groups Are Waging War on the American Dream and How to Fight Back.* New York: Penguin.

Donaldson, L. (1999) *Performance-Driven Organizational Change.* Thousand Oaks, CA: Sage Publications.

Douglas, T.J. and Judge, W.Q. (2001) "Total Quality Management Implementation and Competitive Advantage: The Role of Structural Control and Exploration," *Academy of Management Executive*, 44 (1): 158–177.

Dunleavy, P., Margetts, H., Bastow, S. and Tinkler, J. (2006) *Digital Era Governance: IT Corporations, the State and E-Government.* Oxford, UK: Oxford University Press.

Eastern European E-Government Days. (2008) Prague, Czech Republic. Available at: www.epma.cz/6-sup-th-sup-eastern-european-egov-days-2008-in-prague.html.

Eggers, W. (2005) *Government 2.0: Using Technology to Improve Education, Cut Red Tape, Reduce Gridlock, and Enhance Democracy.* Lanham, MD: Rowman & Littlefield Publishers.

E-Gov, Expanding Electronic Tax Products for Businesses: Available at: E-Gov, The President's goal of utilizing technology to improve how the Federal Government serves you, citizens, businesses and agencies alike. Accessed at: www.whitehouse.gov/omb/egov/.

Elberse, A., Hale, L.M. and Dutton, H.W. (2000) "Guiding Voters Through the Net: The Democracy Network in a California Primary Election," in Hacker, K.L. and van Dijk, I. (Eds.) *Digital Democracy: Issues of Theory and Practice.* London: Sage Publications: 130–148.

Electronic Procurement In Government: More Complicated Than Just Good Business. (2001) Global Co-Operation in the New Millennium, The 9th European Conference on Information Systems. http://is2.lse.ac.uk/asp/aspecis/20010025.pdf.

Ellsberg, D. (2002) *Secrets: A Memoir of Vietnam and the Pentagon Papers.* New York: Viking Press.

"Environment—Quandaries For SMEs," 17th Bled eCommerce Conference, eGlobal, Bled, Slovenia: June 21–23, 2004.

Ernsdorff, M. and Berbec, A. (2007) "Estonia: The Short Road to E-Government and eDemocracy," in Nixon, P. and Koutrakou, V. (Eds.) *E-government in Europe.* Abingdon: Routledge.

Etzioni, A. (1972) "Minerva: An Electronic Town Hall," *Policy Studies*, 3: 457–474.

Evans, J.R. and Lindsay, W.M. (2008) *Managing for Quality and Performance Excellence* (7th ed.). Mason, Ohio: Thomson Southwestern.

Executive Office of the President (Office of Management and Budget). (2002) *The President's Management Agenda: Fiscal Year 2002.* Available at www.whitehouse.gov/omb/budget/fy2002/mgmt.pdf.

Executive Office of the President. (2010) Memorandum M-10-11 to Heads of Executive Departments and Agencies on "Guidance on the Use of Challenges and Prizes to Promote Open Government," by J.D. Zients, Deputy Director for Management, Office of Management and Budget. Washington, D.C.: March 8.

Fairlie, R.W. (2005) *Are We Really a Nation Online? Racial and Ethnic Disparities in Access to Technology and Their Consequences.* Report for the Leadership Conference on Civil Rights Education Fund. Accessed February 3, 2009 at: www.civilrights.org/publications/nation-online/digitaldivide.pdf.

Fang, Z. (2002) "E-Government in Digital Era: Concept, Practice, and Development," *International Journal of the Computer, the Internet and Management*, 10 (2): 1–22.

Feld, L. and Wilcox, N. (2008) *Netroots Rising: How a Citizen Army of Bloggers and Online Activists is Changing American Politics.* New York: Praeger.

Ferrall, G.M. (1999) "The Development of Virtual Education: A Global Perspective," Vancouver: The Commonwealth of Learning. Available at: www.col.org/SiteCollectionDocuments/prelims_contents.pdf.

Florida E-Government: Serving the Public through Technology Miami-Dade County Working Group Report of Findings. Available at: www.co.miami-dade.fl.us/cio/egov/e-government_report.htm.

Flynn, B. and Saladin, B. (2001) "Further Evidence on the Validity of the Theoretical Models Underlying the Baldrige Criteria," *Journal of Operations Management*, 19 (6): 617–653.

Fountain, J. (2001). *Building the Virtual State: Information Technology and Institutional Change.* Washington, D.C.: The Brookings Institution Press.

Freed, L. (2010) ACSI E-Government Satisfaction Index 2nd Quarter 2010. Retrieved November 23, 2010 at: www.foreseeresults.com.

Friedman, T.L. (1999) *The Lexus and the Olive Tree.* New York: Farrar, Straus, and Giroux.

Freidman, T.L. (2005) *The World is Flat: A Brief History of the Twentieth Century.* New York: Farrar, Straus, and Giroux.

Freidman, T.L. (2008) *Hot, Flat and Crowded—Why We Need a Green Revolution— And How It Can Renew America.* New York: Farrar, Straus, and Giroux.

Garson, D.G. (2006) *Public Information Technology and E-Governance: Managing the Virtual State.* Sudbury, MA: Jones and Bartlett.

Gaster, L. and Squires, A. (2003) *Providing Quality in the Public Sector: A Practical Approach to Improving Public Services.* Philadelphia, PA: Open University Press.

Gill, K. (2004) *How to Measure the Influence of the Blogosphere.* Seattle: University of Washington. Available at: http://faculty.washington.edu/kegill/pub/www 2004_blogosphere_gill.pdf.

Giuliani, W.R. (2005) "Efficiency, Effectiveness, and Accountability: Improving the Quality of Life through E-Government," in Blackstone, E.A., Bonanno, M.L. and Hakim, S. (Eds.) *Innovations in E-Government. The Thoughts of Governors and Mayors.* Lanham, MD: Rowman & Littlefield Publishers: 44–55.

Goldenberg, B. (2008) *CRM in Real Time: Empowering Customer Relationships.* New York: Information Today.

Goodsell, C.Y. (2003) *The Case for Bureaucracy: A Public Administration Polemic* (4th ed.). Washington, D.C.: CQ Press.

Gore, A. (1995) *Common Sense Government.* New York: Random House.

Gorman, S. and Ramstad, E. (2009) "Cyber Blitz Hits U.S., Korea: Simple Attack on Government, Businesses Exposes Vulnerability; Pyongyang [North Korea] Suspected," *New York Times,* July 9: A1 and A4.

Greene, J. (2002) *Cities and Privatization: Prospects for the New Century.* Upper Saddle River, NJ: Prentice-Hall.

Grimshaw, D., Vincent, S., and Willmott, H. (2002) "Going Privately: Partnership and Outsourcing in UK Public Services," *Public Administration,* 80 (3): 475–503.

Grönlund, Å. (2002) *Electronic Government: Design, Applications and Management.* London: Idea Group Publishing.

Habermas, J. (1991) *The Structural Transformation of the Public Sphere.* Cambridge, MA: MIT Press.

Hackman, J.R. (2002) *Leading Teams: Setting the Stage for Great Performances.* Cambridge, MA: Harvard University Press.

Hafkin, N. and Huyer, S. (Eds.) (2006) *Cinderella or Cyberella? Empowering Women in the Knowledge Society.* Bloomfield, CT: Kumarian Press.

Hammer, M. and Champy, J. (1993) *Reengineering the Corporation.* New York: Harper Business.

Hardy, C. and Williams, S. (2008) "E-Government Policy and Practice: A Theoretical and Empirical Exploration of Public E-Procurement," *Government Information Quarterly,* 25 (2): 155–180.

Harley, D.S., Lawrence, S., Acord S.K. and Dixson, J. (2010) "Affordable and Open Textbooks: An Exploratory Study of Faculty Attitudes," *California Journal of Politics and Policy,* 2 (1) Article 10. Available at: www.bepress.com/cjpp/vol2/iss1/10.

Hart-Teeter (2003) *The New E-Government Equation: Ease, Engagement, Privacy & Protection.* Washington, D.C.: Council for Excellence in Government.

Heeks, R. (Ed.) (1999) *Reinventing Government in the Information Age: International Practice in IT-Enabled Public Sector Reform.* London: Routledge.

Hellein, R. and Bowman, J. (2002) "The Process of Quality Management Implementation," *Public Performance and Management Review,* 26 (1): 75–93.

Hendricks, J. and Denton, R.E. (2010) *Communicator-in-Chief: How Barack Obama Used New Media Technology to Win the White House.* New York: Lexington Books.

Hernon, P., Cullen, R. and Relyea, H.C. (Eds.) (2006) *Comparative Perspectives on E-Government: Servicing Today and Building for Tomorrow.* Lanham, MD: The Scarecrow Press.

Hertz, N. (2003) *The Silent Takeover: Global Capitalism and the Death of Democracy.* New York: Harper Business.

Herzlinger, R. (1996). "Can Public Trust in Non-Profits and Government be Restored?," *Harvard Business Review*, 74 (2): 97–108.

Hill, S. (2009) "The World Wide Webbed: The Obama Campaign's Masterful Use of the Internet," New America Foundation, *Social Europe Journal,* April 8, 2009. Available at: www.newamerica.net/publications/articles/2009/world_wide_webbed_12862.

Hiltz, R. and Turoff, M. (1978) *The Network Nation: Human Communication Via the Computer.* Reading, MA: Addison-Wesley.

Hindman, M. (2006) "The Real Lessons of Howard Dean: Reflections on the First Digital Campaign," *Perspectives on Politics*, 3 (1): 121–128. Reprinted in Graber, D. (Ed.) *Media Power and Politics.* Washington, D.C.: CQ Press.

Hindman, M. (2009) *The Myth of Digital Democracy.* Princeton, NJ: Princeton University Press.

Ho, Tat-Kei, A. (2002) "Reinventing Local Governments and the E-Government Initiative," *Public Administration Review* 62 (July/August): 434–444.

Hodge, G. and Greve, C. (Eds.) (2005) *The Challenge of Public–Private Partnerships: Learning for International Experience.* Northampton, MA: Edward Elgar.

Holden, S.H., Norris, D.F. and Fletcher, P.D. (2002) "Electronic Government at the Grass Roots: Contemporary Evidence and Future Trends," presented at the Hawaii International Conference on System Sciences.

Holden, S.H., Norris, D.F. and Fletcher, P.D. (2003) "Electronic Government at the Local Level: Progress to Date and Future Issues," *Public Productivity and Management Review*, 26 (3): 1–20.

Holmes, D. (2001) *eGov: eBusiness Strategies for Government.* London: Nicholas Brealey Publishing.

Holzer, M. and Kim, S-T. (2003) "Digital Governance in Municipalities Worldwide: An Assessment of Municipal Web Sites Throughout the World," The E-Governance Institute/National Center for Public Productivity and Global e-Policy e-Government Institute, Newark, NJ and Korea: Rutgers University and Sungkyunkwan University.

Holzer, M. and Kim, S-T. (2008) "Digital Governance in Municipalities Worldwide: An Assessment of Municipal Web Sites Throughout the World." Newark, NJ: The E-Government Institute, Rutgers University.

Holzer, M., Manoharan, A. and Van Ryzin, G. (2010) "Global Cities on the Web: An Empirical Typology of Municipal Websites," *International Public Management Review*, 11 (3): 104–121.

Homans, G.C. (1974) *Social Behavior: Its Elementary Forms.* New York: Harcourt Brace Jovanovich.

Homberg, V. (2008) *Understanding E-Government: Information Systems in Public Administration.* London: Routledge.

Hui, K.H. and Chaun, T.K. (2002) "Nine Approaches to Organizational Excellence," *Journal of Organizational Excellence*, 22 (1): 53–65.

Ishida, T. and Isbister, K. (2000) *Digital Cities: Technologies, Experiences and Future Perspectives.* Berlin: Springer.

Jaeger, P.T. (2005) "Deliberative Democracy and the Conceptual Foundations of Electronic Government," *Government Information Quarterly*, 22 (4): 702–719.

Jeong, K-H. (2006) *The Road to Innovation E-Government: Principles and Experiences in Korea.* Seoul, Korea: Gil-Job-E Media.

Jupp, V. (2003) "Realizing the Vision of eGovernment," in Curtin, G.G., Sommer, M.H. and Vis-Sommer, V. (Eds.) *The World of E-Government.* New York: The Haworth Political Press: 129–147.

Kahler, M. (2009) *Networked Politics: Agency, Power and Governance.* Ithaca, NY: Cornell University Press.

Kamarck, E.C. and Nye Jr., J.S. (2002). *Governance.com: Democracy in the Information Age.* Washington, D.C.: Brookings Institution Press.

Keehley, P., Medlin, S., MacBride, S. and Longmore, L. (1997). *Benchmarking for Best Practices in the Public Sector.* San Francisco, CA: Jossey-Bass Publishers.

Kelly, D.A., Ramkishen, R.S. and Goh, G.H.L. (Eds.) (2006) *Managing Globalization: Lessons from China and India.* Hackensack, NJ: World Scientific Press.

Keren, M. (2006) *Blogosphere: The New Political Arena.* Lanham, MD: Lexington Books.

Kettl, D. (1987) *Government by Proxy: (Mis?) Managing Federal Programs.* Washington, D.C.: CQ Press.

Kettl, D. (1998) *Reinventing Government: A Fifth-Year Report Card.* Washington, D.C.: The Brookings Institution.

Kettl, D. (2002a) *The Global Public Management Revolution: A Report on the Transformation of Governance.* Washington, D.C.: The Brookings Institution.

Kettl, D. (2002b) *The Transformation of Governance: Public Administration for the Twenty-First Century.* Baltimore, MD: Johns Hopkins University Press.

Kettl, D.F. (2009) *The Next Government of the United States: Why Our Institutions Fail Us and How to Fix Them.* New York: W.W. Norton.

King, S.F. (2007) "Citizens as Customers: Exploring the Future of CRM in Local Government," *Government Information Quarterly*, 24 (1): 47–63.

Klofstad, C.A. (2011) *Civic Talk: Peers, Politics, and the Future of Democracy.* Philadelphia: Temple University Press.

Knowles, T. (2005) "Digital Democracy in Alaska," in Blackstone, E.A., Bonanno, M.L. and Hakim, S. (Eds.) *Innovations in E-Government: The Thoughts of Governors and Mayors.* Lanham, MD: Rowman & Littlefield: 131–41.

Kumar, V., Mukerji, B., Butt, I. and Persaud, A. (2007) "Factors for Successful e-Government Adoption: A Conceptual Framework," *The Electronic Journal of e-Government*, 5 (1): 63–76. Available at: www.ejeg.com/volume-5/vol5-iss1/Kumar_et_al.pdf.

Lamb, J. (2009) *The Greening of IT: How Companies Can Make a Difference for the Environment.* New York: IBM Press.

Lang, R.E. and Sohmer, R. (2000) "Legacy of the Housing Act of 1949: The Past, Present, and Future of Federal Housing and Urban Policy," *Housing Policy Debate*, 11 (2): 291–298. *Fannie Mae Foundation.*

Larsen, B. and Milakovich, M. (2005) "Citizen Relationship Management and E-Government" in Wimmer, M.A., Traunmüller, R., Grönlund, Å. and Andersen, K.V. (Eds.) *Electronic Government: Fourth International Conference.* Berlin: Springer-Verlag: 57–68.

Lenihan, G.D. (2005) "Realigning Governance: From E-Government to E-Democracy," in Khosrow-Pour, M. (Ed.) *Practicing E-Government: A Global Perspective.* Hershey, PA: IDEA Group Publishing: 250–288.

Liikanen, E. (2003). "eGovernment: An EU Perspective," in Curtin, G.G., Sommer, M.H. and Vis-Sommer, V. (Eds.) *The World of E-Government.* New York: The Haworth Press: 65–88.

Lips, M. (2010) *The Digital Citizen: New Directions for Citizen-Centric Government and Democracy.* London: I.B. Tauris.

Longley, P.A., Goodchild, M.F., Maguire, D.J. and Rhind, D.W. (2001) *Geographic Information Systems and Science.* Chichester, UK: John Wiley & Sons.

Lowery, D. (1999) "ISO 9000: A Certification-Based Methodology for Reinventing the Federal Government," *Public Performance and Management Review*, 22 (2): 232–250.

Lowi, T. (1964) "American Business, Public Policy Case Studies, and Political Theory," *World Politics*, 16 (2): 677–715.

Lunney, K. (2009) "Obama Names Washington Businessman as Chief Performance Officer," Government Executive.com. Accessed April 28, 2009 at: www.govexec.com/dailyfed/0409/041809m1.htm.

Mattli, W. and Woods, N. (Eds.) (2009) *The Politics of Global Regulation.* Princeton, NJ: Princeton University Press.

Mayer-Schonberger, V. and Lazer, D. (2007) *Governance and Information Technology: From Electronic Government to Information Government.* Cambridge, MA: The MIT Press.

McLuhan, M. (1964) *Understanding Media: The Extensions of Man.* New York: McGraw-Hill.

McLuhan, M., Fiore, Q. and Agel, J. (1967) *The Medium is the Message: An Inventory of Effects.* New York: Bantam Books.

Means, B., Toyoma, Y., Murphy, R., Bakia, M. and Jones, Y. (2009) *Evaluation of Evidence-Based Learning in Online Learning: A Mega-Analysis and Review of Online Learning Studies.* U.S. Department of Education, Office of Planning, Evaluation, and Policy Development, Policy and Program Studies Service. Available at: www.ed.gov/rschstat/eval/tech/evidence-based-practices/finalreport.pdf.

Mehra, B., Merkel, C. and Peterson Bishop, A. (2002) "The Internet for Empowerment of Minority and Marginalized Users," *New Media and Society*, 6 (6): 781–802.

Meier, K. (1993) *Politics and the Bureaucracy: Policymaking in the Fourth Branch of Government* (3rd ed.). Pacific Grove, CA: Brooks/Cole.

Meinhold, B. (2009) "Obama Unveils High-Speed Railway Plan," *Inhabitat*: April 16, 2009. Accessed July 9, 2009 at: www.inhabitat.com/2009/04/16/obama-pledges-high-speed-rail-lines/.

Milakovich, M. (1979) "Effecting Citizen Participation through Advisory Boards," *Carolina Politics*, 1 (2): 67–73.

Milakovich, M. (1995) "Improving Customer Service Standards in the Public Sector," *The Public Manager*, 24 (3): 5–11.

Milakovich, M. (1998) "The Status of Results-Driven Customer Service Quality in Government," *Journal of Organizational Excellence*, 17 (2): 47–54.

Milakovich, M. (2003) "Balancing Customer Service, Empowerment, and Performance with Citizenship, Responsiveness, and Political Accountability," *International Public Management Review*, 4 (1): 61–83.

Milakovich, M. (2004) "Rewarding Service Quality Innovation: Rewards, Charters, and Standards as Catalysts for Change", in Wimmer, M. (Ed.) *Knowledge Management in Electronic Government*. Berlin: Springer: 64–75.

Milakovich, M. (2006a) *Improving Service Quality in the Global Economy: Achieving High Performance in the Public and Private Sector* (2nd ed.). New York: Taylor and Francis/Auerbach Press.

Milakovich, M. (2006b) "Comparing Bush-Cheney vs. Clinton-Gore Performance Management Strategies," *Public Administration*, 84 (2): 461–478.

Milakovich, M. (2009) "From Representative to Digital Democracy: The Internet and Increased Citizen Participation in Government," in Prosser, A. and Parycek, P. (Eds.) *EDEM 2009—Conference on Electronic Government*. Vienna, Austria: 91–100.

Milakovich, M. (2010) "The Internet and Increased Citizen Participation in Government," *JeDEM—eJournal of eDemocracy and Open Government*, 2 (1): 1–9.

Milakovich, M. and Gordon, G. (2009) *Public Administration in America* (10th ed.). Belmont, CA: Wadsworth.

Miller, C.C. (2008) "How Obama's Internet Campaign Changed Politics," *New York Times*, November 7.

Moon, M.J. (2002) "The Evolution of E-Government Among Municipalities: Rhetoric or Reality?," *Public Administration Review*, 62 (July/August): 424–433.

Morgeson, F.V. and Mithas, S. (2009) "Does E-Government Measure Up to E-Business? Comparing End User Perceptions of the U.S. Federal Government with E-Business Websites," *Public Administration Review*, 69 (July/August): 740–752.

Mossberger, K., Tolbert, C.J. and Stansbury, M., with McNeal, R. and Dotterweich, L. (2003) *Virtual Inequality: Beyond the Digital Divide*. Washington, D.C.: Georgetown University Press.

Moulder, E. (2001) "E-Government ... If You Build It, Will They Come?," *Public Management*, 8 (83): 10–14.

Nasif, T. (2004) "Using Customer Relationship Management to Serve Citizens," U.S. General Services Administration, Newsletter issue 14, January.

Neiman, M. (2000) *Defending Government: Why Big Government Works*. Upper Saddle River, NJ: Prentice-Hall.

Nitkin, K. (2005) "Log in and Learn," *NEA Today,* May: 30–31.

Nixon, P. and Kautrakou, V. (Eds.) (2007) *E-Government in Europe: Re-Booting the State.* London: Routledge.

Norris, F.D. and Moon, M.J. (2005) "Advancing E-Government at the Grassroots: Tortoise or Hare?," *Public Administration Review,* 65 (January/February): 64–75.

Noveck, B.S. (2009) *Wiki Government: How Technology Can Make Government Better, Democracy Stronger and Citizens More Powerful.* Washington, D.C.: Brookings Institution Press.

Nugent, D.J. (2001) "If E-Democracy is the Answer, What is the Question?," *National Civic Review,* 90 (Fall): 221–233.

Nyhan, R. (2000) "Changing the Paradigm: Trust and Its Role in Public Sector Organizations," *American Review of Public Administration,* 30 (1): 78–109.

Obama, B. (2006) *The Audacity of Hope: Thoughts on Reclaiming the American Dream.* New York: Random House.

OECD. (2007) "E-Government as a Tool for Transformation." Accessed October 5, 2009 at: www.olis.oecd.org/olis/2007doc.nsf/8d00615172fd2a63c125685d005300b5/c5bfb886ebcafe06c12572ac0057513c/$FILE/JT03224646.PDF.

Oliver, E.L. and Sanders, L. (2004). *E-Government Reconsidered: Renewal of Governance for the Knowledge Age.* Canadian Plains Research Center and the Saskatchewan Institute of Public Policy, Regina, Canada.

Ornstein, N. and Mann, T. (2000) *The Permanent Campaign and Its Future.* Washington, D.C.: American Enterprise Institute for Policy Research and the Brookings Institution.

Osborne, D. and Gaebler, T. (1992) *Reinventing Government: How the Entrepreneurial Spirit is Transforming the Public Sector.* Reading, MA: Addison-Wesley.

Osborne, D. and Plastrik, P. (2000) *The Reinventor's Fieldbook.* San Francisco, CA: Jossey-Bass Publishers.

Parycek, P. and Sachs, M. (2009) "Web 2.0 as a Base for Democracy 2.0," in Prosser, A. and Parycek, P. (Eds.) *EDEM 2009—Conference on Electronic Democracy.* Vienna, Austria: Osterreichisch Computer Gesellschaft.

Paquet, G. (2004) "There is More to Governance than Public Candelabras: E-Governance and Canada's Public Service," in Oliver, E. L. and Sanders, L. (Eds.) *E-Government Reconsidered: Renewal of Governance for the Knowledge Age.* Canadian Plains Research Center and the Saskatchewan Institute of Public Policy: University of Regina, chapter 13, section 4.

Pavlichev, A. and Garson, D. (Eds.) (2003) *Digital Government: Principles and Best Practices.* Hershey, PA: IGI Global.

Pegnato, J. (1997) "Is a Citizen a Customer?," *Public Performance and Management Review,* 20 (4): 397–404.

Perera, D. (2010) "Study Finds Higher Digital IQ among GOP Senators," *Fierce Government,* August 22. Available at: www.fiercegovernmentit.com/story/study-finds-higher-digital-iq-among-gop-senators/2010-08-22.

Perez, T. and Rushing, R. (2007) *The Citistat Model: How Data-Driven Government Can Increase Efficiency and Effectiveness.* Washington, D.C.: Center for American Progress. Accessed June 8, 2009 at: www.americanprogress.org/issues/2007/04/citistat.html.

Peters, G. (2010) *American Public Policy: Promise and Performance* (8th ed.). Washington, D.C.: CQ Press.

Peters, W. and Porter, C. (2001) "E-Government: No Walls, No Clocks, No Doors." Available at: http://usinfo.state.gov/journals/itgic/1100/ijge/gj02.html.

Petroni, G. and Tagliente, L. (2005) "E-government in the Republic of San Marino: Some Successful Initiatives" in Petroni, G. and Cloete, F. (Eds.) *New Technologies in Public Administration,* Amsterdam: IOS Press: 23–37.

Pew Charitable Trusts. (2008) "Being Online is Not Enough: State Elections Websites," Washington, D.C.: The Pew Center on the States. Available at: www.pewcenteronthestates.org/uploadedFiles/VIP_FINAL_101408_WEB.pdf.

Pew Internet and American Life Project. (2010) "Government Online: The Internet Gives Citizens New Paths to Government Services and Information," Aaron Smith, Research Specialist. Available at: http://pewinternet.org/Reports/2010/E-Government.aspx.

Phusavat, K., Anussarnnitisarn, P. and Rassameethes, B. (2008) "Knowledge Management Practices: Progress on E-Government and Preparation for Quality Management," *Electronic Government, An International Journal,* 5 (3): 247–260.

Pirog, M.A. and Johnson, C.L. (2008) "Electronic Funds and Benefits Transfers, E-Government, and the Winter Commission," *Public Administration Review,* 68 (1): 103–115.

Postman, N. (1995) *The End of Education.* New York: Vintage Books.

Powner, D. (2006) "Improvements Needed to More Accurately Identify and Better Oversee Risky Projects Totaling Billions of Dollars," Washington, D.C.: U.S. General Accountability Office, Testimony Before the Subcommittee on Federal Financial Management, Government Information and International Security, Committee on Homeland Security and Governmental Affairs, U.S. Senate. Accessed July 12, 2009 at: www.gao.gov/new.items/d061099t.pdf.

Prahalad, C.K. and Ramaswamy, V. (2001) "Co-opting Customer Competence," *Customer Relationship Management. Harvard Business Review.* Boston: Harvard Business School Press.

Pressman, J. and Wildavsky, A. (1984) *Implementation* (3rd ed.). Berkeley: University of California Press.

Prestowitz, C. (2006) *Three Billion New Capitalists: The Great Shift of Wealth and Power to the East.* New York: Basic Books.

Public Interest Research Group. (2010) "Following the Money: How the 50 States Rate in Providing Online Access to Government Spending Data." Available at: http://cdn.publicinterestnetwork.org.

Putnam, R. (2000) *Bowling Alone: The Collapse and Revival of American Community.* New York: Simon and Schuster.

Raffel, J. (1999) "Privatization and Contracting: Managing for State and Local Productivity," *Public Performance and Management Review*, 22 (4): 430–434.

Rago, W. (1994) "Adapting Total Quality Management (TQM) to Government: Another Point of View," *Public Administration Review*, 54 (1): 61–65.

Report to Congress on the Benefits of the President's E-Government Intiatives, Fiscal Year 2009. Accessed at: www.whitehouse.gov/omb/assets/egov_docs/FY09_Benefits_Report.pdf.

Rho, S. (2007) "An Evaluation of Digital Deliberative Democracy in Local Government," in Al-Hakim, L. (Ed.) *Global E-Government: Theory, Applications and Benchmarking*. Hershey, PA: Idea Group Publishing: 200–213.

Richardson, W. (2006) *Blogs, Wikis, Podcasts, and other Powerful Web Tools for Classrooms*. Thousand Oaks, CA: Corwin Press.

Riley, T.B. (2004) *E-Government: The Digital Divide and Information Sharing: Examining the Issues*, Commonwealth Centre for Electronic Governance, July 2004. Available at: www.electronicgov.net/pubs/research_papers/track04/index.shtml.

Riley, T.B. (2005) *E-Privacy, Anonymity and Public Spaces: What is this All About?* Commonwealth Centre for Electronic Governance, November 2005. Available at: www.electronicgov.net/pubs/research_papers/PrivAnonNymity05.shtml.

Riley, T.B., and Riley, C.G. (2003) *E-Governance to E-Democracy: Examining the Evolution*, Commonwealth Centre for Electronic Governance, June 2003. Available at: unpan1.un.org/intradoc/groups/public/documents/APCITY/UNPAN015436.pdf.

Robbins, M.D, Simonsen, B. and Feldman, B. (2008) "Citizens and Resource Allocation: Improving Decision Making with Interactive Web-Based Citizen Participation, New Perspectives on E-Government," *Public Administration Review*, 68 (3): 564–575.

Rocheleau, B. (2007) *Case Studies on Digital Government*. Hershey, PA: Idea Group Publishing.

Rogers, E.M. (2003) *The Diffusion of Innovations* (5th ed.). New York: The Free Press.

Ronan, J.W. (2000). *E-Government: The Next Revolution*. Washington, D.C.: Council for Excellence in Government.

Rothkopf, D. (2008) *Superclass: The Global Power Elite and the World they are Making*. New York: Farrar, Straus, and Giroux.

Roucheleau, B.A. (2006) *Public Management Information Systems*. Hershey, PA: Idea Publishing Group.

Roucheleau, B.A. (Ed.) (2007) *Case Studies on Digital Government*. Hershey, PA: Idea Publishing Group.

Rubin, R.E. (2003) *In an Uncertain World*. New York: Random House.

Sanderson, I. (2001) "Performance Management, Evaluation and Learning in 'Modern' Local Government," *Public Administration*, 79 (2): 297–313.

Sarbaugh-Thompson, M. (1998) "Change from Below: Integrating Bottom-Up Entrepreneurship into a Program Development Framework," *American Review of Public Administration*, 28 (1): 3–25.

Savas, E.S. (2000) *Privatization and Public Policy Partnerships*. Chatham, NJ: Chatham House.

Seifert, J. (2003) *A Primer on E-Government: Sectors, Stages, Opportunities, and Challenges of Online Governance*. Washington, D.C.: Congressional Research Service. Accessed November 4, 2007 at http://www.fas.org/sgp/crs/RL31057.pdf.

Senge, P.M. (1996) "Leading Learning Organizations," *Training & Development*, 50 (12): 36–37.

Senge, P.M. *et al.* (1994) *The Fifth Discipline Fieldbook*. New York: Doubleday.

Senge, P., Smith, B., Schley, S., Laur, J. and Kruschwitz, N. (2008) *The Necessary Revolution: How Individuals and Organizations are Working Together to Create a Sustainable World*. New York: Crown Books.

Sensenbrenner, J. (1991) "Quality Comes to City Hall," *Harvard Business Review*, 69 (2): 64–70.

Shark, A. and Toporkoff, S. (2008) *Beyond e-Government & e-Democracy: A Global Perspective*. Public Technology Institute and ITEMS International.

Shea, C. and Garson, D. (2010) *Handbook of Public Information Systems* (3rd ed.). Boca Raton, FL: CRC Press.

Shin, M. and Lee, Y. (2009). "Changing the Landscape of Teacher Education via Online Teaching and Learning Techniques," *Connecting Education and Careers*, 84 (1), 32–33.

Signore, O., Chesi, F. and Pallotti, M. (2005) *E-Government: Challenges and Opportunities*. CMG Italy-XIX Annual Conference. Accessed August 14, 2007 at www.w3c.it/papers/cmg2005Italy.pdf.

Skinner, R. (2008) *Full Interoperability Means More Than Just Voice*, Government Technology Online. Available at www.govtech.com/gt/324033?topic=117676.

Smith, P.J. (2004) "New Information Technologies and Empowerment: The Implications for Politics and Governance," in Oliver, E.L. and Sanders, L. (Eds.) *E-Government Reconsidered: Renewal of Governance for the Knowledge Age*. Canadian Plains Research Center and the Saskatchewan Institute of Public Policy, Regina, Canada pp. 135–151.

Solnit, David (Ed.) (2004) *Globalize Liberation*. San Fransisco: City Lights Books.

Srinivas, H. (2002) "Use of Internet for Citizens' Participation in Urban Management: A View From Japan," January 18. Accessed at: www.gdrc.org/icts/jhdp.html.

Stier, M. (2009) "Challenges for the New Chief Performance Officer," *Washington Post*, Wednesday, January 7, 2009.

Stiglitz, J. (2003) *Globalization and Its Discontents*. New York: W.W. Norton.

Stiglitz, J. (2006) *Making Globalization Work*. New York: W.W. Norton.

Stillman, R. (2010) *Public Administration: Concepts and Cases* (9th ed.). Boston: Cengage.

Stubbs, R. (1998) "The Impact of Telematics on Local Governance and Delivery of Services." Available at: www.democracy.org.uk.

Svara, J. (1999a) "The Shifting Boundary between Elected Officials and City Managers in Large Council-Manager Cities," *Public Administration Review*, 59 (1): 44–53.

Svara, J.H. (1999b) "The Embattled Mayors and Local Executives," in Weber, R. E. and Brace, P. (Eds.) *American State and Local Politics. Directions for the 21st Century*. New York: Chatham House Publishers pp. 139–165.

Svara, J.H. (2009) (Ed.) *The Facilitative Leader in City Hall: Reexamining the Scope and Contributions*. Boca Raton, FL: CRC Press.

Swiss, J. (1992) "Adapting Total Quality Management (TQM) to Government," *Public Administration Review*, 52 (2): 356–362.

Thompson, A.A. and Strickland, A.J. (2002) *Strategic Management: Concepts and Cases*. Burr Ridge, IL: McGraw-Hill.

Todd, C. and Gawiser, S. (2009) *How Obama Won: A State-By-State Guide to the Historic 2008 Presidential Election*. New York: Vintage Books.

Tolbert, C.J. and Mossberger, K. (2006) "The Effects of E-Government on Trust and Confidence in Government," *Public Administration Review*, 66 (3): 354–369.

Tolbert, C.J., Mossberger, K. and McNeal, R. (2008) "Institutions, Policy Innovation, and E-Government in the American States," *Public Administration Review*, 68 (3): 549–563.

Traunmüller, R. (2004) *Electronic Government: Third International Conference – EGOV 2004, Zaragoza, Spain, August/September 2004 Proceedings*. Berlin: Springer Verlag.

Traunmüller, R. and Lenk, K. (2002) *Electronic Government: First International Conference*. Aix-en-Provence, France.

Tummala, V.M.R. and Tang, C.L. (1996) "Strategic Quality Management, Malcolm Baldrige and European Quality Awards and ISO 9000 Certification: Core Concepts and Comparative Analysis," *International Journal of Quality and Reliability Management*, 13 (4): 8–38.

United Nations. (2007) *Manage Knowledge to Build Trust in Government*. New York: Department of Economic and Social Affairs. Available at: http://unpan1.un.org/intradoc/groups/public/documents/un/unpan028460.pdf.

United Nations. (2008) *Global E-Government Survey 2008: From E Government to Connected Governance*. Available at: http://unpan1.un.org/intradoc/groups/public/documents/un/unpan028607.pdf.

United Nations. (2010) *E-Government Survey, Leveraging E-Government at a Time of Financial and Economic Crisis*. Available at: http://unpan1.un.org/intradoc/groups/public/documents/un/unpan038851.pdf.

U.S Department of Commerce, *The Emerging Digital E I Report* (1998) (www.ecommerce.gov) and Nielson//Net Ratings, October 1999 (www.nielson-netratings.com).

U.S. Department of Homeland Security: www.safecomprogram.gov/SAFECOM/.

U.S. General Accounting Office. (2000) *Electronic Government: Government Paperwork Elimination Act Presents Challenges for Agencies*. Washington, D.C.: Report to the

Ranking Minority Member, Committee on Government Operations, U.S. Senate.

U.S. General Accounting Office. (2004) *ELECTRONIC GOVERNMENT: Initiatives Sponsored by the Office of Management and Budget Have Made Mixed Progress.* Washington, D.C.: Testimony before the Subcommittee on Technology, Information Policy, Intergovernmental Relations and the Census, Committee on Government Operations, U.S. House of Representatives.

U.S. General Services Administration. (2005) *Improving Citizen Customer Service: Metrics, Benchmarks, Best Practices, and Technology Trends.* Accessed July 10, 2009 at: www.usaservices.gov/bestpractices/pdf_citizens/metricsmitre-1.pdf.

U.S. Government Accountability Office. (2009) *Agencies Need to Improve the Implementation and Use of Earned Value Techniques to Help Manage Major System Acquisitions.* Report to the Chairman, Subcommittee on Federal Financial Management, Government Information, Federal Services, and International Security, Committee on Homeland Security and Governmental Affairs, U.S. Senate, GAO-10-2. Accessed October 30, 2009 at: www.gao.gov/new.items/d102.pdf.

U.S. House of Representatives. (2002) "The E-Government Act of 2002." Available at: www.usaid.gov/policy/egov/egov_2002.pdf.

Van Thiel, S. and Leeuw, F.L. (2002) "The Performance Paradox in the Public Sector," *Public Performance and Management Review*, 25 (3): 267–281.

Veseth, M. (2005) *Globaloney: Unraveling the Myths of Globalization.* Lanham, MD: Rowman & Littlefield Publishers.

Welch, E.W., Hinnant, C.C. and Moon, M.J. (2004) "Linking Citizen Satisfaction with E-Government and Trust in Government," *Journal of Public Administration Research and Theory*, 15: 371–391. Accessed October 18, 2008 at www.jpart.oxfordjournals.org/cgi/reprint/15/3/371.

West, D.M. (2001) "Assessing E-Government: The Internet, Democracy, and Service Delivery by State and Federal Governments, 2000." Accessed at: www.insidepolitics.org/egovtreport00.html.

West, D.M. (2003) *Global E-government, 2003.* Providence, RI: Taubman Center for Public Policy, Brown University. Accessed July 10, 2008 at www.insidepolitics.org/egovt03int.html.

West, D.M. (2004) "E-Government and the Transformation of Service Delivery and Citizen Attitudes," *Public Administration Review*, 64: 15–27. Accessed June 28, 2007 at www.blackwell-synergy.com/links/doi/10.1111%2Fj.1540-6210.2004.00343.x.

West, D. (2005) *Digital Democracy: Technology and Public Sector Performance.* Princeton, NJ: Princeton University Press.

West, D.M. (2006) *State and Federal E-Government in the United States.* Providence, RI: Brown University. Accessed December 12, 2007 at www.insidepolitics.org/egovt06us.pdf.

West, D.M. (2008) *Improving Technology Utilization in Electronic Government around the World.* Washington, D.C.: The Brookings Institution.

Wilson, L. and Durant, R. (1993) "Evaluating TQM: The Case for a Theory Driven Approach," *Public Administration Review*, 23 (3): 137–146.

Wilson, W. (1887) "The Study of Administration," *Political Science Quarterly*, 2 (June). Available at: www.teachingamericanhistory.org/library/index.asp?document=465.

Wimmer, M. (Ed.) (2002) *Knowledge Management in e-Government*. Vienna, Austria: Trauner Druck.

Wimmer, M.A. (Ed.) (2004) *Knowledge Management in Electronic Government*. Berlin: Springer.

Wimmer, M.A. (Ed.) (2005) *E-Government 2005: Knowledge Transfer and Status*. Vienna: Austrian Computer Society.

Wimmer, M., Traunmüller, R., Gronland, A. and Andersen, K. (Eds.) (2005) *Electronic Government*. Berlin Heidelberg: Springer Verlag.

Wimmer, M.A., Scholl J.H. and Ferro E. (Eds.) (2008) *Electronic Government*. 7th International Conference, EGOV 2008. Springer Verlag: Heidelberg LNCS # 5184.

Xavier, M.J. (2002) "Citizen Relationship Management—Concepts, Tools and Research Opportunities." Paper presented in the 6th Research Conference on Relationship Management in Atlanta, Georgia, June.

Zabriskie, F.H. and McNabb, D.E. (2007) "E-Hancing the Master of Business Administration (MBA) Managerial Accounting Course," *Journal of Education for Business*, 82 (5): 226–233.

Zbaracki, M. (1998) "The Rhetoric and Reality of Total Quality Management," *Administrative Science Quarterly*, 43 (3): 602–636.

Zeithaml, V., Parasuraman, A. and Berry, L. (1990) *Delivering Quality Service: Balancing Customer Perceptions and Expectations*. New York: The Free Press.

Index

Page numbers in *italics* denotes a table/figure